SPIES IN THE VATICAN

Spies in the Vatican

Espionage & Intrigue from Napoleon to the Holocaust

David Alvarez

 University Press of Kansas

© 2002 by the University Press of Kansas

Published by the University Press of Kansas (Lawrence, Kansas 66049), which was
organized by the Kansas Board of Regents and is operated and funded by Emporia State
University, Fort Hays State University, Kansas State University, Pittsburg State University,
the University of Kansas, and Wichita State University

Library of Congress Cataloging-in-Publication Data

Alvarez, David J.
   Spies in the Vatican : espionage and intrigue from Napoleon to the Holocaust /
David Alvarez.
      p.   cm.
   Includes bibliographical references and index.
   ISBN 0–7006–1214–9 (cloth : alk. paper)
      1. Espionage—Vatican City—History—19th century. 2. Espionage—Vatican
City—History—20th century. 3. Intelligence service—Vatican City—19th
century. 4. Intelligence service—Vatican City—20th century. I. Title.
   UB271.V38A48 2002
   327.12456'34'009034—dc21   2002008241

British Library Cataloguing in Publication Data is available.

Printed in the United States of America

10 9 8 7 6 5 4 3 2 1

The paper used in this publication meets the minimum requirements of the American
National Standard for Permanence of Paper for Printed Library Materials Z39-48-1984.

For Donna

CONTENTS

ACKNOWLEDGMENTS

This book could not have been written without the advice and assistance of friends and colleagues. Several individuals helped me chase down intelligence records: John Taylor and Greg Bradsher at the National Archives in College Park, Maryland; Monsignors Charles Burns and Marcello Camisassa at the Vatican; Elisabeth Giansiracusa and Roberto Ventresca in Rome; and Vincent Leguy in Paris. John Ferris and Michael Phayer read the manuscript and helped me see where it needed improvement. Two veterans of the intelligence wars in Rome, William Gowen and Martin Quigley, patiently responded to my questions concerning American operations at the Vatican. Cardinal Silvio Oddi recalled life in the papal diplomatic service in World War II. Eva Kuttner shared her memories of Father Robert Leiber. Brian Sullivan repeatedly demonstrated that no one knows more about Mussolini's intelligence services than he. Larry Gray helped me better understand the figure of Felix Morlion. From Charles Gallagher I first learned of Monsignor Joseph Hurley's work for the American government. Mike Briggs, my editor at the University Press of Kansas, believed in this book when it was only an idea.

The Faculty Development Fund at Saint Mary's College of California subsidized research trips to distant archives. No one will be happier to see this work in print than the fund's directors.

My family remained cheerful and patient throughout the process even when I did not. This is as much their book as it is mine.

Spies in the Vatican. The words evoke images of frescoed corridors and crimson-robed prelates, furtive meetings in shadowy crypts and whispered confidences in incense-scented chapels, cunning cardinals and devious monks, political intrigue and dark conspiracy. The words suggest the plot of a hundred thrillers and mysteries, the story line for a dozen screenplays. The words and images are doubly powerful because the popular imagination, convinced of the power of the Papacy, intrigued by the mystery and glamour surrounding the Vatican, and schooled in tales of ruthless and scandalous Renaissance popes, is all too ready to believe that the Vatican has long been a major capital of the secret world of espionage and that popes, no less than kings and prime ministers, presidents and dictators, inhabit a secret world of spies, assassins, saboteurs, and clandestine operations. The images are so powerful that even diplomats, politicians, military officers, and other professional observers of international affairs have often succumbed to the stories and legends of papal espionage.

Historians, whose job description (at least until recently) has included the task of helping people distinguish the accurate historical images from the inaccurate, have been surprisingly uncritical in adopting the popular view of the Vatican's place in the world of espionage. When considering, for example, the Papacy's role in such central events of the twentieth century as the two world wars, the rise and fall of totalitarian fascism and communism, the Holocaust, and the cold war, they have readily assumed that the Vatican, no less than the United States, the Soviet Union, or any other great power, deployed spies, covert operators, and all the other instruments of espionage and clandestine operations in support of its policies and interests. It is common for historians to speak knowingly of the "Vatican intelligence service" and for the especially bold to assert confidently that the pope is the best informed of the world's leaders. This professional consensus is all the more surprising for the notable paucity of evidence to support it. Even the denizens of the secret world leave traces, no matter how faint, visible to sharp-eyed researchers seeking to confirm their presence or track their movements. No one, however, has tracked the rarest specimen of the secret world, the Vatican intelligence service. For all the claims and assumptions concerning papal intelligence, no one has set out systematically to confirm its existence, identify its characteristics, and describe its nature. It is a curious situation, as if a group of ornithologists sat about discussing the merits of a magnificent bird and describing its place in the ecosystem without anyone having actually observed the bird, discovered a nest, heard its call, or run across the smallest feather. A detached observer might be forgiven for suggesting that an expedition into the forest might not be a waste of time.

Intelligence is no longer, as the noted British diplomat Sir Alexander Cadogan asserted after the Second World War, the "missing dimension" of international history. In recent years intelligence history has become a lively field of historical study with all the accoutrements of an academic subject that has "arrived": specialist journals and conferences, national and international professional associations, special lists at academic presses, and electronic discussion groups. Encouraged by the steady, if rather gradual, declassification of intelligence records, historians have been increasingly emboldened to investigate the role of intelligence and intelligence services in the formation and implementation of political, military, and economic policies. These investigations are enriching and in many cases challenging our understanding of historical personalities and events.

For all the growth and vitality in intelligence studies, most research and writing in the field has been characterized by certain biases of focus and periodization. Intelligence historians have tended to focus on the twentieth century, in particular the period 1914–45, in part because that period encompasses such historically significant and dramatic events as the two world wars, the rise and fall of empires and would-be empires, and the origins of the cold war; in part because the era witnessed the emergence and development in many countries of distinct intelligence organizations whose operations could be observed and described; and in part because archival records from the period exist in sufficient quantity and order to provide a documentary base for such descriptions. Historians have further narrowed their focus by concentrating on the intelligence experience of the great powers of the twentieth century. Within this initial concentration there has been a further disposition in favor of two particular powers: the United Kingdom and the United States. This geographic bias reflects the fact that until recently the majority of historians working in the field have been American or British. It also reflects the fact that, again until recently, American and British archival records have been more accessible than those of other countries.

Recently historians have begun to expand their horizons to include other countries and periods. Intelligence history has begun to attract students in Canada, France, Germany, Israel, Italy, the Netherlands, Russia, and other countries, and these scholars have naturally looked close to home for research subjects. Caches of documents have been discovered or have become available in archives and libraries in various cities, including The Hague, Moscow, Oslo, Ottawa, Paris, and Rome. Searching through these collections, historians are discovering that the smaller powers also have rich intelligence histories and that these histories (as well as those of the larger powers) often extend back beyond the First World War. Indeed, some of the most exciting research in the field is now focusing on intelligence services whose existence scholars hardly acknowledged even ten years ago.

This book is an effort to contribute to this new direction in intelligence history by investigating the place of the Vatican, the world's oldest but smallest power, in that history. The result is the first detailed description of the intelligence history of the Papacy in a period (1815–1945) when espionage agencies and operations became increasingly important weapons in the diplomatic and military arsenals of nations. By exposing that history, the study also sheds new and revealing light on important political events of that period. Finally, the study tests the popular and professional perceptions concerning the intelligence capabilities of the Papacy to determine if, in fact, the popes are the best informed of the world's leaders.

The seed of this project was planted several years ago when I visited the Vatican Archive in search of material for a history of Vatican diplomacy in the First World War. Working through the files of telegrams and reports from the papal nuncios (ambassadors) in various countries, I was struck by how many of the pope's representatives were preoccupied by questions of security. References to surveillance, ciphers, and sealed diplomatic pouches littered their correspondence, and the files contained frequent warnings that foreign intelligence services were trying to intercept the pope's confidential communications. Many of the telegrams and reports were encrypted to protect their secrets from unauthorized eyes, and one of the files actually contained a codebook used by the nuncio in Lisbon in the early years of the war. It was the first codebook I had ever seen. As a diplomatic historian, I was aware that governments routinely encrypted their diplomatic communications to circumvent surveillance, but it had never occurred to me that the Vatican would resort to such an expedient.

My curiosity was piqued. At the Vatican Archive researchers are in the habit of passing the seemingly interminable periods between ordering and receiving files in the pleasant café that is an adornment to the archive and the adjoining Vatican Library, but I found myself forsaking espresso and pastries in favor of searching through the finding aids for references to ciphers, communications security, and espionage. The first, rather superficial, sweep turned up a handful of items: another codebook (this time from the late nineteenth century), a handful of ciphers from the period of the old Papal States, a directive to nuncios from the papal secretariat of state concerning proper procedures for protecting the security of messages, a report from the nuncio in Switzerland that confidential letters addressed to him from Rome showed signs of having been opened before their delivery. Gradually my curiosity about papal communications security expanded into a more general interest in questions of espionage and security at the Vatican, and what began as a brief diversion from the main road of diplomatic history turned into a full-scale journey in the direction of intelligence history.

My new interest was further stimulated when Father Robert Graham, S.J., invited me to collaborate with him on a study of Nazi espionage against the Vatican in World War II. Working with Father Graham, an authority on the wartime Papacy, I learned just how deeply involved the Vatican was in the espionage history of the war. I also discovered, however, that the broader aspects of that involvement were obscure. As is often the case with research, the primary and secondary sources raised as many questions as they answered. Was Nazi Germany's intelligence interest in the Papacy unique, or was it shared by other countries, such as Britain and the United States? Were German espionage operations against the Vatican in World War II prefigured by similar operations by Germany or other countries in World War I or even earlier? Was the Vatican a helpless target for espionage, or did it reciprocate the attention of foreign powers with aggressive intelligence operations of its own? What were the intelligence capabilities of the Papacy, and how did they compare with those of other governments? Was the pope really one of the best informed among world leaders?

Answers to such questions were not exactly thick on the ground, but they seemed worth seeking out. The search took me back to the Vatican and to archives in several other countries. This book describes what I found.

I

The End of the Papal States

In appearance there was nothing to distinguish the young man in the simple jacket and blouse of an Italian artisan from the other petitioners who, that July day in 1817, crowded the reception hall of the bishop's palace in Fermo, a quiet hill town in the Marche region of Italy. He refused to state the nature of his business and declined an invitation to speak with a secretary, insisting that he must see the bishop personally. When, finally, the persistent visitor was ushered into the bishop's study, it quickly became apparent that he was no ordinary petitioner.

The young man introduced himself as Paolo Monti, a resident of Fermo, and without further ado he announced that he was a senior officer in a clandestine revolutionary organization committed to overthrowing the pope's rule in the Papal States, the broad swath of territory stretching across central Italy that pontiffs had governed as priest-kings for centuries. Monti explained that earlier that year, at the direction of his superiors, he had prepared a plan for insurrections in the principal cities of the papal domain set to flare upon the death of the seriously ailing pope, the seventy-five-year-old Pius VII. The plan was shelved, in part because Pius recovered (he would vex his opponents by living another six years) and in part because it was far too ambitious for the limited resources of the revolutionaries. Acting on their own, perhaps in the hope of sparking a spontaneous uprising, a band of hotheads in Macerata, a town near Fermo, had attacked police posts on the night of 24 June 1817. The attacks were repulsed, and the only consequence was increased pressure on the clandestine organization as the pope's police flooded Macerata with reinforcements in an effort to suppress the revolutionary underground.

Standing before the bishop of Fermo, two weeks after the Macerata incident, Monti explained that a guilty conscience had driven him to confess his criminal activity, and to prove his contrition he was prepared to reveal everything he knew about the membership and plans of his secret organization. The astonished bishop, more accustomed to dealing with confirmation schedules, the finances of poor parishes, and the peccadillos of errant priests than with self-confessed terrorists, hardly knew what to do with the earnest young man. He decided to pack the penitent off to Rome, the capital of the Papal States and the home of the Curia, the central administration of the Catholic Church.

In the Eternal City Monti was personally interviewed by Cardinal Ercole Consalvi, the pope's secretary of state and chief minister in both foreign and domestic affairs. Cardinal Consalvi passed the erstwhile revolutionary to Monsignor Tiberio Pacca, the director general of the papal police. A secret police officer in clerical costume, Pacca was an old hand at conspiracy.[1] He owed his senior position in part to his success several years earlier in exposing the clandestine channels by which Napoleon Bonaparte, the former emperor of France and scourge of Europe, then living in exile on the small Italian island of Elba, had plotted his return to power with his supporters in France and Italy. Pacca immediately saw an opportunity to penetrate the antipapal underground. Assuming correctly that Monti's former colleagues remained ignorant of his betrayal, the wily police official sent the repentant revolutionary back to Fermo to reestablish contact with them. From his position inside the underground, Monti passed to the papal police intelligence on the membership, structure, and plans of conspiratorial groups in the Marche. With this intelligence the police were able to arrest more than thirty conspirators and deal a serious blow to the revolutionary movement in central Italy.[2]

The image of a papal official in clerical dress and collar directing intelligence operations, recruiting double agents, and penetrating clandestine organizations is somewhat incongruous, but the nineteenth century was a dangerous time for the Papacy, and popes as much as kings and emperors relied on intelligence to anticipate and deflect threats to their power. Since the collapse of the Roman Empire, the popes had successfully claimed the right to rule as temporal sovereigns in central Italy. Expanding or contracting according to the relative strength or weakness of the Papacy, the papal domain allegedly provided the pontiffs the political and financial independence necessary for the unfettered exercise of their spiritual authority. Without his own state, the argument went, the pope would become little more than the chaplain of whatever monarch controlled Rome, dependent on the goodwill of that monarch for the food on his table, the water in his cisterns, the wool in his cloak, the very ink and paper on his desk. Although the popes claimed a place in the councils of kings and potentates on the basis of their spiritual office of Vicar of Christ on earth, this claim was buttressed, especially after the Protestant Reformation, by sovereign control over territory, population, and resources. For both religious and political reasons, therefore, Catholics, both churchmen and laypeople, came over the centuries to believe that the status and prerogatives of the Papacy were inextricably linked with its control of the Papal States. By the nineteenth century, however, that control and the claims that depended on it were under serious assault.

The Papal States proved no more capable than other European principalities of withstanding the wars and political upheavals that followed in the wake of the French Revolution. The revolutionaries lumped the Catholic Church together with monarchy and aristocracy as oppressive elements of the old order that they were determined to sweep away. Remnants of religious practice might survive, but only in a form supportive of revolutionary purposes. In 1796 the Directory, the ruling junta in Paris, had sent into Italy an army under its youngest and most ambitious general, Napoleon Bonaparte, to chastise Pope Pius VI for resisting its effort to subordinate the Catholic Church in France to the revolutionary regime. Despite the occupation of Rome and other papal cities and the imposition of crippling indemnities, including the shipment to Paris of valuable artworks and ancient manuscripts from church buildings and libraries, Pius remained unbowed. In 1798 the eighty-one-year-old pontiff was forcibly removed from Rome by French troops (who interrupted the kidnapping to plunder the Vatican palace) and dragged from one place of temporary incarceration to another until, in 1799, he died in the fortress of Valence in southern France.

The cardinals who were free to travel gathered in Venice under the protection of the Austrian emperor to elect a successor to the martyred pope. Their choice, the Benedictine monk and cardinal bishop of Imola, Luigi Barnaba Chiaramonti, assumed the name Pius VII in memory of his predecessor. Hoping to reach an accommodation with Napoleon, who had in the meantime returned to France to overthrow the Directory and establish one-man rule, the new pope negotiated with the new dictator a concordat (treaty) by which, at least in theory, church and state demarcated their respective rights and responsibilities in French religious life. The pontiff also flattered Napoleon's ego by agreeing to officiate at his coronation as emperor of France in 1804.

Pius, however, refused to ally the Papacy with Napoleon's program of personal aggrandizement and imperial expansion. Insisting on his political neutrality in the constant warfare that was the French emperor's gift to Europe in the years between 1798 and 1815, the pontiff declined to close the ports of the Papal States to the shipping of Britain, France's principal enemy, and categorically rejected Napoleon's request to control one-third of the seats in the College of Cardinals, the body responsible for electing popes. For his part, the emperor was not about to allow a stubborn monk to challenge his power and tarnish his glory. In February 1808 French troops occupied Rome and surrounded the Palazzo Quirinale, the papal residence, where Pius remained defiant behind gates barred and patrolled by his Swiss Guards. The standoff continued until May 1809, when Napoleon, frustrated by the pope's recalcitrance, simply signed a decree incorporating the Papal States into the French empire and allowing the Holy Father to continue to reside in his private palace with an annual allowance of 2 million lire. Refusing to become a ward of the French empire, Pius rejected the terms of the decree and announced the excommunication of all those responsible for formulating and executing the document. Outraged by this new act of defiance, Napoleon decided to remove this affront to his power once and for all.

On the night of 5 July 1809, French troops broke into the Palazzo Quirinale. As one French detachment disarmed the heavily outnumbered Swiss Guards, another descended from the roof into the papal apartments, where they found Pius calmly awaiting their arrival. When the Holy Father courteously but firmly refused the demand of the French commander to renounce his claim to the Papal States, he was pushed into a carriage and rushed out of Rome under heavy escort. Eventually the pope was confined in virtual isolation and spartan conditions in Savona, a small town near Genoa. Pius, who had spent most of his life in Benedictine monasteries, was little discomfited by the rough conditions of his imprisonment. Nor was he impressed when, in the summer of 1812, Napoleon, hoping to substitute the carrot for the stick, transferred him to Fontainebleau, a luxurious château near Paris. Napoleon's blandishments were no more effective than his threats. Pius resolutely refused to renounce the territorial claims of the Papacy or to accept any arrangement that would reduce the Papacy to a chaplaincy of the French emperor. When, upon the fall of Napoleon in 1814, Pius was released from custody to return in triumph to Rome, the pope fully expected to reassume his position as both a secular and a spiritual ruler. Unfortunately, others did not share this expectation.[3]

At the Congress of Vienna, the great international conference convened to reconstitute the traditional European order upon the ruins of Napoleon's empire, Cardinal Ercole Consalvi, Pius VII's brilliant secretary of state, successfully negotiated the return to the Church of its territories and authority in central Italy. However, the odds against the pope or his successors retaining these territories and maintaining that authority were high. Under French occupation or influence almost continuously between 1798 and 1814, the States of the Church had borne the exactions, requisitions, and confiscations that were the unwelcome burden of any territory subdued by Napoleon. The papal territories, however, had also harvested the fruits of French domination, namely, the limited civil and social reforms that allowed Napoleon to justify, systematize, and exploit his conquests. Centuries-old clerical government had been swept away in a flood of decrees and proclamations and replaced by secular administrations staffed entirely by laymen. Civil law was clearly distinguished from ecclesiastical law, and the jurisdiction of the latter was significantly curtailed. Taxes were rationalized, while projects to improve education, transportation, and public order were put in hand. The secularization of politics and society and the reform of administrative institutions struck a responsive chord among the professional and middle classes in the papal territories. While these groups may have applauded the end of French domination, they did not welcome the return of papal power and clerical rule, both of which represented, in the minds of many, obscurantism, inefficiency, and repression.

The reform-minded subjects of the pope were also not immune to the rising national sentiment that looked toward the unification of the ancient and ineffectual principalities of the Italian peninsula into a single nation-state under a popular and progressive regime. Throughout Italy secret societies with such names as Guelfi (Guelphs), Carbonari (charcoal burners), Cavalieri della Libertà (Knights of Liberty), and Giovane Italia (Young Italy) appeared to challenge the traditional order and the regimes that protected that order. With their earnest manifestos, elaborate initiation rituals, and secret passwords, these groups adopted a comic-opera manner that often obscured the deadly seriousness of their revolutionary purpose. With the restoration of clerical rule in central Italy, several such groups committed themselves to the violent overthrow of papal government.

After the Congress of Vienna, ecclesiastical authorities, fearing that political and social reforms were merely the precursors of political and social revolution, had no intention of accommodating challenges to the pope's temporal rule in central Italy and condemned such challenges as dangerously radical and irreligious. A few farsighted individuals, such as Cardinal

Consalvi, were open to cautious change, recognizing that prudent and timely reforms were often a better guarantee against revolution than police repression. At the urging of his secretary of state, Pope Pius instituted several modest reforms aimed at humanizing the government of the Papal States without substantially changing it. Some, such as the separation of civil tribunals from ecclesiastical courts and the reorganization of finances, continued innovations introduced by the French; others, such as the prohibition of torture in judicial proceedings, merely formalized established practice. Unfortunately, reactionary elements in the College of Cardinals and the papal administration, known collectively as *zelanti* (zealots), successfully impeded and undermined reforms that might have removed at least some of the popular discontent and quieted the more strident voices calling for revolutionary change. Even before the death of Pius in July 1823 and the subsequent departure from office of Consalvi, the *zelanti* and their attitudes were in the ascendancy.

Pius's successors were committed to affirming rather than reforming the traditional order. Pope Leo XII (1823–29) was a reactionary who substituted principle for prudence and inflexibility for imagination. He dismissed Consalvi, canceled the administrative and legal reforms instituted by the reforming secretary of state, strengthened censorship of books and newspapers, restored the judicial privileges of the higher clergy, and built a new prison to house those convicted of heresy. To protect civic morality, his administration removed from public view statuary of nude figures, promulgated legislation regulating female dress, prohibited men from walking too closely behind women, and banned the waltz as obscene. Even medical vaccination was denounced as an imprudent departure from traditional practices. In the political realm, Leo endorsed the suppression of political dissent and excommunicated Catholics who joined the secret revolutionary societies.[4]

The pontificate of Pope Pius VIII (1829–30) was too brief to accomplish much beyond affirming the death penalty for revolutionaries. It was left to the next pope, Gregory XVI (1831–46), a pontiff so enamored with the past that he banned railroads from his domain, to face the political storm. Three days after his election a revolt broke out in Bologna, the principal city of the northern Papal States, and quickly spread across the country as the pope's small and ineffectual army fled the rebels or joined their ranks. Within three weeks the new pontiff controlled little beyond the walls of Rome, while inside the Eternal City antipapal conspirators were so active that Gregory considered fleeing to Genoa or Venice. The pope was saved only by the intervention of Austria, which dispatched an army from Austrian-controlled territories in northern Italy to ruthlessly suppress the rebellion. The victory, however, was only a temporary reprieve, since the surviving revolutionaries simply went underground to continue the struggle. The result was a low-intensity conflict of terrorist attacks by revolutionaries and counterterrorist operations by papal security forces that persisted throughout Gregory's pontificate.[5]

Briefly it seemed that Gregory's successor, Pius IX (1846–78), might assuage popular discontent and reverse the deteriorating political situation in the Papal States. A moderate reformer, Pius opened his pontificate by releasing political prisoners and decreeing modest reforms, including the liberalization of press controls and the creation of city and state councils that included laymen. These changes, however, merely fueled popular expectations. When Pius made it clear that the reforms were the limit of his concessions, that he had no intention of moving toward a constitutional monarchy that might compromise in any way his temporal sovereignty, and that he would not join a national crusade to expel the Austrians from northern Italy, popular disorders broke out in Rome. On 15 November 1848 an assassin murdered Pellegrino Rossi, the pope's chief minister. The next day an armed mob swarmed around the Palazzo Quirinale and exchanged gunfire with the Swiss Guards. Several guardsmen were wounded, and Pius's secretary was killed by a musket ball while standing next to the pontiff at a window. Enraged, the mob threatened to storm and destroy the palace unless the pope disarmed his Swiss Guards, accepted a "civic guard" as his new protectors, and granted a popular government. To avoid further bloodshed, Pius reluctantly acceded to these demands. His status uncertain, he remained in his palace under virtual house arrest until the evening of 24 November, when he made a run for it.

Pius began planning his escape even as his new "protectors" were taking up their positions outside his apartments and at the gates of his palace. The French, Bavarian, and Spanish ambassadors agreed to help: the Frenchman undertaking to get the pope out of the palace, the Bavarian to get him across the border to Naples, and the Spaniard to provide a ship to carry him, if necessary, to refuge in Spain. On the evening of 24 November the French ambassador arrived at the Quirinale and informed the civic guards that he had an audience with His Holiness. Admitted to the papal apartments, the ambassador began speaking in a loud voice as if in conversation with someone. This was for the benefit of the guards outside the door. While the diplomat carried on an imaginary conversation, the pope, dressed in the black cassock of a common priest, with his faced obscured by a muffler and dark glasses, slipped out through a secret stairway accompanied only by an aide.

At a side door to the palace, the two "priests" politely greeted the sentry and entered a waiting carriage that looked like any other coach available for hire in the city. The driver, a servant of the Bavarian ambassador but dressed as an ordinary city coachman, set off at a leisurely pace for the center of the city, but once out of sight of the palace, he reversed direction and raced to the Church of Saints Peter and Marcellinus, where the ambassador was waiting in his personal coach. Pius and his aide quickly switched vehicles and set off with the ambassador for the gate of San Giovanni, where the Bavarian used his diplomatic passport to pass the guards. Once outside the walls, the fugitives hurried to the nearby village of Ariccia, where the ambassador's wife was waiting with a heavy traveling coach. Another transfer, and then the fugitives were heading south. As dawn broke, they crossed the border into the Kingdom of Naples, and by midmorning they were in the small town of Gaeta, where Pius established a Papacy-in-exile and appealed to the European powers for help.[6]

By March 1849 Austria, France, Naples, and Spain had agreed to restore the pope to Rome, where the revolutionaries, upon discovering the pope's flight, had decreed the end of the Papal States and the formation of the Roman Republic. Fierce bravado, however, was no substitute for sharp bayonets, and civic guards no match for professional soldiers. In early July French troops assaulted the Eternal City and suppressed the Roman Republic. Pius did not return to his capital until the spring of 1850. Disillusioned by his experience with political reform, the pope now embraced the politically reactionary posture of his immediate predecessors and adopted a policy of repressing rather than accommodating antiregime sentiments. Political dissidents returned to a conspiratorial life of secret cells and clandestine meetings, while papal security forces and the revolutionary bands reopened their war of attacks and reprisals, plots and counterplots.

As the popes struggled to suppress dissent and rebellion in the Papal States, the external world proved no less threatening than the internal. The revolution of 1831, when Pope Gregory had been compelled to request Austrian intervention, proved once and for all that the survival of the Papal States depended on the goodwill of foreign powers. Politically weak and militarily insignificant, the Papacy relied on friendly Catholic powers, especially France and Austria, to ensure its political control over central Italy. In 1832, for example, political disturbances in the pope's lands brought Austrian troops again to Bologna, while French soldiers secured the port of Ancona. Eighteen years later, it was French bayonets that recovered Rome for Pius IX.

The interests of Paris and Vienna, however, often clashed and just as often diverged from the interests of Rome. After the Congress of Vienna,

Austria controlled most of northern Italy, including Lombardy and the Veneto, and it considered the rest of the peninsula a sphere of influence. This political and military presence was a serious irritant to the nationalist sentiments of an increasing number of Italians and a significant obstacle to the dynastic ambitions of the royal House of Savoy, which ruled the Kingdom of Piedmont in the northwest corner of the peninsula but saw itself as the rightful sovereign of all of Italy. To protect their territories in northern Italy and to maintain their political influence in the remainder of the peninsula, the Austrians expected the Italian principalities, Modena, Parma, Tuscany, and the Papal States, to align themselves with Vienna and to acquiesce in the intervention of Austrian troops to maintain the traditional order against internal and external threats. France, concerned to balance Austria, sought to assert its own influence in Italy and restrain the exercise of Austrian power. In pursuit of this policy Paris vacillated between supporting the independence of the Papal States and supporting Austria's archenemy, the Kingdom of Piedmont, whose aspirations were, in the long run, a direct threat to the Papacy. For its part, Piedmont was a constant threat to the territorial integrity of the Papal States and the political independence of the pope as it sought to incorporate all of Italy into a unified kingdom under the House of Savoy.

To navigate between the rocks of internal revolution and the shoals of foreign intervention and aggression, the Papacy needed good intelligence. With accurate and timely information papal authorities could neutralize subversive threats by identifying, locating, and suppressing individuals and organizations conspiring against the pope's government. With good intelligence the authorities could also anticipate decisions in Paris, Turin, and Vienna that would impact the independence of the pope and his territories. Intelligence, however, could not be summoned simply with a wave of a magic wand.

In the early nineteenth century the Papacy, like the other principalities with which it shared the Italian peninsula, did not have formal intelligence or security services in the sense of specialized organizations with trained personnel dedicated solely to the collection of information and the penetration of hostile governments and groups. Various officials and organizations performed intelligence activities, often as an adjunct to their principal responsibilities. In the first half of the century, for example, as many as five organizations had some responsibility for internal security and countersubversion in the Papal States.[7]

For foreign intelligence the Vatican depended primarily on its network of nuncios (ambassadors) and consuls in the various countries with which the Papacy maintained diplomatic or consular relations. The nuncios reported to the secretariat of state, the office in the papal administration responsible for the foreign affairs of the Papacy. The pope's diplomatic representatives were expected to report any information concerning ecclesiastical, political, military, and economic affairs that came their way. Although the account books of a papal nunciature (embassy) might include an entry recording "expenses for secret service of the Secretariat of State," secret agents were not a nuncio's principal sources of intelligence. The pope's diplomatic representatives gathered information primarily through personal contacts in the political and social circles of their host government, and they were much more likely to uncover a news item at a court reception or in a conversation with a socially prominent baron than in furtive, nighttime meetings with paid informants.

By conscientiously cultivating personal contacts, an enterprising nuncio might harvest a surprisingly diverse crop of intelligence. Dispatches from the papal representative in the Kingdom of Naples in the early 1840s, for example, included items on the familial scandals of prominent Sicilian aristocrats, the status of diplomatic negotiations between Britain and China, social unrest in Ireland, an outbreak of cholera in the Aegean Islands, the political situation in France, and the travels of the grand duchess of Tuscany.[8] At times the quantity and quality of intelligence collected by papal diplomats were excellent. More commonly, however, both quantity and quality were, at best, no more than adequate.

Much depended on the initiative and appetites of the papal representative. The Abbé de Salamon, the pope's secret representative in revolutionary Paris in the 1790s, was courageous and resourceful at a time and in a place that required both qualities in large measure. The National Assembly, the popular convention that had displaced King Louis XVI and his ministers as the governing authority in France, had moved to restructure the Catholic Church in France by unilaterally confiscating church lands, abolishing the monastic orders, reducing the number of dioceses, and instituting a civil oath for the clergy. In protest Pius VI had recalled his nuncio, but, reluctant to lose touch with fast-changing events in Paris, the pope directed Salamon to establish himself in the French capital and secretly report developments. It was a difficult period for France and a perilous time for the institutions of the traditional order, particularly the monarchy and the Church. In June 1791 the king and his family were arrested as they fled Paris for Montmédy and the sanctuary of the Austrian Netherlands. In October the increasingly radical assembly reconvened and deliberately adopted a more anticlerical posture. The polemical and legal assaults against the Church culminated in

September 1792 in a series of massacres, which included more than two hundred priests among the victims. Thousands of priests fled abroad, while those who remained in France and refused to pledge loyalty to the anti-clerical regime were forced into an underground existence.

Through all these events, Salomon served as the pope's clandestine eyes and ears in the French capital. He spent his days on the streets and in the shops and taverns of Paris and his nights in a hideout under a kiosk in the Bois de Boulogne. He developed contacts with bishops and priests in the provinces, and he collected newspapers, pamphlets, and broadsheets to include with his detailed reports to the Vatican. To evade the mail surveillance established by the revolutionary regime to expose sedition and espionage, he set up clandestine channels of communication with Rome. Exposed, arrested, and imprisoned, Salomon survived the infamous September Massacres and upon his release from custody immediately returned to his intelligence work for the pope.[9]

Monsignor Francesco Capaccini was another conscientious and industrious observer. During his service as nuncio in Holland (1829–31), Capaccini cultivated a range of contacts in the royal court and the government from whom he acquired useful and, at times, highly secret information. A former director of the Dutch police (who also happened to be the brother-in-law of the papal nuncio in Bavaria) regularly slipped Capaccini confidential information on various members of the States General, the Dutch parliament. A counselor of state provided intelligence "of the highest secrecy" concerning the personal lives of the royal family, particularly the prince of Orange. At times the nuncio was prudently vague about his sources and methods, as when he informed Rome that he managed "to have in my hands for a few minutes" a confidential report from the Dutch ambassador at the Vatican informing his government of recent developments in the Papal States. Monsignor Capaccini's net stretched even beyond the Dutch capital. In the late summer of 1829 he received information that a dozen men had met in the town of Spa to plot subversive activities in the Papal States. The conspirators, who had access to plentiful funds and a printing press, planned to travel separately to the Tuscan port of Livorno, from where they would enter the Papal States under the guise of pilgrims. Once in the pope's territory they intended to distribute revolutionary and antipapal literature. Passing this information to the secretariat of state, Capaccini reported that his source was an artisan who was part of the conspiracy and who claimed to have been moved by religious scruples to expose the plot. The careful nuncio noted, however, that this young man carried a grudge against his compatriots and probably betrayed them as revenge for some slight or insult.[10]

If every papal representative had been as conscientious in the collection of political intelligence as Monsignor Capaccini or the Abbé de Salamon, the nineteenth-century Papacy would have been among the best-informed governments in Europe. Unfortunately, the standards set by Capaccini and Salamon were only occasionally met by their colleagues, who as a group tended to neglect the intelligence element of their responsibilities. The experience of Monsignor Antonino De Luca, who served as nuncio in Munich (1853–56) and Vienna (1856–63), was more typical. Educated in history, philosophy, and theology and fluent in several languages, the Sicilian prelate had been called to Rome in 1829 to edit a theological journal and serve as a learned consultant to various departments in the Roman Curia. In 1845 he was consecrated bishop of Aversa, a town in the southern region of Campania, where his tenure was distinguished by thoughtful initiatives to improve the education and spirituality of the clergy. In 1853 the scholarly bishop was suddenly plucked from his southern diocese and packed off to Bavaria as nuncio, a post for which he was prepared by neither training nor temperament. Three years later he was transferred to Vienna, the most important post in the papal diplomatic service.

Despite his brief apprenticeship in Munich, De Luca had not grasped the fact that the job description of a papal ambassador included the collection of intelligence. Periodically the secretariat of state had to remind its man in Vienna to include in his reports information about political and diplomatic developments in the Austrian capital. When, in February 1859, the British ambassador to France, Lord Cowley, arrived in Vienna for discussions seeking to avert a war between Austria and France over the latter's support for the Kingdom of Piedmont's efforts to expel Austrian influence from the Italian peninsula, Cardinal Giacomo Antonelli, the papal secretary of state, found it necessary to remind De Luca that "since Italian affairs are not extraneous to the diplomatic issues, it would indeed be useful to be kept up to date on the negotiations that are taking place there." The nuncio had so little appreciation of his intelligence responsibilities that he would tack on to the end of a dispatch, almost as an afterthought, the news that a traitorous officer in the Piedmontese army had secretly offered him the plans to fortifications in the Romagna, a region formerly part of the Papal States that had been annexed in 1860 by the Kingdom of Piedmont, which was now styling itself the Kingdom of Italy.[11]

Nuncios like De Luca were often constrained by their education, experience, and outlook to adopt a rather narrow perspective on their responsibilities as representatives of the pope. Learned theologians, pious priests, conscientious bishops, they were often poor intelligence officers. Products of an ecclesiastical culture and education, they were more comfortable with religious issues than with political, military, or economic matters. Since they were responsible for monitoring the health of the Catholic Church in their host country, as well as representing the pope before that country's government, this preference was not entirely dysfunctional. Not surprisingly, their reports on such topics as the state of religious observance in the country, the quality of religious instruction, the piety of the clergy, and the performance of bishops reflected a degree of interest, a measure of detail, and a breadth of understanding not often present in their reports concerning the political scene.

If the quantity and quality of intelligence flowing into the Vatican were restricted by the limitations of the papal diplomatic personnel, it was also restricted by the inadequacy of the papal diplomatic network. In the first half of the nineteenth century the Papacy maintained relations with only a handful of states, the vast majority in western Europe. In 1840, for example, the pope had nuncios in only eleven countries. All but two (Brazil and Colombia) were in western Europe, all but two (Holland and Switzerland) were predominantly Catholic in population and culture, and three (Kingdom of Naples, Grand Duchy of Tuscany, and Kingdom of Piedmont) were neighbors of the pope on the Italian peninsula.[12] There were no nuncios in London or St. Petersburg, capitals of two of the most important powers in the nineteenth century. Entire regions of the globe were without papal representation: Africa, Asia, the Middle East, Scandinavia, North America, and most of South America. For all their inadequacies, the nuncios generated at least some political intelligence, but their concentration in a handful of western European capitals meant that the popes were often ill informed, or not informed at all, about events in other parts of the world.

Occasionally the Vatican tried to overcome this problem by sending special representatives to particular countries or areas. These special missions were temporary and usually focused on the investigation of particular ecclesiastical problems, although their reports might refer to political events. In 1853, for example, Archbishop Gaetano Bedini, a capable papal diplomat with experience in Austria and Brazil, was dispatched on a special mission to the United States to observe the condition of the Catholic Church. For seven months Bedini toured the country, meeting prominent political figures, including President Franklin Pierce; consulting with priests, nuns, bishops, and lay Catholics; and narrowly escaping lynching by anti-Catholic mobs in Cincinnati, Ohio, and Wheeling, West Virginia.

Not surprisingly, the temporary nature of such special missions and their ecclesiastical focus made them poor sources for foreign intelligence. At best

they provided Rome with the equivalent of a snapshot of a place at a particular time, but with no provision for follow-up observations. Moreover, the
snapshot (to continue the metaphor) featured churches and people in clerical garb, but secular personalities and secular institutions appeared only on
the margins, if at all. Archbishop Bedini's experience is a case in point. The
bulk of his final report to the Vatican concerns the condition of the Catholic Church in the United States. Political and economic subjects are touched
upon in a short addendum that focuses primarily on arguments for and
against establishing a papal nunciature in Washington. Bedini's observations on American society, especially its economic potential, were insightful, but they lacked the scope and specificity that distinguished his much
longer treatment of ecclesiastical matters.[13]

Compared with nuncios, papal consuls were only a minor source of intelligence. The Papacy's consular network was not extensive; with the exception of a handful of posts in the Western Hemisphere, the consulates
were located in the ports or commercial centers of the Italian peninsula,
southern France, and Spain. The consuls issued passports, visas, and health
certificates, notarized documents, and generally expedited the foreign trade
and commerce of the Papal States. Since such trade and commerce were
modest, there was little need for a full-time, professional consular service.
Consular duties were usually entrusted to Catholic residents of ports and
cities who performed their duties in moments spared from their regular
employment as lawyers, notaries, or merchants.

Papal consuls communicated infrequently with Rome, and their reports normally contained little intelligence beyond news of arrivals and
departures of merchant vessels and the transit of travelers bound for the
Papal States. Depending on the energy and initiative of the particular consul, a report might contain the occasional piece of political intelligence.
During the American Civil War, for example, the papal consul in New
York, Louis Binsse, included in his annual reports brief surveys of political
and military developments in the United States. His report for 1864, for
example, noted the tightening of the federal naval blockade of the South
and the deteriorating military position of the Confederacy. The report
also indicated that the emancipation of the slaves was progressing and
that the reelection of President Abraham Lincoln signaled the determination of the North to prosecute the war and reestablish the Union at all
costs. Such reports, however, were the exception rather than the rule.
Most papal consuls were content to submit annual or biannual financial
accounts and lists of passports issued and documents registered. In
Binsse's case, one is left with the impression that he included political in-

formation in his one dispatch to Rome each year because he had nothing else to report. Trade between the United States and the Papal States was practically nonexistent, and the work of the pope's consul in New York consisted merely of issuing three or four passports a year. For its part, the pope's secretariat of state, which never solicited political intelligence from its consul, did nothing to encourage their man in New York. It was not unusual for more than a year to pass without a communication from Rome to its New York consulate.[14]

A potential source of political intelligence that was rarely exploited was the network of bishops, priests, and religious orders that stretched around the world. Anticlericals readily imagined a secret army of priests and confessors, more loyal to their pope than to their sovereign, and more committed to their religion than to their country, who assiduously reported to the Vatican the political, military, and economic secrets that reputedly came their way in the course of their religious ministrations to princes and paupers, statesmen and servants. In such fantasies the pope's minions formed an invisible web along whose strands a constant stream of secret intelligence flowed toward Rome from the most distant corners of the globe.

The reality was far different. Information did flow into the Vatican from priests and members of religious orders, but this information related almost exclusively to internal church affairs. The worldwide ecclesiastical network produced very little political intelligence. In a collection of more than twenty-one hundred letters and reports submitted to the Vatican by priests, bishops, nuns, and monks in the United States between 1840 and 1862, there were scarcely a dozen references to political affairs, and even these usually amounted to little more than brief, one- or two-sentence notices. The events and issues that disturbed American politics in this period—the war with Mexico, the political battle over the extension of slavery, the election of Abraham Lincoln, and the outbreak of the Civil War—are barely visible in the mass of letters announcing the death of a bishop, reporting the construction of a new cathedral, requesting the assignment of nuns to a convent school, or seeking guidance concerning the appropriate liturgical formula for the blessing of church bells.[15]

The Vatican made no attempt to mobilize its ecclesiastical resources to collect political or military information. The effort required to organize, coordinate, and process the intelligence activities of tens of thousands of priests, monks, and nuns was beyond the administrative capacity of the inefficient departments of the papal administration. More important, such an effort was also beyond the inclinations, if not the imaginations, of clerics inside the Vatican and in distant ecclesiastical fields, who were accustomed by faith, education, and training to consider their church and its institutions instruments for the salvation of souls rather than the collection of intelligence.

It rarely occurred to a bishop in the United States, a parish priest in Holland, or a missionary in India to be alert for political information to forward to Rome. Even when procedures were in place for reporting to the Vatican, they were rarely turned toward the collection of intelligence. Diocesan reports are a case in point. Since the Counter-Reformation in the sixteenth century, bishops were required to submit reports on conditions in their dioceses. To supplement the periodic reports, each bishop was also required to visit the Vatican every five years to discuss with officials the state of his diocese and to renew his homage to the pope. Potentially such reports and visits were useful devices for collecting a range of information from around the world. In practice, however, they never came close to achieving that potential. For one thing, the requirements were poorly enforced. Bishops from distant dioceses might avoid the journey to Rome by pleading ill health or lack of funds. The written reports were of uneven length and quality and, depending on the diligence of the bishop and the vagaries of nineteenth-century communications, often arrived in Rome late or not at all. These reports focused almost exclusively on spiritual and ecclesiastical conditions in the dioceses. The statement from the American diocese of St. Louis, Missouri, for 1851 is probably typical of the episcopal reports reaching the Vatican at midcentury. In a mere three handwritten pages the bishop provided a cursory history of his diocese, a description of its geography, some statistics on the number of churches, clergy, and practicing Catholics, and an account of diocesan finances. There was no mention of political, economic, or military affairs.[16]

When bishops or clergy did take the initiative to forward political information to Rome, the credibility of this intelligence was often compromised by the political prejudices of the source. During the American Civil War, for example, the Papacy received conflicting accounts from bishops who found it difficult to rise above sectional and partisan loyalties. Initially, Pope Pius IX and his cardinal secretary of state, Giacomo Antonelli, supported President Abraham Lincoln's efforts to preserve the Union through military force. Papal policy depended, in part, on information provided by the archbishop of New York, John Hughes, who appeared unannounced and uninvited in Rome in February 1862, a mere ten months after secessionist forces initiated hostilities by attacking Fort Sumter. Although Hughes told papal authorities that he served no sectional interests and merely wished to provide them a disinterested account of events in the United States, the archbishop was in fact a witting agent and propagandist for Washington. His expenses were paid by the government, and he sent written reports to Secretary of State William Seward, who had charged him with the mission of securing the sympathy of the Papacy by impressing upon the pope the justice of the North's cause. Hughes belittled the military prospects of the secessionists and warned Rome that the Confederacy was planning to attack Mexico and Catholic islands in the Caribbean.[17]

Papal sympathy for the North lessened when Rome began to receive intelligence from different (though no more disinterested) sources. In the spring of 1863, Rome received a long report on the war from Martin J. Spalding, the pro-secessionist bishop of Louisville, Kentucky. According to Spalding, the Southern states had been provoked into secession by their Northern neighbors, who exploited them economically and insisted on an unrealistic policy toward slavery. He assured Rome that the emancipation of the slaves (decreed by President Lincoln in 1862) was the goal of a small but influential movement of fanatic and vindictive Protestant abolitionists, who wanted only to humiliate and punish the South. The bishop warned papal authorities that the slaves, inclined by nature toward sloth and licentiousness, were woefully unprepared for freedom and that emancipation would produce social disorder and seriously compromise the Church's missionary work among blacks.[18]

Papal officials heard similar testimony from Patrick Lynch, the bishop of Charleston, South Carolina, who traveled to Rome in the spring of 1864 on a mission for Judah Benjamin, the Confederate secretary of state. Directed by Benjamin to plead the South's cause and secure, if possible, the pope's diplomatic recognition of the Confederacy, Lynch, who was already known in the Eternal City for his moving reports on the human costs of the conflict, assured the bishops and monsignors in the papal administration that, despite the high-minded rhetoric of President Lincoln, the North was intent on prosecuting a barbarous and destructive war for purely materialistic and ignoble motives. Fearing that the pope and his advisers were being misled by the information provided by Bishop Lynch, Washington felt compelled to launch a major (and ultimately successful) diplomatic offensive in Rome to recover the moral and political advantage.[19]

The reports of Hughes, Lynch, and Spalding revealed that Catholic bishops were no more immune from political and sectional loyalties than farmers, plantation owners, and shopkeepers. In the case of the American Civil War, partisan reports from politically committed sources confused papal authorities and complicated their efforts to develop a consistent policy toward Washington and Richmond. Vacillations in that policy, with the

Papacy initially sympathizing with the North, then sympathizing with the South, and finally turning again to the North, reflect the inadequacies of the intelligence reaching Rome from its American bishops and the inability of papal authorities to determine with any confidence the true state of affairs in North America.

The papal delegates and governors who administered the various provinces and cities of the Papal States in the first half of the nineteenth century were a more fruitful source of political intelligence through their control of local police forces. Preoccupied with domestic order and security in an era when revolutionary movements increasingly threatened the political and territorial integrity of the pope's domain, the delegates naturally focused on internal affairs, particularly countersubversion and the surveillance of dissidents, although those who administered border provinces sometimes collected intelligence from foreign territory.

In addition to special reports on particular events or problems, each provincial administration prepared weekly political bulletins that described police activities in such areas as the censorship of books, newspapers, and public entertainment; the oversight of public employees; the surveillance of foreigners and travelers; and the investigation of political subversion. The bulletins and other reports were forwarded to the secretariat of state, which supervised the collection of foreign and domestic intelligence, or, less frequently, to the directorate general of police in Rome.[20]

The delegates and their police services collected intelligence from secret agents, the surveillance of individuals, and the interception of mail.[21] Lacking a specialized intelligence or security service separate from the regular police, the delegates, more or less haphazardly, recruited agents to collect political information. Most of these informants reported directly to the delegates, although occasionally an agent might report to the police, who separately recruited their own secret sources. The number of such informants varied according to the needs, industry, and luck of the individual delegate. A few administrators built their careers on a reputation for skillful secret service work. Monsignor Tiberio Pacca, whom we have already met interrogating the repentant revolutionary, Paolo Monti, as director of the pontifical police, first came to the notice of his superiors during the Congress of Vienna when, as the delegate in the port of Civitavecchia, he exposed the exiled Napoleon's efforts to set up clandestine communication channels into Italy. As a young delegate in the small town of Rieti, north of Rome, Monsignor Tancredi Bellà uncovered a hitherto unknown conspiratorial group, Fedeltà e Mistero (Fidelity and Mystery), thereby launching a career in secret service operations that would impress even the exacting

Austrians and eventually carry him (via increasingly responsible posts in Spoleto, Perugia, and Ancona) to the College of Cardinals. As delegate in Ancona in the fall of 1859, Bellà achieved his greatest intelligence success by uncovering a major conspiracy to overthrow papal rule in the Marche region with covert support from the Kingdom of Piedmont.

Each delegate controlled ten to twelve principal agents, each of whom recruited his own network of local informants. One such agent was a police inspector in Pesaro who had previously served in the police services of Tuscany and Venice. After the incorporation of the Grand Duchy of Tuscany into the Kingdom of Italy in 1860, he moved to the Adriatic port of Pesaro to ply his trade under papal auspices. He eventually left the pope's service to join the police of the Kingdom of Naples. Another principal agent had worked (under eight aliases) as an informant for the papal nuncio in Florence and for the police in Naples before moving to Pesaro. In addition to serving the delegate in Pesaro, he also reported to the delegate in Ancona and, when his papal superiors were not looking, sold information to his former employers in the Neapolitan police.

Agents collected information on domestic political opinion, the circulation of subversive literature, the membership of revolutionary cells, the morale of papal troops, and political developments in the neighboring states of Tuscany, Naples, and Piedmont. The expense accounts of the delegates suggest the scope of the operations: 21 scudi to an army captain to purchase civilian clothes for undercover work, 45 scudi to support an agent on a journey through Tuscany and Austrian-controlled Lombardy, 1 scudo a day to maintain a "listening post" in Senigallia on the Adriatic coast, 32 scudi to send an agent to Bologna "to implement interesting operations," an unspecified sum to station women at the gates of Ancona to observe and converse with people entering or leaving the city, 26 scudi to send a police officer to meet informants in the mountains of the Marche.

Although the emphasis was on domestic surveillance and security, foreign intelligence often appeared in reports. In the summer of 1814, shortly after Napoleon's exile to the island of Elba, the papal delegate in Viterbo obtained from an agent information about fortifications on the island. Later that year, the police in Civitavecchia learned from travelers disembarking from Corsica that the strength of the Bonapartist Party on that French island was growing.[22] In mid–April 1859, with Austria and Piedmont on the verge of war over the latter's determination to expel Austrian influence from the Italian peninsula, and the world wondering if France would support the House of Savoy, the papal delegate in Pesaro submitted a current intelligence survey that reported that volunteers from all over Italy were flocking to volunteer for the Piedmontese cause; that the revolutionary firebrand Giuseppe Garibaldi was in the northern city of Como organizing a special corps known as the Cacciatori delle Alpi (Alpine Hunters) for service against not the Austrians but the traditionalist regimes in the Papal States and the Grand Duchy of Tuscany; that antipapal exiles in Piedmontese territory were sending death threats to employees of the papal police in the Romagna and Marche regions of the Papal States; and that France was massing troops on its border with Piedmont.[23] Between March and August 1860, the delegate in Ancona received from his agents information on a diverse range of topics, including Garibaldi's health, student unrest in Bavaria, the transfer of French troops to the Levant to protect Catholics from Muslim attacks, and the departure of Garibaldi and five hundred of his men for Sicily.

Of course the accuracy, relevance, and timeliness of foreign intelligence reports were uneven. Many were accurate but trivial, such as a report that Garibaldi had rheumatism or that a Colonel Tornetta of the Piedmontese garrison at Rimini had broken his arm in a riding accident; others were important but inaccurate, such as a message, dated 27 April 1860, that Garibaldi had definitely sailed for Sicily with an armed band when, in fact, he would not depart until 5 May. On the other hand, some intelligence was on target. The report on the Cacciatori delle Alpi correctly identified the name of the unit, its approximate size, its brigade commanders, and its mission. The report erred only in placing the corps in Como when, in fact, the unit was outfitting fifty miles away in Brusaco.

The quality of the foreign intelligence flowing into the Vatican in the first half of the nineteenth century was, at best, uneven. As noted earlier, the quantity and quality of such intelligence were negatively affected by the professional assumptions, characteristics, and preparation of the personnel (nuncios and consuls) upon whom the Papacy largely relied for foreign intelligence. Organizational problems, such as the limited papal diplomatic network, also constrained efforts by the Vatican to remain informed of current events around the world. Even apparently trivial matters, such as the delivery of mail, could significantly impede those efforts.

In the first half of the nineteenth century, all European governments, including the Papacy, routinely kept mail passing through their post offices under surveillance in order to monitor domestic opinion, forestall subversive or criminal activity, and collect intelligence on neighboring states. The Papacy had long been the target of such surveillance. Cardinal Consalvi, the great papal secretary of state, had lost all confidence in the French postal system as early as 1801 when, during negotiations in Paris over a new concordat, the confidential letters between the papal representative in the French capital and the secretariat of state in Rome had been intercepted and opened by French authorities. Indeed, during the Napoleonic Wars the interception of the pope's correspondence was a priority for French intelligence, and this interest did not die with Napoleon's imperial ambitions. Well beyond midcentury the nuncios in Paris continued to complain to Rome that dispatches from the Vatican were "lost" or suspiciously delayed in transit. They suspected (correctly) that French authorities diverted these dispatches so that they could be opened and copied.[24]

The Vatican had even less cause to trust the Austrian mails. During the Congress of Vienna, Cardinal Consalvi's correspondence was closely monitored by his hosts (who were watching *everyone's* mail), and Austria's interest in papal communications continued long after the close of the conference. When representatives of the various Italian principalities gathered in the Austrian-controlled city of Verona in 1822 to discuss, among other topics, a postal agreement, Consalvi told the papal delegation to assume that Austrian intelligence would open all letters. As late as 1860 the nuncio in Vienna feared that any dispatches consigned to the Austrian post office would be opened, and he, too, reported suspicious delays in the delivery of telegrams addressed to the nunciature. When instructed by the secretariat of state, in the summer of 1860, to forward by secure means certain confidential letters for the papal representatives in Brussels and Paris, the nuncio replied that there were no secure communication channels between Vienna and those capitals.[25]

The minor powers were no less a threat to papal communications than Austria and France. Spain and Piedmont routinely intercepted and opened papal dispatches passing through their territory. The nuncio in the Low Countries, Francesco Capaccini, warned the secretariat of state to use the "utmost caution" in communicating with him, since he was certain that his mail was read. In 1829 the enterprising nuncio actually contrived an elaborate stratagem that caught his hosts at their game. An embarrassed official could only assure the pope's representative that his mail was not intercepted and that the whole affair was a terrible misunderstanding. Whatever satisfaction Capaccini derived from this incident was short-lived; within weeks he was again warning the secretariat of state that letters from Rome arrived bearing clear signs of having been opened.[26]

The absence of secure communication channels had serious consequences for papal diplomacy and the administration of a global church. Forewarned through mail surveillance of papal decisions or initiatives, a government such as that of France or Austria could more readily prepare a timely and appropriate response. In diplomatic negotiations, for instance, such forewarning could seriously weaken the hand of the pope's negotiators. Less apparent, but no less significant, was the impact on the process by which papal representatives reported to Rome and, in turn, received instructions from Rome. Aware that their correspondence was intercepted, nuncios did not always speak frankly in their reports. They were especially careful in reporting political intelligence and the sources of that intelligence. They depended on circumlocution and hoped that their superiors in Rome would discern the true meaning of the message by reading between the lines. The secretariat of state was similarly restrained in its instructions to the nuncios. The result, not surprisingly, was confusion and misunderstanding because papal representatives were often unsure of Rome's purposes, while the secretariat of state was uncertain about the true situation on the ground.

To remedy this problem, the Papacy cast about for more secure channels of communication. To avoid postal surveillance, many governments used their own couriers to hand carry dispatches to and from their ambassadors. Unfortunately, the cost of maintaining a network of couriers to link the various papal diplomatic missions with Rome exceeded the capacity of the pope's treasury. The papal postal administration had a handful of special messengers, but they were too few to service regularly the nunciatures and were used primarily to carry official papers within the Papal States. Consequently, nuncios who wished to avoid the uncertainties of the ordinary mails were forced to make ad hoc arrangements.

Personal servants were often drafted into courier service in the expectation that their movements would not attract the attention of police agents. During the Congress of Vienna, when Austrian intelligence closely monitored the mail of all foreign delegations, Cardinal Consalvi successfully evaded surveillance by sending his valet to Rome with an important report. A nuncio in Paris never used the French mail for his most sensitive dispatches, preferring to entrust the letters to his butler, whose trips to Rome on various pretexts, such as family business, aroused little suspicion.

Trusted Catholic laymen were also used. In the early decades of the nineteenth century, the Papacy often called upon the services of Paul van der Vrecken, a pious gentleman from the Dutch town of Maestricht. Well known in ecclesiastical circles, van der Vrecken was recruited into papal service in 1813 through his friendship with Monsignor Tomaso Bernetti, an aide to Pope Pius VII. When Pius had been seized by Napoleon's troops and placed under house arrest, first in Savona and then at Fontainebleau, his loyal cardinals were also seized and held under close surveillance in various

French cities. During these desperate times, as the pope tried to maintain some semblance of control over church affairs, van der Vrecken secretly carried money, letters, and encouragement to the isolated cardinals. At one clandestine meeting on the streets of Liege, Belgium, Bernetti entrusted him with letters for the nuncio in Austria. When van der Vrecken appeared unannounced at the nunciature in Vienna, the nuncio, who had had no news of the pope for more than a year, fainted at the sight of Pius's signature on the letters and, upon reviving, had to be convinced that the young man at his door was not an impostor or provocateur sent by French intelligence to trick him. Melodrama often followed the secret messengers on their journeys. Late one night in the summer of 1860, the household of the nuncio in Paris was awakened by a young man who refused to identify himself but insisted that he must see the nuncio at once. When the nuncio appeared in robe and slippers, the mysterious caller merely handed him a packet of letters from Rome and, without a word, disappeared into the night, never to be seen again.[27]

Secret messengers did not automatically guarantee security because police and intelligence services were aware of the subterfuge. During the Napoleonic period, the French police proved especially adept at ferreting out clandestine couriers. In one month alone (November 1809), the emperor's agents twice caught private citizens carrying letters between Pius VII (then in French custody in Savona) and his officials in Rome. In Paris the police threatened a certain Monsieur Curti with arrest if he carried letters for the Vatican. Arrest and imprisonment were not the only risks: on at least one occasion during the Napoleonic Wars, a secret papal messenger was intercepted and killed.[28]

Aware that even secret couriers did not provide complete security, papal officials adopted various stratagems to protect their correspondence. Assuming that foreign postal authorities routinely monitored all mail to or from certain addresses or individuals, such as the secretariat of state in Rome or the nuncio in Paris, papal officials used cover addresses to hide the true destination of their letters. In 1814 the Vatican, having recalled its nuncio from Paris, arranged for a certain Monsieur Perault to keep it informed concerning events in the French capital. Aware that all letters postmarked "Rome" were opened by French postal authorities before delivery in Paris, Cardinal Consalvi directed that letters to Perault should bear neither his name nor his address. They were to be addressed to Monsieur Bertaud Duvoin, an inhabitant of the southern town of Lyon, who would forward them to Perault or hold them for collection by the papal agent. The cardinal secretary of state had discovered that letters with a Rome postmark were not opened in Lyon, nor were letters arriving in Paris from that provincial city. For his part, Perault would address his reports not to the pope's secretariat of state but to a Roman merchant, Pietro Paolo Paperi, who would deliver them to the Vatican. Fifteen years later Francesco Capaccini would adopt a similar, though more elaborate, subterfuge to protect his dispatches from the Netherlands. Capaccini mailed his reports to a half dozen cover addresses in Rome from whence they would be delivered to the secretariat of state. Before midcentury, many nuncios used banks, particularly a Franco-Italian firm, the Goupy-Busoni, as mail drops. While clever, the use of cover addresses did not necessarily ensure security. The trick was an old one, dating back at least to the seventeenth century, and police services were well practiced in exposing it. During the Reign of Terror, for instance, an elaborate system of cover addresses did not protect the correspondence of the pope's secret representative in Paris, the Abbé de Salamon, from interception by the French authorities.[29]

If the pope could not keep his communications from falling into unauthorized hands, he might still hide them from unauthorized eyes. Like most governments, the Papacy used codes and ciphers to protect its most sensitive communications.[30] This practice had a long, distinguished history at the Vatican. The oldest code in the papal archives dates from the early fourteenth century, and by the sixteenth century the office of cipher secretary had become a prominent fixture in the papal administration. Under two of the earliest cipher secretaries, Giovanni Batista Argenti and his nephew and successor, Matteo Argenti, papal cryptography reached a level of sophistication that made it the wonder of Renaissance diplomacy.

Remnants of past fame survived into the nineteenth century. For a brief period in the 1820s the Papacy employed what was probably the most secure cryptographic system in Europe: the polyalphabetic cipher. A cipher usually replaces (enciphers) each letter in the original message (the plaintext) with another letter to create a new version (ciphertext) of the message. The plaintext "Pope dead" becomes the ciphertext "KLKV WVZW" in a cipher in which a = Z, b = Y, c = X, . . . z = A. The cipher equivalents (Z, Y, X, . . . A) are known as a cipher alphabet. If, as in this example, the same element in the cipher alphabet always replaces the same letter in the plaintext (a always = Z, b always = Y, etc.), then the cipher is said to be monoalphabetic. It is possible, however, to use several cipher alphabets to encipher a single message. The first cipher alphabet would be used to encipher the first letter in the plaintext, the second cipher alphabet would be used for the second letter, the third cipher alphabet would be used for the third letter, and so on until the ciphertext is complete. Beginning with the cipher alphabet a = Z, b = Y, c = X, . . . z = A, a cipher clerk could create additional cipher alphabets simply by shifting the first alphabet one place to the left each time. The second cipher alphabet would be a = Y, b = X, c = W, . . . z = B, while the third would be a = X, b = W, c = V, . . . z = C. Using these three alphabets in rotation, the plaintext "Pope dead" becomes the ciphertext "KKIV VTZV." A cipher that rotates through several alphabets is a polyalphabetic cipher. Increased security could be achieved by increasing the number of alphabets and devising complicated "keys" for determining their composition.

Conceived in the fifteenth century by the great Renaissance polymath Leon Battista Alberti and acclaimed by Matteo Argenti, the famous papal cipher secretary, as "the noblest and greatest [ciphers] in the world," polyalphabetic ciphers were understood to provide a high degree of security because they avoided the fixed replacement of the letters of the alphabet with the same cipher symbols throughout a message (a always = Z, b always = Y, etc.), a practice that renders monoalphabetic systems particularly susceptible to solution by codebreakers. Professional cryptographers, however, generally were reluctant to adopt polyalphabetics because their operation required too much time and concentration.[31] The frequently changing alphabets too easily confused cipher clerks with the result that encrypted messages were often undecipherable by their intended reader. Well into the nineteenth century, governments preferred to use simple, monoalphabetic ciphers or, more commonly, "nomenclators," hybrid systems that combined the features of a cipher and code. A typical nomenclator would have numerical substitutes for each letter of the alphabet (a = 11, b = 42), as well as for a number of commonly used proper and common nouns (Napoleon = 396, Vienna = 368, army = 310).

The Papacy's decision to abandon conventional practice and adopt polyalphabetic ciphers to protect its secret communications was the result of the influence of Monsignor Francesco Capaccini, who, before his assignment as nuncio to Belgium and Holland in 1828, served for several years as a senior clerk in the papal secretariat of state. Capaccini was a cryptographer of some imagination (as nuncio to the Low Countries he would design several cryptosystems for his personal use), and he was convinced that the nomenclators then in service in the secretariat were hopelessly insecure. He persuaded Pope Leo XII, himself a former nuncio with personal experience in ciphering dispatches, that polyalphabetic ciphers provided much more security than other systems. In June 1829 he recalled the experience in a letter to the cardinal secretary of state, Giuseppe Albani:

Since our old ciphers were known to everyone, when I was in the Secretariat of State I composed, with much effort, a new one which is the one I now use. Pope Leo XII laughed at me, saying that no cipher is unbreakable, but when he saw that a professional cryptologist, who was then in Rome, could not break mine and had to give up, he authorized me to use it for correspondence. This cipher, however, is very difficult and requires much time to cipher, and perhaps even more to decipher, as Your Eminence will have already discovered.[32]

The Papacy's polyalphabetic ciphers were probably the best cryptosystems in Europe in the 1820s, and they provided a relatively high degree of security against attacks by the cryptanalytic bureaus (the so-called Black Chambers) of the European powers. In a cryptologic world where the nomenclator was king, few of the professional codebreakers employed by London, Paris, St. Petersburg, or Vienna had any experience with polyalphabetic ciphers, and even fewer were able to unlock their secrets. Ironically, the Papacy abandoned these useful ciphers after only a few years of service. Notoriously laborious and prone to errors in ciphering and deciphering as correspondents tried to keep track of the shifting alphabets, the polyalphabetics frustrated papal cipher clerks, who were often unable to turn the lines of jumbled letters into meaningful language. The margins of dispatches bear witness to this frustration. A dispatch from the nuncio in Madrid concerning his confidential interview with a Spanish politician might bear the marginal notation "Because of a mistake in enciphering it isn't possible to read the name of the person indicated," while the top of a undecrypted report from the nuncio in Vienna might carry the complaint "Armellini gave up trying to decipher this dispatch." Several lines of ciphertext in a letter might remain unintelligible, a sure sign of confusion over the proper cipher key.[33]

It is easy to imagine papal cipher clerks cursing the polyalphabetics and urging a return to the simple ciphers and nomenclators that had served so well in the past. By the late 1830s these voices won out, and the polyalphabetic ciphers were withdrawn from service. Their replacements provided nowhere near the same level of security. In the 1840s, for example, the nunciature in Madrid used three monoalphabetic ciphers, including one in which the letters of the alphabet were replaced by two-digit numerical groups in ascending order (a = 11, b = 12, c = 13, ... z = 36). Such simplistic systems were unlikely to fool for long the professional codebreakers in the various European chancelleries. They certainly engendered little confidence among the nuncios who used them. In 1859, for instance, the nuncio in Vienna warned the secretariat of state that his ciphers provided no protection against the skilled cryptanalysts who worked for the Austrian government.[34]

Insecure communications were not the only factor contributing to the uneven quality of the Papacy's foreign intelligence. Papal intelligence was also undercut by a rather unsystematic approach to collecting information. While the Vatican might occasionally instruct a nuncio to seek a particular item of diplomatic or military information, or direct a provincial delegate to monitor the mail of a suspected dissident, the pope's representatives at home and abroad were largely left to their own devices when it came to determining what intelligence was required in Rome. Consequently, the representatives collected material rather indiscriminately, reporting whatever came their way. Unfortunately, they usually had no systematic way to assess the reliability of their informants or the veracity of their intelligence. Occasionally, a delegate or nuncio might refer to "a trusted informant" or seek to place a report in a larger context, but more commonly he simply passed the raw information to his superiors without comment. Unfortunately, these superiors were ill prepared to assess this information.

The secretariat of state lacked any organizational capacity to process effectively the intelligence reaching Rome. There was no intelligence desk in the small department, and no official was specifically responsible for screening incoming reports for intelligence items, collating these items, comparing the more recent with the older, and developing a coherent intelligence picture. This organizational deficiency was exacerbated by an administrative tradition that reserved all authority and responsibility for the cardinal secretary of state and relegated the staff to purely clerical roles. All dispatches went to the cardinal secretary for his personal attention. Lacking any institutional mechanism for coordinating the collection effort and evaluating its product, this overworked prelate, who, as in the case of Pope Pius VIII's octogenarian cardinal secretary, Cardinal Giuseppe Albani, or Leo XII's septuagenarian Cardinal Giulio Della Somaglia, might carry the burdens of age as well as of office, was left to make what he could of the bits and pieces of information that indiscriminately found their way to his desk. Giacomo Antonelli, who became cardinal secretary of state in 1849 and held the post until his death twenty-eight years later (a term unequaled in papal history), was so jealous of his power and prerogatives that he concerned himself with the smallest details of administration, deliberately surrounded himself with mediocre assistants, and made a point of never consulting with his staff. As a device to maintain personal authority, Antonelli's practice was irreproachable. As a method for producing good intelligence, it left something to be desired.

Not surprisingly, the absence of system and method resulted in frequent lapses in intelligence. Some were merely distracting, as when, in June 1861, reports from abroad convinced the pope and his advisers that Queen Victoria of England was about to convert to Catholicism and that the recently deceased duchess of Kent had converted on her deathbed.[35] Others were more serious. As late as 15 May 1860, Cardinal Secretary of State Antonelli persisted in believing that Garibaldi was in Tuscany gathering forces for an incursion into the Papal States, when in fact (as at least one intelligence report had warned) the famous revolutionary and foe of the Papacy had landed in Sicily with his troops on 11 May and embarked on a campaign that would quickly bring down the Kingdom of Naples, the pope's neighbor and ally to the south. Antonelli was equally surprised in the summer of 1862 when Russia dealt the Papacy a major diplomatic setback by recognizing Piedmont's claim to be called the Kingdom of Italy even though much of the territory of the new kingdom had been seized from the Papacy.[36]

Papal authorities were in general better informed about political subversion and revolutionary activity inside the Papal States than they were about foreign developments. The provincial delegates and police directors understood that one of their principal responsibilities was the surveillance and suppression of dissident groups. If their concentration wandered, there were enough domestic insurrections, attacks on police and troops, and terrorist activities (including, during Easter Week of 1864, a bomb in St. Peter's Square that blew out many windows in the Vatican) to refocus their attention. They knew their territory and controlled an array of agents and informants devoted exclusively to collecting domestic intelligence. Also, the threat to the regime was so immediate and so serious that even the notoriously lackadaisical and inefficient papal bureaucracy was moved to action.

Papal authorities employed a variety of instruments in the war against revolutionary subversion. Loitering near city gates, drinking in taverns, and strolling through marketplaces, undercover police agents collected the latest gossip and rumor. More reliable intelligence came from sources inside conspiratorial movements. Enterprising delegates and police directors sent their agents to penetrate such movements. Making contact with members of a revolutionary cell, an undercover agent would affect a hatred of papal government and a commitment to revolution. If invited to join the group, he would bide his time, earning the confidence of his fellow conspirators and, if lucky, insinuating himself into leadership circles where he could learn details of insurrectionary plots.

The Paolo Monti case (described earlier) was only one of several successful penetrations of the revolutionary underground. In 1859 Monsignor Tancredi Bellà, the papal delegate in Ancona, was able to smash a major conspiracy against the government, arrest dozens of conspirators, and seize secret arms caches along the Adriatic coast because the man selected by the conspirators to coordinate the uprising with antipapal groups in the cities of Bologna and Rimini was actually his agent. Several years earlier a Roman surgeon, a friend of the governor of Rome, agreed to try to penetrate the secret societies. While attending a scientific conference in Naples, the surgeon discreetly let it be known among his professional colleagues that he harbored republican sympathies and was active in revolutionary circles in Rome. As he had hoped, he was soon approached by a furtive colleague who whispered an invitation to attend a secret meeting of self-styled revolutionaries. Further meetings followed at which the conspirators—earnest, though largely harmless, middle-class professionals—compared notes on the state of revolutionary ferment in various parts of Italy. The surgeon loyally reported everything and everybody to Rome.[37]

Some penetrations were major covert operations. In 1860 a shadowy Comitato Nazionale (National Committee) began operating in Rome. Committed to the overthrow of the Papal States and the creation of a unified Kingdom of Italy, the committee covertly recruited members, collected funds, and sought contacts with sympathetic groups in other Italian cities in order to coordinate efforts. Ostensibly the very model of a revolutionary group, the committee was in fact a creature of the papal police whose undercover agents established and ran the organization for several years as an instrument for collecting intelligence on the secret societies and spreading disinformation and provocation among dissidents inside the Papal States.[38]

Perhaps the most important penetration of the revolutionary societies occurred in 1833 when Michele Accursi, a lawyer and activist in the Young Italy movement who had been convicted by a papal tribunal of conspiracy and sedition, offered to turn informer in return for his freedom. Granted an amnesty by the cardinal secretary of state, Tommaso Bernetti, Accursi returned to his old haunts and soon renewed his contacts among Italian political exiles in Geneva and Paris. Since these contacts included a friendship with the leader of Young Italy, Giuseppe Mazzini, the erstwhile revolutionary was able to send Cardinal Bernetti timely reports on the movement's clandestine activities in Italy. Accursi's reports continued until 1836, when he fell under suspicion among his fellow exiles, and his usefulness ended.[39]

Occasionally, papal authorities had recourse to less subtle methods in their war against the secret societies. After the insurrections of 1831, Cardinal Secretary of State Tommaso Bernetti established two paramilitary organizations to bolster internal security and carry the war to the revolutionaries. Bernetti had long believed that the pious and conservative peasantry were the bulwark of the traditional order and the best guarantee of that order in the face of revolutionary challenges from the urban professional classes. Recruited primarily from rural areas, Bernetti's paramilitary groups, known as Centurions and Papal Volunteers, were under the direct authority of the cardinal secretary of state. Mimicking the secret societies that were their sworn enemies, these armed bands were clandestine. The members wore neither uniforms nor insignia but were allowed to carry concealed weapons. Their operations and, often, their very identities were kept secret from local officials, who complained to Rome about a "shadow" police force that undercut their authority and worked at cross-purposes with the regular police.

Conceived as internal security units, the Centurions and Papal Volunteers were supposed to monitor the countryside for signs of activity by the secret societies, gather information on political malcontents, and generally uphold the authority of the papal regime. In practice, they proved useless as sources of intelligence. All too often the armed bands degenerated into strong-arm squads that physically intimidated anyone suspected of liberal sympathies. Effectively beyond the control of local authorities, these auxiliaries often abused their power in pursuit of personal profit or private vendetta. Their arrogance, indiscipline, and propensity to violence alienated the population, but Cardinal Bernetti refused to disband a force that he considered an effective weapon against revolution. It was only under his successor, Cardinal Luigi Lambruschini, that the paramilitary bands were suppressed.[40]

The papal police also relied on surveillance of individuals to produce intelligence. Extensive, if not always efficient, such surveillance covered citizens suspected of subversive activity, foreign diplomats, and prominent visitors to the Papal States. In December 1814, for example, the son of a British duke arrived in the papal port of Civitavecchia from the island of Elba, then the place of exile of Napoleon Bonaparte. The young nobleman immediately attracted the attention of the police, who suspected that he might have met the deposed French emperor. This suspicion was confirmed when the police, having bribed the young man's valet to show them his employer's diary, read an account of the Englishman's conversation with Napoleon. Odo Russell, the British diplomatic agent in Rome from

1858 to 1870, discovered that one of his servants was an informant for the police and informed the Foreign Office in London that police surveillance was pervasive in the Eternal City. From police posts at the various gates to the city, the secretariat of state received immediate word of the arrival of important personages (aristocrats, diplomats, journalists, prelates, and bankers) so that, if deemed necessary, surveillance could be quickly arranged. No dignitary was too exalted to escape attention. When Prince Klemens von Metternich, the Austrian foreign minister, accompanied the emperor of Austria on a state visit to Rome in 1819, Cardinal Consalvi placed several police agents inside the diplomat's guesthouse in the guise of servants. When the czar of Russia, Nicholas I, visited Rome in December 1845, the police insinuated an agent into his entourage to observe his visitors and report his conversations.[41]

Like other European governments, the Papacy maintained surveillance of all communications crossing its territory. Papal delegates were authorized to intercept and open letters addressed to private citizens if those citizens were suspected of subversion. After the establishment of the papal telegraphic service in 1854, the secretariat of state received copies of all telegrams sent or received by the Rome post office.[42] This surveillance was often the source of useful intelligence. During Napoleon's exile on Elba, papal authorities closely monitored all mail to and from that island. This operation revealed that the former emperor was conducting a clandestine correspondence with his supporters on the Italian mainland, including his brother Lucian (the prince of Canino), his uncle, Cardinal Joseph Fesch, and the king of Naples, Joachim Murat. The delegate in Civitavecchia, the port of embarkation for Elba, suspected a certain Captain Taylade of carrying secret messages to and from Napoleon. When Taylade next disembarked in Civitavecchia in transit to Rome, the delegate arranged for several sailors to stage a fight around the traveler's coach. In the tumult and confusion, a police agent stole the captain's valise, which, when opened at police headquarters, contained several letters concerning Bonapartist intrigues. These letters were copied and then replaced in the valise, which was then returned to Taylade by the police, who apologized profusely for the robbery, condemned vociferously the scandalous behavior of the criminal elements of the city, and assured the good captain that such an outrage would not recur. On another occasion papal authorities intercepted a letter from Cardinal Fesch to General Bertrand, one of Napoleon's aides on Elba. The letter alerted the general to the arrival of a shipment of books and recommended for his attention a particular volume in that shipment. When two sealed crates of books arrived in Civitavecchia for shipment to Elba, the

police opened them without disturbing the seals. Inside the pages of the indicated volume were several letters, including two in cipher, addressed to
Napoleon and Bertrand.[43]

Diplomatic mail was no more secure from surveillance than private
mail. Odo Russell was sure that the papal police intercepted his correspondence with the Foreign Office in London. In 1860 the American ambassador to the Papal States protested to the cardinal secretary of state that official letters passing by courier between the American diplomatic missions in
Paris and Rome had been opened by papal customs officers on the transparent pretext that the diplomatic pouch contained contraband. Two years
later the American consulate in Rome informed the State Department that
dispatches from Washington arrived with their envelopes opened.[44]

Intercepted correspondence often included enciphered letters. In an age
when postal surveillance was pervasive, foreign diplomats in Rome, as in
other capitals, routinely encrypted their dispatches to their foreign ministries. Revolutionary cells plotting the overthrow of the papal regime also
turned to ciphers to conceal their secrets. Given the scope of their surveillance effort, it is surprising that papal authorities made no provision for
codebreaking. In the Renaissance papal cryptanalysts had been the scourge
of European communications, cracking with diabolical ease the most difficult codes and ciphers of kings and princes. This tradition, however, was
somehow lost in the seventeenth and eighteenth centuries. As some European states, particularly England and France, strengthened their codebreaking capabilities, the Papacy allowed its to atrophy.

By the nineteenth century it was no longer possible to speak of a papal
Black Chamber. Britain's Foreign Office was so dismissive of the Papacy's
codebreaking capabilities that it allowed the British diplomatic representative in Rome to use an antique cipher that had been in service for almost
half a century.[45] Papal officials were helpless when confronted by an encrypted letter. When an alert delegate intercepted and sent to Rome some
enciphered letters destined for Napoleon on Elba, the secretariat of state
could do nothing but forward them to Cardinal Consalvi, then attending
the Congress of Vienna, in the hope that the cardinal's cipher clerk might
make something of them. The clerk could do nothing, so Consalvi, who
was aware that the Austrians maintained a large codebreaking establishment, turned the unbroken ciphers over to his hosts. On another occasion,
when the papal police intercepted an enciphered communication addressed to a suspected revolutionary, they managed to read the letter only
after ransacking the suspect's house to locate the cipher key. In 1861, the
year in which the Kingdom of Piedmont extended its control over all of

Italy except for Rome and its environs, the papal telegraphic service routinely delivered to the secretariat of state copies of the encrypted telegrams exchanged by the Piedmontese representative in the Eternal City and his foreign minister, Count Camillo Cavour. The secretariat made no effort to decipher these secret messages, even though they may have provided an insight into the house of Savoy's intentions toward the pope and what remained of his territory.[46]

Throughout this period the intelligence and internal security capabilities of the Papacy were enhanced by collaboration with other conservative regimes that shared an interest in suppressing revolution. The papal police established especially close relations with their counterparts in the Kingdom of Naples. The two services routinely exchanged information on individuals suspected of subversion and cooperated in the surveillance of suspects who crossed their common border. The Neapolitan police were particularly forthcoming with intelligence on Young Italy and similar movements, and they often alerted papal authorities to the location of revolutionary cells or the movement of armed bands into the Papal States. This intelligence included the confidential reports of Neapolitan diplomats who monitored the activities of political exiles in Britain, France, and Switzerland. Often these reports provided the details necessary for successful security operations. In 1833, for instance, Naples passed to Rome a report from its consul in Marseilles (a center of exile activity) that identified one Pietro Tocardi as the individual responsible for coordinating the clandestine distribution of revolutionary propaganda in Italy. The report added that the shipment of propaganda materials to Rome and Naples was expedited by a man named del Nero, who was identified as a marble merchant from Carrara.[47]

When, in 1860, the Neapolitan monarch, Francesco II, lost his kingdom to the Piedmontese after an invasion by Giuseppe Garibaldi and his nationalist irregulars, Pope Pius IX allowed the displaced monarch and his supporters to establish a government-in-exile on papal territory where they plotted their return to power. In their efforts to organize a counterrevolution, the exiles were covertly assisted by papal authorities, who allowed guerrilla bands to raid across the border and then return to papal territory to rest and reprovision. The papal police received orders to facilitate the passage across the Papal States of legitimist sympathizers (many of whom were Spanish army officers traveling on false passports to join Francesco's cause) and to ignore the movement of illegal weapons in border areas.

Francesco's counterrevolution failed in large part because it could not attract the sympathies of his former subjects but also because agents of the Kingdom of Piedmont, which was now calling itself the Kingdom of Italy, quickly penetrated exile circles. One Piedmontese agent, the confidant of Francesco's principal representative in Rome, betrayed the decisions of the legitimist leaders almost as soon as they were made. The involvement of papal authorities in the counterrevolutionary plots was no more secret, since the Piedmontese were kept well-informed of Vatican-Bourbon collaboration by their able consul in Rome, Francesco Teccio di Bayo, who assiduously collected intelligence from a network of informants inside the papal administration, including officers in the papal security apparatus.[48]

In intelligence matters the Papacy collaborated most closely with Austria. After the Congress of Vienna, Cardinal Consalvi and Prince Metternich discovered a common interest in suppressing the liberal and nationalist movements that threatened not only the theocratic government of the Papal States but also Austria's control over the north Italian regions of Lombardy and the Veneto. Convinced that the weak police services of the various Italian principalities were incompetent to deal with the revolutionary threat, Metternich had, as early as 1814, proposed a special commissariat of police with headquarters in Austrian-controlled Milan to coordinate a common security effort against the revolutionary groups. Fearing that the proposal would lead to Austrian control of the papal police, the Papacy had joined with the principalities of Modena, Parma, and Tuscany to reject the plan. Common interests, however, encouraged a bilateral exchange of information between the police services of Rome and Vienna.[49]

The collaboration got off to a shaky start in the spring of 1816 when the papal secretariat of state, in a series of alarmist reports that Metternich dismissed as "spectres of a madman," warned Vienna of an imminent invasion of Italy by Turkey, a mutiny by Italian-speaking contingents in the multiethnic Austrian army, and a plot by revolutionaries to overturn the Bourbon monarchy in France. Austria's confidence in its new intelligence partner was further shaken when the director of the papal police proposed that police authorities across Italy deal a mortal blow to the secret societies by arresting simultaneously all their leaders. This ambitious proposal was quietly set aside when the Austrian police minister in Vienna pointed out that no one knew who the leaders of the secret societies were precisely because they were so secret.

Collaboration eventually settled into more productive channels. The secretariat of state recovered some credibility by identifying a postal worker in Austrian Lombardy who was exchanging conspiratorial letters (intercepted by papal authorities) with an employee of the papal post office in Ancona. Soon Rome was passing to Vienna and Milan (the administrative center for Austrian Italy) intelligence that confirmed Bologna as the center of the Guelph organization in Italy, identified a certain General Gifflenga as the military chief of certain revolutionary groups in northern Italy and a Count Aghuti as the liaison between underground centers in Bologna and Milan, and revealed the presence of revolutionary cells in several towns around Venice.[50]

The two governments also cooperated in an effort to track political suspects who moved between Austrian and papal territory. The passports and visas of these individuals were secretly marked in a way that would escape notice by anyone but an alert border official. These marks were usually added to the date of issuance, which was written on the travel document. In March 1841, for instance, papal police authorities informed their Austrian counterparts that for the next trimester travelers suspected of subversive activities would be identified by a small mark over the letter p in *Aprile* (April), the first g in *Maggio* (May), or the second g in *Giugno* (June). The passports of those under grave suspicion would use a comma rather than a simple point to dot the i in each of these words. The documents of harmless travelers would be dated in the normal way without special signs. Through cooperation with the Neapolitan police, the Papacy established similar passport controls along its southern border.[51]

For its part, Vienna shared with Rome intelligence collected by its ubiquitous and efficient police agents whose reach extended across northern Italy and (unbeknownst to the Papacy) into the States of the Church. In 1819, for example, the Austrians rolled up (after long surveillance) a conspiratorial group in the Veneto that had links with similar groups in papal territory to the south. Information from this operation allowed the papal authorities to arrest on charges of subversion eighty-three individuals, including the leader of the underground revolutionary organization in Ferrara.[52] The Papacy continued to benefit from this intelligence partnership well into midcentury. In 1851 the Austrians provided information on the leadership of a revolutionary organization in Faenza that had branches in other papal towns, including Cesena, Forli, and Rimini. In February 1859, just months before they were forced from Lombardy by French and Piedmontese armies in the Second War for Italian Independence, the Austrians were keeping Rome informed of the movements of Carlo Petz, a revolutionary traveling from London to Italy under the alias "Colonel Kupa."[53]

Vienna also shared with Rome some of the fruits of its extensive program of mail surveillance. No European power committed more resources to intercepting communications than Austria, and the Hapsburg emperor's codebreakers were the bane of foreign ministries and conspiratorial groups from Lisbon to St. Petersburg. Security authorities in the Papal States were especially interested in any information concerning the cryptographic practices of the revolutionary societies, since these authorities, lacking a cryptanalytic capability of their own, were usually unable to read the encrypted letters they intercepted. Austrian codebreakers cracked several ciphers used by various revolutionary groups, including the Carbonari and the Guelfi. The Austrians were also aware that the clandestine groups used certain tricks to hide their secret communications, such as using invisible ink to write messages on pieces of linen.[54]

Occasionally, Vienna's surveillance of communications helped the Papacy monitor religious dissidents within the Church. For example, Prince Klemens von Metternich, foreign minister and later chancellor of Austria, passed to Pope Gregory XVI copies of several letters written by Felicité Lamennais, a French priest who criticized the Church's alignment with reactionary regimes and called for an accommodation with political liberalism. Through his newspaper, L'Avenir, Lamennais advocated freedom of conscience, religious toleration, freedom of the press, universal suffrage, and the separation of church and state. This platform did not endear him to conservative religious authorities in Rome. Neither did it thrill Metternich, who had no intention of allowing anyone, least of all an intelligent and articulate priest, to subvert the traditional order with nonsense about toleration and liberalism. When Lamennais traveled to Rome in the spring of 1832 to present his ideas to the pope, the Austrian chancellor directed his intelligence service to intercept the correspondence of the French priest. The letters revealed Lamennais's revulsion at the abuses of ecclesiastical government, the venality of papal officials, and the decline of religious life in the Papal States. Metternich passed these letters to Pope Gregory, and they had the desired effect: in August 1832 the pope issued an encyclical that condemned most of the positions advocated by Lamennais, including religious toleration, freedom of the press, and the separation of church and state.[55]

Despite their close collaboration with papal authorities, the Austrians had a generally low opinion of the pope's police and intelligence services, which they considered corrupt, inefficient, and unsophisticated. Of course the Austrians considered all foreign police organizations inferior to their own, and in the early nineteenth century corruption and inefficiency characterized every police service between New York and Istanbul. Nevertheless, there was, perhaps, little in the traditions of the papal services to engender confidence. Recruited from the criminal elements of the towns and notorious for their venality and violence, the papal police in the seventeenth and eighteenth centuries had been considered social outcasts by the very society they were meant to protect. Reforms in the early nineteenth century, particularly several initiated by Cardinal Consalvi, produced improvements especially in the areas of intelligence and countersubversion that contributed to important successes against the revolutionary groups, but venality and incompetence continued to plague the service. In the 1830s an Austrian official with extensive experience with the papal bureaucracy (which had a continent-wide reputation for inefficiency and ineptness) made a special study of the papal police and reported with amazement, "The chaos surpassed all my expectations."[56]

Unwilling to depend on the pope's police for information on revolutionary nationalist movements in the papal lands that abutted Austria's own Italian territories, Vienna did not hesitate to establish secret intelligence networks in the Papal States. These clandestine networks served the secondary purpose of collecting intelligence on papal affairs. The Austrians had never been shy about spying on the pope. During the Congress of Vienna, Metternich's police assigned a team of operatives to follow Cardinal Consalvi and the personnel of the papal nunciature where Consalvi resided during the conference. The police also infiltrated agents into the nunciature. These operations turned up useful intelligence on a range of topics, including Cardinal Consalvi's credit at Viennese banks (excellent) and his relations with the nuncio (strained). The Austrians' principal informant was the self-styled "Chevalier" Ludovico Freddi-Battilori. This adventurer had at one time been attached to the Vienna nunciature in a minor capacity. Though his tenure in papal service had been brief, he managed to steal from the nunciature certain secret documents that he sold to the Austrian police. During the Congress of Vienna he renewed his friendship with the unsuspecting nuncio in order once again to collect information from inside the papal embassy.[57]

Vienna continued to spy on the Papacy after the restoration of the Papal States. In 1821 the Austrians suborned at least one official inside the central post office in Rome; this agent provided access to the private mail of cardinals, as well as incoming and outgoing official communications.[58] About the same time the Austrians bribed a papal chamberlain to provide information on activities inside the papal household. They also added to their payroll Prince Altieri, a highborn Benedictine monk resident in Rome, who claimed a long acquaintance with Pope Pius VII. The Austrians gladly purchased information from Altieri even though the minister of police in Vienna considered him "immoral, purchasable, and a most dangerous political intriguer."[59]

Austria's most important recruitment may have been in the very heart of the pope's security organization. During the Congress of Vienna, Monsignor

Tiberio Pacca had been the papal governor of Viterbo, in which capacity he demonstrated a flair for intelligence and police work. The diligent monsignor, who was the nephew of the powerful Cardinal Bartolomeo Pacca, was brought to Rome and appointed director general of police with primary responsibility for countersubversion and internal security. From his new position Pacca pursued revolutionary groups with his usual industry and ruthlessness, and he quickly became the strong arm of the pope. The surprise and scandal were all the greater, therefore, when, on the night of 7 April 1817, the police director suddenly fled Rome with his young mistress and tens of thousands of scudi from the public treasury. Pacca may have fled to escape exposure for forging his uncle's signature on several promissory notes.[60] It is likely, however, that he was fleeing from an even more serious charge. During his tenure as director of papal police, Pacca had been an advocate of close cooperation with Austrian intelligence even when his superior, Cardinal Secretary of State Consalvi, suspected Vienna's intentions. Pacca began to pass secret information to the Austrians without Consalvi's knowledge. In Vienna, Metternich considered this intelligence and its source so sensitive that he shared it with only a select circle of officials. Pacca eventually surfaced in Paris, where he immediately resumed his work for Austrian intelligence.[61]

Tiberio Pacca was not the only papal police official to divide his loyalties between Rome and Vienna. Indeed, seduction by the Austrians seems to have been an occupational hazard for the director general of papal police. While holding that post in the 1820s, Monsignor Tomaso Bernetti secretly and without authorization passed to an official of the Austrian embassy in Rome intelligence concerning revolutionary groups inside the Papal States. The future cardinal secretary of state probably did so because he thought his pontiff, Pope Leo XII, underestimated the need for rigorous police measures to suppress revolutionary sentiments.[62] In one of those ironies so common in the history of espionage, the officials responsible for protecting the Papacy against the agents of foreign powers were themselves agents of such a power.

The Austrians were not alone in seeking to penetrate the pope's secrets. Most of the European powers considered the Papacy a legitimate intelligence target and did not hesitate to place informants close to the centers of papal power. Some of these informants were very well placed. During the Napoleonic period, Cardinal Joseph Fesch, Napoleon's uncle, kept Paris abreast of developments in Rome, although his usefulness was compromised by the fact that he was known and despised across the Eternal City as the eyes and ears of his nephew, the French emperor. London had a more discreet source in Lady Elizabeth Foster, the duchess of Devonshire. After the death of her husband, the wealthy duchess had moved to Rome, where she became a fixture of Roman society, entertaining diplomats and members of the papal court, patronizing the arts, and performing good works among the city's neediest. She struck up a close and genuine friendship with Cardinal Consalvi, who came to consider the intelligent and attractive expatriate a confidant. The two friends would exchange daily letters and see each other two or three times a week. The duchess regularly reported the cardinal's views to Lord Liverpool in London, who was not only her brother-in-law but also the British prime minister. Occasionally she made similar reports to the British ambassador in Naples. Lady Foster would have recoiled at any suggestion that she was betraying her friend by acting as an agent for the British government, but her chatty and insightful comments on papal affairs and the attitudes of the pope's powerful secretary of state were London's best source of information on the Papacy in the years immediately following the Congress of Vienna.[63]

Few governments could hope to place an agent next to the cardinal secretary of state. Most had to rely on low-level agents whose work occasionally brought them within range of important people or documents. For example, after the French Revolution, Paris suborned at least one employee of the papal secretariat of state, thereby gaining access to confidential dispatches that came to Rome from around the world. In the 1820s the papal nuncio in Madrid discovered that his Spanish valet was secretly reading his confidential correspondence with Rome. At about the same time the nuncio in Holland was sharing confidential information, including details about papal ciphers, with a fellow Italian with whom the diplomat shared a townhouse. Unbeknownst to the nuncio, his good friend was a spy for the government of Naples.[64]

By midcentury, no government posed a greater threat to the Papacy than the Kingdom of Piedmont because no other government sought to abolish the temporal power of the popes by seizing the Papal States. In 1852, under the direction of its prime minister, the brilliant and unscrupulous Camillo di Cavour, Piedmont embarked on a policy of unifying the Italian peninsula under the House of Savoy. Combining diplomacy, war, and what later generations would call covert action, Cavour pushed the Austrians from Lombardy (1859) and gathered into the Piedmontese fold the principalities of Modena, Parma, and Tuscany and the Kingdom of Naples (1860). Occupying the greater part of the peninsula and claiming as its capital the Eternal City, the symbol of Italian culture and historical greatness, the Papal States could not hope to escape Cavour's attentions.

The Piedmontese prime minister was strongly inclined toward secret operations. His intelligence operatives (including seductive noblewomen who made it their business to befriend foreign officers and diplomats) were present in every court and chancellery in Europe. In papal cities, particularly Rome and Ancona, Piedmontese diplomats and consuls organized intelligence networks that penetrated every corner of the papal administration, particularly the army and police. While his spies collected information, Cavour's secret representatives worked to harness to Turin's expansionist policy the energies of patriotic and nationalist movements across Italy. Seeing in the House of Savoy the vehicle for Italian unification and national rejuvenation, these organizations with their underground cells and thousands of sympathizers in the papal territories became a fifth column that opened the doors of the Papal States to the Piedmontese.

In the spring of 1859, Austria went to war against Piedmont and France, and Vienna withdrew its protecting garrisons from the papal cities of Ancona, Bologna, and Ferrara in order to reinforce its armies along the northern Italian front. Antipapal insurrections broke out immediately, and in response to appeals from the revolutionaries, Piedmont dispatched troops to occupy Bologna, after Rome the premier city in the Papal States. The insurrection spread quickly to other towns in the pope's domain, although Swiss mercenaries in the pay of the pontiff restored a semblance of order in the regions of Umbria and the Marches. The Romagna, however, was permanently lost when a plebiscite, covertly directed by Turin's agents, endorsed the annexation of the region by Piedmont. Worse was to come.

In the spring of 1860 Giuseppe Garibaldi successfully landed a band of revolutionaries near Marsala, Sicily, sparking a popular insurrection that by the late summer had spread to the mainland, overthrown the Kingdom of Naples, and threatened Rome. While publicly denouncing Garibaldi's actions, Cavour secretly supported his enterprise with arms, money, and advice and directed his agents in papal cities to foment disturbances and spread pro-Piedmontese propaganda. With Garibaldi's forces poised to attack the Papal States from the south and popular unrest simmering across the pope's territory, Cavour, in September 1860, sent Piedmontese troops into Umbria and the Marches, ostensibly to help the pope quell the unrest and deter any move by Garibaldi against Rome. This military intervention was barely opposed by the feeble papal army, whose will to resist had been undermined by Cavour's agents, particularly the Piedmontese consul in Ancona, who spent lavishly to undermine the morale of papal troops and police. Of course Cavour intended the occupation of papal territory to be merely the first step in their annexation. By mid-October, Umbria and the

Marches were absorbed into the Kingdom of Piedmont, as was the former Kingdom of Naples, where a plebiscite resulted in a popular majority for inclusion into a united Italy. The pope's state was now reduced to Rome and the rural districts adjacent to the city, and to defend this territory the pontiff depended on a French garrison sent to Rome by Emperor Louis Napoleon to forestall a Piedmontese takeover. The future, however, remained uncertain as the Kingdom of Italy made no secret of its intention to extend its sovereignty over the entire peninsula and establish the national capital in the Eternal City.

The demise of the Papal States, lands that had been in the papal domain for a millennium, was the defining event of the nineteenth-century Papacy, an event that would reverberate in Rome and other European capitals well into the next century. At the time some thoughtful observers, both Catholic and non-Catholic, judged the loss a blessing in disguise, but most Catholics considered it an unmitigated calamity that humiliated the Papacy and threatened to deprive it of the independence it required to exercise its spiritual mission. The loss can be attributed to many factors—the failure of the papal administration to concede needed reforms; the reluctance or inability of European powers to prop up an increasingly anachronistic institution; the inability of the popes to comprehend the political and social forces pushing the Italian peninsula toward unification—but it was not the fault of the pope's intelligence service.

In the first half of the nineteenth century, papal intelligence operations were often unprofessional, frequently disorganized, and always unsystematic, but then so were the intelligence operations of almost every other power. After Napoleon's final defeat at the battle of Waterloo in 1815 and his exile to the South Atlantic island of St. Helena, the intelligence capabilities developed by many European governments during the almost perpetual warfare of the previous twenty years were allowed to atrophy. Governments closed intelligence bureaus, disbanded agent networks, and neglected established informants. During the Napoleonic Wars Britain's annual intelligence budget had never fallen below £100,000; by 1822 intelligence spending had declined to £40,000. In the 1840s Austria, Britain, and France shut down (at least for a time) their deciphering offices and pensioned off their codebreakers.[65] With few exceptions (Austria, perhaps, the most obvious), what remained were feeble, underresourced, and maladministered organizations devoted primarily to internal security, particularly the surveillance of political dissidents who threatened the established power structures. Of course neither the need for foreign intelligence nor the devices required to satisfy that need disappeared completely. In times of diplomatic or military crisis, foreign offices and war ministries rushed to develop lines of information, but these efforts were usually impromptu, jury-rigged expedients that were promptly abandoned when the crisis (and the need) passed. In the decades after Waterloo, the potential value of a standing, professional intelligence service was largely underappreciated in most European capitals. Indeed, the intelligence capabilities of some countries, such as France, were probably weaker in the mid–nineteenth century than they had been a century earlier.[66]

In its Eurocentric focus, its reliance on ill-suited and ill-prepared diplomats, and its inadequate attention to coordination and assessment, the Papacy's foreign intelligence effort was typical of the intelligence practices of European states in the post-Napoleonic era. When compared with the professional, specialized intelligence bureaucracies that began to appear at the turn of the next century, the intelligence experience of the Papacy seems paltry, but in the context of the time, it was usually no worse and occasionally much better than the experience of most other governments.

On some occasions papal intelligence demonstrably outperformed that of even major powers. During Napoleon's brief exile on Elba, no government was more concerned about monitoring his activities on that small island off the Tuscan coast than the restored Bourbon monarchy of King Louis XVIII in Paris. Still, for all their anxiety about an effort by the deposed emperor to return to France and power, the insecure Bourbons could mount only feeble intelligence coverage of Elba. During the several months that Napoleon lived on the island, French agents managed to intercept *only one* of his letters, although the former emperor carried on an extensive clandestine correspondence with his supporters in Italy and France.[67] By comparison, papal intelligence (as we have seen) maintained a closer surveillance of mail to and from Elba, identifying at least some of the clandestine channels used by Napoleon to communicate with his loyalists and intercepting enough letters to identify several of the former emperor's correspondents. Although there is no evidence that papal intelligence had advance word of Napoleon's daring escape in March 1815, it was probably less surprised by the event than the intelligence and police authorities in Paris, London, Vienna, and St. Petersburg.

The internal security and domestic political intelligence operations of papal agencies also exhibited more than a little success. The nineteenth-century papal police may have been corrupt and only marginally competent, but it is unlikely that their deficiencies were much more egregious than those of most police services in a period when professional standards of law enforcement had yet to establish themselves.[68] Furthermore, in the area of domestic intelligence (as opposed to routine law enforcement), the pontifical police demonstrated more than a little initiative, imagination, and ability. In their effort to identify and suppress revolutionary movements, they deployed most of the counterintelligence and countersubversion techniques (double agents, disinformation, mail surveillance, penetration agents, foreign liaison) that would become the stock-in-trade of "modern" internal security services in the twentieth century, and they scored some important intelligence successes against the revolutionary sects. Unfortunately, none of the successes on either the foreign or the domestic intelligence front could save the Papal States.

The Papacy did not lose the Papal States because the popes and their advisers lacked good intelligence. Papal authorities were all too well aware that the Kingdom of Piedmont had aggressive designs on the States of the Church. They were not surprised to discover that central Italy was rife with revolutionary groups seeking to undermine their regime. The Vatican was well aware of the political and social crisis it faced in the decades following Waterloo. It just could not or would not do anything about it. The popes lost their patrimony not because they lacked information but because they lacked the imagination to respond to nationalism and revolution with any policy other than political intransigence; the financial and military resources to make intransigence effective; and the will to reform attitudes, institutions, and procedures that were increasingly anachronistic. The last popes to rule as temporal sovereigns did what they believed God required of them irrespective of immediate political circumstances and consequences. In responding to foreign and domestic political challenges to the temporal power, such popes were more likely to consult their theologians than their intelligence officers. Intelligence can have little influence when the potential consumers of the product have little use for it.

2

Prisoner of the Vatican

The third of February 1878 was a day to test the mettle of any intelligence officer. If reports were to be believed, Pope Pius IX died that day; in fact, if reports were to be believed, he died twice that day. In his office in the Borgo, the Roman neighborhood just beyond the walls of the Vatican, Commissioner Giuseppe Manfroni may well have meditated on the doctrine of the Resurrection as aides rushed in with the latest reports and telegraphers flashed the news across town to the Interior Ministry. A senior officer in the Italian police, Manfroni was responsible for monitoring events and personalities inside the Vatican and informing the Italian government of significant developments in papal affairs. Under any circumstances the death of the pope qualified as a significant development. Two deaths on the same day were, well, nothing less than incredible.

In the first weeks of 1878 few people expected the eighty-six-year-old Pius to survive the year. For years the pontiff had been in declining health, and on at least one occasion the press had reported that he was on his deathbed. Pius always rallied, though each bout with illness left him weaker. In late January he had taken to his bed and canceled most of his official functions. On 2 February he was sufficiently improved that his doctors allowed him to receive a few visitors, all of whom noticed his poor spirits and weak condition. Perhaps sensing that his time was short, Pius that day ordered the special commission of cardinals preparing new rules for a papal election to accelerate their work. There was hardly time. Early the next morning the pontiff's condition suddenly deteriorated. Alarmed and fearing the worst, the physicians immediately sent for Cardinal Giovanni Simeoni, the secretary of state, who abandoned his breakfast to rush to Pius's bedside. Word was quietly passed to several other key prelates, and by midmorning a handful of the pope's closest collaborators had gathered in the papal apartments.

From his confidential sources around the pope, Giuseppe Manfroni had learned of the medical crisis almost at the same time as papal chamberlains were delivering the news to selected cardinals and monsignors. Despite the early hour, the police commissioner immediately mobilized his network of informants inside the Vatican to report every scrap of information concerning the pope's condition. Every half hour Manfroni passed the latest intelligence to the Interior Ministry and his superiors in the directorate of police. At nine in the morning an officious senior officer arrived unannounced from the ministry to inquire why the Borgo office continued to inundate police headquarters with ridiculous reports on the current condition of the pontiff. According to the officer, headquarters had been reliably informed by other sources that the pope had died hours earlier. Manfroni, who knew that the Italian government had no more reliable a source than the network of secret agents he had carefully built up inside the Vatican, angrily dismissed this news as absurd and produced the latest reports, some less than an hour old, that demonstrated conclusively that the pope still lived. The officer, now more subdued, returned to headquarters, but Manfroni had not heard the last from imperious superiors who believed they were better informed than their man in the Borgo. At three in the afternoon, he learned that the pope was slipping fast, and he immediately telegraphed this news to police headquarters. In reply he received a telegram curtly informing him that Pius had died a half hour earlier at precisely two thirty. Once again Manfroni had to convince his bosses to trust his sources over the rumors about the pope that were by now flashing across Rome. Not only was Pius still alive, but he had actually rallied. The resilient pope, who had sat on the Throne of St. Peter longer (thirty-two years) than any of his predecessors, held on until 7 February, when Manfroni had the melancholy duty of informing his superiors that Pius had finally and most certainly died.[1]

Secular governments had always been interested in the death of a pope, but none more than the government of Italy in 1878. Eight years earlier an Italian army had completed the process of unifying the Italian peninsula under the House of Savoy. The withdrawal of French troops from Rome upon the outbreak of the Franco-Prussian War in the summer of 1870 and the diplomatic dislocations resulting from the rapid defeat and collapse of France had provided the government of Vittorio Emanuele II, then reigning as king of Italy from his temporary capital in Florence, an opportunity to move against Rome and the rural districts beyond the city that were all that remained of the once-vast papal patrimony. Since annexing the bulk of the Papal States in 1860, the Italian government had sent secret agents into the remaining papal territories to fan nationalist and antipapal sentiments, and the resulting political unrest, though largely contained by the pope's police, allowed the royal authorities to claim that intervention was required to maintain order in the peninsula and protect the Holy Father from his own subjects.

On 10 September 1870 a representative of Vittorio Emanuele appeared at the Vatican to inform Pope Pius IX that the king intended to march into Rome but that the royal government was prepared to recognize the pope's sovereign inviolability and right to send and receive ambassadors, acknowledge his continued jurisdiction over the so-called Leonine City (the Vatican, the nearby Castel Sant' Angelo, and the Borgo district), guarantee his full liberty of communication with the outside world, and provide a substantial financial settlement to compensate for the loss of revenues from the old papal territories. Pius, who did not believe he had the right to waive sovereign rights or abandon territories that had been in the papal patrimony for more than a millennium, angrily rejected the proposal; indeed, the royal emissary was so discomfited by the pontiff's fury that upon being dismissed from the papal presence he mistook a window for the door and narrowly avoided a serious accident.[2]

On 11 September Italian troops invaded papal territory and within days occupied the port of Civitavecchia and the inland towns of Città Castellana and Viterbo. Papal police and military units offered little resistance, in part because Italian agents, posing as volunteers, had previously infiltrated these forces to subvert discipline and morale.[3] On 19 September the Italians stood before the ancient walls of Rome, and even the pope abandoned hope for a miracle. To avoid any suggestion of complicity in the demise of the Papacy's temporal power and to force his enemies into the ignominious position of firing on the Vicar of Christ, Pius ordered his remaining forces to resist until the city walls were breached. The next morning, Italian artillery batteries bombarded the walls, and infantry forced an entry through the Porta Pia. Pius promptly ordered his troops to lay down their weapons, and he surrendered the city. Within two weeks the occupiers arranged a plebiscite in which the pope's former subjects overwhelmingly voted to join the Kingdom of Italy. The Papal States, Europe's oldest government, were no more.

Pope Pius had no intention of quietly acquiescing in the loss of his temporal power. Pronouncing excommunications against all involved in the seizure of the papal domain and denouncing publicly the usurpation, the pope withdrew into his palace, proclaimed himself the "prisoner of the Vatican," and refused all contact with the new regime beyond his walls. When Italian authorities, searching for a suitable royal residence in what was now the capital of Italy, settled on the Palazzo Quirinale, the onetime papal summer palace on the highest hill in the city, Pius refused to turn over the keys, commenting acerbically, "I'm sure they'll find a way to get in without the keys."[4]

In an effort to settle the controversy, calm church-state relations, and placate Catholics at home and abroad, the Italian government, in December 1870, proposed the so-called Law of Guarantees. This legislation paralleled the earlier settlement offered to Pius before the battle for Rome in its assurances concerning the sovereign prerogatives of the pope as head of the Church, the extraterritoriality of the Vatican and certain ecclesiastical properties in the city, and an annual subsidy from the Italian treasury. The Italian parliament approved the Law of Guarantees, but Pius rejected it and refused to accept any reconciliation with the new rulers of Italy.

With the pope sulking behind the high walls of the Vatican, affirming his traditional rights, and hurling denunciations across the Tiber at the "usurpers" now ensconced in former papal palaces and offices, church-state tensions threatened to unsettle the foreign and domestic politics of the Kingdom of Italy. Pius or his successors might appeal to foreign powers to pressure Rome to restore at least some of the political and territorial prerogatives of the Papacy. Among devout Catholics inside and outside of Italy, attitudes toward the Italian government could not help but be influenced negatively by the plight of the pope. A hostile Papacy, unreconciled with the House of Savoy and the constitutional government, would also provoke anticlericals in the press and parliament to call for more direct and draconian solutions for what was now being referred to as the "Roman Question."

The Italian government needed to anticipate any secret diplomatic initiatives by the pope that might align one or more foreign powers behind the Papacy and its claims, and it needed to identify and encourage more moderate voices inside the Vatican that might counsel accommodation and compromise over resistance and intransigence. Was the pope's hostility implacable? Were there pragmatists around the pontiff who might work for a settlement? What terms would make a settlement more attractive to these pragmatists? Was the papal secretariat of state seeking the intervention of Austria or Spain? Was there any chance that the next pope would be more accommodating? Unfortunately, in the months following their occupation of Rome, the Italians could not answer these questions because they knew almost nothing about what the pope and his officials were thinking and doing.

After the occupation of Rome by Italian troops, Pius had ordered his Swiss Guards to bar the gates of the Vatican to all but ecclesiastics and employees of the Curia, the central administration of the Church. Contacts with the new regime were to be limited to those absolutely necessary for the health and provisioning of the Vatican and its personnel. The pope's self-imposed isolation might have been a futile protest against his loss of temporal power, but it proved an intelligence nightmare for the Italians who were denied access to the personnel and premises of the Holy Father. To remedy this situation, the Kingdom of Italy turned to espionage. Giuseppe Manfroni, an eighteen-year veteran of the royal police who had spent most of his career tracking down brigands in the rural districts of the kingdom, was transferred to Rome to fill the newly created post of police commissioner for the Borgo. Ostensibly, the new commissioner was responsible for maintaining law and order in the city precincts between the Tiber and the Vatican, but his chief responsibility was to spy on the pope.

Manfroni set out to establish an agent network that would have informants at all levels of the Vatican. His first recruit was a monsignor who worked in an important papal office. This cleric was an avid hunter, but he could not secure a hunting permit because the pope forbade any of his personnel to submit documents or applications to Italian authorities, since such submissions might be interpreted as an implicit recognition of the legitimacy of the new regime. Manfroni cultivated the goodwill of this well-placed monsignor by arranging for him to obtain and periodically renew a hunting license without submitting any applications. In return for this favor the cleric passed the occasional item of news or rumor from inside the Vatican to his new friend in the Italian police.[5]

By 1873 Manfroni had established a network of informants that reached into every corner of the Vatican. From this distance it is impossible to identify these contacts, but it is clear that no small number were officials in the various administrative departments of the Church. Most, however, were servants and attendants inside the papal palace who, moving freely but unnoticed through the corridors and chambers, were able to observe visitors or overhear conversations. At least one held a position that required his daily attendance in the pope's private apartments, and this source proved especially valuable during the medical crises that were increasingly common in the final years of the aged pontiff.[6] Manfroni paid each of his informants a small stipend and seized every opportunity to bind them more closely to himself by performing small services for them or their families.

Through his informants Manfroni collected intelligence on the diplomacy, finances, and internal politics of the Vatican, all of which he passed to the Italian foreign ministry and interior ministry. In the months following its occupation of Rome, the Italian government was especially fearful that Pius, in protest against the loss of his territories, would again flee Rome, as he did at the time of the Roman revolution of 1848, and seek refuge abroad. The flight of the Holy Father from the Eternal City to escape "usurpers" and "aggressors" would be a public relations disaster for the House of Savoy and a diplomatic crisis for Italy. Manfroni was directed to report any rumor, conversation, or bit of news bearing upon the pope's intentions. At the time the newly appointed police commissioner had only begun to recruit informants inside the Vatican, but he tasked his handful of agents to report immediately any signs of an imminent papal flight. Recalling that in 1848 Pius had escaped the Roman revolutionaries by disguising himself as a simple priest and slipping out an unattended gate of his palace, Manfroni sent plainclothes police agents to keep every gate, door, and opening in the walls surrounding the Vatican under round-the-clock surveillance. Nothing if not thorough, he also sent agents to patrol unobtrusively the long stretches of wall that faced the open countryside beyond the city, although an escape over walls thirty feet high seemed an unlikely ploy for a man approaching his eightieth birthday.

In early March 1871 there was a scare when Manfroni heard from his sources that the pope had decided to flee and that Paris had been secretly approached about asylum on the French island of Corsica. The commissioner immediately alerted his observation posts, as well as senior officers in the police service; dispatched a lieutenant to organize surveillance at Civitavecchia, the closest port to Rome and most likely place of embarkation; sent out mounted police to patrol the Via Aurelia, the principal road to the sea; and ordered his personal carriage readied for immediate use should he have to give chase. Fortunately, Pius had no intention of leaving the city he still considered rightfully his, and Manfroni was spared the dilemma of choosing between the embarrassment of losing the pope and the embarrassment of detaining him.[7]

Once the Italian government was convinced that Pius would not flee the Eternal City, it shifted its concern to the matter of the pontiff's health. The anxious and insecure government imagined that any number of political crises might follow upon the death of the long-reigning pope. In particular, it feared the international embarrassment that would result if the cardinals, announcing that they could not freely exercise their responsibility to elect the new pope if the conclave were held in "occupied" Rome, decided to meet outside of Italy. A non-Italian conclave might well produce a non-Italian pope, the first since the early sixteenth century. That embarrassment, however, would pale beside the full-blown political crisis that would result if the cardinals elected a zealot who promised to be as intransigent as his predecessor in his posture toward the Kingdom of Italy.[8]

To anticipate the conclave in sufficient time to prepare for, if not deter, its consequences, the government directed Giuseppe Manfroni to monitor closely the pope's health. By recruiting informants inside the pope's household, the police commissioner was able to follow the slightest variations in the pontiff's condition. For example, one day intelligence from the Borgo told of Pius wishing to leave his sickbed to walk in the Vatican gardens only to be deterred by the physicians who insisted that he not further weaken himself. On another day the reports described the pope shuffling about his apartment for two hours before returning to his bed at the insistence of one of his aides. Not wishing to rely solely on informants, Manfroni arranged with a friend to set up a telescope on a property with a distant view of the Vatican gardens. The police commissioner would occasionally visit this observation post to spy on the feeble pope as he exercised. On one occasion, Manfroni was able to report to his superiors, "I had the opportunity through a telescope to observe him for a moment as he passed under an awning in the garden. He was supported by two chamberlains and, shuffling his feet, he walked with difficulty."[9]

The Vatican was aware, at least in general terms, of the intelligence work of the police commissioner for the Borgo. Although one particularly zealous papal aide warned the servants in the pontifical household that he would personally hunt down and punish anyone passing information about His Holiness to outsiders, there was little that papal authorities could do to stem the flow of information to the Borgo. The priests who attended the pope and administered the Vatican departments had little appetite and less aptitude for security matters. Moreover, any attempt to identify and counteract Manfroni's agents would have been stymied by the absence of any security or counterespionage organization inside the papal administration. Eventually, papal authorities reached an unspoken accommodation with the police commissioner. The Vatican would tacitly accept surveillance but would turn that surveillance to its benefit by using police channels to alert the Italian government to issues of concern to the Papacy. In 1875, for instance, a representative of Cardinal Secretary of State Giacomo Antonelli requested a private meeting with Manfroni to inform the police commissioner that the Vatican had learned that Giuseppe Garibaldi had recruited and armed a band of fanatic anticlericals for an assault on the papal palace. The commissioner was skeptical about this alleged plot, but he alerted his superiors and calmed Cardinal Antonelli by personally inspecting the walls and gates of the Vatican and increasing police patrols around the perimeter of the pope's tiny domain.[10]

In a period when the Vatican refused to have any official relations with the Kingdom of Italy, Manfroni became the Italian government's unofficial representative to the pope. He was a back channel through which the two parties quietly communicated while maintaining toward each other a public posture of icy aloofness. Certain cardinals, more pragmatic than some of their intransigent colleagues, cooperated with the commissioner by secretly exchanging information so that each party had some idea of what the other was thinking. By cultivating such highly placed sources, Manfroni gained access to some of the most closely held secrets of the Vatican. For example, he routinely knew the identity and political attitudes of the prelates selected for elevation to cardinal before these honors were publicly announced.[11]

Fortunately for the Vatican, no government was as tireless or successful as the Italian in establishing intelligence coverage of the Papacy. Indeed, few governments even tried. In part, this disinterest reflected the Papacy's reduced importance in international affairs after the loss of the Papal States. It also reflected a more general reduction in intelligence operations across the political landscape. After the Napoleonic Wars, most governments neglected their foreign intelligence capabilities and applied what little attention and few resources that remained to internal security, particularly the surveillance of political dissidents who threatened the established power structures. Even when, in the last third of the century, some powers, such as France after the shock of its rapid defeat in the Franco-Prussian War of 1870 and Britain in response to the demands of imperial defense, sought to refurbish their intelligence capabilities, the focus usually was on military rather than political information.[12]

For political intelligence from the Vatican, the handful of European and Latin American countries with embassies to the Holy See generally relied on their diplomats even in times of crisis. Not necessarily poor intelligence sources, these embassies were limited by the diplomatic customs and practice of the time from extending their search for information beyond a small circle composed of senior officials in the papal secretariat and colleagues in the diplomatic corps accredited to the pope. For example, in the spring of 1898, when Queen María Christina of Spain frantically sought the pope's intervention to avert the looming war between Spain and the United States, her government had no other source of intelligence on Vatican attitudes and intentions than its ambassador at the papal court, Marquis Merry del Val. For his information the ambassador relied exclusively on his formal meetings with the cardinal secretary of state, Mariano Rampolla, a well-placed source and one who made no effort to mislead Merry del Val during the 1898 crisis but who could not be expected to reveal much beyond what the Vatican wanted Spain to know.[13] Governments without embassies to the pope generally had little interest in papal affairs to begin with and usually did not feel the absence of reliable information from the Vatican. When a need arose, these governments would direct their embassies to Italy to collect the necessary information, or they would consult fellow-countrymen bishops or cardinals.

Well into the twentieth century, only the Italians bothered to recruit a network of secret agents inside the Vatican. Not surprisingly, when problems in church-state relations suddenly flared into crisis, most governments were hard-pressed to obtain reliable information about papal policies and intentions. This problem persistently bedeviled French authorities after 1880 when anticlerical politicians such as Jules Ferry and Emil Combes, convinced that reactionary Catholics were intriguing to undermine the Third Republic and reestablish the monarchy, embarked on a program to reduce what they considered the pernicious influence of the Church in French politics and society. The suppression of religious orders, the laicization of education, the abolition of military and hospital chaplains, and the legalization of divorce were only a few of the measures that convulsed relations between Paris and the Vatican for a quarter century. The conflict, which at one point saw French soldiers occupying monasteries and convents and forcibly expelling monks and nuns, culminated in the rupture of diplomatic relations in 1904 and the promulgation of the Law of Separation that abrogated the concordat between France and the Vatican and proclaimed the separation of church and state. Throughout this bitter dispute Paris had few sources besides its embassy at the Vatican on which to draw for inside information on papal attitudes or intentions. Consequently, French authorities (at times, to be sure, willfully blinded by their anticlerical biases) constantly misjudged their antagonist, at times overestimating the opposition, at times underestimating it.

Even at the height of church-state tensions, French intelligence operations against the Papacy were limited primarily to surveillance of the nuncios who served in Paris during the period and interception of the Vatican's diplomatic telegrams and the correspondence of French Catholics suspected of conspiring against the Third Republic. At the Prefecture of Police in Paris, files bulged with reports charting the daily activities, no matter how banal, of the nuncios as they moved about the capital on personal or official business. One such report from 1904 solemnly noted that at ten in the morning on the Avenue Gabriel, just opposite the gardens of the Elysée Palace, the residence of the French president, the vehicle of the nuncio, Monsignor Benedetto Lorenzelli, collided with a passing cyclist and demolished the apparatus without injury to its rider.[14] Telegrams passing between the papal secretariat of state and its nuncios were potentially more valuable sources of intelligence, but French cryptanalysts, though successful against the codes of several countries, including Italy, Spain, and Turkey, were apparently unable to crack the Vatican's codes and ciphers.[15]

French intelligence coverage of the Vatican was so weak that information was often as much the result of serendipity as system. In the spring of 1913, for example, codebreakers in the Sûreté (police) routinely deciphered a telegram from the Italian ambassador in Paris to his foreign ministry in Rome that would prove explosive in Paris. The telegram reported the presence in the French capital of a certain Cardinal Vannutelli and revealed that President Raymond Poincaré and Foreign Minister Stephen Pichon were opening secret conversations with the Vatican, even though relations had been broken off in 1904. French police and intelligence sources had picked up not the slightest hint of such talks, though the discussions were going on right in Paris. When he read the intercepted telegram, Interior Minister Louis-Lucien Klotz was enraged, as much from embarrassment at the failure of police intelligence (for which he was responsible) as from knowledge that Poincaré and Pichon had acted without consulting the cabinet on an important question of church-state relations, still a highly charged subject in the Third Republic. A cabinet crisis was avoided only when an embarrassed Pichon threatened to resign unless Klotz tempered his objections and prohibited his police codebreakers from decrypting diplomatic telegrams in the future—a clear case of punishing the bearers of awkward news.[16]

On one occasion poor or incomplete intelligence forced the French authorities to take drastic action. After the rupture in diplomatic relations and departure of the papal nuncio in 1904, the papal embassy was left in the hands of Monsignor Carlo Montagnini, the nuncio's secretary, who remained in Paris as "chargé for religious interests and custodian of the nunciature's archives," a novel title that had no standing (and, therefore, no protection) in international law or diplomatic custom. Ostensibly little more than a caretaker for the papal property and its files and furnishings, the monsignor was actually the Vatican's unofficial eyes and ears in a France still torn by political combat between clericals and anticlericals. The French police (probably after intercepting incriminating letters exchanged by French Catholics) suspected that Montagnini was secretly fomenting resistance to the anticlerical laws and conspiring with conservative politicians to subvert the republic, but the scope of his activity was unknown. The only way that they could determine what he was up to was to mount a surprise raid on the papal embassy in December 1906 and seize him and his files. Montagnini, who turned out to be something less than a master conspirator, was put on the next train for Rome. The confiscated files proved more embarrassing to certain French politicians than to the Vatican. For instance, the papers included copies of messages Montagnini sent to Rome in his personal cipher reporting that Jacques Piou, the leader of the Action Libérale political party, had suggested that by a judicious distribution of bribes the Vatican could assure the defeat in parliament of new anticlerical legislation. Piou specifically mentioned Georges Clemenceau, the prominent politician who would later lead France to victory in the First World War, as among those who would adjust their position in return for a large sum of money. The Vatican did not pursue Piou's suggestion.[17]

Most governments experienced a diminution in their intelligence resources in the nineteenth century, but in the Papacy's case, the decline was especially severe. The pope's intelligence capabilities had largely disappeared with the Papal States. With the loss of the temporal power, the instruments contrived to protect and maintain that power became superfluous. The espionage networks run by the pope's delegates from their provincial capitals were things of the past. Gone, too, were the agents and double agents of a police service now reduced to a handful of uniformed gendarmes pacing the courtyards of the pope's palace and the pathways of his gardens and controlling the crowds at important ceremonies inside St. Peter's Basilica. Only the nuncios remained of the various sources that had collected political intelligence for the Papacy, but here, too, there were changes.

In 1878, the year of Pius IX's death, the Vatican maintained diplomatic relations with fifteen countries, up slightly from the total at the beginning of his pontificate in 1846. There remained, however, an imbalance in the distribution of the papal nunciatures. Seven of the fifteen countries (Austria, Bavaria, Belgium, France, Holland, Portugal, and Spain) were European states with majority or at least numerically significant Catholic populations. The remaining eight were South American states, but despite their number these governments were hosts to only three nuncios, two of whom had multiple assignments. The nuncio to Argentina was also accredited to Paraguay and Uruguay, while the nuncio in Peru was simultaneously the pope's diplomatic representative to Bolivia, Chile, and Ecuador. Only the nuncio in Brazil had a single assignment.

Clearly there were significant gaps in the papal diplomatic network. Non-Catholic regions were not covered. More important, the pope still had no diplomatic representatives in several major European capitals, including Berlin, London, and St. Petersburg. There was no nuncio in Washington, and none east of Vienna. The Vatican tried to compensate for the inadequacies of its diplomatic network by sending "apostolic delegates" to countries, such as the United States, that declined to establish formal relations with the Holy See. A delegate was simply the pope's representative to the local Catholic Church, not to the government, and as such he had no formal diplomatic standing, although he usually established residence in the capital. Depending on his personality and the circumstances surrounding his mission, a delegate might occasionally treat with government authorities and assume quasi-diplomatic functions, but his mission was primarily to oversee the affairs and adjudicate the disputes of the local Catholic Church. For example, in the United States, which received its first apostolic delegate in 1893, the papal representative had almost no contact with the White House and the State Department. Not surprisingly, the delegates kept the Vatican well-informed about local ecclesiastical affairs but were often less reliable sources of political intelligence.

After the loss of the Papal States, there was also a discernible shift in emphasis from the political to the ecclesiastical in the work of the nuncios, and this shift affected the flow of political intelligence to Rome. In addition to his diplomatic duties as the pope's representative to a foreign government, a nuncio had always exercised a purely ecclesiastical responsibility as the Holy Father's representative to the Catholic clergy and faithful of the country in which he served. In this capacity a nuncio (much like an apostolic delegate) transmitted to local Catholics the directions and instructions of the Vatican in matters of religious observance and discipline, while passing to Rome information concerning the administrative, financial, and spiritual health of the local church. After 1870, as the Vatican found itself on the margins of international affairs, the ecclesiastical role of the nuncios assumed greater importance; consequently, most of the information flowing into the secretariat of state and other curial offices was specifically ecclesiastical. Of course political intelligence still appeared in the dispatches from the nunciatures, if only because many ecclesiastical questions, such as the appointment of bishops or the privileges of Catholic schools, contained a political component in that governments often had to be consulted or, in some cases, confronted. Still, despite improvements in communications, such as the spread of the telegraph and the appearance of professional news services, the Vatican was not always as well-informed about world political affairs in the second half of the nineteenth century as it was in the first.

As a source of political intelligence, the papal diplomatic service had a decidedly mixed record in the decades following the loss of the Papal States. Some nuncios excelled in their ability to keep the Vatican informed of political affairs. During its frenzied (and ultimately futile) labors in the spring of 1898 to avert war between Spain and the United States, the papal secretariat of state was well served by the lucid and informed reports of the nuncio in Madrid, Monsignor Giuseppe Francisca Nava di Bontifé. Between 1879 and 1881 the Vatican's earnest (and also futile) effort to improve relations with France relied, in part, on the accurate reporting of the Paris nuncio, Monsignor Wladimir Czacki, whose charm, discretion, and fluency in seven languages helped him cultivate a wide range of contacts in French government and society.[18]

Unfortunately, political observers of the quality of Czacki and Nava di Bontifé were uncommon in the papal diplomatic service. Like so many of their predecessors in the first half of the nineteenth century, the learned monks and dutiful bishops who represented the Holy See abroad in the second half often possessed neither appetite nor aptitude for political reporting. This was true even of the more important diplomatic missions. For example, despite Monsignor Czacki's distinguished performance, the Vatican was often poorly served by its representatives in Paris during the turbulent years of church-state conflict. The situation was especially unfortunate during the tenure of Monsignor Benedetto Lorenzelli (1899–1904) and his unofficial successor as the Vatican's observer in the French capital, Carlo Montagnini (1904–6). Despite previous diplomatic experience in Holland and Germany, Lorenzelli lacked both the personal tact and the social graces that might have opened doors to ministerial chambers and private salons in Paris, where tact and grace were more highly valued than experience. Speaking no language but Italian, he was so isolated in Parisian society that he was said to live "in a state of virtual social disgrace." Montagnini, his successor, was frivolous, indiscreet, and overly fond of society—unpromising qualities for a confidential agent. The cardinal secretary of state at the time, Raffaele Merry del Val (whose reserve of competent diplomats must have been seriously depleted) had a low estimate of Montagnini's abilities, admitting that his agent was "shallow [and] a complete muff."[19] At times the Vatican had so little confidence in its own representatives that it bypassed them and sought information and advice from local bishops, a practice, as we shall see, that sometimes had unfortunate consequences.

The uncertain flow of intelligence from abroad mattered little in the last years of Pius IX, whose political horizon then did not extend beyond the Monte Quirinale, one of the legendary seven hills of Rome, where King Vittorio Emanuele reigned over Rome and a united Italy from the pope's former summer palace. The ailing and stubborn pontiff did not need the latest dispatches or secret reports to tell him that the house of Savoy was ensconced in his city and on his lands and had no intention of leaving. The situation, however, was different for his successor, who would come to regret the limitations of papal intelligence.

Gioacchino Vincenzo Pecci, the cardinal archbishop of Perugia, was elected to the Throne of St. Peter by the College of Cardinals on 20 February 1878 and took the name Leo XIII. Almost sixty-eight and fragile in health, the new pontiff was not expected to have a long or active pontificate. He thought otherwise. For the next twenty-five years Leo, a moderate conservative, struggled to rescue the church in general and the Vatican in particular from reaction and intransigence and bring both into the modern world. Few aspects of contemporary society, from the condition of industrial workers to the study of the natural sciences, escaped the attention of the elderly but energetic pontiff, who at the age of ninety-two was described by a visiting dignitary as "bubbling with humor" and "lively as a cricket."[20]

In the area of foreign affairs, Leo introduced a new style and purpose into papal diplomacy. No less committed (at least rhetorically) than his predecessor to the recovery of the temporal power, Leo understood that the Papacy's diplomatic interests extended beyond the single issue of the Roman Question. In close consultation with Cardinal Mariano Rampolla, his fourth secretary of state (Leo outlived two of his first three), he intended to return the Papacy to a respected and influential place in world affairs. To accomplish their purposes they adopted a less strident tone with regard to the Roman Question without abandoning any of the claims asserted by Pius IX; worked to secure for the Holy See a place at international conferences and a role in diplomatic questions; and sought to establish correct, if not cordial, working relations with established powers, such as France, and emerging powers, such as the United States.

The results of this diplomatic offensive were, at best, mixed, and the setbacks often reflected, at least in part, the Vatican's inability to secure reliable information concerning the personalities and governments with which it dealt. For example, the pope's failure to prevent war between Spain and the United States over Cuba in the spring of 1898 (a failure that compromised the Vatican's position in both Madrid and Washington) exposed the inadequacies of the papal information network. For some time Spanish-American relations had been troubled by events in Spanish-controlled Cuba, particularly Madrid's inability to suppress a long-simmering popular revolt despite the application of severe repressive measures that inflamed American opinion. In February 1898 two events caused relations to deteriorate precipitously. First through Cuban insurgent channels the American press obtained and published a private letter from the Spanish ambassador in Washington, Enrique Dupuy de Lôme, to a friend in Cuba in which the ambassador expressed contempt for American pretensions and ridiculed President William McKinley. The diplomat resigned, but American sensibilities had been grievously offended. Then, within days, the American battleship *Maine* accidentally exploded and sank during a port visit to Havana, and immediately voices in Congress and the press spoke of Spanish sabotage. By the end of the month the debate in Washington over the future of American relations with Spain was increasingly dominated by those who insisted that if the Spaniards refused to leave Cuba, the United States should force them out.[21]

Having successfully mediated a minor dispute between Spain and Germany over certain Pacific islands, Pope Leo and Cardinal Rampolla were emboldened to offer papal mediation to Madrid and Washington to defuse an even more tense situation. In the absence of formal diplomatic relations between the Holy See and the United States, the Vatican was represented in Washington by an apostolic delegate, who had no formal standing with the American government, while the United States had no representative at all at the papal court. Surprisingly, the Vatican had so little confidence in the abilities of its own delegate that when U.S.-Spanish relations deteriorated, it asked John Ireland, the archbishop of St. Paul, Minnesota, to accept a mission as its confidential channel to the McKinley administration and its eyes and ears in Washington. Ireland's experience revealed some of the dangers inherent in relying on local observers rather than trained professionals for advice and information.

Archbishop Ireland was not a disinterested participant in the secret negotiations that marked the Vatican's intervention in the Spanish-American crisis. By 1898 Ireland was one of the most politically active and prominent clerics in the United States. Long identified with the Republican Party then in power in Washington, he had scandalized certain elements in the American Catholic Church by campaigning for McKinley in the election of 1896. He did not hesitate to remind anyone who would listen, including Cardinal Rampolla, that he had many friends and contacts in the president's administration, and these reminders undoubtedly influenced the cardinal secretary of state's decision to rely on the archbishop of St. Paul rather than the politically isolated apostolic delegate. Moreover, the archbishop of St. Paul nurtured an ambition to be a cardinal, an ambition that relied, in part, on retaining the confidence and friendship of influential figures in Washington. Finally, Ireland was a patriot and a nationalist. From his perspective it was evident that Providence had singled out the United States for great things. Blessed by political democracy, religious tolerance, and economic vitality, the United States was destined to occupy a leading place, perhaps *the* leading place, in world affairs, and, if they were smart, traditional powers, such as Spain (and the Vatican), would accommodate themselves to this destiny.[22]

It is difficult to determine to what extent Ireland's connections and attitudes compromised rather than facilitated his role as papal agent and influenced his reporting to Rome. His loyalties were certainly divided between McKinley and the United States, on the one hand, and Pope Leo and the Vatican, on the other. He wanted to help the Holy Father ensure peace, but he did not want to embarrass the McKinley administration or encourage American Protestants to think that their Catholic fellow countrymen were pro-Spanish or unpatriotic.[23] No one can doubt that he worked earnestly and diligently to secure a peaceful solution to the crisis, but no one can doubt either that the solutions he urged the Vatican to press on Spain were those preferred by the McKinley administration: a declaration by Madrid of an immediate armistice in Cuba as an indispensable first step toward resolving the crisis; Spanish-Cuban negotiations leading toward a prompt and permanent resolution of the insurgency; and binding arbitration by the president of the United States in the absence of a negotiated resolution. These proposals, which envisaged one of the principals in the controversy (the United States) assuming the right to impose a solution on the other (Spain), required Madrid to make all the concessions and (given American sympathy for the insurgents, who were unlikely to agree to any solution short of independence) anticipated an early Spanish withdrawal from Cuba.[24]

The Vatican relied exclusively on Ireland for information concerning events and sentiments in Washington. The papal delegate, whom Ireland contemptuously (and unjustly) dismissed as "afraid of his own shadow," played no role beyond encrypting and decrypting the messages that passed almost daily between Archbishop Ireland and Cardinal Rampolla.[25] The Vatican, consequently, had no independent source against which to check Ireland's information. It had no choice but to accept the archbishop's assurances that President McKinley "desperately desired peace and help to attain it," and that only if Spain acceded to McKinley's desires could the president stave off the pressure for war that was building relentlessly in Congress and public opinion.[26] When the Vatican later realized that the "help" McKinley wanted was concessions by Madrid, not papal mediation, and that the only effort to deter the war party in Congress that the president would make after Madrid conceded an armistice was briefly to remind the legislators of that concession in a long report he submitted to the national legislature on 11 April 1898 seeking authority for military intervention in Cuba, it concluded it had been ill informed by its confidential agent in Washington. Of course there was more than a little truth in the observation of Denis O'Connell, an American priest and friend of Ireland then resident in Rome, that the Vatican misunderstood the constitutional position of the American president, assuming he had more executive powers than he really had, but Ireland (perhaps inadvertently) had contributed to this misperception.[27]

Inadequate intelligence would complicate U.S.-Vatican relations again when, in the summer of 1902, the two parties sought a solution to the Friars' Land Question in the Philippine Islands. The islands had been a Spanish colony for centuries, and under the colonial administration certain Catholic religious orders had grown rich and powerful from their ownership of large agricultural estates, their control of schools, hospitals, and charities, and their role as surrogates for Spanish authority in isolated villages. This wealth and power, combined with certain instances of licentious or dissolute behavior on the part of some of the friars, alienated Filipinos, who saw the friars as symbols of Spanish privilege and misrule. When the United States assumed control of the Philippines after the defeat of Spain in 1898, the new American administration sought to pacify local sentiment, secure the loyalty and affection of the population, and distinguish and separate the activities of church and state in accordance with the American Constitution. The administration hoped to purchase the properties of the controversial religious orders in return for a commitment from the orders to leave the Islands. When the orders declined to cooperate in their own demise, the United States decided to approach the Vatican.[28]

In the negotiations that followed, both parties suffered from inadequate intelligence, in part because both parties relied again on Archbishop John Ireland. Despite reservations concerning his performance during the Spanish-American crisis of 1898, the Vatican again decided to use the archbishop of St. Paul rather than the apostolic delegate in Washington for advice and information. For its part, the administration of President Theodore Roosevelt, lacking a representative at the papal court and remaining perfectly ignorant of papal personalities and procedures, considered the personally familiar and politically sympathetic archbishop a trustworthy guide through the unknown territory behind the high walls of the Vatican. Seeking earnestly again to serve two masters, Ireland would end up again misleading both.

Protestant prejudices against Roman Catholicism in general and the pope in particular created a domestic political environment that forced President Roosevelt and his advisers to approach the friars' land issue with care. The Americans hoped to discuss with the Vatican a resolution of the matter, but without suggesting formal political negotiations. They could not risk any action that, by implying diplomatic recognition of the Holy See or seeming to acknowledge the pope's privileged status among religious leaders, might expose them to charges of sectarian preference or indifference to the strict separation of church and state. For their part, Pope Leo and Cardinal Rampolla, determined to enhance the international status and prestige of the Vatican, believed that direct conversations with Washington would advance their efforts, and, if successful, the discussions might encourage the United States to establish a permanent diplomatic mission to the Holy See. Thus, even before the two parties had opened negotiations, each had a different understanding of their purpose: Washington saw any exchanges as merely a business transaction, while the Vatican saw them as diplomatic negotiations.

Serving as the only channel of communication between the two parties and providing each with information about the intentions of the other, Archbishop Ireland perpetuated the misunderstanding by telling each what it wanted to hear. He assured President Roosevelt that the Vatican clearly understood that Washington wanted only a quick settlement of the particular issue and had absolutely no desire for diplomatic relations.[29] He then told Cardinal Rampolla that Washington was eager for a mutually acceptable accommodation and encouraged the cardinal secretary of state to view the arrival of an American delegation in Rome as a precursor to American diplomatic recognition of the Holy See and the arrival of an American ambassador.[30] The Vatican, at least, should have been wary of this intelligence. One of its officials, Monsignor Donato Sbarretti, a specialist in American affairs in the papal administration, stopped in Washington in March 1902 on his way to assume the post of apostolic delegate in Manila. It took him only a few days to discover that Archbishop Ireland, whom he characterized as a self-interested intriguer, had misrepresented the American position. Sbarretti alerted Rome that some American officials, particularly the influential secretary of war, Elihu Root, whose department was responsible for

Philippine affairs, were especially prejudiced against the religious orders and committed to a radical solution, such as the immediate expulsion of the friars from the islands. More important, American officials showed absolutely no interest in diplomatic relations with the Holy See.[31]

The Vatican ignored Sbarretti's warnings and maintained its confidence in Ireland. When, on 1 June 1902, William Howard Taft, the civil governor of the Philippines, arrived in Rome at the head of a small delegation, he was surprised to be received at the papal palace with all the ceremony reserved for the reception of a foreign ambassador. The Vatican made every effort to publicize the visit of the delegation as an important political development and did nothing to discourage press speculation that the United States was considering relations with the Papacy. For his part, Taft, who was irritated by the suggestion that he was on a formal diplomatic mission, adopted a polite but cool demeanor and emphasized that he was in Rome only to negotiate a land sale.

The Vatican misperceived not only the nature of the American mission but also its goals. Papal authorities believed that Washington's principal concern was the purchase of the friars' land. In fact, the Americans saw the purchase of the agricultural estates as merely a means toward their real goal: the removal of the offending friars from the Philippines. Part of the confusion stemmed from the vagueness of the proposals first submitted by the American delegates to the special commission of cardinals appointed by Pope Leo to represent the Church in the negotiations. The confusion, however, was exacerbated by the lack of reliable intelligence on American intentions. In his zeal to facilitate negotiations by downplaying potentially contentious subjects, Archbishop Ireland had understated Washington's antipathy toward the religious orders. This posture was also adopted by Thomas O'Gorman, the bishop of Sioux Falls, South Dakota, a protégé of Ireland's and a member of the American delegation. When approached privately by a member of the Vatican commission for a clarification of the American position, Bishop O'Gorman confidently assured his visitor that the friars themselves were a secondary concern, that Washington did not envision their expulsion from the islands, but only their withdrawal from their country estates until public sentiment against them had cooled. From the United States Archbishop Ireland confirmed that the fate of the friars was only a negotiating point by assuring Cardinal Rampolla that, if pushed by the Vatican's negotiators, Taft would back down from the demand for expulsion.[32] In fact, the departure of the friars from the Philippines was a priority for Washington, and the papal negotiators were perplexed when their American counterparts steadfastly refused to abandon the point.

The American delegation was as misinformed as the Vatican. Neither the State Department nor the War Department had any sources at the Vatican, so no help could be expected from Washington. Except for Bishop O'Gorman, whose soutane and Roman collar provided some access to ecclesiastical circles, the delegation was largely isolated in its Rome hotel. By default, the bishop of Sioux Falls became the delegation's de facto intelligence officer. No less eager than his mentor, Archbishop Ireland, to facilitate an agreement and foster cooperation between the Catholic Church, the world's oldest power, and the United States, the world's newest, O'Gorman generally limited his contacts to those priests and bishops in Rome who shared his views. He seems to have assumed that these contacts represented broader opinion inside the Vatican, and this assumption led him to underestimate the opposition to a settlement, especially among the religious orders that felt themselves morally slandered by the charges of idleness and licentiousness and economically threatened by the potential loss of their valuable lands. For example, after a conversation with a Spanish priest whose brother was a member of the Vatican negotiating team, O'Gorman confidently assured Taft that the discussions would be successful because Pope Leo had directed his negotiators to accept fully all of Washington's proposals.[33] Such assurances seriously misled Taft, who could not understand why, if the pope had ordered a settlement, the papal negotiators persisted in rejecting his proposals and substituting counterproposals. After four weeks the discussions were at an impasse, and Washington ordered a frustrated Taft to break off negotiations and return home.

Poor intelligence by itself did not cause the negotiations to fail. Washington and the Vatican were, after all, divided by differing interests that could be bridged only by mutual trust, accommodation, and compromise. With better intelligence, however, both sides might have eliminated some of the confusion and misperception that are the enemies of these beneficent impulses. The fact that, a year later, Taft (now returned to Manila as civil governor) and the apostolic delegate in the Philippines successfully negotiated a settlement of the friars controversy suggests that the interests of the Vatican and the United States, while different, were not irreconcilable, and that Taft might have secured a settlement in Rome if only the negotiating environment had not been confused on both sides by misinformation.[34]

Inadequate intelligence also compromised another major diplomatic initiative during the pontificate of Leo XIII. In August 1898 the Russian czar, Nicholas II, proposed an international conference to consider ways to limit world armaments and secure and maintain a just peace. For Pope Leo and Cardinal Rampolla the proposal was another opportunity to advance their plan to reestablish the Papacy as a legitimate voice in international affairs. Since the loss of the Papal States in 1870, the Papacy had been overlooked when governments gathered to consider political, military, and economic questions. If the Vatican participated in the conference proposed by the czar, it would enhance its stature and visibility in the community of nations and reclaim a role in international diplomacy. Furthermore, if the Vatican could convince the conference that the Holy Father's anomalous situation in Rome was an obstacle to securing a just world order, the conference might be a step toward resolving the tiresome Roman Question that made the pope a prisoner in his own palace.[35]

For the next ten months the papal secretariat of state turned all its energies toward securing an invitation to the conference that would eventually convene in The Hague, the capital of the Netherlands, in May 1899. Even when it became apparent that any effort to interest the conference in the Roman Question would be futile, the Vatican continued to seek an invitation for the opportunity to return, at least symbolically, to the "club" of world powers. The nuncio in the Netherlands constantly pestered the Dutch foreign office, which was responsible for issuing invitations, and on one occasion even pulled the foreign minister from a formal ball to press the Vatican's case. The nuncios in other European capitals, especially Paris and Vienna, worked hard to cultivate the sympathy and support of other powers. Unfortunately, no invitation materialized, and, by affirming the diplomatic isolation and weakness of the Holy See, the manifest and humiliating failure of the Vatican's efforts created exactly the opposite impression than that desired by the pope and his secretary of state.

Once again, the failure of a papal diplomatic initiative was the result of several factors, including the hostility or indifference of several important powers, particularly Germany and Italy, and the lack of political resources that might have helped the Vatican attract or compel support for its position. Still, poor intelligence was no small factor in the debacle. Throughout the controversy the secretariat of state had difficulty discerning the true intentions of certain of the European powers whose attitudes significantly influenced events. Of course a world-class intelligence service was not necessary to predict Italy's opposition to papal participation in *any* international conference. The Kingdom of Italy was still sufficiently insecure in its claim to the Eternal City that it would resist any initiative that promised to elevate the prestige of the Papacy and draw attention (and perhaps sympathy) to its grievances. From the moment the proposed conference began to take shape, the Italians made it clear that they would not attend any meeting to which papal delegates were invited. The Vatican anticipated Italian opposition but hoped that support for the Papacy from other powers would isolate Italy and that Rome, finding itself alone, might withdraw its objections.

Russia was especially crucial to papal calculations. As the progenitor of the conference, the imperial government was in a position to influence its agenda and the list of those invited to attend. From the start, Pope Leo and Cardinal Rampolla believed that St. Petersburg desired Vatican participation. Their belief was based on the fact that the Russian foreign ministry had arranged for its ambassador at the Holy See to pass to the papal secretariat of state a copy of the original proposal for the conference. Unfortunately, they seriously exaggerated the importance of this communication. The Russian government had, purely as a courtesy, distributed a copy of the proposal to all states with whom it had diplomatic relations. From its perspective the communication was simply a call for a conference, not an invitation to a conference. The latter would be determined according to other, largely political, criteria once the call was generally acknowledged and accepted. The Vatican (or Mexico, or Siam, or the Ottoman Empire) might be invited, or it might not. The Russians were not opposed on principle to papal participation, but they would not jeopardize the prospects of the conference by pressing the Vatican's case against opposition from other powers, such as Italy, that threatened to boycott the conference should the pope's delegates attend.

Unfortunately, the Vatican did not understand, until it was too late, that St. Petersburg could not be relied upon to overcome Italy's objections to papal participation. Although there was a Russian ambassador at the Vatican, there was no papal nuncio or delegate in the Russian capital to apprise the secretariat of state of Russian intentions. Since the Catholic population of the empire was relatively small (and concentrated mainly in the Polish territories) and barely tolerated by a regime for which the Russian Orthodox Church was the state religion, there were no well-connected Catholic prelates to report unofficially in the manner of Archbishop Ireland during the Spanish-American crisis of the previous year. Consequently, the secretariat received no intelligence whatsoever from St. Petersburg. For information concerning Russian plans, Cardinal Rampolla had to depend on conversations with the Russian ambassador, who (perhaps because he was himself kept in the dark by St. Petersburg) misled him into assuming Russian support when the prospect for such support had long faded. Indeed, Cardinal Rampolla first learned that the Russians had decided to leave the Holy See off the invitation list when the nuncio in the Netherlands reported that the rumor was circulating in The Hague. Even after receiving this discomfiting news, the cardinal secretary of state continued to grasp at Russian straws. He was, for instance, briefly buoyed by a report from "Pierre," a source in Paris who claimed to be close to the local Russian embassy, that St. Petersburg supported the Vatican, but that the Dutch were the obstacle!

The complete lack of intelligence from Germany also confused papal authorities. Ultimately, Germany proved to be Italy's strongest supporter in opposing Vatican participation in the conference. The two countries were bound (along with Austria-Hungary) in the so-called Triple Alliance. Berlin valued the alliance as insurance against any French attempt through war to revenge its defeat by Germany in the war of 1870. The Germans feared that Vatican participation in the conference would weaken the Triple Alliance, the cornerstone of German foreign policy, by compromising the legitimacy and authority of the Italian regime and encouraging political instability in Italy by sharpening church-state conflict.

The papal secretariat of state had trouble discerning the strength of German support for Italy, and this was, again, the result of poor intelligence sources. There was a nuncio in Munich to conduct relations with the Kingdom of Bavaria, a nominally independent German principality that was a constituent part of the German Empire, but there was no papal representative in Berlin. Although several prelates, particularly Cardinal George Kopp, the prince bishop of Breslau, had access to senior German policy makers, the Vatican apparently made no use of them for intelligence purposes. Some indications of German intentions were reported by the nuncios in Munich and Vienna, but generally the secretariat of state relied on guesswork. The guesses invariably proved wrong. Even though Germany had informed the European powers that it would stand by Italy and that an invitation to the Holy See would offend Berlin as well as Rome, Cardinal Rampolla persisted in the belief that German support for Italy was pro forma and subject to modification depending on circumstances. Although the cardinal secretary of state had no information to support this belief, he confidently sent Cardinal Kopp to appeal to the German emperor, Wilhelm II, to reconsider his country's commitment to Italy. The emperor flatly refused. This embarrassing rejection was the best intelligence indicator that his assumptions concerning German goodwill and flexibility required review, but as late as April 1899, only weeks before the conference was scheduled to open, Cardinal Rampolla still nourished hopes that Germany would come around. The hopes were based on vague reports from Brussels and Paris that France would propose a compromise that would allow a papal representative to attend the conference sessions concerned with arbitration of international disputes, and that the French foreign ministry was confident of Russian support and cautiously optimistic concerning German and British support. Lacking his own sources in Berlin, London, and St. Petersburg, Rampolla could only cross his fingers and hope that French predictions were right. Unfortunately, they were wrong. If there was a serious French initiative on behalf of a compromise, it aroused little interest among the other major powers. When the international conference finally opened in The Hague on 18 May 1899, the Vatican was not represented.

In their effort to enhance the international status of the Papacy and recover for the Vatican a significant role in world affairs, Pope Leo XIII and Cardinal Rampolla suffered a series of setbacks. Some of these, such as the failure to avert the Spanish-American War, were merely disappointing. Others, such as the futile pursuit of an invitation to the Hague conference, were embarrassing as well as disappointing in that they confirmed the very image of a diplomatically isolated and impotent Papacy that Leo and Rampolla were working so hard to replace. Of course the harsh truth was that, at the turn of the nineteenth century, the Papacy *was* isolated and impotent. It had yet to recover the moral authority it had squandered during the desperate and reactionary effort to retain the temporal power, and it lacked the armies, fleets, factories, farms, and financial institutions that, in the power calculations of international diplomacy, often substituted for moral authority. Without the relevant political resources to back it up, the ambitious foreign policy of Leo and Rampolla would have faltered even with the support of the best intelligence. Weak intelligence, however, exacerbated the difficulties by distorting or obscuring the view from the pontifical palace. With better intelligence, for example, the Vatican might have seen that, given the attitudes and interests of the major powers, its quest for a seat at a major international conference was, at best, quixotic. With better intelligence the Vatican might have relied less on the alleged goodwill and power of President McKinley and investigated alternate approaches to avert war between Spain and the United States. With better intelligence the Vatican in general might have adopted a more careful and pragmatic foreign policy that accommodated its diplomatic reach to its diplomatic grasp.

Though frustrated at many turns by their lack of reliable information, neither Leo nor Rampolla did anything to improve the intelligence capabilities of the Vatican. Of course in the late nineteenth century, the Vatican had few resources for any activity, let alone espionage, and the secretariat of state was happy just to keep its handful of nunciatures and delegations running. The indifference to espionage, however, mainly reflected a failure of imagination and a certain moral reticence. Like their counterparts in most nineteenth-century governments, papal authorities were blind to the potential value of organizations devoted specifically to collecting and analyzing political information, and like those counterparts they viewed espionage with distaste, considering the practice unworthy of a gentleman, let alone a man of God. It would take a new pope, a dangerous threat, and a ruthless imagination to change the situation.

When the College of Cardinals placed the sixty-eight-year-old Gioacchino Vincenzo Pecci on the Throne of St. Peter in February 1878, observers had predicted a short, uneventful pontificate. Pope Leo XIII finally died on 20 July 1903, after an energetic pontificate of twenty-five years. His successor, Giuseppe Sarto, who took the name Pius X, was in many ways his exact opposite. Gioacchino Pecci was the scion of a noble family, while Giuseppe Sarto was the son of a humble village postman and a seamstress. Pecci was educated in two of the Papacy's most elite schools, the Collegio Romano and the Academia degli Ecclesiastici Nobili, while Sarto was a graduate of a provincial seminary. The future Leo XIII was a career bureaucrat who entered the papal service immediately after his ordination and advanced through various administrative and diplomatic posts. The future Pius X was a country curate and parish priest who was preoccupied with the care of souls even when his piety and ability eventually led to his appointment as Cardinal Patriarch of Venice in 1893. Finally, and most important, the new pope shared none of his predecessor's interest in foreign affairs and preoccupation with reinvigorating the diplomacy of the Holy See. He was much more interested in the interior life of the Church and preferred to focus on issues of religious doctrine and practice. More concerned to be a good shepherd than a good diplomat, Pope Pius X intended to protect his flock from every threat to faith and religious practice. And there seemed to be so many threats.

During the pontificate of Leo XIII, a younger generation of Catholic intellectuals, impressed by the analytic power of the new, more critical, approaches to historical, biblical, and theological studies that emerged during the nineteenth century, began to reconsider many elements of the Catholic tradition. In the field of biblical studies, for example, scholars such as the French priest Alfred Loisy challenged the veracity of many "historical" events in the Old Testament, such as the Creation story and the account of the Flood and the ark, and questioned also the authorship of the Gospels of the New Testament. In theology, writers like Ernesto Buonaiuti and George Tyrrell suggested that, rather than being fixed for all time, Church teachings might be better understood as dynamic and adaptive over time to events and circumstances. Political modernists such as Romolo Murri and

Marc Sangnier called for the Church to reconcile itself with democracy and social action, first by moderating its strict hierarchical and absolutist approach to internal governance, and second by abandoning its traditional identification with monarchy and political conservatism and aligning itself with emerging popular political and social movements.[36]

While never part of an organized movement with a common program, these "modernists" (so called because they wanted the Catholic Church to accommodate itself to the attitudes, insights, and discoveries of the modern world) shared a suspicion of received wisdom, a distaste for intellectual and political absolutism, an openness to innovation, and (like so many reformers) a supreme confidence in their own rectitude. They believed that the administrative and theological structures of the Church often rested on insubstantial foundations and that these structures, established in distant times, were no longer entirely suitable for life in the late nineteenth century. They did not anticipate that certain people, some of them extremely powerful, liked the established structures very much and had no intention of allowing others to muck about with them.

Modernism struck a highly dissonant note at the Vatican, where papal authorities were inclined to use the term as an umbrella covering any number of liberal and reformist (and, therefore, unwelcome) tendencies in church and society. These authorities were alarmed by the implications of modernism because they clearly understood that the scattered articles and essays in learned journals were collectively an attack on the notion of a church directed by a centralized authority with a monopoly on the right to interpret and teach an unchanging corpus of dogma. They had little interest in coming to terms with the modern world, and less in adapting the Church to contemporary society, because to do either would suggest that beliefs and practices (on which they had built a lifetime of faith and professional service) were circumstantial and dependent on the times rather than perfect and permanent.

Pope Pius X was appalled by the implications of modernism, as were the conservative cardinals on whom he relied for advice. He saw the movement as nothing less than a mortal threat to the authority of the pope and the traditions and teaching of the Church, and he was determined to crush it. The writings of modernist scholars such as Loisy and Buonaiuti were placed on the Index of Prohibited Books. Authors, like Tyrrell, who refused to be silenced were excommunicated. Papal decrees and encyclicals excoriated modernist tenets and explicitly called for the purge of modernists from Catholic seminaries and schools, the imposition of an antimodernist oath on all priests, and the establishment of vigilance committees in every diocese to root out the new heresy. Declaring war on the modernists, Pius warned, "These people expect to be treated with oil, soap and embraces. But what they need—and what they will get—is a good fist."[37]

The traditionalists found their fist in Umberto Benigni, an Umbrian priest whose scruples fell far short of his ambitions. With a modest reputation as a journalist and polemicist, Benigni had moved from Perugia to Rome in 1895 to seek his fortune. The Eternal City, however, was as unwelcoming to earnest provincials as any other great capital at the turn of the century. A minor clerkship in the Vatican Library and a chaplaincy in a small religious institute offered Benigni little scope for his ambition and abilities. His prospects improved in 1901 when, on the basis of a monograph on agrarian policies in the old Papal States, he secured an appointment as professor of church history at the Roman Seminary, an elite institution whose graduates often went on to glittering ecclesiastical careers. About the same time he began an association, as writer and then editor, with the ultramontane Catholic newspaper, *La Voce della verità*.

These positions provided an outlet for Benigni's polemical skills and a platform for his reactionary views on religion and society, views that were increasingly fashionable among the "integralists" (traditionalists) in the court of Pius X. Benigni's articles defending the pope's temporal power and opposing political and theological reforms received favorable notice among conservative cardinals, especially Raffaele Merry del Val, the powerful secretary of state, and Gaetano De Lai, the equally influential prefect of the Consistorial Congregation, the Vatican department concerned with the selection of bishops. Within a year Benigni was appointed *minutante* (senior clerk) in the Congregation for the Propagation of the Faith (Propaganda Fide), the curial department responsible for missionary activity, and professor in its university for seminarians from mission lands. The once obscure provincial now became something of a celebrity in conservative intellectual circles in Rome and among the "black" nobility around the papal throne, but even his friends were surprised when, in 1906, he catapulted into the heart of the Vatican with an appointment as undersecretary for extraordinary affairs in the secretariat of state.[38]

It was uncommon for an outsider, inexperienced in diplomacy, to assume a senior position in the papal foreign ministry, but Benigni had assiduously cultivated contacts who could advance his career. The cardinal secretary of state had two deputies, the secretary for extraordinary affairs, who supervised relations with foreign governments, and the "substitute" for ordinary affairs, who ran the administrative side of the department. The undersecretary was the principal assistant of the secretary for extraordinary affairs. At the time, the secretary for extraordinary affairs was Monsignor Pietro Gasparri, who also held the post of director of the Vatican Seminary, where, it so happened, Benigni taught a course in ecclesiastical history in the few hours a week he could spare from his administrative and teaching responsibilities at Propaganda Fide. Gasparri considered Benigni a diligent and intelligent instructor. For his part, the ambitious Umbrian, ever alert for an influential patron, shamelessly courted his superior's goodwill and relentlessly pestered him for a better post. When the incumbent undersecretary was appointed apostolic delegate to Cuba, Gasparri offered the vacant position to Benigni, believing the young instructor to be suited for the post by virtue of his intelligence, industry, and command of languages.[39]

The appointment to the secretariat of state was a major opportunity for Benigni, who had become restless and frustrated at Propaganda Fide. Personally ambitious, committed to the assertion of traditional papal claims in religion and society and convinced that those claims were seriously threatened by the many voices of modernism, he sought a more central and active role in the struggle for what he saw as the life and soul of the Catholic Church than that provided by a university chair or a journalist's column. He wanted to grasp the instruments of power and wield them against the enemies of the Church. He now found that power in the secretariat of state, the prestigious department that directed papal foreign policy and influenced affairs in every corner of the papal administration. At the time, the post of undersecretary was especially important because the secretary, Monsignor Pietro Gasparri, was increasingly distracted from departmental business by his editorial responsibilities in the massive project to revise and publish a new code of church law. With Gasparri otherwise occupied, Benigni would be the principal collaborator of Cardinal Secretary of State Raffaele Merry del Val, who was, in turn, the principal collaborator of Pope Pius. The obscure provincial journalist who had come to Rome to seek his fortune now strode confidently along the corridors of power.

The new undersecretary had barely moved into his office in the Apostolic Palace before he approached the cardinal secretary of state with a bold plan to combat the errors of modernism and its secular equivalent, democratic liberalism. Benigni argued that the agents of modernism had to be rooted out of the institutions of the Church into which they had insinuated themselves, and their tenets had to be discredited. Their lay collaborators in the universities, newspapers, and political institutions of Britain, France, Germany, and Italy had to be identified and isolated. To these ends, he easily convinced Cardinal Merry del Val, who shared his subordinate's repugnance at theological and political innovation, to authorize him to organize a clandestine effort in defense of the Church and the traditional order. This effort would have two elements. A propaganda program would provide an instrument for attacking the arguments of the modernists and dominating the public debate over the future of the Church and society. Separately, a clandestine intelligence operation would recruit secret agents in Europe, North America, and South America to identify the modernists, expose their conspiratorial connections, and frustrate their plans.

Benigni threw himself into his assignment with all the energy of a fanatic. Soon his position of undersecretary became little more than a cover for his secret work, which was hidden from his colleagues in the secretariat of state, including his patron and immediate superior, Monsignor Gasparri. Benigni's first steps were to create instruments to influence public opinion. By the turn of the century many foreign ministries, recognizing the growing power of mass circulation newspapers and news services that could flash a news item to subscribers around the world, routinely sought to manipulate the press in support of official policies. The papal foreign office, however, operated in an administrative environment that was compulsively secretive and suspicious of any outsiders, particularly journalists, and it studiously kept its distance from the secular press. The new undersecretary, however, had launched his ecclesiastical career as a journalist, and before moving to Rome he had edited Catholic newspapers in Umbria and Liguria. He understood, as few in the papal Curia did, the potential influence of newspapers, and he believed that the Vatican could effectively use the press in the battle against modernism and liberalism.

Benigni set himself up as the unofficial press officer of the secretariat of state and made himself available to reporters to whom he provided, off the record, the Vatican "line" on various events and issues. In a practice that a later generation would know as disinformation, he made a point of cultivating the "enemy," correspondents of liberal newspapers and news agencies, in order to place misleading items in their columns and dispatches. He also bribed journalists to ignore or minimize news that reflected well on liberals. Through intermediaries Benigni founded and secretly directed a weekly newspaper, *Corrispondenza Romana,* which attacked modernism and political liberalism while defending the traditional prerogatives of the Papacy. Though the secretariat of state went out of its way to declare that the paper (which soon also appeared in a French edition) was neither an official nor a semiofficial mouthpiece of the Vatican, the *Corrispondenza* was secretly subsidized by Cardinal Merry del Val. Finally, the undersecretary wrote a weekly newsletter containing the integralist perspective on ecclesiastical and political events around the world. He quietly passed this newsletter to certain conservative correspondents of foreign newspapers, who were told to publish the material under their own names without any reference to the source. Through these contacts Benigni was able to spread anti-modernist propaganda through newspapers in various countries, including Argentina, Austria, Belgium, Spain, and the United States.[40]

Propaganda and disinformation operations served to discredit modernism, but Benigni and his patrons inside the Vatican needed to monitor the influence of the movement on religious and secular beliefs, practices, and institutions. Until Rome could divine the presence of the hateful heresy in schools and seminaries, youth and labor movements, and political, social, and cultural organizations, it could take no remedial action. The integralists also needed to identify the adherents of modernism so as to remove them from positions of authority and expose them to ecclesiastical sanctions. Secrecy, of course, was paramount, since the prey would seek cover if they knew they were being hunted. The Vatican's usual sources—bishops, nuncios, apostolic delegates—could not be relied upon to collect and report the required information, especially since some of these sources (particularly among the bishops) were themselves suspected of modernist sympathies. What was required was a secret intelligence organization, closely supervised from Rome and dedicated to infiltrating and exposing the modernist movement. Unfortunately for the integralists, the Vatican had not had a formal intelligence service since the loss of the Papal States. Benigni intended to remedy this situation.

In the months following his appointment the new undersecretary organized a clandestine intelligence service that had no name and no location (aside from the undersecretary's desk in the papal palace). It had no official standing and did not appear in the *Annuario Pontificio*, the pontifical yearbook that listed all Vatican departments and organizations. Its modest expenses were covered by secret subventions from the cardinal secretary of state, Merry del Val, to whom Benigni reported privately. Few, if any, of Benigni's colleagues in the secretariat were aware of his work, and none were a part of it. Benigni was the sole controller: only he corresponded with informants, only he had access to the files, only he read the reports that were soon arriving from Europe and the Western Hemisphere.

Benigni used the same espionage techniques—spies, mail interception, personal surveillance—that were common among the intelligence and police services of secular powers. In a rare instance of collaboration between the Vatican and the Italian government, the secretariat of state, at the undersecretary's suggestion, quietly arranged with the Italian post office to monitor the mail of bishops and priests suspected of theological or political liberalism.[41] In episcopal palaces, sacristies, refectories, and seminary class-rooms across Europe and (to a lesser extent) North and South America, informants secretly opened mail, transcribed lectures and sermons, and reported incriminating conversations. Though many of these sources were zealous traditionalists who spontaneously denounced superiors and colleagues to Rome, some operated under Benigni's direction.

Though the full range of Benigni's espionage network remains obscure, some operations have surfaced. In 1909, for instance, the undersecretary concluded that there existed in Rome a ring of young modernist priests who corresponded with Antonio De Stefano, a noted medievalist and former priest who, Benigni believed, directed an international modernist network from his home in Geneva, Switzerland. To penetrate this alleged conspiracy against orthodoxy, Benigni sent a young priest, Gustavo Verdesi, to ingratiate himself with the reform-minded clerics and report on their activities. To expose the Swiss end of the conspiracy, the undersecretary recruited Father Pietro Perciballi, a former classmate of De Stefano at the Roman Seminary. At the seminary Father Perciballi had also come to know other important modernists, including Ernesto Buonaiuti, whose books were condemned as heretical by the Holy Office, the Vatican department responsible for enforcing Catholic orthodoxy.

Supplied by Benigni with money, a passport, and a camera, Perciballi traveled to Geneva, where, under the guise of a reunion of old school chums, he called on De Stefano. The unsuspecting historian, who was distracted by plans to launch a modernist magazine, the *Revue moderniste internationale,* invited his old friend to extend his visit to Geneva as his house guest. Perciballi repaid this kindness by taking advantage of his host's absences from the house to examine the contents of his desk, photograph some of the papers and transcribe others, including correspondence with Buonaiuti, and make a list of books in the library. He also took every opportunity to engage his host in frank and leading conversations to elicit his views on theological and political issues and to discover his contacts beyond Switzerland. When Perciballi returned to Rome, he carried all this material to Benigni, who shared it with the Holy Office. Later, during one of his many hostile interviews at the Holy Office, Buonaiuti would be amazed to discover that his questioners had before them copies of his private correspondence with De Stefano.[42]

Benigni directed most of his espionage against internal threats to Catholic orthodoxy, and his files soon bulged with reports on reformist bishops, liberal seminary professors, and suspect intellectuals. One report would identify a "very modernist" chaplain at a Catholic boarding school in Tournai, Belgium, who allegedly bristled at the very mention of the Vatican; a second document denounced a candidate for the chair of history at the Catholic university of Lille, France, for criticizing in his lectures the Catholic clergy at the time of the Reformation; yet another report noted that a politically active priest in Paris consorted with known Freemasons.[43] By 1910 the Vatican's de facto intelligence director had established a wide-ranging internal surveillance apparatus that ferreted out real and imagined critics of the authority of the Vatican and the teachings of traditional Catholicism. Once identified, these individuals frequently were threatened with ecclesiastical and professional penalties if they did not submit. Professors lost their posts in Catholic faculties; writers found their books on the Index of Prohibited Books; priests were transferred to distant parishes or suspended from their religious duties. Especially recalcitrant individuals were excommunicated. Nobody was safe from Benigni's spies. The list of those denounced included Cardinals Amette (Paris), Ferrari (Milan), Mercier (Brussels), and Piffle (Vienna), as well as the rectors of the premier Catholic universities of Louvain, Paris, and Toulouse. Benigni even secretly investigated his immediate superior in the secretariat of state, Monsignor Pietro Gasparri.

For all his attention to ecclesiastical affairs and religious orthodoxy, Benigni did not neglect the world of politics. Committed to the defense of the traditional order in the secular as well as the spiritual realm and convinced that political liberalism was a threat to all authority and the "accomplice of Revolution," the undersecretary collected political intelligence almost as avidly as he did ecclesiastical intelligence.[44] As undersecretary he routinely saw the dispatches of the pope's nuncios and delegates around the world, but he supplemented this information with reports from his private sources. The reports ranged widely across borders and topics. From a source in Berlin he learned of current developments in the German Reichstag and the situation of the Catholic Center Party. Information from France covered the activities of "Sillon," a Catholic student-worker organization devoted to social reform and the reconciliation of Catholics to the Third Republic. A report from Uruguay warned that the new president of that South American republic would support the separation of Church and state and the suppression of religious holidays. News from Russia described the religious persecution of Catholics and tensions between Lithuanian and Polish subjects of the czar.[45]

In the beginning Benigni's informants were largely priests, seminarians, and conservative laypeople who shared his traditionalist views on religion and papal authority, but soon he began to seek recruits in such disparate areas as the Italian ministry of public works and the Rome police department. Clearly the undersecretary, who had developed a taste for the clandestine world, intended to expand his operations beyond a narrow focus on defending religious orthodoxy to a broader intelligence program that included among its targets secular governments, such as Italy. He even began to penetrate the Roman Curia, the administration of Vatican City, and the papal household itself. Junior officers in certain nunciatures kept him informed through back channels of events at their diplomatic posts. Pope Pius's private secretary commented on the pontiff's visitors and described his latest concerns. There were even reports from an employee in the office of the pontifical gardens.[46] No rumor, no bit of corridor gossip, no report from abroad was insignificant. No individual, no matter how exalted, was beyond suspicion. Perhaps Benigni suspected enemies everywhere, even at the heart of the Papacy; or, perhaps, he hoped to build his personal power on a foundation of secret files; or, more likely, espionage had become an obsession, and he now pursued betrayal, intrigue, and secrecy for their own sakes.

This secret work had the tacit approval of both Pope Pius X and Cardinal Secretary of State Merry del Val, as well as other high Vatican dignitaries, such as the reactionary Cardinal Gaetano De Lai, the powerful head of the Vatican department concerned with the appointment of bishops, and the half-mad Cardinal Jose Calasanzio Vives y Tuto, the director of the department responsible for Catholic religious orders. A traditionalist in religion and conservative in politics, Cardinal Merry del Val supported the war against modernism and liberalism, and he had explicitly endorsed Benigni's proposal for a secret intelligence service when the new undersecretary began his work in the secretariat of state in 1906. Although probably unaware of the specifics of Benigni's apparatus, the cardinal saw the undersecretary every day and was privy to much of the information collected by his subordinate. The knowledge and complicity of the pope can also be assumed. Among his opponents (and victims) inside the Vatican, Benigni was considered the pontiff's "evil genius."[47] Pius secretly subsidized Benigni's paper, *Corrispondenza Romana*. More significantly, he provided moral support and legitimacy to Benigni's enterprises by twice granting an "apostolic benediction" to the Sodalitium Pianum, an antimodernist organization established by Benigni in 1909 as a front for his secret operations. For his part, Benigni passed information and files to Pius through Cardinal Merry del Val or through Monsignor Giovanni Bressan, the pope's private secretary, who was a close ally of the undersecretary.[48]

Because Benigni was widely known to have friends and protectors in the highest circles, the surprise was all the greater when, on 7 March 1911, the Vatican newspaper, *L'Osservatore Romano,* carried a brief item announcing that Monsignor Umberto Benigni had been promoted to the post of "protonotary apostolic" and that Monsignor Eugenio Pacelli, a junior officer in the secretariat, would be the new undersecretary for extraordinary affairs. In the frescoed corridors of the Vatican the news set off a flurry of rumor and speculation that soon spread across Europe. The College of Protonotaries Apostolic was an anachronistic institution that had neither duties nor powers. Appointments to the college usually went to elderly, worthy ecclesiastics upon their retirement when long service to the Papacy required symbolic reward. For a forty-eight-year-old undersecretary in the prestigious secretariat of state, transfer to an honorific society of superannuated priests was hardly a promotion. Undersecretaries could usually expect to move up to a higher post in the secretariat or to an important nunciature in the papal diplomatic service. The College of Protonotaries was little more than a kick upstairs to an honorable but empty sinecure.

Although the *Corrispondenza Romana* loyally described Benigni's reassignment as a "high distinction," most observers concluded that the erstwhile undersecretary had been disgraced and purged. Some believed that Benigni's increasingly strident and irresponsible propaganda campaign against modernism and liberalism had become a liability. Others were aware that, whatever his aptitude for intelligence work, he was a dismal failure as a diplomat. For all his preoccupation with espionage, Benigni was still the undersecretary in the pope's foreign ministry, and in this capacity he committed several gaffes that embarrassed the Papacy and adversely affected the Vatican's relations with several governments, including those of France, Germany, and Bolivia. The latter, for example, recalled its ambassador from the Vatican over an intemperate diplomatic note Benigni had drafted and dispatched without first clearing it with either his immediate superior, Monsignor Gasparri, or Cardinal Merry del Val. More alarming were rumors (never confirmed) that the undersecretary had been discovered passing secret papal documents to representatives of the imperial Russian government.[49]

In fact Benigni, ever the conspirator, had orchestrated his own removal. In June 1910 he had approached Cardinal Merry del Val with a plan to advance his secret work. Explaining that the propaganda and espionage operations required more and more of his time and energy, Benigni asked his superior to allow him to resign his office in the secretariat in order to pursue these operations full-time. He further proposed that he receive a modest, but respected, title so as to counter the inevitable rumors that he had been demoted. The title should come with no duties or responsibilities that might distract him from his important work. To facilitate his intelligence work, he should be allowed continued access to the facilities, documents, and personnel of the secretariat of state. Finally, he asked for a salary of 7,000 lire a year (a raise from his undersecretary's salary of 5,100 lire) and several hundred additional lire per month to support his intelligence activities.[50]

Although it is not clear that Benigni received all that he asked for, there can be little doubt that his departure from the secretariat of state was not the abject disgrace that his enemies desired. Superficially, his stature among the reactionaries of the papal court remained undiminished, and his intelligence work continued unabated. He remained in close and frequent correspondence with important prelates, such as Cardinal De Lai. He occasionally exchanged information with the secretariat of state on political and ecclesiastical matters, and his former employer often asked him to vet individuals under consideration for promotion or papal honors. For example, in the spring of 1912 Monsignor Pacelli, Benigni's replacement as undersecretary, asked his predecessor if he had any information concerning a certain priest who had been nominated by his bishop for a special papal award. Several weeks later Pacelli contacted Benigni to inform him that the secretariat was preparing a statement on the German labor movement and to update him on the search to replace a recently deceased German archbishop.[51]

Still, there was a decided shift in his status and influence. His relations with Cardinal Merry del Val, for instance, cooled noticeably. Though as committed to the war against modernism as his undersecretary, the cardinal secretary of state had always had less appetite for the clandestine surveillance, disinformation, and anonymous denunciations that were the routine weapons in this war. So long as Benigni's work remained secret, the cardinal suppressed his reservations, but by 1911 the Umbrian's cover had been blown, and rumors about his control of a secret organization committed to spying on clerics and lay Catholics were spreading within ecclesiastical circles. The rumors were seemingly confirmed in the spring of 1911 when the liberal Catholic journalist Guglielmo Quadrotta interviewed a former priest (since converted to Methodism) who had served as Benigni's private secretary; this man acknowledged his former employer's espionage and admitted that he personally had been sent to infiltrate a circle of Italian priests suspected of modernist tendencies.[52]

Increasingly, Merry del Val had to calm cardinals and bishops who were alarmed by such stories or insulted by scurrilous attacks in the *Corrispondenza Romana*. On one occasion he barely averted a major scandal. Adopting the tactics of their opponent, a group of liberal Belgian and German Catholics launched a secret investigation of Benigni's cover organization, Sodalitium Pianum, by infiltrating a Dominican friar, Foris Prims, into the organization. Prims ingratiated himself with one of Benigni's principal collaborators, a Belgian lawyer named Jonckx, who lived in Ghent. From the trusting lawyer Prims learned much about the organization and activities of Sodalitium Pianum. The rather naive Prims, who apparently did not know that Benigni had powerful protectors inside the Vatican, traveled to Rome intent upon warning the pope that there was a clandestine organization within the Church that was sowing pain and suspicion among Catholics. Merry del Val saved Benigni (and himself) from embarrassment by blocking Prims's attempt to secure an audience with the pope and refusing to pursue the matter unless the friar could produce documentary evidence to support his charges.[53]

Umberto Benigni was becoming a liability, and the cardinal secretary of state was probably relieved when his undersecretary asked to resign his post. If nothing else, Benigni's resignation would distance the Vatican from the increasingly troublesome spymaster. To increase that distance, Merry del Val ceased his secret financial support for the *Corrispondenza*, and in 1912 he ordered Benigni to close the newspaper. As a further sign that Benigni's star was falling, Pope Pius failed to grant formal recognition to the Sodalitium Pianum. Such recognition would have legitimized and empowered the association (and its founder), but the pope, despite intensive lobbying by Benigni among well-placed supporters, such as Cardinal De Lai, preferred merely to send periodically his "apostolic blessing" to the association, each more brief and less enthusiastic than the one preceding.[54]

Benigni was apparently undismayed by these small but unmistakable signs of disfavor. After his departure from the secretariat of state, he withdrew ever more completely into a murky world of clandestinity and paranoia. From his Roman apartment on the Corso Umberto I, he tried to maintain the networks of informants that, by now, had made him notorious in ecclesiastical circles. In a curious case of mirror imaging, the Vatican's erstwhile spymaster convinced himself that modernist spies were attempting to penetrate his organization and that his movements were monitored. Believing that modernist agents in French, German, and Italian post offices were secretly intercepting and opening his mail, Benigni communicated with his now dwindling band of agents in a private code, and he directed his correspondents to avoid using his name on envelopes but, rather, to send their reports to "Cesare Naturelli" at the Corso Umberto address. To avoid the enemies he imagined dogging his every step, he adopted various aliases when he traveled to meet his informants, and he arranged elaborate procedures to ensure that his presence in Brussels or Geneva or Paris remained secret. In the years following his departure from the secretariat of state, however, fewer and fewer people, including the modernists, were interested in his activities.[55]

By 1914 Umberto Benigni had slipped to the margins of papal affairs, and the once fearsome spymaster had become a pathetic paranoid who could find purpose and direction in his life only by conjuring threats and intrigues. He had envisioned a papal intelligence service the equal of those employed by such secular powers as France and Russia, but the vision was chimerical. Benigni got no further than creating a private intelligence net that he put at the disposal of the Vatican. He personally recruited informants, personally directed their activities and read their communications, personally arranged and secured the files, personally reported to the cardinal secretary of state, and personally performed all other tasks except, perhaps, polishing the floor around his desk. He recruited and trained no assistants, delegated no tasks, established no administrative procedures and routines, and obtained no authority beyond a wink and a nod from one or two cardinals. In short, he failed to build an organization that would survive him. What the Vatican got was an intelligence *officer,* but not an intelligence *service,* and when the officer departed, the Vatican was left with an intelligence capability no better than it had before he arrived. Furthermore, the ruined careers, broken friendships, and pervasive suspicion that resulted from Benigni's notorious program of secret informants and anonymous denunciations discredited the very idea of an information service. Unfortunately, as Benigni's star dimmed along with his vision of a papal intelligence service, the world was moving closer to a conflagration that would rudely reintroduce the Vatican to the unseemly world of intelligence operations.

3

The Great War

Pius X's death on 21 August 1914 came as a surprise in a month of unpleasant surprises. Although the seventy-nine-year-old pontiff had been in precarious health for some time, his death still caught a distracted world off guard. In July Italian intelligence, preoccupied as always with matters of papal well-being, had reported that the Holy Father's physicians found him in good health. In July and early August the "Reports on the Vatican" filed with the Directorate General of Public Security (DGPS) by Police Commissioner Cesare Bertini, the officer responsible for covert surveillance of the Vatican, indicated that the pope maintained his regular schedule of audiences with diplomats and church officials. As late as 18 August, Bertini assured his superiors in the DGPS that, though indisposed with an undisclosed ailment, Pius was in stable condition, and there was no cause for concern.[1]

Normally the death of a pope would merit banner headlines in newspapers around the world, but Pius's departure from this world had to compete for space on the front pages with more alarming news. Austrian outrage at the assassination in Sarejevo of the Hapsburg heir apparent, Archduke Franz Ferdinand, and his wife on 28 June 1914 had escalated in a flurry of ultimatums and mobilization orders into the gravest European crisis since the Napoleonic Wars. By 4 August, barely three weeks before Pius's death, Germany and Austria-Hungary were at war with the British Empire, France, Russia, Serbia, and Belgium. The first reports of casualties and destruction that reached the papal secretariat of state from Brussels, Berlin, and Vienna may have been too much for the frail pontiff. Although the doctors listed pneumonia as the official cause of death, the more pious denizens of the papal palace insisted that the saintly pope had succumbed to a heart broken by the unfolding of a truly global war.

In the last week of August, as the cardinals assembled in Rome for the conclave to elect the new pope, the war bulletins announced attack and counterattack, advance and retreat. In the west, British, French, and Belgian armies fell back under the relentless pressure of a German offensive that threatened to overwhelm Allied resistance and end the war before autumn. Brussels had fallen to the Germans as Pius X lay dying, and by 29 August, as British and French troops retreated to the Marne, barely thirty miles northeast of Paris, authorities in the French capital prepared for a siege by bringing beef cattle to graze in the Bois de Boulogne and requisitioning the city's taxis for emergency transport. In the east, where Russian forces repulsed an Austrian invasion of Russian Poland and launched their own offensive into German East Prussia, Allied prospects temporarily seemed brighter. But hope gave way to disappointment after the devastating Russian defeat at the battle of Tannenberg (25–30 August), where the Germans repulsed the czarist army, which lost more than 120,000 men (including 92,000 taken prisoner) and six hundred pieces of artillery.

The sounds of distant cannon echoed in the frescoed corridors and marbled chambers of the Vatican. On 1 September, as the princes of the church filed into the Sistine Chapel for the first day of voting, the German cardinal Felix Hartmann of Cologne turned to the Belgian cardinal Désiré Mercier of Malines and said, "I hope that we shall not speak of war." The Belgian, who had recently learned of the destruction by German soldiers of the University of Louvain, his country's premier university and a cultural center of international reputation, hissed in reply, "And I hope we shall not speak of peace."[2]

The belligerents certainly saw the papal conclave as an extension of the political battlefield. The election of a pope in the midst of a war that had already spread beyond Europe was much too important to be left to chance or the intervention of the Holy Spirit. Because of his moral authority, an unsympathetic, let alone hostile, pontiff could seriously complicate the war effort of any belligerent, but especially those such as Belgium, France, Germany, and Austria-Hungary that counted large numbers of Catholics among their population. The funeral ceremonies for the dead pope were hardly over before the powers began to intrigue to ensure a friendly replacement.

At the instigation of their government, which hoped to seize the moral high ground and preempt action by Britain and France, German Catholics took the highly unusual step of sending the cardinal electors a formal statement explaining Germany's grievances and justifying its recourse to war. In reaction, Belgian and French Catholics (no doubt inspired by their own governments) submitted a counterstatement justifying the position of Belgium and France. Unwilling to rely solely on public manifestos, certain belligerents tried to influence the election directly. Before their departure for Rome the five cardinals of the Austro-Hungarian Empire were advised by the Austrian foreign minister to vote for neither Cardinal Giacomo Della Chiesa, the archbishop of Bologna, nor Cardinal Domenico Ferrata, the former papal nuncio in Paris. Both cardinals were identified with the pro-French posture of the late Cardinal Mariano Rampolla, Pope Leo XIII's longtime secretary of state, and Vienna feared that the election of either would undercut Austria's influence at the Vatican and advance the cause of France and its allies. Of the two, the better-known Ferrata was a more immediate threat than Della Chiesa, who had labored diligently but obscurely in the pastoral fields of Bologna and who had been a cardinal for only three months. Before the conclave the French government advised Cardinal Amette of Paris that Ferrata was France's preferred choice, and the French foreign ministry directed its embassy in Rome to orchestrate a discreet press campaign on behalf of the former nuncio.[3] For its part, the Austrian government pushed the candidacy of Cardinal Domenico Serafini, a pious and unworldly Benedictine monk, who could be trusted to focus on spiritual matters and avoid inconvenient political or diplomatic initiatives. Encouraged by Berlin, Cardinal Hartmann was also active in undermining the prospects of politically unattractive candidates, including the allegedly Francophile dark horse, Cardinal Della Chiesa.[4]

To the consternation of both Berlin and Vienna, Cardinal Della Chiesa emerged after ten ballots as the choice of the conclave, and he accepted election under the name Benedict XV. The outcome surprised most observers, including Italian intelligence, which had tried without success to penetrate the secrecy of the conclave. In Rome and other capitals, officials discovered that they knew relatively little about the personality or the attitudes of the new pontiff, and they scrambled for indications of his political sympathies.[5] In fact, in selecting the low-profile archbishop of Bologna, the cardinals reacted as much to ecclesiastical as to international considerations. By 1914 the harsh and relentless orthodoxy of Pius X and the integralist movement he patronized had disillusioned all but a handful of the cardinals. The majority of cardinals (including the Austrians, who, despite the instructions of their foreign ministry, placed the interests of their church above the interests of their empire) sought a pope of moderate inclination and modern sensibilities with the pastoral and diplomatic experience to heal the divisions among the faithful while guiding the Church through the vicissitudes of war.[6]

Ironically, Giacomo Della Chiesa's election pleased none of the belligerents, both sides believing that the new pope favored their enemies. Austria-Hungary and Germany were stunned by the selection of a cardinal they had actively opposed for his past association with Cardinal Rampolla and the policy of accommodation with republican France. For their part, Britain and France found little solace in the outcome of the conclave despite the new pope's Francophile reputation in Berlin and Vienna. In France, where the anticlericalism of Jules Ferry and the Laws of Separation remained virulent and church-state controversies still inflamed public life, elements of the press did not hesitate to brand Benedict the *Pape boche* despite his appointment of Pietro Gasparri, another disciple of Cardinal Rampolla and the policy of *raillement*, as cardinal secretary of state.[7] In Britain the reaction, while more restrained, was no less apprehensive. The concern extended beyond questions regarding the sympathies of the new pope; the biases of the papal administration were also suspect. Within weeks of the conclave Cardinal Aidan Gasquet, the only British cardinal resident in Rome, warned London that, whatever the personal sympathies of Della Chiesa, "the whole sentiment of ecclesiastical Rome was distinctly pro-German."[8]

Concerned but uncertain about the future direction of papal policy, the various powers needed as much information from the Vatican as they could acquire. Good intelligence would alert a government to upcoming papal decisions and initiatives in sufficient time to prepare a response. It would also expose any efforts by hostile countries to influence or manipulate the papacy in their favor. Finally, it would allow a government to contrive policies well suited to appeal to the attitudes and interests of the pope and his administration. To secure good intelligence, a government required a capable and experienced team of overt representatives and covert agents working at the Vatican. In the competition for intelligence, the Central Powers were first off the line.

Diplomatically Berlin and Vienna were well represented at the papal court. Germany was especially well positioned, since, owing to an unusual arrangement dating from the nineteenth century, the Reich had two ambassadors at the Vatican, one representing Prussia and the other Bavaria. The Prussian ambassador, Otto von Mühlberg, was an accomplished and energetic diplomat, while his Bavarian colleague, Otto von Ritter, was especially admired inside the papal palace for his piety and modest demeanor. For its part, Austria was ably represented by Prince Schönberg, scion of a prestigious family that had served church and state for centuries. These conscientious ambassadors assiduously cultivated the curial cardinals and monsignors, as well as the Catholic press in Italy. In contrast to the stellar lineup of the Central Powers, the diplomatic team of the Allies was decidedly minor league. Britain and France had no diplomatic relations with the Papacy and no representatives at the Vatican at all. The only Allied ambassadors at the Vatican were an elderly Belgian, who was passing the time until retirement, and an enervated Russian, who was effectively marginalized by his passivity and a longstanding suspicion in clerical circles that his government and the Russian Orthodoxy it defended were greater threats than Protestantism to Catholic Europe.[9]

To counter the influence of the Central Powers, Cardinal Gasquet, ably assisted by his secretary Dom Philip Langdon, became an informal agent and propagandist for the Allies. Best known as an authority on English monasticism, Gasquet revealed an aptitude for political action surprising in one who had spent his life in the sheltered cloisters of Benedictine abbeys. Patriotic and energetic, he never doubted the righteousness of the Allies or the perfidy of their enemies. He showered London with letters describing Austro-German efforts to capture and manipulate Vatican sympathies and urging the Foreign Office to open quickly a British embassy at the Vatican to counter enemy intrigues. In the early months of the war these letters were London's principal source of intelligence from inside the Vatican, and they significantly influenced the Foreign Office not only in its perceptions of a Germanophile Vatican but also in its decision, in November 1914, to send to Rome Sir Henry Howard, a retired diplomat and a Catholic, as His Majesty's special representative to the pope.

Even after the arrival of the British diplomatic mission, Gasquet missed no opportunity to advance the Allied cause. Equally at home in musty archive, papal antechamber, and secular drawing room, the cardinal was everywhere in Rome, cajoling, debating, and encouraging. He advised Sir Henry on the nuances of Vatican politics and guided him through the Byzantine complexities of papal protocol and ceremonial. He organized lavish receptions in his residence to introduce the new British mission to ecclesiastical Rome, and earnestly spread Allied propaganda among foreign and Italian journalists. Indeed, the cardinal's apartment in the Palazzo San Calisto, a papal building in the Trastevere neighborhood, became so well known in Rome as a center for Allied sympathizers that Benedict had to caution Gasquet to be more discreet lest the social gatherings cause political scandal and compromise papal neutrality.[10]

London was well-advised to attend to affairs at the Vatican, since the Central Powers were working assiduously to manipulate the Papacy for their own ends. In the early months of the war Berlin and Vienna relied on their ambassadors to the Holy See, who, until the arrival of Sir Henry Howard in December 1915, had the diplomatic playing field largely to themselves. These ambassadors and their respective staffs labored tirelessly, requesting audiences with Pope Benedict, meeting weekly the cardinal secretary of state, Pietro Gasparri, and his deputies, hosting curial officials and prominent ecclesiastics at dinners and receptions, and cultivating editors and journalists from the Catholic press. Initially they worked overtly to take the measure of the new pope and his principal collaborators and to explain and justify the war policies of the Central Powers while denigrating those of the Allies. Soon, however, a threat began to emerge that would require measures more cunning and clandestine than formal audiences, dinner soirees, and tea parties.

By January 1915 the war of maneuver in which armies advanced, wheeled, and retreated along broad fronts and generals dreamed of capturing cities and encircling opponents, had given way, particularly on the western front, to a war of stalemate in which opposing forces attacked from uninterrupted lines of heavily fortified entrenchments, and success was measured in yards rather than miles of territory gained. Both sides now looked for new allies in the hope that fresh armies and new fronts would break the stalemate and provide the key to victory.

Though a member of the Triple Alliance and, therefore, nominally an ally of Germany and Austria, Italy had remained on the sidelines when its partners marched to war in August 1914. Italian leaders were naturally reluctant to expose their country to the uncertain fortunes of war. They also understood that the opposing sides would bargain hard for Italy's support and that the price for Italian belligerency might well include the *terre irredente*, Italian-speaking territories in the Trentino districts of the Austrian Empire, whose absorption into the Kingdom of Italy had long been a goal of Italian foreign policy. Rome's opportunistic posture placed the Central Powers, particularly Austria, in a difficult position. It cost the Allies nothing to purchase Italy's support with any number of promises concerning the disposition of Austrian territory after the war. The Austrians, however, could satisfy Italian demands only by sacrificing their own territory, a step that was doubly repugnant, since it might encourage Poles, Hungarians, Slovaks, and other linguistic and religious groups in the multinational empire to imagine their political and cultural future outside the imperial fold.

As the new year opened, the German and Austrian embassies at the Vatican were hearing from their sources inside the papal palace that the Italian government was increasingly inclined toward intervention on the side of the Allies. These sources also indicated that the Vatican was appalled at the prospect of a war between Austria and Italy that presaged disaster beyond the unspeakable loss of life and property no matter what the outcome. The Vatican doubted the capacity of the Italian state to survive the political and economic tribulations of a major war, especially should that war turn against Italy. Defeat might undermine the legitimacy of the regime, create civil unrest, and ignite the flames of social revolution with consequences for Italy and the Church that no one could predict. On the other hand, Italian victory might fatally weaken the Austro-Hungarian Empire, the principal Catholic power in central Europe and the traditional bastion against the encroachments of hateful Russian Orthodoxy and Pan-Slavism.[11] These fears provided a fertile field for German intrigue.

In February 1915 Italian intelligence observed the arrival in Rome of Mathias Erzberger, the leader of the Catholic Center Party in Germany and a figure well-known and respected at the Vatican. During this and subsequent visits to the Italian capital in the spring of 1915, Erzberger attended meetings at the German and Austrian embassies, called frequently at the Vatican, and occasionally slipped off to visit out-of-the-way churches and monuments. Suspecting that the German politician, who had assumed an important role in his country's propaganda effort, was on a clandestine mission on behalf of the Central Powers and that this mission in some way involved the Vatican, the Italian police kept him under close surveillance.[12]

The Italians were right to be suspicious, for Erzberger was indeed on a special mission. Reluctant to add yet another country to the list of enemies fighting the Central Powers, Germany had dispatched the Center Party leader to Rome to ask the Vatican to deter an Austro-Italian war by pressing Vienna to give up at least some of its Italian-speaking territories as the price for Italian neutrality. Even before his trip to Rome, Erzberger had quietly floated an ambitious proposal in which Austria would transfer the Trentino to the pope, who would then cede the territory to Italy in exchange for the creation of an independent papal enclave around the Vatican and a papal corridor to the sea. Although both Pope Benedict and Cardinal Gasparri dismissed this plan as hopelessly unrealistic, neither required much encouragement to urge Vienna to compromise, since both men had, by early 1915, concluded that only by abandoning the Trentino could Austria prevent Italy from joining the Allies. In this instance at least, Vatican and German interests were parallel. Throughout the spring the Papacy worked in tandem with Berlin to avert an extension of the war by pressing

Vienna to accommodate Italian territorial ambitions, and the whole time Erzberger served as a facilitator and communication channel between Berlin and the Vatican.

Erzberger, however, carried more than diplomatic proposals on his visits to Rome. There was, for instance, the matter of secret German contributions to the papal treasury. Although the status of papal finances in 1914 remains a subject of controversy among historians, there is no doubt that the war posed a serious threat to those finances.[13] The Vatican categorically refused to accept from the Italian government the annual indemnity provided by the Law of Guarantees (1871) as compensation for the loss of the Papal States. Instead, the Vatican relied on the contributions of pilgrims and tourists and the income from "Peter's pence," a special collection for the maintenance of the Holy See instituted in Catholic parishes around the world. Unfortunately, the war effectively killed tourism and interrupted the flow of contributions from Catholics, while increasing the financial demands on the Papacy for humanitarian assistance to civilian and military victims of the fighting. The Vatican may not have been facing bankruptcy, but it could hardly be complacent about its financial future.

Recognizing an opportunity to ingratiate itself with the Vatican at the very time it required papal support for Italian neutrality, Germany, through Erzberger, moved swiftly to save the pope from financial embarrassment. Dangling the prospect of Prussian titles and decorations before potential donors, the Center Party leader toured Germany, collecting large sums from wealthy landowners and businessmen, Protestant as well as Catholic. The German foreign ministry helped with secret subsidies from its covert propaganda fund, and the Austrian government made at least one secret contribution. In April 1915 Erzberger was able to present a delighted Benedict with a large financial gift and a promise of additional sums in the future.[14]

After Erzberger's initial gift, German funds, invariably described as Peter's pence, were secretly channeled to the Vatican through Swiss banks. Italian intelligence, which believed that Benedict had inherited an empty treasury in 1914 and now wondered how the pope was keeping the Vatican financially afloat, became aware of this activity as early as April 1915 and monitored the money trail from Germany with growing suspicion. The surveillance only fueled suspicions in Rome that the Papacy was in the pocket of the Central Powers.[15]

Erzberger did not limit his largesse to the Holy Father. In addition to his overt visits to the Vatican, the Center Party leader consulted frequently with Franz von Stockhammern, a diplomat at the German embassy in Rome, who upon the outbreak of war assumed direction of his country's intelligence and propaganda operations in Italy. Together, Erzberger and Stockhammern collaborated on a clandestine program to anticipate Rome's diplomacy and prevent Italy's entry into the war by collecting political intelligence, fanning antiwar sentiments, and supporting the initiatives of neutralist politicians. The program depended on the judicious distribution of German propaganda and, more important, German money. It also relied on the cooperation of the Vatican and influential ecclesiastics.

Given the neutral posture of the Holy See, it is not surprising that Catholic newspapers were among the loudest voices in Italy speaking against Italy's entry into the war. At the end of 1914 the Austrian embassy in Rome informed Vienna that among the fifty significant newspapers in the country, the Catholic journals were almost the only ones friendly to the Central Powers and opposed to belligerency.[16] To support these voices, Franz von Stockhammern provided secret subsidies to the papers and sought the advice of pro-German clerics in composing antiwar articles that would impress Catholic readers. Sir Henry Howard, the newly appointed British minister to the Holy See, had hardly unpacked his bags before hearing rumors of sinister sessions at Stockhammern's apartments in the elegant Hotel Russie, where the German diplomat consulted daily with various ecclesiastics. Sipping champagne provided by their host, the visitors, who included at least one cardinal, the abbot of a Roman monastery, and various monsignors connected with the Vatican, wrote articles, corrected proofs, and generally acted as an editorial advisory board for Stockhammern's propaganda offensive.[17]

Stockhammern's covert propaganda activities produced a flood of anti-Entente and pro-neutrality articles and inflammatory political cartoons in various Catholic newspapers. The press attacks became so vituperative that Sir Henry Howard protested to Cardinal Gasparri. Agreeing that the campaign in the Catholic press was unseemly, the cardinal secretary of state promised to admonish the editors. If the papers persisted, they would be officially reprimanded in the pages of the Vatican's own newspaper, *L'Osservatore Romano.* Despite these assurances, little was done to rein in the Catholic press, although on one occasion the secretariat of state financially compensated a paper that agreed not to publish an issue containing an especially scurrilous cartoon.[18]

While Stockhammern worked the press, Erzberger cultivated Antonio Lapoma, a pro-German priest from the city of Potenza who had important contacts in political and ecclesiastical circles in southern Italy. On behalf of the German embassy, Father Lapoma spread neutralist propaganda, compiled reports on political opinion in the south, distributed German money in the form of "mass offerings" to the impoverished rural clergy of Basilicata and Calabria, and encouraged southern bishops to pressure parliamentary deputies from their dioceses to oppose war.

By the spring of 1915 Italy's leaders had concluded that a deal with the Allied powers promised Italy the greatest spoils. In early May, as Prime Minister Antonio Salandra and Foreign Minister Sidney Sonnino prepared to push through cabinet and parliament the agreement they had secretly negotiated in London in April to enter the war alongside Britain and France, Father Lapoma put Erzberger in touch with Pasquale Grippo, the minister of education in Salandra's cabinet, who was willing to sell information and influence to Germany. Through Lapoma, who would pass the information to Erzberger during clandestine meetings in out-of-the-way churches in Rome, Grippo revealed that, despite the arguments of Salandra and Sonnino, the majority of the ministers remained uncertain about the wisdom of entering the war, and that two members, the minister of posts, Vincenzo Riccio, and the minister of agriculture, Giannetto Cavasola, were strongly inclined toward neutrality.[19]

Pasquale Grippo's information suggested to Berlin and Vienna that there was still a chance to avert Italian belligerency. As rumors of Italy's imminent entry into the war spread through Rome, the Germans and Austrians pinned their hopes on Giovanni Giolitti, a wily politician whose political acumen had five times propelled him into the prime minister's office and whose political influence in the country and in parliament remained strong. Giolitti, who was away from Rome as the crisis over belligerency peaked, believed that Italy's territorial ambitions could be secured more easily and cheaply through clever negotiation than through war. If a decision for war could be delayed until Giolitti's return to the capital, then perhaps the elder statesman could use his influence to turn the tide in parliament and block the plans of the war party.

To buy time, the German embassy tried to create divisions in Italian political circles. For a price, the treacherous Pasquale Grippo promised to sow dissension in the cabinet. Of course, if bribes could purchase a cabinet minister, they might purchase any number of lesser politicians; thus Erzberger received from Berlin 5 million lire to be distributed among parliamentary deputies to influence their votes. For their part, the Austrians already had several parliamentarians on their payroll. Meanwhile, Stockhammern's tame journalists increased the volume of their attacks against the Entente, while Father Lapoma scurried off to collect the signatures of southern bishops on a peace petition. Friendly ecclesiastics, particularly Father Fonck, the director of the Jesuit Biblical Institute, and Monsignor Boncampagni, a curial official with important family connections in the Roman aristocracy, urged their friends in Italian society to oppose war.[20]

To further their delaying tactics while masking their direction of these schemes, the German representatives in Rome enlisted the support of the Holy Father. Late on the night of 6 May, Franz von Stockhammern slipped quietly into the Vatican without being observed by the Italian police, who maintained round-the-clock watch on the pope's territory. Normally, the entrances to the Vatican were closed by the Swiss Guards at nine o'clock, but Monsignor Giuseppe Migone, the pope's private secretary, whose friendship Stockhammern had prudently cultivated, met the German intelligence officer at a little-used gate and led him to the papal apartments, where Benedict was waiting.

The pope was well aware that Italy was on the brink of war. He also believed that Sonnino had callously maneuvered the country into this perilous position by hiding from the cabinet and the parliament the extent to which Austria, pressed by both the Papacy and Germany, was prepared to make territorial concessions to appease Italy. In fact, despite intense diplomatic pressure from Berlin and the Vatican, Vienna was prepared to promise only modest territorial concessions to Rome, but only after the war and a time-consuming survey of borders (an awkward fact upon which Stockhammern did not encourage the Holy Father to dwell). But Benedict was convinced that the spirit of compromise should not be extinguished. When the German intelligence officer suggested that the antiwar faction in the cabinet would be strengthened in its resolve if it was made aware of Austria's willingness to accommodate Italian interests, Benedict readily agreed to arrange for Pasquale Grippo (whose pecuniary relationship with the German embassy Stockhammern considered an item too trivial to mention) to receive all the intelligence from Vienna then available to the Vatican. Having enlisted the Holy Father in his covert scheme to interfere in Italian politics and derail the Italian war party, Stockhammern left the pontiff's apartments as quietly as he had entered. Benedict immediately summoned to the papal palace two individuals in his confidence, who, as dawn broke over the roofs of Rome, were briefed on the Vatican's efforts to secure concessions from Austria and instructed to secretly pass this information to Grippo before the next cabinet meeting.[21]

All these secret machinations were unavailing. German and Austrian bribes, propaganda, and secret agents could not reverse the rush to war, and in the end Giolitti and the neutralists had neither the will nor the power to challenge the decision to join the war alongside Britain and France. The struggle over Italy's neutrality, however, had a deleterious political impact on the Vatican. Although Italian intelligence failed to detect Benedict's last-minute collaboration with Stockhammern to influence secretly the cabinet, it could hardly miss the constant visits of prominent ecclesiastics to German embassy officials and the active participation of priests in German propaganda efforts. The fact that these ecclesiastics acted without the sanction of the Vatican remained a fine point that Italian authorities refused to credit. By the time that Italy declared war on Austria (23 May 1915), Italian police and intelligence officers were increasingly inclined to believe that the Papacy supported the Central Powers and would work hand in glove with Berlin and Vienna to undermine Italy's war effort.[22] These suspicions were seemingly confirmed in 1916 when Italian counterintelligence began to unravel a conspiratorial skein whose threads led to the very heart of the Vatican.

When Italy entered the war, Berlin and Vienna closed their embassies in the Eternal City and recalled their diplomats. The German and Austrian embassies to the Holy See relocated to Lugano, Switzerland, where they tried to maintain long-distance relations with the Vatican. Franz von Stockhammern also moved his espionage operations to Switzerland, where, from the security of neutral territory, he organized intelligence networks inside Italy. One of his early recruits was Archita Valente, a sometime informant for the Italian police, who agreed to collect information for Germany in return for a monthly stipend and bonuses for special assignments. Valente communicated with his German controller through a jargon code in the lonely hearts column of the newspaper *Giornale d'Italia*. Apparently innocuous messages (to "Giuliano" from "Zingara") actually contained coded references to people (UNCLE = General Luigi Cardona), places (JEALOUS WOMAN = France), and events (JOURNEY = military offensive). Thus, the message "Uncle will soon begin his journey" alerted Stockhammern that General Cadorna, the commander in chief of the Italian army, was about to launch an offensive.[23] By means of these secret messages and occasional visits to Switzerland, Valente reported on such subjects as Anglo-Italian and Vatican-Italian relations, the alleged war-weariness of the Italian population, and equipment shortages and troop movements in the Italian army,

In April 1916 Italy's Directorate of Public Security received a visit from Antonio Celletti, a lawyer and friend of Archita Valente. Celletti had noticed that his formerly impecunious friend now gambled and lost large sums at cards, exhibited an inordinate interest in the personals column of the *Giornale d'Italia*, and received packets from men he encountered on the street. Suspecting some criminal activity, Celletti approached the police, who expressed a certain skepticism about the lawyer's story and limited their action to suspending Valente's passport. In May Valente, now unable to travel abroad, asked a friend, Giuseppe Grassi, who was also known to Antonio Celletti, to carry several letters to a certain Baron Stockhammern in Lucerne, Switzerland. He was to introduce himself with the famous opening lines of Dante's *Divine Comedy* ("Nel mezzo del cammin di nostra vita").

Uneasy about this strange assignment, the rather ingenuous Grassi confided in Antonio Celletti, who promptly volunteered to go to Switzerland in Grassi's place provided that Valente remain ignorant of the switch in messengers. Collecting the letters and recognition signal from Grassi, Celletti set off for Lucerne, where he met the unsuspecting Stockhammern and his Italian deputy, Mario Pomarici, a Germanophile journalist who, after accepting Berlin's money in return for writing anti-interventionist articles during the debate over Italian belligerency, had moved to Switzerland, where he offered his services to German intelligence. During this trip Celletti learned enough about Stockhammern's operations (including the coded messages in the *Giornale d'Italia*) to confirm his suspicions about Archita Valente. Upon his return to Rome, he denounced his friend, who was immediately arrested by the police. Under interrogation Valente admitted his contacts with Stockhammern and Pomarici but insisted that they were merely efforts to develop leads for the Italian police for whom, the suspected spy insisted, he had always been a loyal and industrious informant.

After three days of questioning, Valente was released, but he remained under police surveillance while the authorities pursued leads in Italy and Switzerland. By July 1916 counterintelligence officers had enough evidence to submit a report implicating Valente and Mario Pomarici in espionage. Unaccountably, further action was delayed until November, when the authorities filed formal charges of high treason against the two. Valente was arrested, but in his Swiss refuge Pomarici was beyond the reach of Italian law.

When Italian security authorities studied the coded messages placed by Valente in the *Giornale d'Italia*, they uncovered traces of another clandestine communications channel between Stockhammern and his agents inside Italy. Valente, for example, had once asked Pomarici to send him funds "by the agreed upon method," while on another occasion he suggested communicating either through "cav[aliere] A" or through "G." Under interrogation Valente revealed that "A" was Giuseppe Ambrogetti, a Roman lawyer who served as a shipping agent for the Vatican and as a general business agent or "man of affairs" for several cardinals and bishops. A longtime intimate of Giacomo Della Chiesa from the days when the future pope was a senior official in the Vatican's secretariat of state, Giuseppe Ambrogetti had received from his old friend, now enthroned as the successor to St. Peter and the vicar of Christ on earth, a high papal decoration for his services to the Church. A team of police investigators was dispatched immediately to Ambrogetti's apartment overlooking the ancient Pantheon in the center of Rome, where the papal functionary sat calmly under a large, inscribed photograph of Pope Benedict while the police searched the rooms and carried off bundles of letters and documents.[24]

Ambrogetti would not have been so composed if he had known that Valente, in an effort to save his own skin, was talking faster than the police secretaries could record his words. He confessed that he had collected intelligence for Franz von Stockhammern and that he had received his payments through Giuseppe Ambrogetti. The news that a close friend of the pope was a bagman for German intelligence stunned Valente's interrogators. The German spy, however, had an even more dramatic revelation. He told the police that the mysterious "G" referred to in his communications with Switzerland was in fact Monsignor Rudolf Gerlach, a Bavarian priest who was private chamberlain and confidant of the pope. The trail of espionage had led the Italian police to the doorstep of the papal palace.

According to Valente, during the period of Italian neutrality Monsignor Gerlach had been a conduit for covert German payments to various anti-interventionist newspapers, particularly *La Vittoria* and *Il Bastone*. Gerlach would pass the money to Ambrogetti, who would deposit it in a special bank account for later distribution in support of German propaganda. Valente also asserted that Stockhammern had assured him that Gerlach could be used as a channel for secure communication between Rome and Switzerland, and the accused spy also claimed to know that Gerlach had corresponded secretly with the German spymaster. Since any such correspondence would have had to circumvent the strict Italian censor who opened all private letters entering or leaving Italy, the implication of Valente's charges was that Gerlach communicated with Stockhammern by using the papal diplomatic pouch, which, theoretically, was immune to search.

Italian intelligence had long had its eye on the papal chamberlain. Educated for the papal diplomatic service, Rudolf Gerlach was ambitious and intelligent, but during his term at the prestigious Pontifical Ecclesiastical Academy there had been disturbing rumors about his character and the sincerity of his vocation. A probationary appointment to the nunciature to Bavaria was quietly set aside when the nuncio, Archbishop (later Cardinal) Andrea Frühwirth, refused to have the young priest on his staff. Gerlach hung around Rome and first met Giacomo Della Chiesa when the then archbishop of Bologna came to the Eternal City to receive his cardinal's hat. They met again three months later when Della Chiesa returned for the conclave that would elect him pope. Gerlach successfully ingratiated himself with the new pope, who took him into his service despite warnings from various quarters that the young Bavarian was an unscrupulous adventurer.[25]

Not surprisingly, Gerlach's nationality and his association with Austrian and German diplomats in Rome raised questions among Italian authorities about his loyalties. As early as 22 November 1914 the director general of public security requested information about the papal chamberlain and received a report from Commissioner Bertini, the police official responsible for surveillance of the Vatican, that Gerlach had so far aroused no suspicion. Appraisals, however, soon changed. By February 1915 the police were noting that the Bavarian priest was in frequent contact with Franz von Stockhammern of the German embassy, to whom he was passing information about Vatican affairs.[26] By the spring of that year, as the debate over Italian neutrality intensified, Gerlach's behavior had become so indiscreet that political circles in Rome openly questioned his allegiances. The British ambassador to Italy, Sir James Rennel Rodd, warned the foreign minister, Sidney Sonnino, that the Bavarian priest was "one of the most dangerous German agitators," while the British representative at the Vatican concluded that he was "an undoubted German agent."[27] The Italian police intensified their surveillance of Gerlach, at one point substituting police officers for the regular waiters at a dinner at the Hotel Russie attended by the papal chamberlain and, coincidentally, Giuseppe Ambrogetti.[28]

Surveillance reports, Archita Valente's confession, disclosures by Giuseppe Ambrogetti under questioning, and papers discovered during the search of the latter's residence convinced the Italians that Monsignor Rudolf Gerlach was at the center of German intelligence operations in Italy. The government, however, did not relish the prospect of an espionage scandal in which a personal assistant of the pope would be pushed into the witness box and, perhaps, in front of a firing squad. The Vatican had been quietly informed of the evidence accumulating against the papal chamberlain, and on 5 January 1917 Gerlach was driven to Rome's central station and placed in a first-class railway carriage by Italian police officers, who escorted the priest to the Swiss border. Thus, when Archita Valente, Giuseppe Ambrogetti, and several other Italians who had been implicated in the conspiracy appeared before a military tribunal in the spring of 1917 on charges of treason and espionage, Gerlach was not present, even though he was charged in the indictment and the testimony. The evidence against him was sufficient for the tribunal to convict him in absentia and sentence him to life imprisonment. Valente was condemned to death, while Ambrogetti received three years in prison.

The Gerlach affair rocked the Vatican. From its sources inside the papal palace, Italian intelligence learned that the charges against his assistant, Gerlach, and to a lesser extent his friend, Ambrogetti, had so affected the pope physically and psychologically that Benedict had fallen into a deep depression.[29] The cardinal secretary of state, Pietro Gasparri, wrote to Gerlach in his Swiss refuge expressing Benedict's deep chagrin that one of his closest collaborators might have engaged in espionage, and urging the Bavarian to give the Vatican a frank account of his actions. Of course the consequences of the affair extended far beyond personal feelings. Although the military tribunal explicitly exonerated the Vatican from any complicity in the espionage scandal, papal officials were well aware that Gerlach and Ambrogetti had seriously compromised the Papacy's efforts to cultivate a public image of strict neutrality. From the earliest days of the war, critics in London, Paris, Rome, and Washington had been ready to insinuate that the Vatican sympathized with the Central Powers and worked secretly for their victory. Now the Gerlach affair seemed to confirm these charges. Equally disturbing was the implication that the pope's chamberlain had used the papal diplomatic pouch to pass information to foreign agents. If believed, this charge would only encourage the belligerents, especially Italy, to monitor more closely papal communications with the outside world.

Although Monsignor Gerlach was not represented before the military tribunal that ultimately convicted him, the Vatican secretly paid a large fee to the attorney representing one of the other defendants in the hope of overturning the entire case. It also quietly approached General Luigi Cardona, the chief of the general staff, in the vain hope that he would suspend the proceedings of the military court.[30] To undermine the accusation that Gerlach was a German paymaster, the secretariat of state submitted to the tribunal a memorandum explaining that the pope routinely received from foreign bishops contributions to support missionary and charitable work and to offset the operational expenses of the Vatican. Before the war the German bishops had personally delivered their contributions to the pope. With the onset of fighting and the consequent restrictions on travel, these bishops now sent their checks to Monsignor Gerlach because, as the most prominent German in the papal household, he was known personally to the German bishops. In turn, Gerlach merely asked Ambrogetti to deposit the checks for him.

In the matter of the alleged abuse of the papal diplomatic pouch, the Vatican took the unprecedented step of sending a senior official from the secretariat of state to provide a deposition to the military tribunal. Monsignor Federico Tedeschini, the substitute secretary of state, testified that he supervised the preparation of the Vatican's diplomatic pouch, which, in conformity with Italian censorship guidelines, was restricted to the official correspondence of the secretariat of state. According to Tedeschini, it was impossible for unauthorized items to escape his scrutiny and find a place in the pouch. He admitted that in late 1915 and early 1916 Monsignor Gerlach had occasionally exchanged correspondence with various German officials, including Matthias Erzberger and Franz von Stockhammern. This correspondence, however, was specifically authorized by Pope Benedict and was meant to facilitate certain confidential initiatives of the Holy Father, such as proposals to prevent the bombardment of cities and to secure hospitalization in Switzerland for seriously wounded French and German soldiers.[31]

From his neutral asylum Gerlach proclaimed his innocence and challenged his accusers. He steadfastly denied having worked as an agent for Berlin. The monsignor admitted receiving money from Germany but insisted that the funds were merely contributions from German Catholics to the Holy Father. Gerlach had endorsed the checks to Giuseppe Ambrogetti because, as an enemy alien working at the Vatican, he was uncertain if he could legally receive money from his homeland, and he hoped to avoid complications at the bank. Gerlach admitted that, through Ambrogetti, he had passed money to *La Vittoria,* but only because he wanted to support an impecunious Catholic newspaper. The Bavarian also acknowledged that Archita Valente had once asked him to include a letter to Franz von Stockhammern in the Vatican diplomatic pouch for Switzerland. When he learned that the letter contained information about Italian politics, he suspected some conspiratorial affair and broke all contact with Valente. As for his own contacts with Switzerland, Gerlach strenuously denied that he maintained an illegal correspondence with German diplomats in that neutral country.[32]

Despite Gerlach's protestations of innocence and the Vatican's assurances of propriety, there can be no doubt that the papal chamberlain was a German paymaster. He admitted that he passed money to *La Vittoria* (a newspaper secretly established and maintained by Berlin to advocate Italian neutrality), and his claim that he intended nothing more than to support a struggling Catholic journal rings hollow, especially in light of Matthias Erzberger's reports to Berlin, which clearly indicate that the Bavarian monsignor was the principal covert channel for dispensing German subsidies to other papers, such as *Corriere d'Italia,* which received 22,000 lire a month from Berlin. In the final days before Italy cast its lot with Britain and France, Erzberger authorized Gerlach to distribute 5 million lire to ecclesiastics, journalists, and politicians in a last-ditch effort to preserve Italy's neutrality. After Rome's entry into the war, the papal chamberlain continued to receive large sums of money from Stockhammern. Some of this money may have been distributed in ecclesiastical circles in an effort to encourage sympathy for Germany. In November 1915, for example, Stockhammern informed Erzberger that 200,000 lire had been paid to various ecclesiastics, including Father Antonio Lapoma, the Basilicatan priest who continued his pro-German activities, and Monsignor Francesco Marchetti-Selvaggiani, the papal diplomatic representative in Switzerland. Stockhammern specifically instructed Gerlach to disguise these funds as contributions from German Catholics. This effort to launder the covert funds may have misled the Vatican as to the true origin of the money arriving from Germany.

The espionage case against Gerlach is less certain but still compelling. During the period of Italian neutrality, Gerlach was a back-channel link with the Austrian and German embassies in Rome. Pope Benedict and his secretary of state, Cardinal Gasparri, often used the papal chamberlain to carry messages and the latest information between the Vatican and the Austrian and German diplomats who were negotiating with the Italian government. After Italy's entry into the war, Gerlach continued to serve as a private channel between Benedict and Berlin. In this capacity he often communicated with Matthias Erzberger, passing on the pope's thoughts and ideas. These messages were enclosed in the papal diplomatic pouch for delivery to the papal nuncio in Switzerland, who then passed them to the German and Bavarian ambassadors to the Holy See, who had relocated their embassies to Lugano when Italy declared war on Germany. Though these contacts were authorized, it would have been easy for the pope's chamberlain to add his own appraisal of the situation, and in so doing provide Berlin intelligence about attitudes, events, and personalities at the Vatican. Gerlach undoubtedly passed such information in the *unauthorized* correspondence he maintained (unbeknownst to the pope) with Erzberger and Stockhammern, neither of whom was connected with either the German or the Bavarian embassy to the Vatican.[33]

After the recall of German diplomats from Rome in May 1915, Gerlach was Berlin's primary source of intelligence on the Vatican. Indeed, for all the charges of espionage against Italy, the Vatican rather than Italy seems to have been the Bavarian's principal victim. Erzberger considered Gerlach's exposure a calamity for German intelligence, since Berlin had lost a source at the very heart of the Papacy.[34] A letter from Gerlach to Erzberger in April 1916 is probably typical of the political intelligence passed to Berlin by the papal chamberlain, and it suggests why his loss so discomfited the Germans. In this communication Gerlach reported a conversation with the sister and brother-in-law of the Belgian king, Albert. Gerlach informed Erzberger that the couple was favorably inclined toward the Central Powers and had intimated that King Albert would not be averse to a separate peace between Belgium and Germany, although his government would probably oppose such a project. The papal chamberlain advised Erzberger that Berlin might have an opportunity to separate Belgium from the Allies by offering to restore the country to full independence in return for a peace agreement. He added that the Vatican would probably support any proposal that offered the Belgians reasonable terms.[35] For the German foreign ministry, hoping to reduce its enemies by detaching Belgium from the Allies, this would have been priceless political intelligence.

Despite the scandal, Gerlach retained the confidence of the Holy See even after his expulsion from Italy. The Vatican not only rejected all the charges against the Bavarian priest but also continued to seek his advice in matters concerning German-Vatican relations.[36] For his part, Gerlach seemed little discomfited by the scandal. He moved freely between Switzerland and Germany and enjoyed the company and patronage of German politicians and diplomats in Bern, Berlin, Munich, and Vienna. In Berlin he visited the kaiser, Wilhelm II, and in Vienna he had an audience with the emperor, Karl I. He soon abandoned the priestly life and adopted the lifestyle of a cosmopolitan man of affairs. By the end of the war, the governments of Austria, Germany, and Turkey had bestowed medals on the erstwhile priest, gestures that spoke more eloquently of his services to the Central Powers than any testimony in an Italian court.[37]

The Gerlach affair only confirmed the Italian government in its suspicion that the Papacy sympathized with Italy's enemies, and strengthened its resolve to monitor the Vatican for any signs of political threat. Italian police and intelligence agencies, which had long considered the Vatican an important target, intensified their surveillance of the pope and his projects. Vigilance was required to ensure that the Central Powers did not use Vatican facilities and personnel for espionage, but the government was also haunted by the prospect of the Vatican finding amid the political dislocations of the war an opportunity to raise anew the Roman Question and to seek restoration of at least some of the papal territory lost in 1870. The government was so alarmed by this prospect that Foreign Minister Sonnino insisted that the Treaty of London, which formalized Rome's adherence to the Allies, include a secret clause (Article 15) pledging London, Paris, and St. Petersburg to support Rome in refusing the pope any role in a future peace conference. The need to anticipate papal policy and expose papal intrigues demanded aggressive intelligence operations. By the end of the war only Austria, Italy's principal military antagonist, rivaled the Vatican as the main target of Rome's intelligence services.

For some of its information on the Vatican the Italian government relied not on the deceptions and clandestine activities of secret agents but on the routine work of an unassuming individual who moved undisguised in the striped pants and stiff collar of a government functionary, and who entered the papal palace without stealth through the main entrance. Officially, Baron Carlo Monti was director of the office of Affari di Culto, the section in the Italian Ministry of Justice concerned with all matters affecting relations between church and state. Unofficially, he was the government's channel to the Vatican, a role facilitated by a friendship with Pope Benedict that began when they were schoolboys in Genoa. An intimate of the Holy Father and, effectively, Italy's representative to the Vatican, Monti was in a position to collect important information on papal attitudes and intentions. His activity was overt and without subterfuge. The information that came his way was volunteered by the pope or his collaborators, often in exchange for insight into the position and perspectives of Italian political leaders, but with the certain knowledge that the news would reach the government. Predictably, some of the information, such as the intentions of the papal administration to seek an exemption from military conscription for the personnel of the papal police force, was trivial or of fleeting interest. Occasionally, however, the baron picked up useful political intelligence, as when, in February 1917, the Vatican shared with him its intelligence on the deteriorating conditions inside Russia or, in May of the same year, acknowledged that the pope would not pursue any polices that might antagonize the British government.[38]

Although intelligent and diligent, Baron Monti was constrained by his relationship with the Holy Father and the protocol surrounding his semiofficial position from aggressively pursuing the secrets that the Papacy preferred to withhold from the Italian government. The baron was not privy to the pope's private conversations with cardinals, or to the confidential instructions dispatched to papal representatives abroad, or to the deliberations of papal committees, but it was precisely such information that would most accurately reveal the real intentions and motives of the Vatican. To uncover those secrets, the Italians had to rely on the classic methods of espionage.

The Directorate General of Public Security remained responsible for surveillance of the Vatican and its personnel in Rome. To that end, Cesare Bertini, police commissioner for the Borgo, the Roman neighborhood that encompassed the Vatican, deployed a large force of officers and agents. Observation posts monitored the various entrances to the Vatican and recorded the arrival and departure of diplomats, journalists, and high ecclesiastics. Plainclothes police agents patronized two cafés inside the Vatican (one inside the barracks of the Swiss Guard and one in the offices of the papal police) where, over glasses of wine and plates of pasta and sausages, they collected useful news, especially concerning visitors to the papal palace and changes in security arrangements. In October 1915, however, the police lost these companionable intelligence oases when the papal administration, seeking to deny foreign intelligence services the very access sought by the Italians, closed the cafés to all but those living or working inside the Vatican.

The police commissioner also depended on a swarm of informants who provided details concerning events and personalities inside the walls of the papal city. Most of these informants were menials, guards, or minor functionaries, who passed to Bertini and his lieutenants current rumor and gossip in return for small sums of money. Occasionally these low-level sources were well placed to collect important intelligence. For instance, Cardinal Gasparri's butler regularly provided the police with information about the cardinal secretary of state's visitors and their conversations.[39] Some of Bertini's sources were papal dignitaries, although most of these individuals were not conscious agents of the police, and most would have blanched at the suggestion that they were betraying the Vatican to the Italians. Collaborators of the late pope, Pius X, were an especially fruitful source of information. Known as the Vaticanetto, this group, which included Cardinal Merry del Val, Pius's secretary of state, Monsignor Nicola Canali, Merry's deputy in the secretariat, and two papal chamberlains, Monsignors Carlo Caccia-Dominioni and Arborio Mella di Sant'Ellia, who held on to their titles in the new pontificate, became the more or less loyal opposition to Benedict. Shunted into honorific or marginal posts (Benedict appointed Merry del Val archpriest of St. Peter's Basilica and "promoted" Canali to the position of secretary to the Sacred Congregation for Ceremonies), the clique wreaked revenge for its fall from power and perceived humiliation by gleefully and maliciously leaking information and sharing gossip about Benedict and his entourage with anyone who would listen.[40]

As in any intelligence operation, the results of Bertini's penetration of the Vatican were mixed. Much of the information was trivial. It is unlikely, for example, that anyone in the Italian government was interested in a report in March 1915 that the pope's Swiss Guards had postponed the purchase of new rifles.[41] Some of the information was simply false, such as a report from September 1916 that the chaplain of the Swiss Guards was collaborating in espionage with several Austrian diplomats, who were hiding in the Spanish embassy, and that Rudolf Gerlach had organized teams of priests to replenish Austrian submarines off the Italian ports of Ancona and Bari. An equally improbable report had the commandant of the Swiss Guards and the director of the Vatican pharmacy collecting intelligence for the Central Powers.[42] Occasionally, however, the intelligence alerted the government to important developments behind the walls of the papal palace. During the debates over Italian belligerency in the spring of 1915, the government knew about Matthias Erzberger's plan for Austria to cede the Trentino to the Papacy shortly after the Vatican received the proposal. Italian authorities were also well aware from Bertini's reports that Benedict was pressing the Austrians to purchase Rome's neutrality with territorial concessions. Indeed, the tempo of the pope's efforts in the spring of 1915 to keep Italy out of the war could be measured by the daily reports recording the number of visits to the Vatican by German and Austrian diplomats. As Italy moved closer to war, Bertini accurately reported that the king of Spain had invited the pope to take refuge in Spain should Italian belligerency make the pontiff's position in Rome untenable. In November 1915 the police commissioner alerted the government to the fact that the pope was soliciting the opinion of various cardinals as to whether the Vatican should seek a seat at the peace conference, the very scenario the government hoped to avoid.[43]

The Directorate General of Public Security was not the only Italian agency collecting intelligence on the Vatican. The intelligence branch of the Italian army, the Servizio Informazioni Militari (SIM), was responsible for foreign intelligence operations, and some of its efforts were directed against the papal nuncios in European capitals. For example, SIM placed an agent inside the nunciature in Spain, one of the Vatican's major diplomatic posts. This agent not only provided information about the affairs of the nunciature but also so ingratiated himself with the nuncio that he was able to influence the diplomat's attitudes and reports. The papal representative in Switzerland was also under close surveillance by military intelligence.[44]

Switzerland was a fertile field for Italian intelligence operations against the Papacy in large part because Italian military intelligence had convinced itself that the Alpine confederation was the center for a clandestine committee that secretly controlled the pope and determined the policies of the

Vatican. The Italians believed that this shadowy group was directed by a triumvirate made up of the papal delegate to Switzerland, the Father General of the Jesuits, who had relocated the headquarters of his famous religious order to Switzerland for the duration of the war, and (most improbably) the bishop of Coire, a small diocese in the Romansch region of Switzerland. Throughout the war SIM received reports that the Papacy's major diplomatic initiatives, particularly various plans in 1917 to mediate a negotiated settlement of the war, were contrived or at least approved by this secret directorate, which, in turn, had clandestine connections to Berlin and Vienna.[45]

The idea that the pope was controlled by a conspiratorial triumvirate secretly manipulating international events from Alpine castles would have readily appealed to anticlericals, not a few of whom were to be found in Italy's police and intelligence services. The idea was, of course, preposterous, as was pointed out by the British ambassador to the Holy See, who, noting the propensity of Italian military intelligence to collect information "with much industry, but less discrimination," scoffed at the very notion of a secret authority in Switzerland and reminded London that few officials had less latitude for personal initiative and independent action than papal officials.[46] The inclusion of the obscure bishop of Coire in the fanciful scenario struck the ambassador (and other objective observers) as especially curious. A blameless and scholarly individual, who before his elevation into an enemy of the state by Italian military intelligence was known primarily for composing poetry in Romansh, the native dialect of his diocese, the good bishop attracted the attention and ire of Italian intelligence because of his efforts to prevent the dissemination of irredentist propaganda among Italian stonecutters in his Swiss diocese. Instigated by Rome, this propaganda sought to cultivate among Italian-speaking populations on the wrong side of Italy's borders with Austria, France, and Switzerland a nationalistic wish to be included (territorially as well as culturally) in the motherland. Convinced of the bishop's anti-Italian sentiments, intelligence officers were prepared to believe the most outlandish rumors of his involvement in sinister plots. Many of these rumors originated in a private intelligence service, Defesa Interna, organized by a patriotic, if slightly eccentric and excitable, Italian, Pietro Lanino, who collected information from a variety of unidentified sources. This information was then distributed to various government agencies and foreign embassies in Rome. The well-informed British ambassador to the Vatican, a recipient of Lanino's newsletters, belittled the reports and warned London that the purported intelligence had to be taken with "many grains of salt."[47]

When not sending agents to skulk around the episcopal palace in Coire or to follow the movements of the Jesuit general, SIM targeted the papal diplomatic pouches that carried diplomatic reports and confidential correspondence between the Vatican and its representatives around the world. Before the war the Vatican had routinely sent official correspondence by ordinary mail, although especially sensitive material would be entrusted to a priest or bishop traveling to or from Rome. With the outbreak of war, international mail service was disrupted as the belligerents imposed postal controls that allowed government censors to open all correspondence. To protect the confidentiality of its communications, the Vatican turned to the diplomatic pouch, whose immunity from search and seizure was theoretically guaranteed under international law. Unfortunately, the Vatican had neither the personnel nor the resources to maintain an independent network of diplomatic couriers, so it had to accept the hospitality of other governments. In the summer of 1915 the papal secretariat of state accepted an offer from the Swiss foreign ministry to place its Bern–Rome diplomatic bag at the disposal of the Holy See. An official of the secretariat delivered the Vatican "pouch" (usually one or more large envelopes with wax seals on their flaps) to the Swiss legation in Rome for the twice-weekly courier service to Bern, where it would be delivered to the papal representative. Papal dispatches for destinations beyond Switzerland were carried by Swiss couriers or the couriers of other countries who, as a courtesy to the Holy Father, opened their diplomatic bags for the buff envelopes sealed with wax impressions of the keys of St. Peter.[48]

Although diplomatic bags were theoretically protected from search and seizure, Italian military intelligence cared little about the niceties of international law. The Vatican's confidential correspondence was too tempting a target, especially when that correspondence moved to and from enemy territory and contained information from this denied area. By the last year of the war, SIM's agents in Switzerland had somehow gained clandestine access to the Vatican pouch on the Munich-Bern-Vatican circuit. The pouch was surreptitiously opened, the correspondence copied, and the pouch resealed and sent on its way. Unfortunately, the Italian operatives were sometimes sloppy. The papal representative in Switzerland reported to the secretariat of state that often the pouch arrived at his office torn or suspiciously disturbed. Of course the Italians were not alone in their desire to peek into the pope's diplomatic pouch. The Austrians had the pouch of the nuncio in Vienna under close surveillance, while that same nuncio warned the Vatican that it should assume that any confidential mail passing through German hands was completely compromised.[49]

Italy's best intelligence on the Vatican came not from spies but from a small group of studious men scribbling away on sheets of lined paper behind a door at army headquarters marked Reparto Crittografico (Cryptographic Bureau). For centuries governments had protected their confidential communications from prying eyes by using codes and ciphers to disguise those communications. For almost as long, intelligence services had sought to strip away such disguise by employing codebreakers to solve the codes and ciphers. During the First World War, all the major powers and many of the small powers maintained "signals intelligence" organizations to intercept and decipher the secret communications of friends, enemies, and neutrals. The Italians, however, were latecomers to the game. Although Western cryptology had practically been invented in their peninsula in the early Renaissance, the Italians had lost touch with that heritage, and it was only in late December 1915, several months after the declaration of war against Austria-Hungary, that the Italian army organized a small unit of codebreakers inside the military intelligence service. The personnel were untrained and had to learn the arcane craft of cryptanalysis as they went along, but within a year they were decrypting their first coded messages. These were Vatican messages.

It is little wonder that the Italians scored their first cryptanalytic success against the Vatican, since the cryptosystems used by the papal secretariat of state were so simple that they provided hardly more than token protection for the messages passing between the secretariat and papal representatives around the world. In the first year of war, each nuncio had a codebook of 700 to 800 three- and four-digit numerical groups, each representing a word or phrase (e.g., 471 = message received, 7015 = France). These small codes were seriously deficient for wartime service, not the least because they lacked code equivalents for such words as *submarine, airplane, artillery, refugee, offensive,* and *armistice,* terms that would quickly become part of the working vocabulary of wartime diplomats. More seriously, many of the codebooks had been in service for so long (some up to ten years) that the nuncios had grave reservations about their security and were reluctant to entrust their most sensitive messages to their protection. At times, nuncios delayed passing important pieces of information to the Vatican until they could arrange more secure channels of communication.[50]

By the last year of the war, Italian codebreakers were routinely intercepting and reading the confidential telegrams passing between the Vatican and its diplomatic representatives in Austria-Hungary, Belgium, Germany, the Netherlands, Spain, Switzerland, Turkey, and the United States.[51]

Possessing neither a telegraph nor a radio service of its own, the Vatican relied on the Italian post office to transmit and receive enciphered papal messages. The Italian postal authorities secretly provided the army crypt-analysts copies of every papal telegram, thereby ensuring comprehensive coverage of papal telegraphic communications.

The success of the codebreakers provided Italian intelligence access to the deepest secrets of Vatican diplomacy: reports from the nuncios on polit-ical attitudes and conditions in their host countries; summaries of confi-dential conversations with foreign leaders; instructions to the nuncios from the cardinal secretary of state concerning changes in Vatican policy; alerts concerning new diplomatic or military initiatives by the Allies or the Cen-tral Powers. Little remained hidden. The cryptanalysts must have smiled at the irony as they decoded the warning "Destroy this message and maintain absolute secrecy in this matter" in a telegram from the cardinal secretary of state to the nuncios in Austria-Hungary and Germany concerning an op-portunity to detach Italy from its wartime allies.[52]

The decrypts proved especially useful in the summer of 1917 when, on 1 August, Pope Benedict circulated to the belligerents a call for a nego-tiated peace based on the mutual evacuation and restoration of occupied territories, mutual renunciation of war indemnities, freedom of the seas, diminution of armaments, international arbitration of disputes, and nego-tiation of rival territorial claims. Although the Vatican had, in July 1915, publicly called on the belligerents to come to the negotiating table, and had on several occasions quietly encouraged peace initiatives, the August proposal was the most serious, though ultimately unsuccessful, effort by the Holy See (or any other government) to negotiate an end to the war. Benedict and Gasparri had been considering a major peace initiative since the spring of 1917, and by the early summer the time seemed opportune. The entry of the United States into the war on 6 April 1917 lifted the spirits of the Allies, but it would take time for the newest belligerent to mobilize its resources, raise and train an army, and transport its troops to the front. In the meantime, the two sides continued the war of attrition that they had pursued without success for more than two years. On both sides the will to battle was weakening. In May and June there were large-scale mu-tinies in the French army, with troops refusing to move to the front. In Russia, where in March the czar and his regime had been swept away by popular disturbances and replaced by a "provisional government," the military situation was desperate. The new government had promised its allies that it would continue the war, but desertions, insubordination, and outright mutiny were now so common among Russian troops on the eastern front that the commanders were unable to conduct effective military operations. War-weariness was appearing even in Germany. In the spring of 1917 the imperial chancellor, Theobald von Bethmann-Hollweg, had opened secret discussions with the papal nuncio, Monsignor Eugenio Pacelli, on possible terms for a negotiated settlement, and in July a majority of the national legislature (Reichstag) startled the war leaders by passing a peace resolution.[53]

Lacking effective intelligence sources at the Vatican, London, Paris, and Washington knew nothing of Chancellor Bethmann-Hollweg's secret meetings with Nuncio Pacelli, and they were caught completely off guard by the pope's peace proposal, which was distinctly unwelcome in the Allied capitals. None wished to open peace negotiations except from a position of strength, a posture that eluded the Allies in the summer of 1917. Each also had its own reason for opposing Benedict's démarche. Assuming that the pope was pro-German, France automatically distrusted any initiatives emanating from the Vatican and did not even deign to respond to the proposal. Britain found the papal proposal untimely and limited its response to a polite acknowledgment. From the United States, President Woodrow Wilson, who resented anyone claiming the moral lead in the wartime drama when he himself was auditioning for the role, replied that the German rulers simply could not be trusted to honor any commitments or agreements they might make.[54]

The Italians were equally hostile to the papal initiative. In part, Rome continued to fear any diplomatic initiative that would enhance the international prestige and visibility of the Papacy, especially one that might lead to papal participation in an international peace conference. More immediately, however, Italy was the only Allied power with effective intelligence coverage of the Vatican, and its secret sources provided ample reason to suspect the papal initiative. From its interception of messages passing between the Vatican and Monsignor Eugenio Pacelli in the spring and summer of 1917, Italian intelligence was aware that the nuncio was secretly discussing peace terms with Germany. Since the Vatican was not engaged in similar discussions with any of the Allied powers, the decrypted messages strengthened the conviction, already established by the Gerlach affair, that the Papacy favored the Central Powers.

Reluctant to pursue any settlement that did not satisfy its territorial ambitions, the Italian cabinet was further fortified in its opposition to the peace proposal when the decrypts revealed that in its eagerness to sell its plan to the Allies, the Vatican exaggerated the extent to which Berlin and Vienna were prepared to make political and territorial concessions. In late

September 1917 Cardinal Gasparri had confidentially assured an emissary of the Italian cabinet that as part of a comprehensive peace settlement Germany was definitely prepared to reestablish Belgium and pay an indemnity to Brussels, and that Austria was open to recognizing some of Italy's territorial aspirations in the Trentino. However, the Italian foreign minister, Sidney Sonnino, knew from the decrypts he received each day from army intelligence that the nuncio in Germany had actually warned the Vatican that Berlin's position on Belgium remained vague and equivocal, while the nuncio in Austria had reported that Vienna absolutely excluded any territorial concessions. To already suspicious Italian minds, the decrypts suggested that the Vatican was playing a double game.[55]

Good intelligence also allowed Italy to deflect another potentially troublesome papal diplomatic initiative at the end of the war. For some time the Vatican had been aware that Article 15 of the Treaty of London bound Britain, France, and Russia to support Italy in excluding the Vatican from any peace negotiations. Although publicly disclaiming any interest in a place at the peace conference, Pope Benedict and Cardinal Gasparri quietly directed a campaign to mobilize Catholic opinion in Allied and neutral countries against Article 15 and convince authorities in London, Paris, and Washington that nonbelligerent powers, such as the Vatican, had a right to be heard at a conference that would not only end the war but also arrange the postwar world. Once again, Italian intelligence exposed the Papacy's diplomatic plans by deciphering the secret messages that flashed between the Vatican and its representatives abroad. Forewarned by his codebreakers, Sonnino was able to launch a diplomatic counteroffensive to block such papal maneuvers as a plan to stimulate an international press campaign against Article 15 and an effort to enlist the sympathies of the British monarch, King George V.[56]

Decrypted papal messages permitted Italian intelligence to monitor not only the activities of the Vatican but also political developments in enemy territory. The telegrams of Monsignor Pacelli allowed the Italians to chart the growing influence of the military in German politics and to follow the political maneuvers in Berlin that led, in July 1917, to the replacement of Theobald von Bethmann-Hollweg as chancellor by Georg Michaelis, and the latter's removal the following November in favor of Georg von Hertling. By the fall of 1918 the reports of the nuncios in Germany and Austria were revealing the deteriorating economic and political situation of the Central Powers and providing early indications of the overthrow of the Wittelsbach dynasty in Bavaria and the creation of a socialist republic in Munich.[57]

Occasionally, the Vatican's diplomatic telegrams contained items of military interest. This was especially true in the fall of 1917, when Italy faced its greatest military crisis of the war. After Italy had declared war against Austria in May 1915, the Italian army had scored some limited successes along the river Isonzo and the Dolomite Mountains. These advances, however, were soon contained and, in some cases, reversed by the Austrians. The conflict then settled into a pattern of offensive and counteroffensive as the belligerents won and lost obscure mountain peaks along a front where rough terrain and inclement weather had to be fought as much as the enemy. The stalemate ended in late October 1917, when Austrian armies, stiffened with German reinforcements, smashed through the lines and sent the Italians reeling in disorderly retreat after a decisive defeat at Caporetto, a small Italian town at the center of the battle. By the second week in November the invaders had captured most of northeastern Italy and threatened Venice.

From Bern, Munich, and Vienna papal diplomats cabled daily reports on the offensive and the scope of the Italian debacle. Based on official bulletins, contacts in the host governments, and conversations with colleagues in the local diplomatic communities, these reports included references to the situation on the front ("Colle di Lana lost, province of Belluno threatened, Italians retreating along a front of 150 kilometers"); Italian losses ("From 24 October to 1 November, 250,000 prisoners and over 2000 pieces of artillery"); the direction of the enemy advance ("On the lower Piave German troops are nearing the Vidor bridge"); and the intentions of Italy's enemies ("Probably the plan is to separate Italy from France in order to aggravate Italy's economic and military situation").[58] Delivered each day to the foreign ministry, these decrypts were especially useful to Foreign Minister Sonnino, since the Italian High Command deliberately issued misleading or false reports to civilian authorities to obscure the scope of the debacle and the incompetence of the general staff.[59]

The papal secretariat of state was not blind to the threat of signals intelligence. It was well aware that its encrypted telegrams were intercepted and studied by foreign governments, particularly Italy. It also recognized that the codes it had in service in 1914 were woefully inadequate for the conditions of a world war. Unfortunately, the immediate preparation and distribution of new codes were tasks beyond the capabilities of the small secretariat where, among the staff of fourteen, a single official was responsible for codes and ciphers. It was only in 1916 that the secretariat was ready to distribute new codebooks, "larger and more complete" than the earlier books. The papal foreign office also took additional steps to improve communications security. The more important nunciatures, such as Vienna and Madrid, received two codebooks to allow the nuncios to vary the cryptography of their messages, and these codes were now replaced as frequently as every six months rather than every eight or ten years as was the practice before the war. Cipher clerks were required to adopt more secure procedures for handling cryptographic material and encrypted messages.[60]

Though steps in the right direction, the secretariat's efforts did not secure papal communications against surveillance. The Italian cryptanalysts were able to reconstruct the new codes as fast as the Vatican introduced them. Indeed, the threat to papal communications increased as additional governments began to intercept and decrypt papal messages. By 1917 the Swiss and the Germans were reading at least some of the encrypted traffic of the nuncio in Germany.[61] Security began to improve in January 1918 when the secretariat of state introduced an encipherment for use with new codebooks issued to papal representatives in Austria, Germany, Spain, and Switzerland. The new system, which added a second layer of encryption to a message, was reserved for the most confidential communications; the old codes remained in service for less confidential ones. Papal officials expected the improved cryptosystems to provide "full and absolute" security for their secret correspondence.[62]

The new enciphered codes immediately began to cause problems for Italian codebreakers. While continuing to read many coded telegrams passing between the Vatican and its representatives in Austria, Germany, and Switzerland, they were unable, well into the summer of 1918, to crack the new system that protected the most sensitive messages. Important political intelligence now escaped Italian surveillance. For example, Monsignor Pacelli in Germany used the new enciphered code in the spring of 1918 to discuss with the secretariat of state Austria's interest in a negotiated peace, discussions that apparently escaped the scrutiny of Rome's codebreakers. Similarly, reports in September 1918 from the pope's representative in Switzerland concerning renewed Austrian peace overtures remained hidden from Italian eyes. By the last month of the war, Italian signals intelligence had recovered sufficiently to read some of the telegrams from Bern, but one of the nuncio's enciphered codes remained unbroken, as did at least one of the codes of the nuncio in Vienna.[63]

Despite its problems with later papal ciphers, Italian intelligence was remarkable for the scope and overall success of its operations against the Papacy. No country came close to matching its record. Burned by the Gerlach affair, Germany did not seek new informants within the papal administration. From the security of neutral Switzerland the Austro-Hungarian intelligence services organized espionage and sabotage operations against Italy, but none of these operations targeted the Vatican.[64] Both Berlin and Vienna obtained some information concerning papal affairs from covert surveillance of papal mail crossing their territory, and German codebreakers solved at least one of the Vatican's ciphers. The Germans also dealt a mortal blow to the intelligence activities of Monsignor Umberto Benigni by closing down one of the few remaining networks of the erstwhile papal spy chief.

Benigni, the once fearsome paladin of the Vatican traditionalists, had fallen upon hard times. The death of Pope Pius X in August 1914 had marked the end of the antimodernist crusade and the marginalization of its remaining warriors. The new pope was no friend to the integralists. Giacomo Della Chiesa knew Benigni from their service together in the secretariat of state, and as substitute secretary of state and, subsequently, archbishop of Bologna, he had had ample opportunity to observe the ruinous effect upon the Church of the crusade against political and religious liberals. Unsympathetic toward Benigni's goals and methods, the new pope had no intention of encouraging or supporting the zealous monsignor. He made his position clear immediately upon his election by announcing, "The era of secret denunciations is over."[65]

Driven by his reactionary impulses and addicted to the clandestine world, Benigni could not abandon his secret war against modernism and liberalism, although his struggle was increasingly lonely and pathetic. With the new regime in the Vatican repudiating past practices and the immediate demands of war displacing theological and ecclesiastical controversy in the minds of the pope and his advisers, the lists of suspected modernists, the furtive trips to meet informants, the code names and false addresses all seemed to have less and less purpose. Benigni tried to maintain his former connections to the secretariat of state, but the sympathetic Merry del Val had been replaced as cardinal secretary of state by the disapproving Pietro Gasparri, a former and now disillusioned patron who regretted that day in 1906 when his recommendation brought the devious Umbrian into the secretariat and launched his career of espionage and intrigue. The Sodalitium Pianum, the cover organization for his espionage operations, had been disbanded upon the death of Pius X, and the once extensive network of informants was now reduced to a handful of die-hard antimodernists. One of these loyalists would unwittingly contribute to the demise of his master.

In March 1915 Heinz Brauweiler, the editor of the *Dusseldorfer Tageblatt*, a prominent German newspaper, alerted the military government of

German-occupied Belgium to a dangerous conspiracy against the Central Powers. The alleged conspiracy revolved around the Catholic integralists who had set themselves in opposition to Catholic modernists. According to Brauweiler, these conservative Catholics were not, as they claimed, a purely religious movement committed to resisting the encroachments of modernism in Church teachings and rituals but a political movement secretly controlled by Russia and directed against the interests of Germany. The editor claimed that a book, *La Guerre allemande et le Catholicisme,* recently published by French Catholics charging that German absolutism was the principal enemy of the Church, was merely the latest example of an organized effort to compromise Germany in the eyes of world opinion. Brauweiler claimed to have secret documents, obtained from a Catholic priest, which proved that Monsignor Umberto Benigni, one of the most dangerous leaders of this movement, was actually a Russian agent. The documents also indicated that a certain Jonckx, a lawyer in Ghent, a town in German-occupied Belgium, was one of Benigni's principal agents. Brauweiler urged the authorities to act quickly against this subversive conspiracy.

The rumors of espionage for Russia and anti-German sentiments that had swirled around Benigni in 1910–11 and forced, in many people's mind, his retirement from the papal secretariat of state clearly had reached the offices of the *Dusseldorfer Tageblatt.* Brauweiler may also have come into possession of some of the documents obtained by Father Floris Prims when that Dominican priest infiltrated Jonckx's circle to expose the plots and machinations of the Sodalitium Pianum. Whatever its source, Brauweiler's warning was taken to heart by the German administration in Belgium. On 18 May 1915 military police appeared at the door of Jonckx's residence and demanded admission. There is some question about what happened next. The story that eventually reached the Vatican was that the police forced themselves into Jonckx's house and at gunpoint made the lawyer reveal information concerning his relations with Monsignor Benigni and the code used by Benigni to communicate with his contacts. The German version of the story maintained that Jonckx received his visitors amiably, voluntarily answered their questions, readily acknowledged that Monsignor Benigni had once visited him in the company of a certain Baron Sonthoff (whom the Germans suspected of being a Russian agent), and at the end of the interview allowed them to remove a collection of documents.[66]

The Jonckx raid was a disaster for Benigni. The Belgian lawyer had been one of the monsignor's principal agents and most loyal supporters, and his exposure meant that his usefulness was ended. More important, the papers seized from Jonckx revealed to the Germans (and anyone else with whom the Germans wished to share the information) the inner workings of Benigni's operations and handed his enemies ammunition for their ongoing battle to expose and punish him. It was a professional setback and personal embarrassment from which the onetime "evil genius" of the Vatican would never recover.

Despite suspicions among certain Germans that Vatican agents were working hand in glove with czarist agents, Russian intelligence completely ignored the Vatican during the war. In fact, aside from Italy, the countries aligned against the Central Powers did not aggressively conduct clandestine intelligence operations against the Vatican. The smaller partners in the Allied coalition, such as Belgium and Portugal, were content to rely on their embassies in Rome for whatever news of the pope they required. Britain also seems to have relied primarily on its diplomatic mission to the Holy See for news of papal affairs. At the "other" British embassy in Rome, the one accredited to the Italian government, an officer responsible for collecting political intelligence occasionally included in his reports to the Foreign Office items concerning papal affairs, but the Papacy was not among his priorities. Clandestine espionage figured not at all in London's dealings with the Vatican. The British secret service seems to have paid no systematic attention to the Vatican, while British codebreakers, who cracked the wartime diplomatic ciphers of many countries, including Austria, Germany, Greece, Japan, Spain, and the United States, completely ignored the Vatican.[67]

Aside from Italy, France was the only Allied power to mount a serious clandestine intelligence effort against the Papacy. Initially Paris was at a disadvantage in the intelligence competition at the Vatican. Since the rupture in diplomatic relations in 1904, there had been no French representative at the Vatican. Occasionally the French ambassador to Italy sent Paris items concerning papal affairs, but "Vatican watching" remained a distinctly secondary responsibility of the embassy. Obsessed with the possibility of anti-republican conspiracies among French Catholics, the police of the Third Republic had for some time routinely monitored the activities of French bishops and various Catholic groups and personalities inside France, but the intelligence and security services exhibited little interest in political affairs at the Vatican.

Upon the outbreak of war, France moved quickly to improve its intelligence coverage of the Papacy. Convinced that the Vatican was no more prepared than Paris to forgive and forget the church-state struggles over the Law of Separation, French authorities persuaded themselves that the pope and his advisers harbored a special animosity toward France and would neglect no opportunity to collaborate with Germany to discredit or weaken the Third Republic. From this twisted perspective every papal nuncio was a German agent and every religious order, particularly the hated Jesuits under their allegedly Francophobe general, Father Wladimir Ledochowski, was a willing instrument of Teutonic propaganda and subversion. To expose and thwart their nefarious intrigues, Paris needed some spies at the Vatican.[68]

France's first step to improve its intelligence was modest and overt. The foreign ministry recruited a well-known journalist, Charles Loiseau, and assigned him to the Rome embassy with the responsibility of opening unofficial contacts with the papal secretariat of state. Loiseau met occasionally with Cardinal Gasparri and other papal officials and mingled with ecclesiastical society in Rome. His mission, while unofficial, was open and well-known in Roman diplomatic circles, and his reports differed little from routine embassy dispatches. It was not long before Paris realized that something more was required. While valuing Loiseau as a communications channel to the Vatican, the Quai d'Orsay believed it needed the kind of secret information not likely to result from an appointment with the cardinal secretary of state, tea with the abbot general of the Benedictines, or dinner with the Contessa di Montebouno. To obtain such information the foreign ministry detailed two officers in the Rome embassy to organize a covert operation to collect intelligence on personalities and affairs inside the Vatican. This intelligence cell gradually recruited a network of informants who generated reports on a broad range of subjects. Some, such as a report in January 1918 concerning Cardinal Gasparri's attitude toward the Vatican's role in a future peace conference, dealt specifically with papal affairs. Others, such as a report from March 1918 that the nuncio in Germany had informed the Vatican that Berlin remained confident of victory, but Vienna was losing heart, had wider implications for the war effort.[69]

Invariably attributed to "a secret but reliable source," these reports were passed to the Quai d'Orsay with little effort to confirm the information or sift the intelligence wheat from the chaff. Whatever the sources, they were not always as reliable as the embassy would have the foreign ministry believe. On one occasion, for example, the embassy reported confidently that a certain Monsignor Giuseppe Aversa was in Washington conducting mysterious negotiations with the American government. In fact, at the time of his alleged intrigues, Monsignor Aversa was in Rio de Janeiro conscientiously performing his duties as papal nuncio to Brazil.[70]

In the summer of 1917, if not earlier, the embassy secured a more reliable source when it gained access to some of the confidential communications of the papal secretariat of state. Ambassador Camille Barrère was able to send to Paris extracts from the letters and telegrams passing between Cardinal Gasparri and the nuncio in Germany, Monsignor Pacelli. By early 1918 Barrère was including items from Gasparri's communications with the papal delegate in Washington, Monsignor Giovanni Bonzano. The embassy probably received this material from Italian intelligence, which was intercepting and decrypting papal communications on a large scale. Apparently, Barrère had access to only the occasional papal message, but the intercepts, particularly those that revealed that the Vatican was discussing peace terms with Germany (but not the Allies) in advance of announcing Pope Benedict's peace proposal of August 1917, probably fueled French suspicions concerning the Papacy's sympathy for the Central Powers.[71]

The foreign ministry was not the only French agency spying on the Papacy. During the war French military intelligence also developed a network of informants at the Vatican. Some of these sources were priests, although to protect their identities the reports refer only to "Monsignor X" or "Monsignor Y." At least one, described as "the most intelligent and frank of the leading personalities at the Vatican," seems to have been well placed. Like the sources available to the embassy, the informants reporting to French army intelligence provided information on Vatican personalities and affairs, as well as a range of broader political and military topics. However well placed these sources, they could, intentionally or not, mislead their French contacts. A military intelligence summary dated 21 May 1918 included a report from "Monsignor X" of his recent conversation with the Austrian ambassador to the Vatican, then performing his duties from the safety of neutral Switzerland. According to Monsignor X, the ambassador had confidentially assured him that, contrary to rumor, an Austrian offensive on the Italian front was not in the works. Three weeks later, the Austrians launched one of their biggest offensives of the war, with fifty-five divisions attacking from the Asiago Plateau, while another fifty-one divisions threw themselves across the Piave River.[72]

Not content to collect intelligence from papal circles, the French also launched covert operations to discredit the reputedly pro-German pope and confound his alleged machinations against the Third Republic. Throughout 1917, for example, the French embassy in Rome worked assiduously behind the scenes to create the impression that the Vatican was intriguing with Joseph Caillaux, a former premier and longtime power broker in France, whose reputation for political opportunism and pro-German sympathies attracted the attention of French police and intelligence services, which suspected his loyalty and patriotism. Caillaux's personal and political reputation had been seriously compromised when, just months before the war, his wife shot and killed a newspaper editor for publishing intimate letters revealing an adulterous affair with Caillaux when both had been married to other partners. Though his wife was acquitted, the one-time prime minister fell from political grace and struggled to regain the pathway to power, in part by becoming the unofficial leader of an incipient peace faction in the French parliament.

Caillaux arrived in Rome at the beginning of 1917 (his notoriety preceding him), and immediately political offices and private salons were abuzz with rumors that the French politician was pursuing any number of intrigues aimed at peace with Germany at any price. There were whispers of surreptitious contacts with pro-German journalists, meetings with Italian politicians, and special audiences at the Vatican. The rumors varied in their details, but they shared a theme of sinister machination. In most the Vatican figured prominently as a conspirator with Caillaux in vaguely described but presumably perfidious plots against the honor of France and the interests of the Allies. Needless to say, the Vatican, still reeling from the scandal of the Gerlach affair, was not amused by these stories, which further impugned the political neutrality of the Holy See and perpetuated the myth of papal intrigue and manipulation that had haunted the Papacy since the Renaissance.

Most of the rumors originated in the French embassy in Rome, where the anticlerical ambassador, Camille Barrère, hoped to discredit the pope and preempt any effort to reestablish diplomatic relations between Paris and the Vatican. The covert propaganda campaign against the Vatican culminated at the end of 1917 in the publication by the Parisian paper *Petit Temps* of certain documents purporting to reveal the Vatican conspiring with Monsieur and Madame Caillaux to separate France and Italy from their allies and realign the two countries with the Central Powers in a new war against Protestant England and Orthodox Russia. In return for the Vatican's support for this breathtaking scheme, Caillaux, who expected to return to power in Paris to lead France in this bold, new direction, allegedly promised the pope that he would reestablish diplomatic relations and negotiate a new concordat that would return the Catholic Church to a privileged position in France. According to *Petit Temps,* the accuracy of the story had been confirmed by reliable and knowledgeable sources, including the British ambassador in Rome, Rennel Rodd; the Italian prime minister, Antonio Salandra; and the Italian foreign minister, Sidney Sonnino.

The story had something to outrage everyone: anticlericals in France who feared the reassertion of religious influence in society, French and

Italian patriots who anticipated a dishonorable peace, British politicians and citizens who feared betrayal by their allies, and bigots in any country who were convinced that political conspiracy was one of the sacraments of the Catholic Church. Fortunately for the Vatican, the story was quickly exposed as a complete fabrication. The incriminating documents were in fact forgeries. The British representative at the Holy See, who was well aware of the clandestine efforts by the French to smear the Vatican, dismissed the account as untrue. Both Ambassador Rodd and Foreign Minister Sonnino denied any knowledge of the Caillaux-Vatican conspiracy to detach France from the Allies. Premier Salandra rose in the Italian senate to denounce the story as "pure fantasy." A Canadian horse dealer, who claimed (somewhat improbably) to have seen a secret memo detailing Caillaux's discussions with the pope when he (the horse dealer) visited the American embassy in Rome, promptly fled the Eternal City when the story began to collapse and the outraged American ambassador ridiculed his claims.[73]

Though burned by the failure of the Caillaux affair, the French did not abandon the tactics of disinformation and covert political warfare. The foreign ministry deployed these weapons again in the summer of 1918 when the Vatican and China agreed to establish diplomatic relations. In a tradition extending back to the reign of King Louis XIV, France had acted as protector of the Catholic Church in China. Less interested in religion than politics, Paris valued the protectorate as a symbol of French power and an excuse to intervene in Chinese politics. By the late nineteenth century the Vatican considered such protectorates anachronisms and obstacles to the health and growth of the church in the missionary lands, and it increasingly preferred to abandon intermediaries and deal directly with the authorities in these lands. For their part, the Chinese embraced any approach that would buttress their sovereignty and weaken the claims of the Great Powers for special privileges in China.

In 1886 the Vatican had announced its intention to establish direct relations with Peking by sending a nuncio to the Chinese court. France, however, successfully pressured Pope Leo XIII to abandon this plan by threatening to break off diplomatic relations. In 1918 Pope Benedict XV decided to try again. In July the Vatican announced that it had established diplomatic relations with China and had appointed Monsignor Giuseppe Petrelli, the apostolic delegate in the Philippines, the first nuncio to Peking. Paris immediately moved to block the papal initiative. The Vatican had recently announced its intention also to forsake French protection of Catholics in the Middle East, so the China affair seemed the second stage in an evolving papal program to undermine French prestige and authority in distant lands. At a time when France was fighting for the survival of homeland and empire, these challenges to its imperial stature were more than petty annoyances and had to be nipped in the bud. Unfortunately, Paris was in the curious position of claiming the right to represent the interests of the Catholic Church in China (and the Middle East) at the very time that it refused to have any diplomatic relations with the Vatican. To avoid awkward questions about the legality or logic of its position, the French foreign ministry turned to disinformation.

French embassies in London, Rome, Peking, and Washington began circulating false information purporting to show that Monsignor Petrelli, the nuncio-designate, was a stalking horse for German intrigues in the Far East. According to French sources, Petrelli was a close friend of Admiral Paul von Hintze, who had been appointed German foreign minister about the same time that Petrelli received his appointment to China, a conjunction of events, Paris hinted darkly, that was something more than simple coincidence. The fact that Monsignor Petrelli had not been outside the Philippines since 1906, that his contacts with Admiral von Hintze had been limited to social exchanges when the admiral paid a courtesy visit to Manila before the war, and that, according to the American governor general of the Philippines, he had exhibited no pro-German sympathies during his tenure as apostolic delegate in the islands were inconvenient issues that figured not a bit in the scenario peddled by Paris to its allies. To improve that scenario, the French embassy in Rome put it about that the intermediary who brought the Vatican and China together was a certain Count Capello, envoy to the pope from the principality of Monaco, who was connected (at least in the French version of events) with various defeatist or pro-German personalities, including the notorious Bolo-Pasha, who would be executed in France for trafficking with the enemy. In Peking, the French ambassador assured his American counterpart that the Quai d'Orsay had conclusive proof that Petrelli's appointment was the product of German intrigue, although the ambassador never got around to producing that evidence.[74]

For all the improbability of its story, Paris was able to convince its allies to pressure China to refuse to accept Monsignor Petrelli. The Italians, of course, opposed any papal diplomatic initiative on principle, while the Americans seemed to have succumbed completely to the French disinformation campaign. For their part, the British, smelling a rat, kept their distance from the affair but humored the French in the name of Allied unity. Ironically, at the very time that Paris was insisting that Petrelli's appointment was part of a plot to project German propaganda and intrigue into the

Far East, Berlin protested to the Vatican against the good monsignor's appointment on the grounds that the establishment of relations with China, following upon the Vatican's reopening of diplomatic relations with Portugal, was an anti-German initiative, since both China and Portugal were among the Allied powers aligned against Germany.[75]

Perplexed and more than a little annoyed by the French campaign against Petrelli, which no amount of denials from the secretariat of state could quell, the Vatican withdrew his name and proposed as his replacement Monsignor Giuseppe Pisani, an official in the Vatican department responsible for selecting bishops. It was a shrewd move to disarm French opposition. Pisani was from Vercelli, a Piedmontese city whose clergy were famous for their patriotism and their loyalty to the Italian monarch. In Rome he was known as a friend of Britain, and he was close to Aidan Gasquet, the British cardinal, and Sir Henry Howard, Britain's representative to the Vatican in the early years of the war. Papal authorities undoubtedly believed that their new candidate's political sympathies were so beyond question that there could be no objection from the Allies to his appointment to Peking. They were wrong.

Within days of the announcement of Pisani's selection, the French foreign ministry began a new disinformation campaign aimed at blocking his mission. Once again the Quai d'Orsay conjured the specter of German intrigue. According to the French, Monsignor Pisani's apparently pro-Allied sentiments were nothing more than a facade behind which he hid his sympathy for Germany. Paris purported to know that his appointment was due to the machinations of the conservative Cardinal Gaetano de Lai, whose commitment to the cause of the Central Powers had fortunately not escaped the notice of vigilant French intelligence, although it apparently escaped everyone else's. Warning the United States of the new threat, the Quai d'Orsay concluded, "It is even considered that he would be more dangerous than [Petrelli] being cleverer and more intelligent."[76] Of course, the stories of German intrigue were deliberate fabrications intended to hide France's self-interested policy of maintaining its political privileges in China. In fact, the only intrigues apparent in the whole affair were those emanating from Paris. France would have opposed *any* person as nuncio. Realizing this and acknowledging that it did not have the diplomatic influence to challenge the French position, the Vatican withdrew Pisani's name and dropped the idea of diplomatic relations with China.

France's success in convincing the United States to support its position in China was due, in large part, to the fact that Washington had a distorted picture of the Vatican. When war broke out in August 1914, the United

States was poorly prepared to collect intelligence on anyone, but political coverage of the Vatican was practically nonexistent. The State Department and its embassies were the primary source of foreign political intelligence, while military information was the responsibility of small offices in the War and Navy Departments. The United States still had no embassy to the pope, and since the Taft mission of 1902 Washington had avoided all diplomatic contact with the Vatican. Consequently, the White House and the State Department lacked up-to-date information on the pope, his policies, and his personnel.

The American embassy in Rome was unable to repair this deficiency. The anti-Catholic ambassador, Thomas Nelson Page, was deeply suspicious of the Vatican and given to speculating publicly about the nefarious influence of the "Catholic conspiracy" in international affairs. On one occasion during the war, Page scandalized the diplomatic community in Rome by speaking at a demonstration at the Porta Pia to commemorate and celebrate the collapse of the Papal States. His colleagues in Rome's diplomatic community considered him hostile toward the Vatican, and the papal secretariat of state suspected (with some justification) that in his reports to Washington the ambassador distorted the Vatican's position on a range of issues from submarine warfare to peace proposals. In fact, Page was not well-informed about the Vatican. He had no personal contact with ecclesiastical authorities, and his embassy had no informants inside the papal palace. For information on the Vatican the ambassador relied primarily on Gino Speranza, a journalist and part-time informant for the embassy, who ran about Rome collecting whatever bits of information he tripped over. Speranza shared with Page a conviction that the Papacy preferred the Central Powers and worked actively for their victory, and his reports tended to confirm rather than challenge the ambassador's prejudices.[77]

Characterized more by ignorance and religious bias than by accuracy and insight, the reports from the Rome embassy did nothing to educate American policy makers, most of whom shared the genteel anti-Catholicism of their colleagues in the Eternal City. The reports certainly did not encourage President Woodrow Wilson and his foreign policy advisers to reconsider their suspicions of pro-German sympathies inside the Vatican. Throughout the war Washington did not have a policy toward the Vatican so much as an attitude, one based on prejudice rather than sound intelligence. This attitude contained two elements: a belief that the Papacy was a reactionary, obscurantist force in world affairs that, even if it was not a conscious instrument of German militarism, could not be counted among the supporters of liberal democracy; and a conviction, especially in the White House, that as head of this retrograde institution Pope Benedict was not a fit spokesman for the values and aspirations that should guide humanity into the postwar world. In the face of such assumptions, Pope Benedict's early efforts to work with the president to maintain American neutrality and, after the United States' entry into the war in April 1917, to support papal peace initiatives were dismissed as, at best, misguided and, at worst, treacherous attempts to advance the cause of Berlin and Vienna.[78] When other powers, such as France or Italy, raised the specter of German intrigue to block papal initiatives they found embarrassing or inconvenient, they found a gullible friend in a United States already predisposed to believe the worst of the Vatican and lacking reliable intelligence to test the substance of such charges.

Curiously, the State Department was more concerned about the quality of the Vatican's intelligence concerning the United States than the quality of its own information on the Vatican. By the fall of 1917, in a judgment that mirrored the Vatican's concerns about the accuracy of information reaching Washington, the State Department concluded that the Vatican was misinformed about American attitudes and policies. Believing (incorrectly) that the papal delegate in Washington, Monsignor Giovanni Bonzano, was pro-German, and that his biases distorted his reports to the papal secretariat of state, the department sought an alternative channel to the Vatican.[79]

For domestic political reasons the United States could not follow the Foreign Office in opening a diplomatic mission at the Vatican. Instead, in the fall of 1917 the department supported a proposal by Cardinal James Gibbons of Baltimore to send his assistant and confidant, Father Cyril Fay, to Rome, ostensibly on humanitarian work for the Red Cross but actually to advise the Vatican on American affairs. The department also took the extraordinary step of asking the Foreign Office to assign to the British embassy at the Vatican a British citizen who was informed about American affairs, including the attitudes of American Catholics. The Foreign Office accepted the request and, in December 1917, ordered Robert Wilberforce, an officer in the British consulate in New York City, to proceed immediately to the Vatican.[80]

The special missions of Monsignor Fay and Robert Wilberforce may have marginally adjusted the Vatican's perspective on the United States, but they did little to improve the flow of intelligence from Rome to Washington. Neither had the time or the opportunity to develop good sources inside the Vatican, although Fay in particular worked to disabuse Washington of some of its prejudices and tried to introduce a more open-minded approach to the Papacy.[81] Secure in the conviction that the information provided by the American embassy in Rome was sufficiently accurate and voluminous for the purposes of American policy, neither the State Department nor the White House felt any need to improve intelligence coverage of the papacy. At the end of the war, Washington was scarcely better informed about events at the Vatican than it was at the beginning of the war, with the result that American decisions in such areas as the papal peace proposal of 1917 or the imbroglio over Chinese–Vatican relations were misguided by ignorance as much as prejudice.

For its part, the Vatican also struggled throughout the war to develop reliable sources of intelligence. The information networks developed by Monsignor Umberto Benigni before the war, while focused primarily on sniffing out heresy and suppressing internal dissent within the Church, were potentially the nucleus for a political intelligence service. Monsignor Benigni was inclined to develop that potential, but neither Pope Pius X nor Cardinal Merry del Val exhibited much interest in political intelligence. By the outbreak of war in 1914, the networks had so atrophied that a major effort would have been required to resuscitate them. Memories of the human pain and institutional discord that had resulted from the Vatican's most recent experience with intelligence services were so fresh that neither Pope Benedict nor Cardinal Gasparri had any appetite for such an effort. Benigni may have harbored a hope of being rehabilitated and recalled to the secretariat of state to run intelligence operations against the belligerent states, but the call never came. There would be no more papal spymasters, and the Vatican would navigate the shoals of war without the help of an intelligence service.[82]

Once again, the burden for supplying the Vatican with political intelligence fell upon the nuncios and delegates in foreign capitals. In the past, the performance of these representatives had been uneven mainly because the secretariat had too often filled its diplomatic posts with learned theologians and capable bishops who had been plucked from their seminaries and dioceses and assigned to nunciatures or delegations with little consideration for their preparation or suitability for diplomacy and political reporting. Beginning in the time of Leo XIII and continuing through the pontificate of Pius X, the secretariat of state had moved to improve the quality of its diplomatic reporting by taking various steps to professionalize papal diplomacy. There was a serious effort to build a career service where nuncios and delegates would reach their positions of responsibility only after service as junior officers in various capitals or in the secretariat. Entrants into the service would be selected from promising students in seminaries and pontifical universities and then sent for two years of specialized study in law, history, and languages at the Pontifical Academy for Noble Ecclesiastics, once a finishing school for well-connected or wealthy young men of the old Papal States, now reserved for the training of prospective papal diplomats.

It would take some time to fully establish the program, but by 1914 the first fruits were visible. During the war the Vatican was well served by several nuncios who were the products of the new system: Giuseppe Aversa and Eugenio Pacelli in Germany, Raffaele Scapinelli di Leguigno in Austria, Francesco Marchetti-Selvaggiani and Luigi Maglione in Switzerland, and Giulio Tonti in Portugal. The nuncios did not develop networks of secret agents but relied on formal and informal conversations with officials in their host governments, a close reading of the local press, and exchanges with the diplomats of other governments. Infrequently, Catholic prelates would volunteer some information about events or personalities in their country. For example, when, in early 1915, the Vatican was seeking to convince Austria-Hungary to purchase Italian neutrality with territorial concessions in the Trentino region, the cardinal primate of Hungary warned the nuncio in Vienna that Hungarian politicians would oppose concessions. On another occasion, the bishop of Mohilea, a diocese within the czarist empire, repeated to the Vatican what the Russian interior minister had said to him about the prospects for a negotiated peace.[83] Better sources meant that the secretariat of state was better informed about political events in Europe, particularly in Germany and Austria, than at any time since the loss of the Papal States.

For all the improvements in political reporting, diplomatic coverage remained uneven. Asia was covered only poorly, and Africa hardly at all. Most significantly, reliable intelligence from Allied capitals was scarce. The Vatican still had no representatives in London, Paris, and St. Petersburg, and informal sources, such as the archbishop of Paris or the archbishop of Westminster, were inadequate substitutes for professional observers. There was an apostolic delegate in Washington, but he was often ignored by Cardinal Gasparri, who considered the cardinal archbishop of Baltimore, James Gibbons, a more effective channel to the American government. This confidence was misplaced. The octogenarian archbishop lacked the energy, initiative, and appetite for political reporting. He was preoccupied with fears that American Catholics would be considered unpatriotic by their Protestant countrymen, and he wanted above all to avoid any action that might suggest tension between the United States and the Holy See. He made little effort to use his (admittedly modest) access to American leaders to inform the secretariat of state of attitudes and intentions in Washington, and preferred to limit his activity to delivering papal messages to the White

House. Inadequate representation in Britain, France, Russia, and the United States meant that the Vatican was always better informed about the Central Powers than the Allies. Because of this imbalance in intelligence coverage, Pope Benedict and Cardinal Gasparri frequently misjudged political conditions and opinions in London, Paris, and Washington and consistently underestimated the genteel anti-Catholicism and deep suspicion of "popish plots" that characterized diplomats and politicians in these capitals. Ironically, what suspicious leaders in the Western coalition saw as a pro-German and Austrian bias in papal diplomacy may have been, at least in part, a tendency to engage those governments and issues where, because of more complete information, Pope Benedict and Cardinal Gasparri were more sure of the political situation and confident about what to expect.

In the late nineteenth century Pope Leo XIII had dreamed of returning the Papacy to a position of international respect and influence. He never imagined that it would take a great and bloody war to achieve that dream. During the First World War the Vatican was more centrally engaged in international affairs than it had been at any time since the Napoleonic era. This engagement reflected, in part, a conscious decision by Pope Benedict and his secretary of state, Cardinal Gasparri, to intervene actively in such issues as peace diplomacy and Italian neutrality, but it also reflected a growing awareness among other powers that in a total war where moral legitimacy and public opinion were as much weapons in a nation's arsenal as cannon and aircraft, the Papacy possessed important political resources. Countries, such as the United States, that had rarely given the Papacy a thought now found themselves studying the pope and his intentions, often with little information to guide their considerations. Other countries, such as France and Germany, that had usually relied on traditional diplomatic channels to inform their relations with the Papacy, now found those channels inadequate for the purpose of anticipating and, more important, influencing the Vatican's actions. The search for information, both to inform and to influence, made the Vatican a center for international espionage and intrigue as well as traditional diplomacy.

It is commonplace to describe the First World War as a war that changed the way people and their governments thought about everything from military strategy to personal morality. The adjustment was particularly evident in the area of intelligence. Governments rediscovered a truth that many had once learned but had forgotten: that diplomacy and military operations required information concerning the capabilities, dispositions, and intentions of other governments, and that, in turn, such information required aggressive collection operations by specialist intelligence organizations. It was difficult for even the belligerent powers to relearn this lesson, but it was especially difficult for the Vatican, which was less accustomed than most governments to worrying about spies, traitors, ciphers, and disinformation. Such unwelcome concerns were the hidden costs behind the newfound international status, and those costs would only increase in the postwar world.

4

Facing the Dictators

It was still dark on the morning of 21 April 1926 as the tall, slim figure in nondescript civilian clothes slipped out the rear door of his Moscow hotel. Hoping that the early hour and inconspicuous departure would cloak his movements from the police agents who had dogged his steps since his arrival in the Russian capital three weeks earlier, the figure hurried the short distance to St. Louis-des-Français, the only Catholic church still open and functioning in the city. It was a curious destination for anyone seeking to escape the notice of police spies, since it stood directly across the way from the Lubyanka, the infamous headquarters, prison, and execution block of the Obyeddinenoye Gosudarstvennoye Politicheskoye Upravleniye (OGPU), the dreaded secret police of the Soviet regime. Despite the early hour, there were already two pious parishioners praying before the altar: a middle-aged woman in the rough clothes of a cleaning woman, and a well-dressed young man with Mediterranean features. The three worshipers sat quietly, and as the minutes turned to hours, it was apparent that they were waiting for something. Four hours into their vigil, the church door opened, and a robust peasant in a sheepskin jacket entered and stood in the nave looking about uncertainly, as if for a sign. The tall stranger stood and moved rapidly to bar the doors against further entry. Then, joined by the other two worshipers, he approached the nervous peasant, who was probably confused and frightened by this strange behavior. This was, after all, the capital of a regime that had repeatedly proclaimed its hatred of religion and gave substance to those proclamations by seizing Church property and persecuting those who refused to abandon their faith. It was risky for a Russian even to be seen inside a church. Were these three strangers police agents? Provocateurs? Had he, a simple visitor from the provinces, been lured into a trap?

Standing before the peasant, the tall stranger leaned forward and in a conspiratorial whisper disclosed the purpose that had brought four strangers together in a small Catholic church in the shadow of a police fortress. He introduced himself as Michel d'Herbigny, a Catholic bishop sent by Pope Pius XI to Moscow on a clandestine mission to establish an underground church hierarchy and administration to replace the bishops and priests exiled or imprisoned by the Communist authorities. He revealed that he knew that the rough-clad man was not a peasant but a Catholic priest, the French-born Father Pie Eugene Neveu, whom the French ambassador in Moscow had summoned without explanation to the capital from his residence in Makejevka, a town in the Donets Basin. If Father Neveu was surprised by the stranger's initial comments, he was flabbergasted by what followed. Bishop d'Herbigny announced that the Holy Father had selected Neveu to be the first secret bishop and that he had traveled to Moscow from Rome to perform the ceremony of consecration. Since d'Herbigny had received a summons to appear that very afternoon at the office of the city administration, a summons he assumed was a preliminary to his expulsion from the Soviet Union, the ceremony would take place immediately, in St. Louis-des-Français, with d'Herbigny's two silent associates as witnesses. The woman, Alice Ott, was the church's sacristan; the young man, Lieutenant Bergera, was the military attaché from the Italian embassy and a friend of Pope Pius from the period just after the First World War when the then Monsignor Achille Ratti had been papal nuncio in Warsaw and Bergera had been attached to the Italian embassy in the Polish capital. The visitor from Rome gave Neveu a few minutes to prepare himself spiritually and emotionally and then hurried through the ceremony that culminated when d'Herbigny handed him a formal letter of appointment drafted in elegant Latin and signed by the cardinal secretary of state, Pietro Gasparri, and placed a copper ring on the new bishop's finger as a symbol of his episcopal authority, including the authority to ordain priests and consecrate other bishops.

There was little time for celebration; police agents kept St. Louis-des-Français under surveillance, and an alert observer might begin to wonder why people entered the church but did not leave. As the four prepared their departure, d'Herbigny handed Neveu a packet of money from the pope and whispered some last-minute instructions. He was to locate the priests Alexander Frison and Boleslas Sloskans, show them his credentials, and secretly consecrate them as bishops. Frison was priest to a small Catholic congregation in Odessa, on the Black Sea, while Sloskans ministered in Leningrad. Then it was time to go. Neveu was overwhelmed with emotion and could hardly credit the morning's events. He had scarcely seen another Catholic priest in years, let alone a bishop fresh from Rome. He entered St. Louis-des-Français a poor and obscure priest and departed a bishop of the Roman Catholic Church. As d'Herbigny bid him a hurried good-bye, Neveu could barely speak. "You have made me a successor to the apostles," he whispered. He might have recalled that all but one of the apostles had been martyred for their faith.[1]

Secret missions and clandestine meetings in hostile territory were uncommon expedients for the Vatican, but the years after the First World War were uncommon times. On 10 November 1918 German representatives, meeting their Allied counterparts in a railway carriage on a siding in the French forest of Compiègne, had signed an armistice that finally silenced the guns on the western front. Following closely upon the capitulation of Turkey (30 October) and Austria-Hungary (3 November), the German action, effectively a surrender, ended four years of global war. In the spring and summer of 1919, the specific terms of that surrender were hammered out at the peace conference that convened amid the splendors of the palace of Versailles outside of Paris.[2] From the Vatican's perspective the Treaty of Versailles was deeply flawed and the peace it enshrined inherently unstable. By placing blame for the horrific war squarely (and only) on the shoulders of the defeated, by exacting retribution in the form of territorial and financial indemnities, and by breaking the Austro-Hungarian Empire into several small states, which neither alone nor in concert could be expected to assume the old empire's role of counterweight to Germany and Russia, the vengeful peace settlement was both morally unjust and politically shortsighted. The Vatican feared that resentments would grow not only among the aggrieved losers but also among disappointed victors who concluded that the spoils of victory did not justify the sufferings of war, and that traditional social and political institutions, shaken if not destroyed by total war, would be unable to contain these resentments.[3] Even before the guns had quieted, radical political movements had appeared to challenge traditional institutions and propose revolutionary responses to the grievances and the suffering. Some of these movements—Bolshevism, Fascism, Nazism—would seize power and seriously threaten the postwar world in general, and the Papacy in particular.

The Vatican had cautiously welcomed the Russian Revolution of March 1917. Under the czars (whose governments were closely allied with Russian

Orthodoxy, the state religion), the Catholic Church in Russia had been subject to official discrimination that ranged from administrative harassment to outright persecution. The revolution of March 1917 that overthrew the czar and brought to power a liberal-democratic "provisional government" promised a better future. The provisional government immediately adopted a conciliatory attitude toward the Papacy and the Catholic Church in Russia. New legislation, such as a law granting Church authorities sole control over religious buildings, recognized the Vatican's administrative prerogatives in ecclesiastical affairs, while other legislation, such as laws allowing the Church to open seminaries and religious schools and to operate printing presses, facilitated the practice and propagation of the Catholic faith.[4]

The promise of tolerance faded, however, when the Bolsheviks under Vladimir Lenin seized power in the revolution of November 1917. On the rarefied level of Marxist theory, religion was just another weapon in the capitalist armory that defused class conflict by offering the exploited masses solace and the promise of a better life in the hereafter. The Bolsheviks, therefore, had nothing but contempt for religion. In the new classless society it would lose its purpose and wither away. To the extent that religious believers refused to reconcile themselves to that new society, they would have to be smashed just like the aristocracy, the bourgeoisie, and other class enemies. On 23 January 1918 a decree of the Council of People's Commissars, the executive authority of the new government, announced the regime's attitude toward religious institutions. While guaranteeing freedom of religion and worship ("as long as it does not disturb public order"), the decree forbade religious instruction in schools and churches, deprived churches of state support, prohibited churches from soliciting donations from their adherents, and stripped churches of their legal personality, thereby making them incapable of owning property. Subsequent decrees in 1918 and 1919 prohibited religious instruction for children even in private homes, nationalized church properties, and stripped clerics of their civil rights. Bolshevik authorities even spoke about future regulations requiring priests to be elected by their congregations, a major violation of Catholic ecclesiastical law. Harsh regulations were reinforced by arrests of recalcitrant priests, harassment of churchgoers, and interruptions in communications between the Vatican and the Soviet Union.

In its response to this antireligious program (which affected all religions inside the Soviet Union), the Vatican vacillated between compromise and resistance. Initially it adopted a wait-and-see posture in the hope that, once settled in power, the revolutionary regime would abandon its more radical attitudes. By 1920 there were signs that Lenin and his associates were indeed prepared to moderate their policy. Devastated by civil war and famine and shunned by the international community, the Soviet Union desperately needed to break out of its diplomatic isolation and secure foreign economic assistance. To obtain such assistance, Lenin and his associates were prepared to temper their rhetoric and adjust their foreign and domestic policies. Assuming that the Papacy commanded enormous riches and that its attitude would influence the behavior of other governments, especially those with large Catholic populations, Moscow opened secret contacts with the Vatican that held out the possibility of new freedom for Catholic worship and missionary activity in the Soviet Union in return for diplomatic recognition and papal economic assistance for the starving people of Russia. Of course the Soviets seriously exaggerated the wealth and political influence of the Papacy, while the Vatican seriously misjudged the commitment of the Soviets to religious toleration. In one of his last major decisions before his death on 22 January 1922, Pope Benedict approved a plan to send a papal relief mission to the Soviet Union. The mission was delayed for several months while Moscow considered the plan and amended the wording of the agreement with the Vatican to ensure that the members of the mission restricted themselves to humanitarian relief and avoided missionary activities. A small and underfunded team of thirteen priests under the direction of an American Jesuit, Father Edmund Walsh, eventually sailed from Italy in the summer of 1922 to distribute food and clothing in Moscow and two or three other Russian cities. At the same time, the Vatican opened secret negotiations with Soviet representatives, first in Rome, then in Berlin, aimed at securing, if not a formal agreement and exchange of ambassadors, at least a long-term modus vivendi that would allow the Church to operate inside Russia with a modicum of freedom.

The experiment in accommodation was short-lived. For the Soviets, who had not abandoned their antireligious prejudices but merely put them in storage for a later day, the experiment had never been more than a tactical retreat required by circumstances. When circumstances improved, the prejudices were easily retrieved. Moscow, which had anticipated tens of millions of dollars in aid from the pope, had been disappointed by the paltry level of papal economic assistance and saw little need to purchase such aid with concessions, especially after 1923, when the worst of the national famine had passed. By that time diplomatic recognition by the Holy See was no longer important, since the Soviet Union had already breached the diplomatic wall that had isolated it from other countries. In the spring of 1922 Russian and German representatives, meeting in the Italian resort of Rapallo, signed a treaty establishing diplomatic relations between the former enemies and laying the groundwork for future economic cooperation. Other governments would soon follow suit. The Vatican had lost what little leverage it had, and the consequences were severe.

In the spring of 1923 three senior Catholic prelates and twelve priests were arrested by the secret police and (in one of the first of the "show trials" that would later become a distinguishing characteristic of Soviet justice) condemned for counterrevolutionary and anti-Soviet activities. Two, Archbishop Jan Cieplak and his vicar general (executive officer) Konstanty Budkiewicz, were sentenced to death and the remainder to prison. Cieplak's sentence was commuted to ten years' imprisonment, but Budkiewicz was executed in Lubyanka prison on Easter night, 31 March 1923. As the Church's senior leadership was decimated, a new wave of persecution swept up Russian Catholics. Churches, schools, and seminaries were closed, and priests were arrested, harassed, or driven into exile. By 1924, the year of Lenin's death, the senile Bishop Zerr of Tiraspol was the only Catholic bishop alive and at liberty inside the Soviet Union. That year the Vatican recalled its economic aid mission in anticipation of an expulsion order. Within months of the mission's departure, the Soviets established a mass organization called the League of the Godless to direct antireligious propaganda and agitation across the country.[5]

Many voices inside the Vatican urged Pius XI, who had been elected the successor to Benedict XV on 6 February 1922, to condemn publicly the antireligious policies of Moscow and mobilize international Catholic opinion against the godless Communists. The pontiff held his hand, although in an address to the cardinals in December 1924 he did refer to the "extremely great danger and very certain evil" of Communism and assured his listeners that he was "very far from endorsing" the Soviet government.[6] His actions, however, were more subtle than his words. Even before his speech, Pius had instructed his nuncio in Germany, Monsignor Eugenio Pacelli, to continue the secret talks with Soviet diplomatic representatives that had been going on for almost a year in Berlin. Further talks could do no harm. The Soviet foreign minister, Georgij Chicherin, was a leading pragmatist in Moscow and was thought to favor a modus vivendi with the Papacy. Though a comprehensive agreement on church-state relations was extremely unlikely, Pacelli might secure some modest concessions concerning the appointment of new bishops and the release of imprisoned priests. In the meantime, the Vatican would hedge its bets by launching a secret operation to secure its position in the Soviet Union regardless of the course of the Berlin negotiations.

Father Michel d'Herbigny was the Vatican's leading authority on Russian affairs. He had entered the Society of Jesus (Jesuits) at the age of seventeen and had developed an interest in Russian culture and history during his studies in Paris and Trier. He was a man of both thought and action, capable of writing prizewinning works on Russian philosophy and committed to participating personally in the rebirth of religion in a new Russia. As Russia figured more and more prominently in Vatican deliberations, it was only a matter of time before d'Herbigny's work and reputation drew the notice of Rome. In 1922 he was summoned to Rome to direct the new Pontifical Institute for Eastern Studies and to serve as a consultant to the Congregation for the Eastern Churches, the papal department responsible for ecclesiastical affairs in Russia and other Slavic lands. By the mid-1920s these affairs were in considerable disarray.

The Vatican was poorly informed about conditions inside the Soviet Union. With neither a nuncio nor an apostolic delegate in Moscow, the papal secretariat of state had no professional reporter on the scene to cover political and ecclesiastical developments. The bishops were in prison or exile, and the remaining priests were subject to such police surveillance and intimidation that they could not have reported much to the Vatican even if there were functioning channels of communication that circumvented the pervasive postal censorship. The Vatican was not even sure how many priests were still ministering in this time of persecution. While resident in Moscow as director of the pontifical relief mission, Father Edmund Walsh, an American Jesuit who fancied himself a political observer of some acuity, sent the Vatican (via the German embassy in Moscow) regular reports on personalities and conditions in the Soviet Union, including at least one report on the Red Army.[7] Since Soviet authorities strictly limited Walsh's movements in Russia and closely monitored the activities of his relief team, the American Jesuit relied on conversations with foreign diplomats in Moscow and occasional official contacts with Soviet authorities for most of the information he forwarded to Rome. Father Eduard Gehrmann, a German priest who succeeded Walsh, continued the practice, but even this modest source was lost when the relief mission was withdrawn in the summer of 1924. Occasionally an ecclesiastical refugee would appear in Rome with news from Bolshevik lands. In April 1924, for example, when the secret police suddenly released Archbishop Cieplak from prison and expelled him from the country, the prelate traveled immediately to Rome to report to the pope. By 1925, however, ecclesiastical refugees were few and far between, and eyewitness testimony was increasingly scarce. The Vatican needed to create its own eyewitness.

In the fall of 1925 Pope Pius sent Michel d'Herbigny into the Soviet Union. The pendulum of Soviet religious policy had swung back toward accommodation, and the director of the Pontifical Institute for Eastern Studies had received an invitation from a prominent Russian Orthodox prelate to visit his church council, an invitation that certainly had the approval of the Soviet authorities. On his visa application, Father d'Herbigny described the purpose of his trip as a "private journey for vacation and study." The Jesuit traveled openly, in clerical dress, and though his six-day visit was confined to Moscow, he held discussions with various Western diplomats, senior prelates of the Orthodox Church, and at least one member of the Soviet leadership, Minister of Education Anatoli Lunarcharski. When he returned to Rome, his report was the first account by a reliable source that the Vatican had received from Russia in months. While the Jesuit affirmed that persecution had eased and that religious conditions were, at least for the moment, relatively relaxed, he found that the organizational status of the Catholic Church remained desperate, with no way to replace lost bishops or augment the declining number of priests. The situation was so bad that one poor individual found himself the only surviving Catholic priest in an area the size of Italy.

While Soviet-Vatican negotiations dragged on in Berlin with little progress, Pope Pius decided on measures to buttress the collapsing structure in Russia. Bishops were the key, for only bishops could ordain the priests who would say the masses, baptize the babies, marry the couples, and anoint the dying. Furthermore, under ecclesiastical law only bishops could exercise legitimate authority over the myriad of administrative, financial, and ceremonial issues that arose routinely in local church affairs. It was not for nothing that the secret police went after the bishops so ruthlessly. The Soviet government would surely resist any effort by the Vatican to appoint new bishops, and any bishop so appointed would just as surely receive the immediate attention of the secret police. Subterfuge was required if the pope was to fill the bishoprics that had fallen vacant during the persecution.

Pope Pius had briefly considered sending priests into Russia clandestinely in 1924 when the papal relief mission was withdrawn. It was not a new idea. In the mid–nineteenth century, during one of the periodic persecutions by the czarist regime, the Vatican had secretly dispatched Jesuits into Russia disguised as traveling tradesmen with false papers and portable altars hidden in their baggage. These brave priests (at least one of whom was exposed and sent to prison) replaced native clergy arrested by the czar's police.[8] In 1926, influenced by d'Herbigny's depressing report, which described religious conditions more bleak than any imposed by a czar, Pius returned to the idea in conversations with his advisers. Initially he hoped that religious orders in Germany might provide priests who had some experience in engineering or technical matters and who could be infiltrated as laymen into the factories that the Germans (as a consequence of the Rapallo Treaty) were constructing in Russia. Presumably, certain of these priests would be consecrated as bishops before their departure, and they would secretly exercise their ecclesiastical office in the evenings or in moments stolen from the factory floor or the construction site. The pope was soon convinced to abandon this improbable plan. Perhaps suitable candidates for the clandestine mission were not forthcoming. Papal advisers may also have realized that foreign engineers and technicians were subject to intense police surveillance, and the OGPU would soon notice any newcomers who sought to mingle with Russians. Bishops would have to be found among the worthy and intelligent priests who still survived in the country.[9]

Father Pie Eugene Neveu had gone to Russia in 1907 to minister to a congregation of French and Belgian mining engineers in the service of the czar near the town of Makejevka in the Donets Basin. Neveu had stayed at his post during the upheavals that attended the Bolshevik Revolution of 1917 even though the engineers had returned to Belgium and France. Ministering to a declining flock of Russian parishioners, harassed and interrogated by the police, destitute, and cut off from the outside world, he had managed, in 1922, to get a message to the Vatican that he was still alive and functioning, adding somewhat drolly that he would appreciate receiving a new pair of pants and a current map of the world. Neveu was courageous, stubborn, and cunning, attributes that were marginally useful for a bishop in, say, Paris or Washington, but absolute prerequisites for survival, let alone success, in Moscow and Leningrad. Pius decided that Neveu was just the man the Vatican needed and that Michel d'Herbigny would go to Russia to tell him so.

On 11 February 1926 Pius summoned d'Herbigny to the papal apartments and astonished the French Jesuit by announcing that he had been selected for a secret mission. He would be made a bishop and then would be sent to the Soviet Union to establish a clandestine Catholic hierarchy and church administration by consecrating secretly Father Pie Eugene Neveu and, perhaps, other Russian priests. As a Jesuit, sworn to obey the pope in all matters, d'Herbigny accepted the mission without question. In early March he departed for Paris, where he secured an entry visa for Russia from the Soviet embassy, explaining his purpose as a "ministerial journey" to attend to the spiritual needs of Catholics in Moscow's foreign diplomatic community. He then traveled to Berlin, where in great secrecy he was consecrated a bishop by the nuncio, Monsignor Pacelli, who was himself a bishop (as were all nuncios). In the meantime, the Vatican secretly informed the French government of its plans. The French foreign ministry instructed its ambassador in Moscow to summon to the Russian capital Father Neveu, who was a citizen of France. Since the embassy assumed that its correspondence with French nationals living in Russia was monitored by the secret police, the letter to Neveu revealed nothing about the purpose of the summons.

Carefully hiding the fact that he was a bishop, Michel d'Herbigny reached Moscow on 1 April 1926 and promptly set out to live his cover story. It was Easter week, and the Jesuit called at the various embassies to remind the diplomats of their religious obligations. He made himself so visibly officious and acted so well the part of the earnest parish priest that at least one ambassador, Germany's Count Ulrich von Brockdorff-Rantzau, suspected that there was more to the priest's visit than pastoral work. When he received an unexpected summons to appear at the offices of the city administration, d'Herbigny concluded that the police had somehow stumbled upon his secret mission, and this fear lent a special urgency to his clandestine meeting with Father Neveu in St. Louis-des-Français on 21 April. When he called at the city offices, however, he was relieved to learn that the authorities merely wished to give him certain documents to facilitate his request to travel to regions in southern and western Russia. Convinced that the St. Louis-des-Français meeting had escaped the notice of the secret police and that the permit to travel beyond Moscow indicated that the authorities had bought his cover story and had no inkling of his clandestine purposes, d'Herbigny became overconfident. Affecting the peaked cap of a worker but retaining his white clerical collar, he embarked on the second stage of his mission by traveling openly with Neveu to Kharkov, and then alone to Odessa, Kiev, and Leningrad. Along the journey he met with the various priests who had been selected by the Vatican as the new bishops and ecclesiastical administrators of the secret Catholic hierarchy in the Soviet Union. Two future bishops, Father Boleslas Sloskans of Leningrad and Father Alexander Frison of Sevastopol, were told to make their way to Moscow by the first week in May. On 10 May, four days before his departure from Russia, d'Herbigny again joined Madame Ott and Lieutenant Bergera behind the locked doors of St. Louis-des-Français, this time to consecrate Sloskans and Frison as the second and third of the pope's secret bishops.[10]

It is unlikely that any of this activity escaped the notice of the Russian secret police. Michel d'Herbigny was a babe in the clandestine woods, and his efforts at security were amateurish. By courteously facilitating the Jesuit's travel beyond Moscow while all the time monitoring his movements, the authorities were able to identify his contacts and place them under surveillance. The Soviet Union was a police state with controls on travel and residency, but whether from innocence or hubris, d'Herbigny did not stop to wonder why the authorities, normally so hostile to Catholic clerics, would allow priests such as Neveu, Sloskans, and Frison to travel without question or impediment to and from Moscow. D'Herbigny's secret mission and the Vatican's secret hierarchy had been compromised from the start.

Three weeks after Michel d'Herbigny's departure from Moscow, the OGPU struck its first blow against the clandestine hierarchy by arresting several priests, including one who had been secretly installed by the Jesuit bishop as "apostolic administrator" for a district in the western Soviet Union. This warning that its clandestine operations were known to Moscow went unheeded at the Vatican. In August d'Herbigny returned a third time to Russia, this time openly as a bishop. Again the announced purpose of the visit was to serve the religious needs of the foreign community in Moscow, but once more some diplomats suspected that this was a pretext for some other, more secret, activity. They were right. In the second week in August he made a lightning visit to Leningrad, having (he believed) first misdirected the police by ostentatiously inquiring in his hotel about a tourist visit to the famous fair in the town of Gorki, while a friend in the French embassy reserved a seat for him on the Leningrad train.[11] In the former imperial capital, behind another set of locked doors, in another French church, Notre Dame de France, he consecrated his fourth secret bishop, Father Antoni Malecki, who had recently been released from prison.

The secret police monitored d'Herbigny even more closely on this visit, and it is unlikely that they were deceived by his crude efforts to throw them off the scent. They also staged various incidents in an effort to provoke the French Jesuit into compromising himself. Strangers would appear unannounced at his hotel, seeking to entrust to his care letters to foreign countries or, on at least one occasion, alleged military secrets. He successfully sidestepped these provocations. Finally, the police decided they had had enough. D'Herbigny's visa expired on 4 September 1926. On 28 August he requested an extension and permission to visit the Ukraine. The authorities immediately granted a temporary extension until 12 September and promised to consider the request concerning the Ukraine. Three days later, however, an official appeared at d'Herbigny's hotel shortly after midnight to awaken the Jesuit and inform him that his presence in Russia was no longer welcome. His passport would be delivered to the hotel that afternoon (a Saturday), and he would be placed on the first available train for the border.

The expulsion order was most untimely because d'Herbigny had been entrusted by the Vatican with certain important documents for Bishop Neveu, who, at the Vatican's direction, would establish himself in Moscow. D'Herbigny had been waiting for Neveu to arrive in the capital, but now that he had only a few hours left in the city, it seemed unlikely that the Jesuit could complete his mission. With nothing to do but pack his clothes and await the arrival of his passport from police headquarters, he went to St. Louis-des-Français to say his morning mass. In the middle of the ceremony, the church doors opened, and in walked Bishop Neveu, who for this journey had replaced his peasant's fleece coat with the leather jacket and pants of a worker. Immediately, d'Herbigny (who for security in Russia always carried important documents on his person in a flannel pouch especially sewn by his mother) handed the papers to Neveu, who must have marveled at how a particular Jesuit and a particular church had suddenly come to play such a pivotal role in his life.[12] Wishing his countryman good luck, d'Herbigny returned to his hotel to wait for the police. He waited through Saturday and then through Sunday. Finally on Monday the passport arrived. Accompanied as far as the border by a police agent, the French Jesuit departed for Finland and, eventually, the Vatican.[13]

The Soviet authorities now began slowly and systematically to dismantle the secret hierarchy that the Vatican had hoped would nurture the Russian Church in its time of peril. The renewed persecution reflected, in part, the rise of new leadership in Moscow. After Lenin's death in 1924 there had been a quiet struggle for leadership among his lieutenants. Within a year Josef Stalin had emerged as the leading force, and within two years he had imposed himself on his party colleagues and his nation. To secure his position as unchallenged leader of the Soviet Union and to ensure that Russia was prepared militarily and economically to withstand the hostility of the capitalist world (goals that often were in conflict with each other), Stalin embarked on radical programs of industrial modernization and agricultural collectivization, while relentlessly seeking out and smashing real and imagined internal threats to his rule. With varying emphases, he would pursue these goals until his death in 1953, but the effort was especially energetic in the early years of his long dictatorship.

In the years following Stalin's ascension to power, the Vatican and the Catholic Church in Russia were seen as serious threats to both of the dictator's goals. For someone schooled in Marxism-Leninism and accustomed to conspiracy theories of history, the Papacy was a reactionary power allied with other anti-Communist powers in an effort to contain and ultimately destroy the Soviet experiment. This perspective would be reinforced when the Vatican signed treaties with Fascist Italy (1929) and Nazi Germany (1933), two of the governments most hostile to the Soviet Union. Domestically, Russian Catholics were a potentially subversive force that resisted the claims of the totalitarian society Stalin intended to put in place. They affirmed allegiance to a foreign potentate sitting on a jeweled throne in Rome, who sent clandestine agents into Russia to establish secret ecclesiastical structures that could just as easily be networks for intelligence and subversion. Especially strong among the peasants in western and southwestern Russia, Catholicism was one of the traditional institutions of hearth and village that had to be smashed to bend the farmers to the collectivist will of the Soviet state. In the strategic western districts of the country, where most believers were Polish or Ukrainian in language, culture, and historical identity and Catholicism was intricately connected to nationalism, the religion of Rome could easily become an instrument of foreign powers and a destabilizing force on Russia's western frontier.

On 15 October 1926, just weeks after d'Herbigny's expulsion, the Council of Ministers adopted a resolution prohibiting further entry of "foreign servants of religion." There would be no more visits by Michel d'Herbigny. In December, Monsignor Vincent Ilyin, whom d'Herbigny that April had secretly appointed apostolic administrator in Kharkov, was arrested for carrying foreign newspapers. Within months, Bishop Sloskans, who had publicly (and rather imprudently) announced his episcopal status in November 1926, was arrested on trumped-up charges of espionage on behalf of Poland and sent to a hard labor camp near the Arctic Circle. Another bishop, Teofilus Matulionis, was arrested and sent to an Arctic labor camp only weeks after his supposedly secret consecration by Bishop Neveu in February 1929. This loss was especially untimely, since the Vatican expected to hold Matulionis in reserve should the police seize Bishop Malecki again. That year also saw the arrest of Bishop Frison, one of d'Herbigny's original band of underground prelates.[14] Subsequent years would witness the arrest and imprisonment (and sometimes execution) of bishops and apostolic administrators and the constant surveillance and harassment of the few prelates who remained free. These measures were death blows to the Russian Church. In 1924, the year of Lenin's death, there were still approximately two hundred Catholic priests in the Soviet Union. By 1936 the number had been reduced to about fifty. The next year there were only ten. In 1938 there were two.[15]

Occasionally there would be breathing spells when Stalin would lift the persecution as a tactic to secure some other goal. For instance, in 1931, when the social and economic debacle of agricultural collectivization threatened Russia with another famine at the same time that Moscow again found itself isolated diplomatically, the Soviet Union moved to improve its international reputation and curry favor abroad. Religious services now were permitted to proceed without interference, and several bishops and priests, including Bishop Frison, were released from incarceration. Relief, however, was only temporary. As soon as the crisis passed, services were again harassed, and the clerics went back into the concentration camps or execution cells. Bishop Frison, for example, was imprisoned again and, in 1937, executed.

As its bishops and priests disappeared one by one into the camps or early graves, the Vatican gradually lost what little touch it still had with events inside the Soviet Union. Mail intercept and censorship by postal authorities made communications with the surviving clerics tenuous and unreliable. The papal secretariat of state received occasional items of political news from the German and French embassies to the Holy See, which passed on information from their counterparts in Moscow. After 1926, however, the Vatican's principal source of intelligence was Bishop Neveu in Moscow, who as a French citizen was more secure against arrest than his Russian colleagues. Every two weeks Neveu sent Michel d'Herbigny in Rome a report outlining the latest developments in religious and political life in the Soviet Union. The French-born bishop handed his reports to the French embassy in the Russian capital for inclusion in the diplomatic pouch for Paris. From Paris the reports would be forwarded to the French embassy to the Holy See for delivery to d'Herbigny. The Jesuit treated these missives from Moscow as strictly confidential and would share them only with Pope Pius XI during weekly meetings in the papal apartments. Through the reverse channel, d'Herbigny sent Neveu letters of advice and encouragement that included the latest news and gossip from the Vatican. There was also clandestine traffic of a different sort between Moscow and the Vatican. Neveu assiduously acquired Russian icons as well as rare religious manuscripts and books for the Pontifical Institute for Eastern Studies. These items were forwarded directly to Rome in the diplomatic pouch of the Italian embassy in Moscow. Perhaps as a return for this service, Bishop Neveu passed to the Italian diplomats some of the same political news he was sending d'Herbigny, although the Jesuit in Rome was unaware that his Moscow source was sharing information with others.[16]

Neveu's customers (he was probably also passing information to his fellow countrymen in the French embassy) received little intelligence of value from the prelate. Doubly suspect as a foreigner and a religious leader, the bishop was always under close surveillance by the police, who prohibited him from traveling beyond Moscow. Of course his contacts with party and political circles were nil, and his interaction with ordinary citizens hardly greater, since few Russians would risk attracting the attention of the police by visiting a foreigner who was also a priest. For information Neveu relied on the comments and gossip of his Catholic parishioners in the local diplomatic community and the occasional rumor that reached Moscow by word of mouth from the countryside. The Vatican lost even this poor source in 1936 when Neveu, after traveling to France for medical treatment, was permanently denied permission to reenter the Soviet Union.

If the Vatican was poorly informed of developments inside the Soviet Union, Moscow was no better informed about events at the Vatican. During the 1920s, Russian intelligence considered the Catholic Church primarily a domestic threat to the Bolshevik regime and concentrated on monitoring bishops and priests and penetrating Catholic circles inside the Soviet Union. By the end of the decade, however, the OGPU concluded that the Papacy posed an international threat and that the proceedings inside the Vatican were worth as much attention as those inside St. Louis-des-Français.

A series of events encouraged the Soviet authorities to direct attention to Rome. In June 1926 Pope Pius XI announced the formation of a special Vatican office, the Commission for Russia (Pro Russia), to deal with Russian affairs under the direction of Michel d'Herbigny. Coming only a few weeks before d'Herbigny's third (and last) visit to the Soviet Union and placed in the context of the French Jesuit's clandestine activity, this announcement may have struck the suspicious (not to say paranoid) minds inside the Kremlin as a preliminary step toward an organizational framework for future clandestine operations against the Soviet state. The same minds, whose own clandestine experience and doctrine predisposed them to assume that any secretive activity must be directed toward espionage or political subversion, readily interpreted d'Herbigny's visits, with their secret meetings to consecrate new bishops, as little more than missions to establish spy networks and counterrevolutionary cells. Suspicions were only fueled when, in 1929, the Vatican established the Russicum, a pontifical college in Rome devoted to preparing priests for future missionary work in the Soviet Union. The new college's program of study, with its emphasis on total immersion in Russian language, history, and culture (to the point where the students spoke only Russian and affected the long beards of Russian Orthodox clergy), probably raised eyebrows in the offices of the OGPU, where intelligence officers may have wondered if this was a seminary or a training school for spies. Michel d'Herbigny did not help matters with his indiscreet talk in Roman salons and ecclesiastical offices of reconverting Russia. At one diplomatic reception he startled the guests by asking the Polish military attaché about the possibility of parachuting priests into the Soviet Union.[17]

Suspicious minds would also have been alarmed when, in 1929, the Vatican and Italy signed the Lateran Agreements, a series of accords that settled the Roman Question and seemed to indicate that the Papacy had come to an understanding with the Fascist regime of Benito Mussolini. Coming on the heels of agreements with Poland (1925), Lithuania and Romania (1927), and Czechoslovakia (1928), the Lateran accords suggested that the Vatican was aligning itself with a variety of states, some of which (Poland and Italy) were strongly anti-Soviet, and all of which had reason to fear and contain a strong Russia. Suspicions peaked in February 1930 when Pope Pius decided to speak out publicly against the religious persecution inside the Soviet Union. In a strongly worded statement (composed by d'Herbigny), the pontiff roundly condemned the "vicious attacks" by the Bolsheviks and reproached those European governments that ignored the suffering of believers in their opportunistic pursuit of diplomatic and trade relations with the Soviet Union. In an appeal that found an echo in the pulpits of Protestant chapels and churches across Europe, Pius proclaimed a "crusade of prayer" against the godless regime in Moscow.[18]

For a regime that was inclined to think of itself as perpetually embattled against a host of hostile, capitalist states, the pope's words rang alarms. Moscow heard the call for a crusade and dismissed the distinction between a spiritual crusade and a political crusade as irrelevant. The situation clearly called for defensive measures. Although the party paper *Izvestia* defiantly proclaimed, "The Pope is assuming the role intended for him by the international plutocracy as leader in the struggle against the Soviet Union," and party agitators organized mass protests against religion in general and the Papacy in particular, the regime temporarily scaled back the administrative and police harassment of believers.[19] It also took steps to improve its intelligence coverage of the Vatican.

Apparently the OGPU had no sources reporting from the Vatican in the 1920s. When it tried to remedy this deficiency after 1930, it encountered particular problems. The ecclesiastical denizens of the papal administration loathed Communism and its works and were inclined to consider its representatives as quite literally the minions of the devil. In countries such as Britain, France, Germany, and the United States, Soviet intelligence could rely on local Communist parties for assistance, but this expedient was out of the question at the Vatican. Expatriate Russians might be convinced to serve the motherland, either from misplaced patriotism or for fear of police reprisals against relatives inside the Soviet Union, but there were precious few Russians circulating in Vatican circles. One of these few, however, was close to Michel d'Herbigny and the pontifical Commission for Russia.

Alexander Deubner was born in St. Petersburg in 1899. His father, an official in the czarist government who had secretly converted from Russian Orthodoxy to Roman Catholicism, sent him to Belgium to be educated by the Assumptionist Fathers, a religious order with particular connections to Russia. In 1921 the Assumptionists transferred Deubner to their seminary in Turkey to prepare for the priesthood and a missionary career. After five years of study, however, he was dismissed from the seminary, the reverend fathers having decided that he was unsuited for the priestly life. With neither money nor prospects, the ex-seminarian drifted about, ending up in Poland, where Archbishop Andreas Sheptyckyi, a prominent prelate and old friend of his father, agreed to ordain him. The archbishop then assigned Deubner to a Russian émigré congregation in Nice, but the new priest went instead to Paris, where he unaccountably converted to Russian Orthodoxy. This religious enthusiasm lasted only a brief time; by 1928 he had repented his apostasy and relocated to Rome. Once again Archbishop Sheptyckyi intervened on behalf of his protégé and eventually arranged for Michel d'Herbigny to give him a post as a research assistant at the newly opened Russicum. The new researcher must have impressed d'Herbigny because the Vatican's resident Soviet expert invited the young Russian to coauthor with him a monograph on Russian Orthodox bishops; soon Deubner was acting as d'Herbigny's aide in matters concerning the Vatican's Commission for Russia. In the summer of 1932 d'Herbigny entrusted him with a confidential mission to report on ecclesiastical affairs in Poland. This is where things began to go wrong.

For some time Bishop d'Herbigny had been convinced that, despite the Bolshevik dictatorship, the religious conversion of Russia was possible, but only if the Vatican was prepared to adapt its religious customs and practices to Russian culture in every respect except dogma. To be successful in Russia, Catholicism had to mask its Latin face and become "Russified." This approach was very controversial, not only among traditionalists, who opposed any change in customary practices but also in Poland, where the national identity was intricately connected with *Roman* Catholicism. Most of the Catholics in the Soviet Union were ethnic Poles caught by history on the wrong side of the border, and Warsaw saw Russification, even in the name of religion, as a device to distance these "separated brethren" from their national origins and culture and assimilate them into Russian society. Since the Soviets were seeking to do just that, d'Herbigny's approach seemed to be playing into the Communists' hands. As far as Warsaw was concerned, the Soviets had to be fought, not converted. D'Herbigny and his Commission for Russia were seen as a threat to Polish interests, and senior Polish prelates worked diligently to undermine the French Jesuit and confound his schemes.

During his visit to Poland, Alexander Deubner attracted the attention of the security police, who were interested not only in his connections with d'Herbigny but also in his connections with the Soviet Union. Deubner's father had been arrested by the Bolsheviks shortly after the Revolution and sent to Siberia. His French mother lived in Moscow, as did his aunt, who actually had a flat inside the Kremlin, where her husband (Deubner's uncle and the son of the prominent German Communist Clara Zetkin) worked for the regime. There was also the interesting fact that while traveling to Poland d'Herbigny's representative had stopped for a time in Berlin, where he met Clara Zetkin and struck up a friendship (purely platonic, according to the young priest) with a young woman who worked for the German police. These disparate facts formed no particular pattern, but they were enough to arouse the suspicions of the Polish police, who refused to extend Deubner's visa and required him to leave the country.[20]

Deubner returned to Rome at the end of 1932 just in time to assume a central role in an emerging espionage scandal. Diplomatic and ecclesiastical circles were abuzz with rumors that secret documents had been stolen from the files of the papal Commission for Russia, and the press was pursuing the story. Deubner's name did not feature in these rumors, but the young priest, who had hardly unpacked from his trip to Poland, suddenly fled Rome without a word of explanation to anyone, including his superior and patron, Michel d'Herbigny. It seemed an admission of guilt, and newspapers across Europe went wild: "Soviet Spy Deubner Flees the Vatican"; "D'Herbigny's Secretary a GPU Agent"; "To Moscow with Stolen Files."[21] In fact the young priest fled to Berlin with a suitcase of clothes. In times of trouble Deubner's invariable practice was to turn for advice to a priest, preferably one with connections. This time the choice was Father Eduard Gehrmann, onetime director of the pontifical relief mission to Russia, who was serving as a special adviser on Russian affairs to the papal nuncio in

Berlin. Gehrmann was surprised to find the alleged spy on his doorstep, and even more surprised when Deubner confessed that he had come to Berlin to marry the young woman he had met on his recent trip to Poland. Since Deubner was an ordained priest, this purpose further complicated an already knotty situation. Gehrmann urged the hapless fugitive to reconsider his situation and arranged for the Jesuits in Berlin to take him into one of their houses. Deubner did not stay long.

In late February 1933 a Communist allegedly set fire to the Reichstag (the German parliament) and sparked a political as well as material conflagration. Adolf Hitler had just come to power, and the Nazis, seizing the opportunity to smash once and for all the hostile German Communist Party, launched a ruthless dragnet that netted more than a thousand party members or alleged sympathizers in twenty-four hours. Within days of this anti-Communist sweep, Deubner fled Berlin. He did not get far. Apparently he was on a police watch list because as he attempted to cross into Austria, he was arrested by German border guards "on suspicion of political intrigues." Incarcerated for more than two months while the police investigated his case, Deubner was eventually released in late May when the authorities could turn up no evidence of any connections with Soviet intelligence. The peripatetic priest next surfaced in Yugoslavia, where he sought out Bishop Franz Grivec, an expert on the Russian church, who helped him compose a press release denying the accusations of espionage and advised him to return to Rome.[22]

Through all the accusations and rumors that attended Deubner's movements, the Vatican had tried to minimize the affair by denying that secret documents were missing and insisting that Father Deubner was merely a temporary, and not very important, employee of the Commission for Russia. Both of these statements were false, but papal authorities probably assumed that without further fuel the scandal would burn itself out. Deubner's reappearance in Rome in July 1933, just as things were quieting down, must have surprised and embarrassed these authorities. Michel d'Herbigny hustled his repentant aide off to a monastery to reflect on his actions, perform penance, and, above all, remain out of sight. Predictably, whatever resolution the penitent might have had to return to the priestly path soon dissipated. In the fall of 1933 he abruptly fled the monastery and walked the seventy miles to Rome. If he hoped to return to the good graces of Bishop d'Herbigny, he was sadly disappointed; his patron, the powerful director of the Commission for Russia and sometime papal secret agent, had been driven from Rome in disgrace.

Michel d'Herbigny had made many enemies who resented his celebrity status in Roman society, his influence over Pope Pius, and his romantic vision of reconverting Russia. By 1933 these enemies were increasingly numerous and powerful, and they worked assiduously to undermine the position of the French Jesuit. Polish bishops, who detested d'Herbigny and all his works, were especially active in this regard, and they had an influential ally in their fellow countryman Vladimir Ledochowski, the Father General of the Jesuit order and d'Herbigny's religious superior. The sequence of events remains shrouded in secrecy, but on 29 September 1933, during their regular weekly meeting, Pope Pius put aside some photos of priests in Soviet labor camps that had arrived from Moscow in Bishop Neveu's latest packet. Without preamble he told his Soviet expert that he had been informed by Father Ledochowski that d'Herbigny required rest and perhaps surgery for a serious medical condition and that he would be leaving within a few days for an indeterminate stay at a Belgian clinic. This was news to d'Herbigny, whose health was sound save for some troublesome hemorrhoids, but he was bound, as were all Jesuits, to obey without question the will of the Holy Father, and he recognized an order when it was given. Three days later d'Herbigny departed for Brussels to await the pope's pleasure. Any hope he may have had of returning to Rome ended in late October when he received a preemptory letter from the Jesuit father general, Father Ledochowski, stating that it would be "convenient" for the Vatican to receive his resignation from all his positions. Ever dutiful and obedient, d'Herbigny complied with this request.[23] Until his death in 1957 he lived in isolated Jesuit houses, prohibited by his superiors from publishing or speaking publicly. He never returned to Rome and never again held a position of responsibility in his order or his Church.

Arriving in Rome penniless and without prospects, only to find his patron disgraced and banished, Alexander Deubner had recourse to his usual emergency procedure: he threw himself on the mercy of priests, whose charitable impulses outweighed any suspicions they may have had concerning the purposes and character of the petitioner at their door. Clerical friends found Deubner a bed in a public dormitory for the indigent and provided small sums of money for food, clothes, and other necessities. After only a brief stay in the hostel, however, Deubner found the means to rent a private flat. He explained to his benefactors that he had secured a job in the library of the Pontifical Institute for Eastern Studies and required no more assistance. This story may have satisfied Deubner's friends, but the Italian police did not buy it.

Recalling the accusations of espionage that attended his flight from Rome the previous December, security authorities had placed Deubner under surveillance when he reappeared in the Italian capital. The surveillance turned up some interesting facts. Soon after his arrival in September, Deubner visited the Russian embassy, usually not a popular venue for Catholic priests. Then there was the matter of his new job at the Pontifical Institute for Eastern Studies. The police discovered that, despite his claims, Deubner was not employed in the institute's library and that he merely frequented its reading room and charged out books. Though he now lived in a private apartment, he had no visible source of income. All this was suspicious; what followed was damning. Informants reported that the priest had visited the Russian embassy to apply for permission to return to the Soviet Union. The Russians, who were aware of their countryman's past connections with the recently departed d'Herbigny and the papal Commission for Russia, refused to issue the necessary travel documents but instead offered the priest a monthly stipend if he agreed to collect information concerning personalities and activities inside the Vatican. Deubner accepted the offer.[24]

Italian police authorities considered alerting the Vatican to Deubner's connections with Russian intelligence, but they decided instead to expel the errant priest from Italy. Expulsion was delayed for several months by bureaucratic red tape as the Division of Political Police exchanged memorandums and agent reports with the Division for Confidential Affairs, which, in turn, communicated with the Frontier Police. The Soviet embassy also intervened with a request that the police suspend any action until arrangements for Deubner's repatriation to the Soviet Union could be finalized. Of course, the Russians had no interest in returning their informant to his homeland. They needed Deubner near the Vatican and simply hoped to delay his expulsion as long as possible by creating imaginary administrative proceedings in Moscow. Unfortunately, action could not be delayed indefinitely. In late 1934, the Italian police escorted Deubner to the French border.[25]

Alexander Deubner was definitely a Soviet agent in the fall of 1933, but by then he had no position at the Vatican and access to neither documents nor deliberations of the papal Commission for Russia, the principal target for Soviet intelligence in the early 1930s. He would have been, at best, a minor source. Was he working for the Russians in 1932 when confidential documents went missing from the files of Pro Russia? Probably. His precipitous flight from Rome when the loss was discovered suggests guilt, although it does not prove it. More damning was his admission to a journalist in Paris after his expulsion from Italy that he passed information to the Russians while in Vatican service.[26] After his flight from Rome he never again worked for the Vatican, so his confession must refer to the period leading up to the scandal of the missing documents. Deubner may have agreed to work for Soviet intelligence to protect his family in Russia. It may be more than a coincidence that his mother, who had lived undisturbed in Moscow since the Bolshevik Revolution and the arrest of his father, was arrested by the secret police in 1934, shortly after Deubner was expelled from Italy and lost whatever value he still had for the OGPU. Soon thereafter, his father, who had for years been an inmate of a labor camp, was executed by the secret police, although the official notice said he had been killed by marauding bandits who, the family was supposed to believe, were so dim-witted that they attacked a slave labor camp to rob and murder the wretched prisoners.

Moscow recruited another source inside the Commission for Russia, but it is unlikely that he passed documents to Soviet intelligence in 1932. Monsignor Eduard Prettner-Cippico entered Vatican service as an archivist in the Commission for Russia in late 1932, just as the affair of the missing files surfaced and Deubner fled Rome. He later worked in a similar capacity in the papal secretariat of state until 1948, when he was dismissed from papal service, allegedly for illegal financial dealings. At some point in his career he began photographing documents and passing the prints to Soviet intelligence. If Monsignor Prettner-Cippico, not Father Deubner, was the agent behind the espionage scandal of late 1932, he would have had to have started his work for Moscow almost from his first day in the Vatican. This is possible, but it is more likely that Prettner-Cippico was recruited later by the Russians, perhaps as a substitute for the departed and discredited Deubner.[27]

Just as the Vatican silently applauded the fall of the czar, so, too, did it greet the rise of Mussolini and Fascism with cautious optimism. Italy had fought with the Allies in World War I, but in the immediate postwar period it seemed more a victim than a victor of the conflict. Disappointed by its failure at the Versailles peace conference to secure its territorial ambitions, weakened by the economic dislocations of the war, racked by increasingly violent class conflict, and administered by a corrupt and discredited political class that placed personal advantage over the public good, Italy drifted politically from crisis to crisis. In the elections of 1921 Giovanni Giolitti, the prime minister and chief of the liberal party, arranged an electoral alliance with Benito Mussolini, the fiery journalist who had led a new political movement, the so-called Fascists, from the margins to the center of Italian political life. Until then the highly chauvinistic and nationalistic Fascists (who favored black shirts and black ties, with pistols, clubs, and daggers as accessories) had largely limited their political activity to street fighting and strong-arm tactics against their opponents, but the election gave them thirty-five seats in parliament and a new legitimacy. Giolitti and his successor as prime minister, Ivanoe Bonomi, tolerated Fascist violence because they needed Mussolini's political support and because they believed they could control him. They were wrong.

Political violence (largely fueled by the Fascists) escalated, and the police often looked the other way. Parliamentary government could neither maintain order nor articulate a coherent and compelling strategy to deal with the country's ills. Since liberals and moderates seemed paralyzed politically by fear or personal feuds, many non-Fascist conservatives in the royal court, the military and police, the civil administration, the business sector, and the Catholic Church began to see Mussolini as the only personality who could end the disorder and return the country to peace and stability. The Fascist leader openly scorned the ineffective government and flaunted the lawlessness of his "blackshirts." On 24 October 1922 he addressed a mass rally of armed followers and boldly proclaimed his intention to march on Rome and seize the reins of power. As Fascist squadrons mobilized across the country and violence flared anew in northern and central Italy, the government lost its nerve. Although the general commanding the garrison in Rome assured the government that he would happily and easily deal with the Fascists and their upstart leader, King Vittorio Emanuele III, recoiling from the prospect of bloodshed and fearing that at the hour of crisis the army would not defend his throne, refused to sign a decree imposing martial law. In fact, the heralded "march on Rome" was largely a bluff, and the ill-disciplined and poorly armed blackshirts would have collapsed in the face of resolute authority. The king compounded his initial mistake by meekly acceding to Mussolini's demand that he be appointed prime minister with the power to form a new government.

Although his first cabinet contained representatives of all political groups except the Socialists, Mussolini made it clear that Fascism was in power and would tolerate no opposition. With little or no protest from other political parties or from other political institutions such as parliament, the monarchy, or the military, he instituted a series of repressive measures that emasculated the legislature, curbed the press, marginalized the king, flouted the constitution, elevated political violence to a routine instrument of politics, and set Italy on an increasingly authoritarian path. The handful of brave individuals who raised their voices in protest, such as the parliamentarian Giacomo Matteotti, were physically intimidated into silence or (as was the fate of Matteotti) simply murdered. By 1926 the "Duce," Mussolini's preferred title, was the undisputed dictator of Italy.[28]

Like other institutions in Italian life, the Vatican made little protest against the imposition of an authoritarian state, although it deplored the "excesses" that were a disturbing feature of that state. A fundamentally conservative institution, it viewed with trepidation the social and political disorder of the postwar years and (with the experience of Russia firmly in mind) by 1922 had come to believe that a firm hand on the rudder was necessary if the Italian ship of state was to sail safely between the Scylla of social anarchy and the Charybdis of leftist political revolution. The Vatican viewed the "march on Rome" with some satisfaction, believing that among the leading political personalities Mussolini was most likely to provide that firm hand.

The view from the papal palace was also influenced by the fact that the aspiring dictator actively courted the Papacy's support. Early in his career, during the radical Socialist phase of his political development, Mussolini had been an enthusiastic anticlerical, writing scurrilous polemics against religion and publicly describing priests as "black microbes who are as fatal to mankind as tuberculosis germs."[29] The early manifestos of the Fascist movement were also explicitly anticlerical, calling for the expropriation of Church property and the eradication of religious influence from Italian society. These positions, both personal and organizational, were cast aside by 1922 as Mussolini and his movement sought the favor of the Vatican in order to bolster their political position at home and abroad. Upon assuming power, the Duce impressed the Vatican with several pro-Church measures, including the introduction of religious education in state primary schools, the placement of crucifixes in public buildings, the provision of state funds for the restoration of churches, and state intervention to rescue the tottering Banco di Roma, an institution in which the Vatican had a significant financial interest. Most important, he demonstrated a firm intention to settle once and for all the Roman Question, the contentious issue of regularizing the pope's status in Italy in such a way that guaranteed his independence. Since the occupation of papal Rome by Italian troops in 1870, this issue had poisoned relations between the Papacy and the Italian government and had been the cause of no end of recrimination and suspicion. By the mid-1920s both sides were ready for a settlement. Fascist and papal representatives began preliminary exchanges on the subject in the summer of 1926, and these unofficial talks continued in great secrecy until the fall of 1928, when sufficient progress had been made that both sides were prepared to announce "official" negotiations. The negotiations culminated in February 1929 when Cardinal Pietro Gasparri and Benito Mussolini signed the so-called Lateran Agreements, three documents that established Vatican City as an independent and neutral state, regulated church-state relations in Italy, and provided the Vatican financial compensation for the loss of the Papal States in the preceding century.[30]

Even before the Lateran Agreements, the Vatican had taken steps to defuse Catholic political opposition to the emerging dictatorship that was so willing to accommodate Church interests. Mussolini had hardly announced his first pro-Church measures when the papal secretariat of state began to press the Partito Populare Italiano (Popular Party), a Catholic political party founded shortly after the war and led by an anti-Fascist priest, Luigi Sturzo, to adopt a more conciliatory attitude toward the Fascist regime. In 1923 the Vatican required Sturzo to resign from the party and quietly leave Italy. The following year it forbade priests to belong to political parties, and it publicly distanced itself from the Popular Party, which finally collapsed in 1926. The Vatican also refrained from criticizing Mussolini for the political terrorism unleashed by the Fascists against their enemies. During the so-called Matteotti Crisis of 1924, when the public outcry against the murder of the anti-Fascist politician shook the regime, the Vatican deplored the murder but declined to blame the Duce and urged an end to allegations and recriminations.[31]

Assuming (somewhat unimaginatively) that Italy faced a choice between social chaos or Fascist authoritarianism, the Papacy initially bet on dictatorship as the lesser of two evils. The general détente in Church-state relations in the 1920s, culminating in the Lateran Agreements, suggested that the pope and his advisers had wagered wisely. They were soon disabused of this attitude. For Mussolini, accommodation with the Catholic Church was simply a means to an end. The dictator wanted to harness the Vatican to Fascism in order to buttress the legitimacy of his regime at home and abroad and disarm a potentially significant political opponent.

The ink was hardly dry on the ceremonial copies of the Lateran Agreements before the Duce adopted a more hostile and polemical tone in his public references to religion, while his government launched an attack against Catholic Action, an umbrella organization that supervised a variety of Catholic lay associations such as Catholic boy scouts and Catholic university students. Catholic Action had been organized to invest Italian associational and professional life with Christian principles, but with the collapse of the traditional political parties and the "fascisization" of youth, student, and professional groups, it remained the only independent organization in the country and as such became a home for opponents of the regime. The Fascist attack on Catholic Action, and the broader threat to the independence of the church represented by that attack, compelled Pope

Pius XI in June 1931 to issue an encyclical, *Non abbiamo bisogno,* criticizing the regime's assault on Catholic associations, rejecting its claim to control all aspects of private life, and condemning the glorification of the state and the cult of violence.

The conflict over Catholic Action was eventually defused by an agreement that allowed the organization to continue but with a focus on spiritual and religious purposes and an explicit prohibition on political action broadly defined, but the "Crisis of 1931" set the pattern for Church-state relations in the 1930s. The Papacy and the Fascist regime coexisted in an uneasy relationship marked by tension and distrust.

Unlike the Bolsheviks, when the Fascists seized power, they did not have to scramble to organize intelligence coverage of the Papacy. Italian intelligence agencies had closely monitored the Vatican since the Kingdom of Italy established itself in Rome in 1870, and the informant networks that permeated the papal palaces were now at the service of the new regime. Under the Fascists, espionage against the Vatican actually intensified, in part because of the insatiable appetite for information about real or imagined opponents that is a characteristic of every modern authoritarian regime, and in part because several additional intelligence agencies took the field after 1922 to feed that appetite. Traditionally the police service had monopolized espionage against the Vatican, although the military became involved in certain operations (e.g., codebreaking) during the First World War. Under Mussolini, however, agencies as disparate as the foreign ministry, the ministry of popular culture, and the dictator's private office took an active interest in what went on in the shadow of St. Peter's Basilica.

Between 1922 and 1939, Italian intelligence interest in the Papacy focused primarily on tracking the Vatican's attitude toward the Fascist regime and its policies. Mussolini realized that a hostile Vatican could seriously challenge his authoritarian rule and complicate his effort to expand Italian influence in the Mediterranean and beyond. To deter this challenge, the Duce's intelligence officers had to collect enough information to allow the regime to anticipate the reaction of Pope Pius XI and his cardinal secretary of state to regime initiatives, such as the assault on Catholic Action; assess the political sympathies of the various cardinals (especially those considered in the running to succeed Pius); and monitor the activities and influence of known anti-Fascists inside the Vatican, particularly those in a position to influence Catholic opinion in Italy and abroad. Secondarily, Italian intelligence focused on monitoring the Vatican's relations with those powers, such as France, Germany, Spain, or Yugoslavia, that figured prominently in Fascist foreign policy. Operationally, this required access to the papal secretariat of state and to those prelates who were in a position to influence the Papacy's diplomacy.

The identities of most Italian agents inside the Vatican and the precise character and extent of the Italian networks working against the Papacy are obscured by a fog of pseudonyms ("Diana," "195") and unsigned intelligence reports, but it is possible to discern in the mist their general outlines. It is apparent that Fascist intelligence had no one in the immediate circle of the pope. It is also clear that no cardinal or senior official consciously worked for Italian intelligence, although their comments and observations were often reported by acquaintances, subordinates, or servants who did. The Italian agents inside the Vatican were mainly junior officials in the papal administration, journalists, or denizens of "black society," the group of aristocrats, would-be aristocrats, businessmen, and Catholic expatriates who visited and entertained along the fringes of ecclesiastical society.

Monsignor Enrico Pucci straddled the worlds of journalism and papal administration. Although his position was never formalized, Monsignor Pucci was effectively the press officer for the Vatican. He wrote and published a regular newsletter that covered events and personalities inside the Vatican, and he sold that newsletter to any individual or organization that needed to keep up with affairs inside the pope's city-state. He also worked as a freelance journalist, writing articles on papal affairs for newspapers in Italy and abroad. Because of his apparent access and expertise, journalists often approached him with inquiries concerning a particular cardinal or a particular papal policy. By the late 1920s, Pucci had become the unofficial spokesman for the Vatican. Aware of his newsletter and his wide contacts among Italian and foreign correspondents, papal authorities frequently turned to him when they wished unofficially to leak information to the press or place a particular story in circulation.

Strolling the corridors and courtyards of the apostolic palace, popping into the anterooms of the various congregations to chat up the *minutanti* and *addetti* at their desks, dropping into the café for coffee and conversation with clerks from the archive or copyeditors from *L'Osservatore Romano,* stopping on his way home for a few words with the Swiss Guards on duty at the Porta Santa Anna, Pucci was constantly on the prowl for the latest rumor, gossip, or inside tip. Some of this information went into his newsletter for distribution to his subscribers, but the best items, the secrets and surprises he uncovered in the corridors, antechambers, cafés, and streets of Vatican City, he kept back for some very special clients.

Enrico Pucci was one of Italy's more important agents inside the Vatican. He had been personally recruited in 1927 by Arturo Bocchini, the chief of police, and though his political sympathies were pro-Fascist, his motives were always financial rather than ideological. Reporting as agent "96," Pucci passed to police intelligence information on a variety of topics from the health of the pope to developments inside the secretariat of state. Occasionally the monsignor bypassed police channels and reported information directly to the private office of Mussolini. In the spring of 1929, for example, Pucci secured for Mussolini the text of Cardinal Bonaventura Cerretti's private memoir of his secret negotiations with Prime Minister Orlando in a futile attempt to settle the Roman Question in 1919. At a time when the Fascist leader was coming under fire from anticlericals for allegedly betraying the spirit of 1870 by signing the Lateran Agreements, evidence that pre-Fascist cabinets had also negotiated with the Vatican was a useful and timely political tool to disarm his critics. It is not clear if Bocchini was aware of Pucci's separate arrangement with the Duce, although the police director was aware that his industrious agent had a sideline selling information to various foreign embassies in Rome.[32]

Rumors of Pucci's work for Italian intelligence must have reached papal authorities, but apparently they did nothing to interrupt his trade in information. Of course the Vatican was notoriously lax in matters of internal security, and it lacked the capacity to investigate any rumors or allegations of espionage. Monsignor Pucci may also have had a powerful protector. The Italian police received certain confidential reports that connected the monsignor with Cardinal Gasparri, the influential secretary of state, while other reports suggested that he received special protection from unnamed patrons.[33] It may also be possible that the Vatican was aware of Pucci's activity and turned it to its own purposes. Perhaps he was a back channel through which the Vatican received from the Italian police information too confidential for more routine channels, or perhaps the secretariat of state, aware of his contacts with the police and foreign embassies, used him to plant stories and thereby manipulate the impressions that other governments had of papal policies. Whatever his true role, Enrico Pucci survived the Fascist regime he served and was still peddling his news bulletin in the late 1940s.

Enrico Pucci was a rare example of the Italians recruiting a priest to spy on the Vatican; more commonly, they sought out well-placed lay employees of the papal state. Stanislao Caterini, Giovanni Fazio, and Virgilio Scattolini were examples of middle-level papal officials who worked for Italian intelligence. Caterini, a longtime employee of the secretariat of state, was recruited in 1929. He was probably one of Italy's most important sources inside the Vatican, since his duties in the secretariat of state included work in the cipher office, where he was in a position to provide his controllers in

Italian intelligence information concerning papal ciphers and communications procedures.[34] He was summarily dismissed from papal service in 1931, almost certainly because evidence of his betrayal reached his superiors. Giovanni Fazio was a senior officer in the Vatican police (and the son-in-law of its commander), a position with access to certain confidential information, including particulars of the limited security procedures in effect inside the papal palace. Recruited in 1929, he served Italian intelligence until 1942, when he, too, was suddenly dismissed. Virgilio Scattolini was a journalist and the assistant to Monsignor Mario Boehm, the editor in chief of L'Osservatore Romano, in the late 1930s. He was recruited by the police to report on the activities of the circle of anti-Fascist journalists, including Monsignor Boehm, who worked for the Vatican daily under the protection of its director, Count Giuseppe Dalla Torre. Scattolini left Vatican service, perhaps of his own free will, in 1939.[35]

Besides the several spies who worked inside the Vatican, Italian intelligence used a number of sources that were not employed in the papal administration but were close to individuals who were. A few of these sources, such as the journalist and film critic Iacopo Comin, have been identified. Comin had many contacts in the French community in Rome, including friends in the French embassy, and he used these contacts to monitor the activities of Bishop Michel d'Herbigny in the late 1920s and early 1930s. Italian intelligence was very interested in d'Herbigny, believing (incorrectly) that the French Jesuit used his position as director of the papal Commission for Russia to maintain a vast espionage network in the Soviet Union and eastern Europe that he placed at the service of France, Italy's competitor for influence in countries such as Poland, Yugoslavia, and Romania.[36]

Tommaso Arrigo Pozzi was another journalist who wrote for the police as well as the newspapers. A former member of the Catholic Popular Party and a frequent contributor to the Catholic press, Pozzi was well-known in ecclesiastical circles in Rome and other Italian cities. He was the principal source of intelligence on Father Agostino Gemelli, the founder of the Catholic University of Milan and a leading Catholic intellectual. He also filled the police files with reports on Monsignor Celso Costantini, the former papal delegate to China, and since 1935 the pro-Fascist executive secretary of the Congregation for the Propagation of the Faith (Propaganda Fide), the department responsible for missionary affairs. Since the Fascists hoped to extend Italy's influence in Africa and the Near East through Italian missionaries and their schools and hospitals, the affairs of Propaganda Fide greatly interested Italian intelligence.[37]

Most of these peripheral sources, however, remain unidentified. For example, Italian intelligence had two sources close to a bitter and aggrieved Cardinal Pietro Gasparri in the months after the elderly secretary of state was pushed into retirement in 1930, but these sources are hidden behind the code numbers "35" and "40." Similarly, someone was close enough to Monsignor Luigi Maglione, the nuncio in Paris from 1926 to 1935, to report the papal diplomat's increasing disenchantment with Fascism, but this source remains unidentified.[38] These anonymous sources—journalists, academicians, socialites, servants—in their unknown numbers make it impossible to detail the scope of Italian intelligence coverage of the Papacy between the world wars.

In the 1920s and 1930s informants remained the principal source of information on the Vatican for Italian intelligence, but their information was usually secondhand ("Monsignor X told me . . .") or thirdhand ("Monsignor X reports that Cardinal Y said . . .") and often unreliable. Quite innocently, stories might be garbled in the telling and retelling. From fear or a desire to please, agents might embellish their reports or, in extreme cases, make them up out of whole cloth. Avaricious sources might even market their information to several "customers." Information collected through the surveillance of communications avoided most, if not all, of these traps. Clandestine mail, telephone, and telegraph intercepts allowed intelligence authorities to eavesdrop directly on papal officials as they communicated with each other. So long as the targets remained ignorant of the surveillance, the information collected was free from distortion and contrivance. Also phone taps, unlike informants, did not demand more money, throw temper tantrums, suffer fits of remorse, or decide suddenly to live with an elderly mother in Palermo.

Although papal operators routed calls within Vatican City, all telephone connections between the papal city-state and the world beyond St. Peter's Square passed through Italian switchboards and along Italian lines. Since most papal officials, including the vast majority of the cardinals attached to the Curia, lived not in the Vatican but in the Borgo, Trastevere, Monte Mario, or other districts of Rome, the telephone lines running over the high walls of the pope's domain or between the apartments of prelates and papal functionaries were always alive with business and social calls. Italian intelligence had never been able to resist eavesdropping on these conversations, but surveillance increased dramatically under Mussolini.[39] The listening service in the Ministry of the Interior monitored the telephone conversations of Father Pietro Tacchi Venturi, the Jesuit priest who often served as a confidential channel between the Vatican and the Fascist regime; Monsignors

Giuseppe Pizzardo and Alfredo Ottaviani, senior officers in the papal secretariat of state; the director of *L'Osservatore Romano* and the editor of *Civiltà Cattolica*, the Jesuit journal that was widely believed to reflect the posture of the secretariat of state; and various clerics associated with Catholic Action. The listeners also targeted several cardinals. Most of the conversations recorded were purely social and without intelligence value, but occasionally there were useful items. During the discussions preceding the Lateran Agreements, phone intercepts provided Mussolini with insights into the Vatican's negotiating strategy and the attitudes of the pope and his cardinal advisers. For example, in January 1929, as the two sides were haggling over the borders of the proposed Vatican territory and the amount to be paid the Vatican in compensation for the papal lands absorbed by the Kingdom of Italy in the nineteenth century, the eavesdroppers recorded a conversation between Cardinal Granito Pignatelli di Belmonte and Father Tacchi Venturi. The cardinal reported that he had just visited Cardinal Secretary of State Gasparri, who had revealed that the pope was impatient for an agreement and was willing to be more flexible in the negotiations in order to secure one.[40]

Telephone conversations were not the only communications vulnerable to surveillance. Most Vatican mail and (until 1931, when Vatican Radio was established) all Vatican telegrams passed through Italian post offices and telegraph offices. Since the Vatican had no regular courier system of its own, the secretariat of state entrusted its diplomatic mail to the Italian foreign ministry for delivery by Italian diplomatic couriers. During the First World War, despite assurances from the Italian government, papal mail, both ordinary and official, had been subject to at least occasional surveillance, and the practice continued when the Fascists came to power. In the spring of 1930, for example, Italian intelligence copied a dispatch from Monsignor Maglione, the nuncio in Paris, to Cardinal Gasparri detailing the French government's attitude toward Italian efforts to suppress anti-Fascist exiles in France.[41] The Vatican certainly did not trust postal channels. When it had especially sensitive correspondence, it entrusted the letters to a bishop or priest who was traveling to or through the city of the addressee.

Before 1931 the Vatican had no radio or cable facilities, so incoming and outgoing telegrams were consigned to Italian offices. This process was insecure, since the telegraph and cable offices routinely passed copies of all foreign diplomatic telegrams (including those of the papal secretariat of state) to military intelligence, the Servizio Informazioni Militari (SIM). When Vatican Radio went on the air in 1931, the situation did not improve. SIM's main radio intercept station, Forte Boccea, was within sight of Vatican

Radio's antenna and easily scooped from the ether all radio messages transmitted or received by the pope's station. Like other governments, the Vatican enciphered its confidential communications in order to escape the surveillance of organizations such as SIM. The effort was not entirely successful. During the First World War Italian codebreakers had cracked several papal ciphers, and they registered similar successes in the 1920s and 1930s.[42] Their work was probably made easier by Stanislao Caterini, the Italian spy inside the papal secretariat of state, who had access to the secretariat's cipher office and its cabinet of codebooks and cipher tables.

In the years between the world wars, Italian intelligence enveloped the Vatican in a web of agents, informants, and eavesdroppers. As should be expected, the intelligence collected by this network (like that collected by any espionage network) varied greatly in quality. Inevitably, many items, such as a report that Cardinal X was departing for a visit to Madrid or that Cardinal Y was a learned student of church law, were trivial. Some, such as the claim that Michel d'Herbigny was running a vast espionage operation in eastern Europe, were wildly inaccurate. Occasionally, the sources failed to provide warning of an important development, such as Pius XI's antiregime encyclical, *Non abbiamo bisogno*. In general, however, Italian intelligence provided Mussolini and his regime with a copious and steady flow of information from inside the Vatican. In dealing with the Papacy, no other world leader, not even the powerful German dictator, Adolf Hitler, could boast of such an advantage.

When, after his rise to power in 1933, Adolf Hitler turned his attention to the Papacy, he found that Germany had few intelligence sources at the Vatican. Under the so-called Weimar Republic (the democratic government established in Germany after the First World War and named for the Thuringian city that was its capital), German intelligence capabilities were much reduced. There was no civilian foreign intelligence service, and the minuscule intelligence office tucked away in the "Troops Department" of the small post-Versailles German army focused on military intelligence from Poland, Russia, and France.[43] Weimar was diplomatically engaged with the Papacy on a variety of fronts, but for intelligence on papal attitudes and intentions it had to rely almost exclusively on its embassy to the Holy See. The ambassador, Diego von Bergen, was an accomplished and respected professional who before the war had served in the old Prussian embassy to the Holy See, but for inside information on papal affairs the embassy relied on Monsignor Rudolf Steinmann, the embassy's ecclesiastical counselor. Ostensibly, Steinmann advised the German embassy on fine points of church doctrine and ecclesiastical law, but with his soutane and clerical collar he could mingle in ecclesiastical circles more easily than the ambassador, who was a Protestant, as were most of his staff.[44] Monsignor Steinmann's contacts inside the Vatican were aware of his position at the German embassy, so his information gathering was largely overt. Weimar's only clandestine source for papal affairs was Father Eduard Gehrmann, the German priest who for a time directed the short-lived pontifical relief mission to the Soviet Union. After the recall of the mission and a brief sojourn in Rome to report on his impressions from Russia, Gehrmann in 1925 was assigned to Berlin, where for the next twenty years he worked inside the papal nunciature as an advisor on Russian affairs and confidential secretary to successive nuncios. In 1924, motivated by patriotism, he began passing to the German foreign ministry confidential information concerning Vatican policy toward Russia. He was still a secret source for Weimar in 1925, but it is impossible to determine how long his espionage continued after that.[45]

These rather feeble intelligence resources apparently were sufficient for the Weimar Republic, which enjoyed relatively cordial relations with the Vatican, but they were entirely inadequate for the Nazis, who had a quite different relationship with the Papacy. Adolf Hitler and the National Socialist movement he led to power in 1933 considered the Catholic Church a serious threat to their ideological claims and their political ambitions for the same reasons Benito Mussolini and his Fascists feared the Church. By affirming the primacy of divine and natural law over human law, by insisting that there was an authority above the state and the leader to which citizens were responsible, and by claiming the right to educate and guide the consciences of individuals, the Church was always a rival for the "hearts and minds" of the German people. Moreover, the German Church's extensive network of schools, newspapers, publishing houses, charitable organizations, youth groups, and confraternities challenged the Nazi Party's effort to build a totalitarian state that controlled every corner of civic and associational life. Under any conditions the Catholic Church's moral leadership and institutional vitality would have been troublesome to a regime with totalitarian aspirations, but the danger seemed all the more sinister to Nazi loyalists, avid students of the conspiratorial school of history who believed that the primary allegiance of German Catholics was to the pope in Rome, who worked his will in Germany through a disciplined legion of clerical agents, most notably that dangerous corps of papal Janissaries, the Jesuits.

Initially Hitler (like his fellow dictator, Mussolini) extended toward the Vatican an open hand of friendship that soon closed into a fist of repression. In his early speeches as chancellor of Germany, he piously committed his government to Christian values and the family, confirmed the rights of the Catholic Church in education, and promised good relations with the Holy See. In conversations with Catholic prelates he reiterated his desire to cooperate with the Church and distanced himself from the anticlerical pronouncements of prominent Nazis such as Alfred Rosenberg, the party theoretician. In the summer of 1933 the Vatican and Berlin negotiated a concordat that regularized church-state relations by defining the legal status of the Catholic Church in Germany. Like the concordats that the Vatican negotiated with more than a dozen other countries in the 1920s and 1930s, the German concordat set out the rights and responsibilities of the contracting parties and bound them to certain modes of behavior in religious affairs. Pope Pius XI and his cardinal secretaries of state, Pietro Gasparri and Eugenio Pacelli, believed that such agreements were the best way to protect the church and its religious mission. They were wrong. For the Nazis (as for the Fascists in Italy), the concordat was little more than a propaganda device to legitimize their regime and favorably impress Catholics at home and abroad by association with the Vatican. They had no intention of abiding by the agreement, and when the time came to smash the Church, they would not be deterred by a legal document. That time came very quickly.[46]

Even before the ratification of the Reich concordat, the Nazis had embarked on a program to dominate the German Catholic Church through a program of polemical and physical intimidation.[47] After ratification of the treaty that was supposedly to protect the church behind a moat of legal rights and contractual obligations, the attacks only accelerated. Although the intensity of the persecution waxed and waned according to the shifting priorities of the regime, its political fortunes, and its perceptions of international opinion, Nazi religious policy relentlessly moved along three paths throughout the 1930s. The first aimed at securing administrative control of the German Catholic Church by frightening or seducing the bishops into subordination and acquiescence so that they would become little more than religious auxiliaries of the state. This goal required not only the intimidation of the bishops but also their isolation from the moral support, institutional authority, and financial and political resources of the Vatican. The second line of attack sought to undermine the popularity and moral authority of the church and its representatives. This effort took the form of highly publicized "morality trials" at which priests, nuns, and monks were prosecuted for alleged sexual offenses or financial crimes. International religious orders, such as the Benedictines, Franciscans, and Jesuits, were especially vulnerable to trumped-up charges of violating currency regulations, since they routinely transferred funds from their headquarters in Rome to their monasteries and religious establishments in Germany and other countries. The final line of attack concentrated on eliminating independent Catholic lay organizations that could provide an institutional base for anti-Nazi activity. This approach required the suppression of Catholic newspapers and publishing houses, the prohibition of Catholic youth and student associations, and restrictions on public religious ceremonies such as pilgrimages and processionals.[48]

To be successful, the Nazi program required intelligence concerning the attitudes and plans of the German bishops, their communications with each other and with the Vatican, and the membership and financial resources of Catholic religious orders and lay associations. To secure such intelligence the regime turned to the Sicherheitsdienst (SD), the party intelligence service. It was a good choice. The director of the SD, Reinhard Heydrich, an intelligent psychopath who hid his brutality and ruthlessness behind a veneer of conventional culture that included a devotion to classical music, was convinced that the pope and his minions inside Germany were hatching all manner of plots against the Reich. He believed that this threat was so severe that its destruction took precedence over operations against Communists, Jews, Freemasons, and other "Transnational Powers" that were the mortal enemies of the National Socialist state. Recalling Heydrich's hatred of "political Catholicism," a former officer in his service noted, "It was almost pathological in its intensity and sometimes caused this otherwise cold and calculating schemer to lose all sense of proportion and logic."[49] For the chief of the SD, the contest against the Catholic Church was a struggle to the death, and he could be counted on to fully mobilize the intelligence resources under his command to ensure a Nazi victory in that struggle.

In 1933 the then fledgling Sicherheitsdienst had established in its Munich headquarters a small intelligence unit to collect information on the organization of the German Catholic Church and its leading personalities. The unit's first director, Wilhelm Patin, a former priest and theologian with a penchant for historical scholarship, was temperamentally unsuited for intelligence work, and the unit accomplished little. When the SD relocated its headquarters to Berlin in 1934, Patin was replaced by Martin Wolff, but within months Wolff was reassigned to the Communist desk, and responsibility for Church intelligence fell to his deputy, Albert Hartl.

Hartl was one of the apostate or renegade priests and monks who appeared with distressing frequency on the rolls of Nazi intelligence and security services. He began working for the SD as a paid informant in 1933, when he was prefect of students at his alma mater, the Catholic seminary in Freising, and he promptly denounced Father Josef Rossberger, his best friend and superior at the school, for anti-Hitler remarks. His testimony against Father Rossberger at the subsequent trial (at which the anti-Nazi priest was convicted and sentenced to prison) caused a sensation in Bavaria and a scandal among German Catholics. Imagining that vengeful Catholics would punish him for his betrayal, Hartl sought protection from Reinhard Heydrich, who was just beginning a career that would carry him to the pinnacle of the German security and intelligence empire. Perhaps perceiving in the thirty-year-old priest the streak of amoral opportunism that was a prerequisite for success in the rapidly expanding Nazi security apparatus, Heydrich offered him a full-time job in the SD. Hartl accepted with alacrity, abandoned the priesthood, and embraced police intelligence with the fervor of a convert.[50]

Hartl's first assignments were relatively mundane. He collected information on Nazi Party members suspected of maintaining close connections with the Catholic Church; prepared an inflammatory report on the Inquisition for use in the party's anti-Catholic press campaign; and completed a study of the history and organization of the Jesuits, a religious order much admired and feared by Nazi police leaders for its asceticism, discipline, and purpose. He worked diligently, but these research projects smacked uncomfortably of the academic environment he had abandoned. It was only when he found himself unexpectedly promoted to director of the SD's church desk that he revealed a vision and industry that would make him the scourge of the Vatican and the German Catholic Church.

When Hartl assumed its direction, the church desk was one of several sections in Amt II, the domestic intelligence division of the Sicherheitsdienst. Since the desk was responsible for monitoring all religious organizations and movements in Germany, its operations against the Catholic Church were relatively modest in scope. The ambitious new director, however, was determined to enhance his unit's (and, of course, his own) standing in the party security service by expanding its operations and focusing on the target he knew best: the Catholic Church. Unfortunately, this field of church intelligence was not entirely unoccupied, and another agency had the same target in its sights. The Geheime Staatspolizei (Gestapo), the state political police who, at the time, were administratively separate from the SD, also had a church desk. The Gestapo's church specialists recruited low-level informants inside the Catholic Church to provide evidence for prosecutions of religious personalities and organizations in the infamous morality and currency trials. Hartl had little interest in such pedestrian investigations and was content to leave what he considered petty police work to the detectives of the state police. He intended to operate on an entirely different level. Reflecting Reinhard Heydrich's obsession with "political Catholicism," the SD's church unit would target the Catholic Church as a political threat to the party and the state, and seek intelligence concerning its antiregime activities and its conspiracies with foreign enemies of the Reich. It would seek this intelligence not among the sacristans, chaplains, and parish bookkeepers so attractive to the Gestapo but among the bishops, diocesan administrators, and higher clergy who communicated with the Vatican and directed the affairs of the German Catholic Church.[51]

Between 1935 and 1939, Albert Hartl relentlessly pursued his intelligence war against the Catholic Church. The Sicherheitsdient's small church desk grew in staff and resources. Eventually every SD office in the Reich had a church affairs officer who had completed a specialized course of training at the SD school in Berlin. These officers and their staff were expected to monitor the local religious press, surveil church services and meetings, and recruit networks of well-placed contacts who could provide information about ecclesiastical affairs. The officers could draw on liberal expense accounts to wine, dine, bribe, or otherwise cultivate the goodwill of their informants. At SD headquarters Hartl and his assistants processed the intelligence that poured in from the field offices and distributed regular surveys of church affairs to the Nazi Party chancellery and the propaganda, interior, and foreign ministries. In response to specific requests from its "customers," the church desk also prepared special reports on such topics as the financial assets of the Vatican, the influence of the Jesuits in various countries, and the Catholic press in Europe. Whenever the Vatican appointed a new bishop to a German diocese or a university hired a scholar to fill a chair in Catholic theology or history, Hartl's office compiled a detailed biography of the individual.

By 1939 the SD's church desk had thoroughly penetrated the German Catholic Church. Albert Hartl met daily with Josef Roth, a onetime priest and professor of theology, who directed the Catholic section of the Reich department for religious affairs. Roth's position brought him into frequent contact with German bishops, abbots, and Catholic lay personalities. He also controlled the distribution of foreign currency to bishops and priests traveling to the Vatican on ecclesiastical business and theologians traveling abroad to academic conferences. Roth made a point of meeting these travelers upon their return to discuss the results of their trips and to remind them of the source of the travel support they enjoyed. Through Roth, Hartl received a stream of information about religious affairs and personalities in Germany and the Vatican that helped the SD officer direct his intelligence networks.

One network of informants extended into the Catholic faculties of German, Austrian, and (after the Munich Agreement of 1938) certain Czech universities. These professors prepared for the SD scholarly studies of issues in church-state relations and passed on information gleaned from their contacts in the academic circuit of conferences, seminars, and research institutes. Another network covered the German and Austrian monasteries and houses of various religious orders, an operation that was advanced by the fact that several of Albert Hartl's aides were renegade monks who maintained contact with friends from their former lives and were aware of foibles or weaknesses that made some of those friends potential targets for recruitment by the SD.[52]

Academic conferences, faculty common rooms, and abbey cloisters are rarely hotbeds of secret intelligence, so while Hartl's networks in the universities and monasteries were useful, they were not likely to uncover the political conspiracies Reinhard Heydrich and like-minded security officials were convinced the church was plotting. To expose these activities, the SD required sources in the diocesan offices and episcopal palaces of the German bishops, as well as the offices in the Vatican that dealt with German affairs. Central to Hartl's operations, therefore, were the twenty to thirty ecclesiastical sources the SD's church desk recruited in each German diocese. Most of these sources were parish priests or chaplains to convents or hospitals who reported little beyond the latest gossip and rumor, but some were sufficiently well placed to secure copies of the confidential correspondence that passed between the Vatican and the German bishops, while others provided informed observations on the political attitudes of the bishops. By 1938 Hartl was receiving a copy of the confidential minutes of the German bishops conference that convened annually in the town of Fulda. At these important meetings the prelates considered the condition of the German Catholic Church, reviewed finances, debated strategies for evading or countering Nazi surveillance and controls, and discussed the latest directives from the Vatican. Access to these proceedings gave the SD a full and authoritative insight into the attitudes and plans of the bishops and the Vatican.[53]

The precious source that provided the SD with the minutes of the Fulda conferences remains unidentified. Within the conference secretariat and the various diocesan administrations, a number of private secretaries, advisers, and printers would have had access to such material, and one of these functionaries might have passed documents to the SD. Of course the penetration may have reached much higher. As a matter of course, the bishops would have sent the papers of their annual conference to the papal nunciature in Berlin. Hartl had at least one informant inside the nunciature, and this source may have had access to the papers. It is also possible that one of the bishops betrayed his colleagues.[54]

For all Hartl's success in placing agents inside the German Catholic Church, there were still significant gaps in the Sicherheitsdienst's intelligence coverage of Catholic affairs. For instance, on Palm Sunday 1937, when bishops and priests across Germany stepped into their pulpits to read a new papal encyclical, *Mit brennender Sorge,* in which the irrepressible Pius XI protested Berlin's persistent violations of the concordat of 1933 and explicitly condemned the Nazi glorification of race and state, the SD and the regime it served were taken completely by surprise. Aware of the pervasive police surveillance inside the Reich and certain that the security services would go to any length to suppress a papal statement so critical of National Socialism, the Vatican had prepared the encyclical in great secrecy, printed the German-language edition outside of Germany, and distributed the document by special courier rather than the postal system as was usually the case. Many priests received the document only on the morning of Palm Sunday, the day they were directed to read it to their congregations. For all the Vatican's efforts at security, however, word of the encyclical and its provocative contents leaked out in Rome; the British ambassador to the Holy See, for example, learned about it from a Vatican source and alerted London to expect a bombshell on either Palm Sunday or Easter Sunday.[55]

The Sicherheitsdienst, however, had no sources at the Vatican. The Nazi security and intelligence authorities were convinced that the Vatican was their natural enemy and that German Catholics received secret support and direction from Rome (convictions reinforced by the propaganda disaster of *Mit brennender Sorge*), but they lacked the resources in the 1930s to extend their intelligence operations into the Vatican. They also lacked the authority, since throughout the decade the foreign ministry and, to a lesser extent, the military intelligence service constantly asserted their claim to monopolize foreign intelligence and resisted efforts by upstarts such as the SD to intrude upon their domain. Aside from efforts (largely unsuccessful) to expose the clandestine channels by which the Vatican communicated with its bishops in Germany, the Sicherheitsdienst's church intelligence operations were domestic in their focus. The death of the pope, however, provided the SD an opportunity to extend its reach into the Vatican.

By the time of his death on 10 February 1939, Pius XI had abandoned whatever hopes of coexistence with the dictators he once had nourished and had become a resolute opponent of the authoritarian regimes. As Europe staggered from political crisis to political crisis in what would prove to be the last year of peace before a new world war, the question of which cardinal would replace the old pontiff preoccupied chancelleries around the world. What would be the political sympathies of the new pope? Would he continue Pius's growing opposition to the militarism and nationalism of Germany and Italy, or would he accept an accommodation with Hitler and Mussolini? Would he be a "political" or a "spiritual" pope? Such questions, with their obvious implications for the political balance of power in Europe, worried politicians and diplomats around the world, but they were especially pressing for authorities in Berlin, London, Paris, and Rome.

The Great Powers could not be indifferent to the identity of the next pope. On the very day of Pius's death, the French foreign minister, Georges Bonnet, suggested to the British ambassador in Paris, Sir Eric Phipps, that Britain and France should cooperate to secure the election of a cardinal whose sympathies would favor the democracies against the dictatorships. The foreign minister was thinking in particular of the late pontiff's secretary of state, Cardinal Eugenio Pacelli. London agreed on the need to secure the election of "the right man," but they were uncertain how to proceed. When asked his opinion, the British representative to the Vatican, d'Arcy Osborne, confirmed that Pacelli should be Britain's first choice, but he thought there was little that London could do to influence the outcome. The French were more decisive, and their ambassador at the Vatican, François Charles-Roux, met frequently with the French cardinals and their Francophone colleagues from Canada and Syria to measure the appeal of the likely candidates and to press France's desire for a pope who would stand up to the dictators. All the French cardinals except Cardinal Tisserant (who believed Cardinal Maglione, the former nuncio in Paris, would be more reliably anti-Fascist and anti-Nazi) agreed on Pacelli as the best choice.[56]

Just as Britain and France consulted on the papal election, so, too, did Germany and Italy. The Italian ambassador to the Vatican, Bonifacio Pignatti, spoke with his German counterpart, Diego von Bergen, about Berlin's preferences. Bergen said he was advising Berlin that Cardinal Pacelli was the best candidate. The German ambassador's recommendation is surprising in view of British and French support for the cardinal secretary of state, but Bergen (whose sympathy for the Nazi regime he served was, at best, lukewarm) undoubtedly concluded that among the viable candidates the Germanophile Pacelli, who had served as nuncio in Germany for twelve years, spoke perfect German, and surrounded himself with German advisers and housekeepers, was Berlin's best bet.[57]

Ambassador von Bergen did not know it, but he was not the only observer advising Berlin on the election. The Sicherheitsdienst finally had its man at the Vatican. When Pius XI died, one of its informants, Taras Borodajkewycz, volunteered to go to Rome to report on the conclave. Born in Vienna of Ukrainian parents, Borodajkewycz had briefly studied theology and claimed to have good contacts in Roman ecclesiastical circles. Seizing the opportunity to extend its reach into the Vatican at the very time that senior officials in Berlin were clamoring for intelligence from Rome, the SD accepted Borodajkewycz's offer and dispatched him to the Eternal City with a generous expense account. Unfortunately, the erstwhile theologian's vaunted contacts failed him because his reports to SD headquarters proved completely unreliable. His assurances that Cardinal Idlefonso Schuster, the pro-Fascist archbishop of Milan, would be elected to succeed Pius XI were hopelessly wide of the mark. Indeed, the archbishop, who had often embarrassed the Vatican and his colleagues with his public support for Mussolini, was one cardinal who had absolutely no chance of election.[58]

While Taras Borodajkewycz merely charged the SD the cost of a comfortable sojourn in the Eternal City, a second source nearly fleeced it of a small fortune. Shortly after Pius's death Albert Hartl was approached by an individual who claimed to report from inside the Vatican. This contact assured Hartl that bribes amounting to 3 million gold marks would be sufficient to convince a majority of the cardinals to support a candidate favorable to Germany: either Cardinal Maurilio Fossati of Turin or Cardinal Elia Dalla Costa of Florence. This was too big for the chief of the SD's church desk, so Hartl reported this offer to his superiors, who, in turn, immediately forwarded it to Hitler's office. Intrigued by the possibility of swaying the papal election, the Führer sought the advice of Hartl and Josef Roth, the chief of the Catholic section in the Reich department for religious affairs. Roth advised the Nazi leader to seize the opportunity and authorize payment of the large sum. Hartl, however, was cautious. While believing that the offer was genuine, the SD officer feared the international political and propaganda calamity that would result if the scheme were later exposed. Hitler accepted the advice of caution and vetoed the bribery proposal.[59]

It was the smart choice. The unsolicited offer was almost certainly a ploy by a confidence trickster to extort a small fortune from the German government. On its face the proposal was absurd, and it is a measure of how little the Nazis understood the Papacy that the proposal went as far (and as high) as it did. This was, after all, the twentieth century, not the tenth. The days when a papal election could be purchased were long past. Though differing in piety, intelligence, and sophistication, the sixty-two members of the College of Cardinals were conscientious trustees of the Church and well aware of their responsibilities. If one or two weak individuals might have succumbed to the lure of Nazi gold, it is impossible to imagine that forty-two cardinals (the two-thirds majority then required to elect a pope) would have collaborated in the subversion of the conclave. Furthermore, if so many prelates were prepared to sell their votes, the various foreign embassies would surely have heard at least whispers of the fact; after all, anyone seeking a bribe must make his interest and availability known, no matter how discreetly. The diplomatic dispatches from Rome (including those of the German embassy) contain no hint that the election might be purchased. When British and French diplomats considered ways to influence the outcome of the conclave, bribery was not even considered an option, less from moral scruple than from that option's sheer implausibility.

The names of the two allegedly pro-German cardinals, either of whom could be elected with Nazi gold, would have raised eyebrows in Berlin if the SD had better intelligence about papal affairs. In the past neither had exhibited sympathy toward Nazi Germany. Though respected by all his peers, Cardinal Fossati of Turin appeared on no one's list of possible candidates, and his attitude toward the totalitarian regimes was, if anything, distinctly cool. Fascist authorities in Turin often complained to Rome that Fossati displayed a most uncooperative attitude and was inclined to endorse such politically unfashionable values as the dignity of the individual, the rights of the family, and the peace of Christ. In submitting their evaluation of their cardinal, these authorities simply took it for granted that in the papal election his candidacy would be politically unacceptable to the Fascist regime. From the perspective of the dictators, Cardinal Dalla Costa was no less problematic. The Florentine cardinal's cold and austere demeanor endeared him to few, and his political sympathies were a mystery even to professional observers. In Florence he maintained good relations with the Fascist administration, but Ambassador Charles-Roux (who did not consider him a desirable candidate) shrewdly advised Paris that Dalla Costa's well-known moral rectitude and rigidity might well make him "a more bitter adversary to governments with a totalitarian morality than a [political] pope with liberal and democratic ideas."[60]

On 2 March 1939 the conclave elected Cardinal Eugenio Pacelli, who took the name Pius XII. Within months of his election the new pope would confront the daunting challenge of guiding the Papacy and the Catholic

Church through another global war. This world war, a mere generation after the first, would exceed its predecessor not only in the scope of military operations, the scale of casualties and destruction, and the barbarity of its genocidal impact on Jews but also in the importance of intelligence operations. In the competition for political, economic, and military information, governments would mobilize and deploy intelligence resources on a scale undreamed of even in the last years of peace. In this intelligence war there would be no sidelines, no safe areas; even neutrals would find themselves engaged as victim or aggressor. Much against its will, the Vatican would find itself a combatant in this secret war, and, as in the preceding years of peace, the dictators would prove the most immediate threat.

5

Men in Black

The short, stocky civilian who stepped down from the overnight train from Munich blended effortlessly into the crowd moving through the Stazione Termini to the tram stops and taxi ranks on the bustling Piazza dei Cinquecento. Germany had attacked Poland several weeks earlier on 1 September 1939, and Britain and France had leaped to the Poles' defense, thereby setting the stage for another world war before memories of the first had dimmed. In the first autumn of the war Italy was still neutral, so traveling foreigners, especially Germans, would have received only routine attention from the plainclothes security officers assigned to Rome's central train station. Perhaps the officers would have been more attentive if one of them had overheard the nondescript visitor give an address to a taxi driver and recognized the number and street as that of the Rome offices of the Abwehr, German military intelligence.

Josef Müller was a familiar though rather mysterious figure to the officers and clerks at the Abwehr station, who knew only that their visitor was attached to their sister office in Munich and that he occasionally visited the Eternal City to question certain unnamed sources at the Vatican about political topics, particularly potential peace initiatives by the Allies. Aside from wondering, perhaps, why Berlin headquarters troubled to send an officer to work the Vatican, always a low-priority target for German military intelligence, the station staff gave him little thought. His visits were brief, often no more than overnight, and his contact with the Rome station rarely extended beyond a request to use the phone.

He would call an unidentified party, say simply, "I am here," listen for a moment, then hang up and with a friendly smile take his leave.

Anyone who had thought to follow the mysterious officer would have discovered that he spent much of his time in Rome in the company of German-speaking priests and monks. Some, such as Monsignor Ludwig Kaas, the exiled former leader of the defunct German Center Party now serving as archpriest (administrator) of St. Peter's Basilica, and Monsignor Johannes Schönhöffer, a Bavarian priest in the Congregation for the Propagation of the Faith (the Vatican department for missionary affairs), had connections in the papal Curia. Others, such as Father Hurbert Noots, the abbot general of the Premonstratensian Fathers, were prominent among the religious orders. To a suspicious observer, these priests, whom Müller would meet in quiet restaurants or the Birreria Dreher, a beer garden that was a gathering place for the German community in Rome, might well have been the unnamed "Vatican sources" that allegedly were the object of Müller's visits to Rome. The Bavarian's occasional visits to the archaeological excavations under St. Peter's or to some of the more obscure Roman churches could be nothing more than the innocent diversions of an officer making the most of a few free hours in the Eternal City. Of course there were those curious nocturnal visits to the Pontifical Gregorian University, a large building that loomed over the tiny Piazza della Pilota, just steps from the famous Trevi Fountain, but the university was staffed by the Jesuit Fathers, and perhaps Müller had cultivated a source in that secretive organization whose members had sworn an oath to serve the pope without question.

A polite inquiry at the porter's lodge would have turned up the interesting fact that the Jesuit priests in residence at the university included a German professor of ecclesiastical history named Robert Leiber. That name would have raised eyebrows in any group familiar with ecclesiastical Rome and the Vatican of Pope Pius XII. Personal assistant and confidant of Eugenio Pacelli since the pontiff's earlier tenure as nuncio to Germany, denizen of the papal apartments, where he spoke privately with Pius two or three times a day, keeper of the deepest secrets of the Papacy, Father Robert Leiber, S.J., was much more than a history professor. But, then, Josef Müller was much more than a junior officer in the Abwehr.[1]

In the waning days of the Polish campaign, two senior Abwehr officers, Colonel Hans Oster and Major Hans Dohnanyi, conceived a plan to use Pope Pius XII to establish clandestine contact with the British. Fervent anti-Nazis and members of the anti-Hitler resistance circle around retired General Ludwig Beck, Oster and Dohnanyi hoped that the pope would serve as a discreet channel for determining London's attitude toward a negotiated end to the war based on a change of regime in Berlin. The disparate and disorganized resistance to Hitler had long considered the removal of the Nazi dictator, but the military members of the conspiracy, who hoped to be seen as patriots rather than traitors, wanted assurances that London and Paris would not seek military advantage in the confusion and violence of a coup in Berlin and that the new, non-Nazi government could make an honorable peace without fear of the sanctions and humiliations that accompanied the peace of 1918. The conspirators anticipated that the Allies would be more attentive and less suspicious if the initial approach was made through the pope.

To open the secret channel to the Vatican, Oster and Dohnanyi turned to Josef Müller.[2] A prominent lawyer in prewar Munich, Müller was a devout Catholic and a fervent anti-Nazi. He was also well known in ecclesiastical circles for his many services as a financial and legal adviser to the Catholic Church in Germany. On more than one occasion before the war, German bishops, suspecting that their mail was subject to covert surveillance by the Gestapo, used the Munich lawyer to carry sensitive documents from diocese to diocese and from Germany to the Vatican. Without hesitation Müller offered his services to the conspiracy. To provide their man with a modicum of protection and to explain his frequent visits to Rome, Oster and Dohnanyi arranged for his induction into the Abwehr, where ostensibly he was responsible for collecting information on the Papacy.

Müller made his first trip to Rome in late September 1939 to consult with Monsignor Kaas on the best way to approach Pope Pius. Kaas suggested that he contact Father Robert Leiber, the pope's confidential assistant, whom the Bavarian lawyer had met before the war. In a brief meeting with the papal aide Müller explained the purpose of his visit to Rome and expressed the hope of the German opposition that His Holiness would help them communicate with London. Leiber was noncommittal but agreed to carry the message to the Holy Father. Müller, fearful of attracting attention by lingering in the Eternal City, returned immediately to Munich.

The secret emissary returned to Rome in mid-October to receive the pope's decision. Father Leiber had good news. After listening to his trusted aide explain Müller's mission, Pius had declared, "The German opposition must be heard in Britain" and promptly volunteered to be the channel of communication.[3] The pontiff's decision launched Josef Müller on a clandestine odyssey that over the following months would see him shuttle between Berlin and Rome with the various proposals, queries, and clarifications of two ostensibly hostile parties wary of each other but searching for common ground. The messenger never dealt directly with the pope. Carrying instructions from Oster and Dohnanyi, he would arrive in Rome and from the security of the local Abwehr office telephone Father Leiber. Without identifying himself, he would say simply, "I am here." The priest would respond with the time at which they should meet. At first, the meetings were in Leiber's apartment at the Gregorian University, but later, for greater security, they shifted to a small Jesuit church on the outskirts of Rome.[4]

At their brief encounters, which continued into the spring of 1940, Müller explained the German conspirators' latest position to Leiber, who then carried the message to the pope. Pius then summoned Sir d'Arcy Osborne, the British minister to the Holy See, to the papal apartments and orally repeated the information. Osborne passed this information by diplomatic pouch to the Foreign Office in London. London's response reached Berlin through the reverse channel.

The "Roman Conversations" were never more than exploratory and in the end amounted to nothing. London suspected treachery, having already been burned in November 1939 when German intelligence kidnapped two British intelligence officers who had been lured to the Dutch border town of Venlo on the pretext of meeting anti-Nazi conspirators.[5] London was also skeptical about the credibility and motives of the alleged conspirators inside Germany, who seemed reluctant to abandon the political and territorial claims of a "greater Germany" with as much readiness as they were prepared to abandon Adolf Hitler. Ultimately, the contacts proved irrelevant because the conspirators could not bring themselves to rise against the Nazi regime before Germany's invasion and conquest of France and the Low Countries in the spring of 1940 solidified Hitler's support among the German officer corps and civilian elite and made a successful coup less likely.

Having agreed to serve only as a communication channel, Pope Pius soon found himself dangerously enmeshed in espionage. By the spring of 1940 the pope was passing to London not only the peace conditions of the German opposition but also the military secrets of the German government. Even before German troops had subdued the last pockets of organized resistance in Poland, Hitler had begun preparations for a massive invasion of France, a campaign that would include attacks on Belgium, the Netherlands, and Luxembourg. In a desperate effort to demonstrate to London its goodwill and forestall Hitler's planned military operations against western Europe, the resistance circle in the Abwehr leaked word of these operations to the Vatican in the expectation that Pius would warn the intended victims. On several occasions, as Hitler would first set a date for the offensive, then postpone it, Josef Müller rushed to Rome to alert the pope to the latest invasion schedule.

The most dramatic and eventful warning was the final one in May 1940. Müller arrived in Rome on the first of the month with word that Hitler was about to attack France, Belgium, and the Netherlands. The news set off a flurry of activity in the papal apartments. Pius immediately directed his secretariat of state to alert the papal nuncios in Brussels and The Hague and order them to warn the Belgian and Dutch governments of the impending attack. At a private audience with the Italian crown prince, Umberto, and his Belgian wife, Princess Marie, the pope spoke so insistently about the danger to the Low Countries that the alarmed princess immediately sent a special courier to Brussels to warn her brother, King Leopold. Pius permitted Father Leiber to alert the Belgian ambassador at the Vatican, Adrien Nieuwenhuys, who cabled the information to the Belgian foreign ministry on 2 May and again on 4 May, adding to the last message the information that the warning came from an emissary of certain German generals. Meanwhile, at the papal secretariat of state a senior official summoned the British and French ambassadors to inform them that Germany would strike before the week was out.[6] The warnings were accurate but futile, since the countries concerned, which had received several false alerts in the past, responded with insufficient energy and urgency. On 10 May 1940 German armies swept into France, Belgium, and the Netherlands in a campaign that would, within weeks, carry German tanks to the shores of the Atlantic and make Adolf Hitler the master of Europe.

The failure of the Roman Conversations greatly disappointed the pope, who had decided to act as a secret link between London and the German resistance in order to hasten the end of the war and facilitate the removal of a vicious political regime that threatened to extend its antireligious and inhuman policies across Europe. It had been a very risky decision. By collaborating in secret negotiations to subvert a foreign government, and by passing that government's military secrets to its enemies, Pius seriously compromised the traditional neutrality of the Vatican and exposed himself and the Papacy to political retaliation. Exposure could mean disaster, so Pius took great care to protect the secrecy of his involvement with the Allies and the German resistance. Nothing was committed to paper. Inside the Vatican, knowledge of the pope's clandestine contacts was so closely held that even Pius's principal diplomatic advisers, the cardinal secretary of state, Luigi Maglione, and the cardinal's two deputies, Monsignors Domenico Tardini and Giovanni Montini, were unaware of the activity. Father Leiber was the only point of contact with the Germans, and Pius always dealt personally with the British contact, Osborne. To avoid attention, Osborne's meetings with the Holy Father were quietly arranged not through the routine protocol of the secretariat of state but through the pontiff's personal *maestro di camera,* who knew nothing of the clandestine affair but must have wondered why he had been instructed to admit the British diplomat to the papal apartments immediately and without question even outside normal audience hours.

The pope's efforts to maintain secrecy proved unavailing. The brave but indiscreet Josef Müller shared information about his mission with an old friend and fellow Bavarian, Monsignor Johannes Schönhöffer, a priest in the Vatican department for missionary affairs. Schönhöffer, in turn, confided in Monsignor Paul Maria Krieg, the chaplain of the pope's Swiss Guard. Two other German priests, Ivo Zeiger, a Jesuit at the German-Hungarian College in Rome, and Augustine Mayer, a Benedictine monk teaching at his order's College of San Anselmo, also learned something of the business. Father Leiber, normally the very model of discretion, felt obliged to inform his nominal superior, Father Vincent McCormick, the American rector of the Gregorian University where Leiber was a professor of history, and the superior general of the Jesuits, Father Wladimir Ledochowski, both of whom, though strongly anti-Nazi, blanched at the risks of the operation. By the spring of 1940 a rather alarming number of people in Roman ecclesiastical circles were aware of Müller's real mission at the Vatican and Pius's secret connections with the German resistance. In June the Italian ambassador to the Vatican asked Monsignor Montini at the secretariat of state if his office had any information about a certain Josef Müller who reportedly was carrying secret messages between Germany and the Vatican. Montini honestly answered that he knew nothing about Müller.[7] If rumors about Müller's activity had reached the Italian foreign ministry, it was only a matter of time before the Nazis had the story.

Herbert Keller was wily, ambitious, and unscrupulous, qualities unattractive in any person, but especially so in a Benedictine monk. A member of the ancient abbey of Beuron, Keller had been, before the war, briefly exiled by his religious order to a desert monastery in Palestine as punishment for using irregular methods to secure election as abbot. Returning to Germany, he became an occasional informant for the Abwehr and the Sicherheitsdienst (SD), the intelligence service of the Nazi Party. In return for rather lavish travel expenses, Keller passed to his controllers whatever political or ecclesiastical intelligence he picked up while traveling in France, Germany, and Switzerland in search of medieval manuscripts to photograph for his abbey's library. Upon the outbreak of war Keller, who seemed to have found his monastic duties increasingly tiresome, abandoned his monastery and agreed to work full-time for German intelligence. His career move may not have been good for his soul, but it immediately paid off for his new employers. On his first mission for the Abwehr, he visited Switzerland, where he unexpectedly encountered an old acquaintance from Germany who, unbeknownst to the monk, was a member of the anti-Nazi resistance. In the course of a convivial evening of brandy and cigars, this individual, demonstrating the indifference to security that seemed to be a prerequisite for membership in the hapless German opposition, confided to his drinking companion that German military officers were conspiring to depose Hitler and that an Abwehr officer named Josef Müller was in regular contact with the Vatican to arrange on behalf of the conspirators a negotiated peace with the Allies.

As it happened, Keller knew Müller and despised him. The two had been bitter enemies ever since the Munich lawyer had helped the Benedictines expose the political chicanery that had caused Keller to be exiled from Beuron to Palestine. Hoping for revenge and an opportunity to impress his new masters in German intelligence, the renegade monk rushed to Rome to uncover the conspiracy.[8] Although his reputation as an unscrupulous adventurer was sufficiently widespread that the papal secretariat of state felt compelled to warn one of his Roman contacts against associating with him, Keller managed in only a few days of conversations in ecclesiastical circles to expose the main outlines of Müller's mission.[9]

Keller hurriedly returned to Germany to inform his Abwehr and SD controllers of his discovery. The report was so inflammatory that it went immediately to the desk of Reinhard Heydrich, now the chief of the Reichssicherheitshauptamt (RSHA; Reich Main Security Administration), Nazi Germany's new central police authority, of which the SD was now a part. The police chief was sufficiently impressed that he summoned the Benedictine monk for a personal interview. Heydrich had long nurtured a violent antipathy to the Papacy, which he suspected of plotting incessantly against the Nazi regime, and here was evidence that confirmed his worst suspicions. The presence of Josef Müller in the cast of alleged conspirators lent a special credibility to the story. Heydrich had had his eye on Müller since 1936, when the Bavarian's legal work for the Catholic Church had first attracted the notice of the secret police. From that time the Nazi security chief had been convinced that Müller was a secret agent of the Vatican. Indeed, Heydrich persuaded himself that the Munich lawyer was actually a disguised Jesuit who had received from the pope special permission to marry, father children, and live a secular life in order better to cover his clandestine work for the Vatican.

Evidence of the Roman Conversations and the pope's collaboration with the anti-Nazi resistance was now in the hands of the Church's worst enemy in Germany. Reinhard Heydrich was probably the most feared and ruthless man in Hitler's service (a title for which the competition was fierce), and as chief of the security services he had demonstrated an unswerving commitment to exposing and smashing the enemies of the Nazi regime. He could be counted on to act without hesitancy or leniency. Disaster was averted when Arthur Nebe, the chief of the criminal police in the RSHA, leaked word of Keller's report to Admiral Wilhelm Canaris, the director of the Abwehr, who intervened immediately to protect the conspirators. Canaris, an enigmatic figure who sympathized with the resistance and turned a blind eye to the activities of its members inside military intelligence, advised Müller to prepare a report indicating that while on an intelligence mission at the Vatican he had uncovered evidence of an anti-Hitler conspiracy directed by Generals Werner von Fritsch and Walter von Reichenau. In fact, neither of these officers had any connection with the resistance. As Canaris was well aware, General von Fritsch had conveniently died in the Polish campaign and so could not be questioned. For his part, General von Reichenau was notorious throughout the German officer corps for his fanatic belief in Hitler and the Führer's vision for the Third Reich. As Canaris anticipated, when Hitler was told that Reichenau, his most slavishly loyal general, was involved in a conspiracy with the pope, he dismissed the report as "rubbish," thereby discrediting in advance any suggestion (such as Keller's) of plots at the Vatican.

Canaris had diverted suspicion from the pope and Müller, but only temporarily. In the summer of 1940 German intelligence again ran across traces of the Roman Conversations. When, in early May, the Belgian ambassador at the Vatican, Adrien Nieuwenhuys, had telegraphed to Brussels the pope's warning of the impending German offensive in the west, the enciphered telegrams had been intercepted by the Forschungsamt (Research Office), one of Germany's several signals intelligence services. Having earlier cracked the Belgian diplomatic cipher, the German codebreakers were able to read the warning from Rome that, according to the Belgian ambassador, originated in the German general staff. Outraged by this evidence of treason, Hitler ordered the Abwehr to investigate, a move that Reinhard Heydrich (Father Keller's report fresh in his mind) snidely likened to "sending a goat to guard your garden."[10] As if to confirm the police general's appraisal, Admiral Canaris promptly appointed Josef Müller to direct the Abwehr investigation.

The Bavarian lawyer returned yet again to Rome, this time to consult with Father Leiber on a means to disarm suspicions in Berlin. They contrived a story in which Italy's foreign minister, Count Galeazzo Ciano, had learned of the planned western offensive from a source in the entourage of his German counterpart, Joachim von Ribbentrop, and that the information had then leaked from Ciano's circle to a certain Father Monnens, a Belgian Jesuit then in Rome but since departed for an isolated Catholic mission station in Central Africa, who had passed it to his countryman, Ambassador Nieuwenhuys. Since Monnens (somewhere in Africa) and Nieuwenhuys (somewhere inside Vatican City) were beyond the reach of German interrogators, the conspirators hoped that this fabrication would provide a satisfactory explanation and divert attention from Müller and his visits to Rome.[11] They were wrong.

Lieutenant Colonel Joachim Rohleder, a senior officer in the Abwehr's counterespionage section, was not a member of the resistance cell inside military intelligence, but he was a capable and conscientious officer. The vague explanations of the leakage of secret information in Rome, with their shifting cast of unidentified Italian diplomats, mysterious Jesuit missionaries, and traitorous generals, left him unconvinced and only more determined to get to the bottom of the mystery. Studying the intercepted Belgian telegrams, Rohleder noticed that in his second warning Ambassador Nieuwenhuys had mentioned that his German source had left Berlin on 29 April 1940, arrived in Rome on 1 May, and remained in the Eternal City until the third of the month. Reviewing the list of Germans who had crossed the frontier into Italy during this period, the colonel noticed that an Abwehr officer, Josef Müller, had entered Italy on 29 April and returned on 4 May. Rohleder contacted the Abwehr station in Munich (Müller's nominal post) hoping to determine if the officer had traveled to Rome on the days in question. He was disappointed. Müller had covered his tracks by leaving the impression in Munich that his destination was Venice. The wily Bavarian had also gone to the trouble of securing from a friendly Italian customs officer an official rubber stamp that he used to smear the entry and exit dates on his passport.[12] Momentarily checked, but increasingly convinced that Müller and his ecclesiastical contacts at the Vatican were the keys to the mystery, Rohleder bided his time waiting for an opportunity to probe church circles in Rome. His opportunity arrived when the Abwehr station in Stockholm took an interest in an itinerant Catholic journalist.

Siegfried Ascher had first visited Rome in 1935 when he secured a post as secretary to Father Friedrich Muckermann, a German Jesuit famous throughout Europe for his anti-Nazi polemics. Through Father Mucker-mann, Ascher was introduced to ecclesiastical Rome, and soon the per-sonable secretary was on friendly terms with abbots, superior generals, and monsignors from the papal Curia. He accompanied Muckermann when the Jesuit relocated to Vienna in 1937, but the next year, when Austria's merger with Germany in the so-called *Anschluss* forced his employer to flee to the Netherlands, he resigned his post and moved briefly to Switzerland before returning to Rome as the Vatican correspondent for the Swiss newspaper *Basler Nachrichten*. He did not stay long. Fearful that the Fascists would em-ulate their Nazi partners and promulgate severe racial laws, Ascher (who had converted from Judaism to Catholicism and changed his given name to Gabriel) once again abandoned Rome, this time for Stockholm, where he lived on the margins of poverty by accepting remittances from his old em-ployer, Father Muckermann, and contributing the occasional article to the *Basler Nachrichten* and the *New Catholic Herald* in London.[13]

Gabriel Ascher's prospects improved in late 1940 when he found a new benefactor: Lieutenant Colonel Joachim Rohleder. The Abwehr counter-espionage officer had not abandoned his search for the traitor who had betrayed German military secrets to the Vatican, and he was confident that the key to unmasking the culprit would be found in the Italian capital. With his anti-Nazi credentials secured by his earlier association with Father Muckermann and with his many connections in ecclesiastical Rome, As-cher seemed well suited to penetrate the conspiracy. The details of his re-cruitment have been lost, but by January 1941 Ascher was preparing to go to Rome for German military intelligence. From the chief editor of the *Bas-ler Nachrichten* he secured a letter appointing him the newspaper's Vatican correspondent, having first falsely assured the editor that his salary and ex-penses would be covered by the Holy See, which allegedly wanted to in-crease coverage of papal affairs in the German-language press. On the strength of this letter of appointment, Ascher then obtained a letter of in-troduction from the Catholic bishop of Stockholm, Johannes Erich Müller, who (in words he would later regret) described the subject as "an excellent man, a solid and conscientious Catholic, and an intelligent journalist who perfectly understands the attitude of the Holy See."[14]

At the end of April, Ascher traveled to Berlin, where he consulted with Lieutenant Colonel Rohleder and received funds for his trip to Rome. He also called on Archbishop Cesare Orsenigo, the papal nuncio, who kindly provided another letter of introduction, this one addressed to Monsignor Giovanni Montini, the influential Substitute (deputy secretary) in the papal secretariat of state.[15] Upon reaching Rome on 3 May, Ascher embarked on a hectic schedule of visits and phone conversations in an effort to renew old contacts and make new ones. On the strength of his letters of introduction, he was received by Monsignor Montini at the secretariat of state, Father Leiber at the Gregorian University, and Monsignor Kaas in his apartment next to St. Peter's Basilica. For many, his credentials as a reporter for a Swiss newspaper hoping to increase its coverage of church affairs explained his curiosity and persistent questions about personalities and events at the Vatican in the early months of the war. Others, however, were more wary. Some wondered how a Jew (though a convert) was permitted by Nazi authorities to travel unmolested across Germany. The abbot general of the Benedictines warned at least one of his aides to be careful in his conversations with the reporter.[16] Father Leiber asked a Swedish journalist of his acquaintance about the new arrival from Sweden and was told that the word from Stockholm was that he was a German informant. Suspicions soon hardened into certainty. On 24 June Leiber alerted Monsignor Montini that confidential information from Berlin indicated that Ascher had reported to German intelligence the substance of all his conversations in Rome. The pope's confidential assistant concluded that the journalist was "an extremely dangerous agent of the Gestapo."[17]

Actually, Gabriel Ascher was an extremely dangerous agent of the Abwehr, and Leiber's warning came too late. Despite the reserve with which he was received in some circles, Rohleder's agent was able to uncover the main lines of Josef Müller's mission to the Vatican, and he returned to Berlin convinced that the Bavarian lawyer had passed word of Germany's impending offensive in the spring of 1940 to the pope and, at least indirectly, to Brussels, The Hague, London, and Paris. Finding Ascher's report "logically convincing and conclusive," Rohleder carried it to Admiral Canaris. The Abwehr chief was well aware of the accuracy of Ascher's charges and their explosive potential should they find their way into the hands of the security police. He could not, however, simply dismiss the accusations out of hand without offending Lieutenant Colonel Rohleder, who had already demonstrated a relentless and rather alarming commitment to the truth. For form's sake Canaris allowed Rohleder to question Müller, who insisted that he traveled to Rome only to collect intelligence on the Vatican, categorically denied that he had betrayed state secrets, and asserted that he was the innocent victim of unknown enemies in Rome who might well be connected to British intelligence and who hoped to compromise his secret intelligence work at the Vatican. On the basis of this inconclusive interview, Canaris told his counterespionage chief that the evidence corroborating Ascher's story was too flimsy to justify distribution of the report to the

Gestapo or the SD. The report was filed in the archives, and at least for the time being, Müller, the conspirators, and the Vatican again slipped through the fingers of the Nazis.[18]

The dramatic events surrounding the Roman Conversations were early evidence that, whatever its wishes, the Vatican could not avoid being drawn into the clandestine world of spy and counterspy that would influence the Second World War even more than it had the First. As far as the Papacy was concerned, Germany remained the most dangerous denizen of that secret world. Since their accession to power the Nazis had considered the Catholic Church in general and the Vatican in particular a major political threat to their nationalist and totalitarian aspirations. Throughout the 1930s, the Nazi security services had pursued an aggressive program of intelligence operations aimed at exposing and disarming this threat. With the outbreak of war these operations intensified. Convinced that the Vatican sympathized with the Allies and contributed secretly to their war against the Reich, German authorities demanded the intelligence that would allow them to expose the perfidy of the Papacy and devise appropriate countermeasures. The Vatican would be an important front in Germany's intelligence wars, but first Berlin would have to find soldiers to defend that front.

When war broke out, the Abwehr, the primary organization responsible for collecting foreign military and political intelligence, did not have a single spy inside the Vatican. Before the war, German military intelligence had evidenced little interest in the Papacy. The small Abwehr station in Rome, concerned almost exclusively with maintaining liaison with Italian intelligence authorities, had made no effort to recruit sources inside the Vatican or the ecclesiastical community. As a result, Germany's principal intelligence agency could tell its government nothing about what the Vatican was thinking or planning after the unprovoked invasion of Catholic Poland threatened to cast all of Europe, including Italy, into the cauldron of war.

In the first weeks of the war, as German armies smashed Polish defenses and ruthlessly absorbed yet another country into the Greater Reich, the Abwehr, scrambling to establish some sort of coverage of the Papacy, ordered its Munich station to send an officer to Rome to begin operations again the Vatican. This officer had barely time to find an apartment before he was peremptorily recalled to Germany. Having decided to use the pope as a channel to the British and seeking a reason to justify the frequent visits to the Vatican by their representative, Josef Müller, Hans Oster and Hans Dohnanyi, the energetic leaders of the secret anti-Hitler cell inside military intelligence, arranged for Müller to be the Abwehr's new man at the Vatican.

Of course Josef Müller was a conspirator, not a spy, and he collected no intelligence for Berlin during his frequent visits to Rome. The fact that no one inside the Abwehr noticed this curious lapse on the part of the officer specifically responsible for establishing intelligence coverage of the Papacy suggests either that German military intelligence was not exactly preoccupied with events at the Vatican or that Oster and Dohnanyi could insulate Müller's activities from scrutiny. When, after the collapse of the Roman Conversations in the spring of 1940 and his near exposure as a resistance courier, Müller ceased visiting Rome, the Abwehr was slow to send a replacement to the Eternal City. When it did, the new man was surprisingly similar to the old.

Paul Franken arrived in Rome in February 1943. Ostensibly a new history teacher for the German-language school on the Via Nomentana, he was in fact an Abwehr officer charged with collecting intelligence at the Vatican. Franken maintained a low profile, avoiding the German embassy and the offices of the local Abwehr station and living quietly in a clinic run by the Grey Sisters, an order of German nuns, near the Basilica of Santa Maria Maggiore. His contacts were mainly German ecclesiastics, many of whom had been close to Josef Müller, including Monsignors Kaas, Krieg, and Schönhöfer at the Vatican and the Jesuits Robert Leiber and Ivo Zeiger. Franken, however, had more in common with Müller than friends. An activist in the Catholic student and labor movements before the war, Franken had actually been arrested by the Gestapo and imprisoned for two years for political offenses against the Nazi regime. After his release he maintained connections with the remnants of the liberal labor opposition in Germany, one of whose leaders, Jakob Kaiser, arranged his induction into the Abwehr, where he would be beyond the reach of the secret police. One of Kaiser's contacts inside the intelligence service then arranged Franken's assignment to Rome.[19]

Like Müller, Paul Franken was more concerned with anti-Hitler conspiracies than espionage. To keep up appearances and to justify occasional visits to Berlin for "consultations," Franken would collect bits and pieces of ecclesiastical gossip, but he saw his main task as representing at the Vatican the more liberal, labor branch of the anti-Nazi opposition. Twice a week Monsignor Kaas visited the clinic of the Grey Sisters for treatment of a stomach disorder, and before leaving he would pay a friendly call on Franken. Every Sunday morning, the Abwehr officer would take coffee at Kaas's apartment inside the Vatican. Most Sundays, Father Leiber would join his two countrymen, and occasionally he would invite Franken (whom he knew to be an Abwehr officer) to his rooms at the Gregorian University.

These apparently innocent social encounters provided an opportunity for Franken to update the German priests on the opposition inside Germany and obtain insights into the Vatican's appraisal of the chances for a negotiated settlement of the war. Leiber would quietly take notes as his friend explained the opposition's latest thoughts on the composition of the post-Hitler German cabinet or its plans for postwar Austria. The Jesuit would then carry the information to Pope Pius, who on at least one occasion after reading his aide's notes lit a candle that stood on his desk and burned the potentially incriminating papers.[20]

The purpose of this clandestine activity is difficult to discern. In its typically haphazard manner, the fragmented opposition probably did not know or could not decide what it expected of the Vatican. Franken's mission seems to have been limited to keeping the pontiff informed of opposition thinking. Apparently, little, if any, of this information went beyond the papal apartments. Having risked so much to no effect during the Roman Conversations of 1939–40, the now cautious pontiff had little appetite for a return to the days of secret messengers and clandestine meetings with foreign representatives.

Caution was especially necessary after 25 July 1943, when King Vittorio Emanuele III, supported by army generals and some high Fascist leaders, dismissed and arrested Benito Mussolini and appointed army field marshal Pietro Badoglio as the new chief of government. The bombastic dictator's dreams of a new Roman empire had dissolved in a series of military debacles that exposed the incompetence of the Fascist regime and the hollowness of its military pretensions. The Allied invasion of Sicily on 10 July, with its promise of future landings on the Italian peninsula itself, had been the final straw. Militarily exhausted and politically bankrupt, the Italians sought a way to extradite themselves from the war without bringing down the wrath of Hitler upon them. Upon the fall of Mussolini the Germans, anticipating a general Italian collapse, had quietly begun to move troops into northern Italy. When, on 8 September, the Badoglio government announced an armistice to coincide with American and British landings in southern Italy and then, accompanied by the royal family, promptly fled Rome to seek refuge with the invaders, German forces immediately moved into the Eternal City.

Hitler's intentions remained unclear. Rumors flew about the city that the Führer, convinced that Pius had conspired in the fall of Mussolini and Italy's abandonment of the Axis, would order his troops into the papal palace to seize the pontiff and transport him to Germany. Papal authorities had no illusions that the Nazi dictator would respect the neutrality of Vatican City or the person of the Holy Father. Fear of a German attack was very real inside the Vatican. Even before the Italian armistice there had been alarming signs. In the spring of 1941 the secretariat of state learned that at a meeting with Count Galeazzo Ciano, his Italian counterpart, Foreign Minister von Ribbentrop had suggested that the Italians forcibly remove the pope from Rome because, "in the new Europe there would be no place for the papacy." The cardinal secretary of state, Luigi Maglione, was sufficiently alarmed by this threat that he sought and received assurances from Mussolini and the chief of the Duce's secret police that the Vatican had nothing to fear. While welcome, these assurances did not assuage the cardinal's concerns. He convened a special meeting of the Congregation for Extraordinary Ecclesiastical Affairs (a committee of cardinals with diplomatic experience who advised the cardinal secretary on important issues) to consider contingency plans to confer special ecclesiastical powers on certain nuncios in the event that the Vatican was no longer able to communicate freely with its representatives abroad. In subsequent months alarm was fueled by intemperate remarks by certain German officials, such as one who commented after attending Holy Week ceremonies in the Sistine Chapel, "The ceremonies have been very interesting, but this is the last time for them; next year they won't be celebrated again," or another who publicly remarked that in Nazi-dominated Europe the Vatican would be reduced to a museum.[21]

Against such a backdrop the rumors that circulated in the fall of 1943 were taken very seriously inside the Vatican. As German paratroopers patrolled the perimeter of St. Peter's Square under the apprehensive eyes of the pope's Swiss Guards, key staff in the secretariat of state were ordered to keep a suitcase packed at their residence and another at their desk in preparation for a sudden evacuation, while archivists hid sensitive documents in obscure corners and under the marble paving of the papal palace. Anticipating a German assault, Allied diplomats resident in Vatican City burned their ciphers and confidential files.[22] Papal officials also steeled themselves for an attack. The commandant of the Swiss Guards was informed orally that to avoid bloodshed the Holy Father had decided that his guards should not resist an attack. Mindful both of his sworn oath to defend the pope even at the risk of his life and of his place in history should he be the first guard commander to meekly allow his pontiff to be seized, the officer refused to accept any such order unless it was given in writing. It was.

In fact there was no German plan to seize the Holy Father. Upon learning of Mussolini's fall and assuming the pope's complicity in the event, Hitler went into a rage and threatened to take over all of Italy, including the Vatican. Once his temper cooled, however, the Führer recognized the impracticality of an operation against the Vatican and accepted the advice of his propaganda chief, Josef Goebbels, that any such operation would have a devastating impact on world opinion. There never was any serious threat against the life or liberty of the Holy Father, but neither the pope nor his advisers knew this.[23] As far as they were concerned, the months after the Italian armistice were no time for risky anti-Nazi adventures with conspirators inside Germany.

Talk about a non-Nazi government in Berlin negotiating a peace with the Allies was not only dangerous but quixotic. In January 1943, at a conference in Casablanca, Morocco, President Franklin Roosevelt and Prime Minister Winston Churchill had agreed to accept nothing short of the unconditional surrender of Germany. Though dismayed by this policy, which he believed would only prolong the fighting and suffering, Pius saw little evidence that Washington or London was interested in abandoning unconditional surrender in favor of conditions proposed by an underground opposition that had yet to come to power. Moreover, by 1943, the tenth year of the Nazi regime, Pius was losing patience with the fractured German opposition, which earnestly drafted plan after plan for a postwar German government without specifying how or when it would remove the current one. At one point a frustrated Leiber, who was undoubtedly relaying the pope's attitude, blurted out to Franken that the opposition had to stop talking and start acting.[24]

Paul Franken returned permanently to Germany in May 1944, a month before the Allied armies pushing up the Italian peninsula captured Rome. His work for the opposition had become too risky, and his position in the Abwehr could no longer protect him. In February 1944, after a series of intelligence failures capped by the defection to the Allies of a senior Abwehr officer in Turkey, Hitler had signed a decree subordinating the Abwehr to the Reichssicherheitshauptamt, the Nazi-dominated organization that increasingly controlled all police and nonmilitary intelligence operations. Admiral Canaris was shunted into a meaningless job in the department responsible for economic warfare. In the meantime, the Gestapo had grown increasingly interested in the rather curious contacts and activities of certain Abwehr personnel. Even before Franken's return from Berlin, the opposition cell inside the Abwehr had been exposed and Hans Dohnanyi and Hans Oster arrested. They would eventually be executed for treason. The Gestapo net would also eventually sweep up Canaris, who also would go to the hangman. Though arrested and brutally interrogated, Josef Müller steadfastly refused to incriminate either himself or others; he was one of the few active resisters to escape death.

Paul Franken was also among this select group. Declining offers of refuge from sympathetic friends, Franken managed to resign from the Abwehr without attracting the attention of the secret police and secure employment as an interpreter for Italian "guest workers" in the Rhineland. When police operations against opposition elements increased after the unsuccessful "July 20 Plot" (when on 20 July 1944 a bomb planted by the military opposition at Hitler's daily staff meeting wounded the Führer and killed or wounded several of his aides), Franken quietly went to ground near Bonn and remained in hiding until the end of the war.

With Abwehr officers too busy plotting against Hitler to provide him with any intelligence on the Vatican, the handful of diplomats at the Reich embassy to the Holy See became by default Berlin's best source of information on the Papacy, especially in the early years of the war. However, several factors, some beyond its control, compromised the embassy's ability to collect information concerning the pope and his policies. With the onset of war, the secrecy that normally surrounded papal administrative departments became even stricter. To avoid any questions about its neutrality, the Vatican adopted a posture of correct but reserved relations with the belligerents. It became difficult for any diplomat, Allied or Axis, to pry information from contacts inside the papal departments. In the case of Germany this reserve took on a particular chill due to continuing church-state tensions over Nazi policies in the Reich and in German-occupied territories that the Vatican deemed anti-Catholic or contrary to divine and natural law. When German diplomats called upon Cardinal Maglione or Monsignors Montini and Tardini, the conversations, potentially a useful source of information, were all too often limited to presenting or receiving protests concerning violations of the 1933 concordat or the dismal condition of church-state relations. By 1943 the German embassy was so frustrated that it frankly admitted to Berlin, "It is impossible to drag any information out of responsible sources."[25]

Under these conditions German diplomats were hard-pressed to sustain a flow of reliable intelligence to Berlin. They scrutinized the columns of the Vatican daily newspaper, *L'Osservatore Romano,* for indications of papal policy and compared notes with colleagues at other embassies, although the growth of the Allied coalition reduced the circle of accessible colleagues to those representing Axis (Italy, Japan, Hungary, Romania, and Slovakia) or neutral (Ireland, Portugal, and Spain) governments. Social encounters with German-speaking ecclesiastics resident in Rome, such as Bishop Alois Hudal, the pro-Nazi rector of one of the German religious colleges in the Eternal City, turned up the occasional item of ecclesiastical gossip or rumor. Additional tidbits were available from the small army of mercenary journalists, professional tipsters, and purveyors of private news services that lurked about the fringes of the diplomatic community, but these sources were notoriously unreliable, and some did not shrink from fabricating items for the intelligence marketplace.

Constrained by a shortage of reliable sources, the embassy's intelligence collection efforts were further undermined by the attitudes of the two ambassadors who directed the Vatican embassy during the war. Diego von Bergen, the ambassador at the outbreak of the war, was an intelligent and prudent diplomat who had represented Germany at the papal court since 1920. No other ambassador in Rome could match his experience, reputation, or contacts. His friendship with Pope Pius XII, for example, extended back to the First World War, when he was responsible for the Vatican desk in the German foreign ministry and the then Monsignor Eugenio Pacelli was the papal nuncio in Germany. He retained the respect and even affection of the monsignors in the papal secretariat of state, even though these same officials considered the antireligious policies of the government he represented nothing less than satanic. In short, Bergen was perfectly positioned to report on papal affairs. If he could not discern the direction of Vatican policy, or anticipate the mind of the pope, or expose the secrets of the Roman Curia, no one could.

Unfortunately, its ambassador failed Berlin just when it needed him the most. Socially and politically a product of the old, imperial Germany, Bergen had always found it difficult to summon enthusiasm for the new Germany of National Socialism. By late 1940 he had abandoned the effort. Disenchanted with the regime he served, unimpressed by the string of military successes that had extended German power across Europe from the Arctic waters of Norway to the forested slopes of the Pyrenees, plagued by poor health, and weary of a mission whose principal task had become the defense of his government's antireligious policies, the sixty-eight-year-old ambassador increasingly delegated the direction of the embassy, particularly political reporting, to his deputy, the embassy counselor Fritz Menshausen, a competent officer but one whose experience and connections in no way matched those of his superior. By the second year of the war, Bergen was rarely seen at the Vatican except for occasional ceremonial events in St. Peter's Basilica and the Apostolic Palace.

By the summer of 1943 it was apparent to Berlin that, physically and emotionally, Bergen was no longer up to the job. He was retired and replaced by Ernst von Weizsäcker, the state secretary in the German foreign ministry, who had actively sought the Vatican mission, in part to escape an increasingly unbearable position as the principal deputy to the arrogant and fatuous foreign minister, Joachim von Ribbentrop, but also to pursue a pet scheme he had been nurturing for some time.

By the time of his appointment to Rome, Weizsäcker had concluded that the war had turned irrevocably against the Axis powers. In January American bombers appeared for the first time in the skies over Germany, joining British aircraft that had been assaulting German cities and industry for months. In February the remnants of the German Sixth Army surrendered to the Red Army at Stalingrad, marking the beginning of the end of Hitler's ambitions in Russia. In May all German and Italian forces in Africa capitulated to the British and Americans, leaving the Allies in control of the southern littoral of the Mediterranean and exposing the southern rim of Axis-controlled Europe to inevitable attack. That same month heavy losses required the German navy to recall temporarily all its U-boats from the North Atlantic convoy routes. Even as the Reich's new ambassador to the Holy See packed his bags for the journey to Rome, reports from the Eternal City described the fall of Mussolini and Allied successes in Sicily. Convinced that these reversals were merely precursors of ever greater disasters, that Germany could never prevail against the increasingly powerful and confident Allied coalition, and that a prolonged war would result in his country's utter defeat and ruin, Weizsäcker saw a negotiated settlement as the only hope for his fatherland. The problem was to find a middleman who would be credible to both sides and who could ensure the proper degree of secrecy, especially during the delicate early contacts. He believed that the Vatican was the best choice for the role, but he also thought that the Nazi leadership would accept papal mediation only if it was convinced of the pope's sympathy for Germany.

Of course Weizsäcker's dream of ending the war through papal mediation went nowhere, largely because neither side was interested in ending the war short of victory, but the fantasy had an unexpected and deleterious impact on German political reporting from Rome. To enhance Berlin's confidence in the Vatican, the new ambassador deliberately distorted the intelligence he forwarded to the Wilhelmstrasse to make the Papacy appear more sympathetic to Germany than it really was. For example, the reports routinely portrayed the Vatican as obsessed with the prospect of the Sovietization of Europe, convinced that only a strong Germany could serve as a bulwark against this threat, and committed to inducing the Allies to negotiate peace with Berlin as a preliminary to a common front against the Soviet Union.[26]

Weizsäcker's reports were a caricature of Vatican attitudes. Certainly the pope and his advisers were under no illusions concerning the Soviet

Union, which they considered (on the basis of some experience) an implacable foe of the Catholic Church and all it held dear. They were also concerned about the westward extension of Soviet influence into Europe. Furthermore, papal officials believed the Allies' insistence on unconditional surrender would only prolong the war, since it gave Germany no incentive to surrender. Nevertheless, the Vatican never allowed its anti-Communism to influence its policy toward Berlin. Reports that the pope wanted a coalition of the Western Allies and Germany against the Soviet Union were complete fabrications. At no time did the papal secretariat of state propose such a course to American or British representatives. When Ambassador Weizsäcker suggested to the Vatican that London and Washington underestimated the importance of Germany as a bulwark against Soviet expansion, papal officials did not rise to the bait. Indeed, on one occasion, when the German representative went on at some length about the dangers to the Church and European civilization inherent in a Russian victory, Cardinal Secretary of State Maglione responded curtly, "Unfortunately, the antireligious policies of Germany have provoked anxieties just as serious."[27] Weizsäcker was careful to keep such criticisms of Germany out of his reports, with the result that Berlin was often seriously misinformed about the true state of Vatican attitudes.

Ironically, Weizsäcker's misleading dispatches had little effect in Berlin because Hitler had no intention of negotiating peace through anyone, least of all the hateful Vatican, but also because Joachim von Ribbentrop instinctively distrusted all reports from his ambassadors, whom as a group he considered excessively timid and insufficiently Nazi. The foreign minister was more inclined to rely on information collected by intelligence networks run directly from the Wilhelmstrasse by trusted cronies such as Rudolf Likus. A semiliterate alcoholic, Likus had ingratiated himself with Ribbentrop when the future foreign minister was Hitler's ambassador in London in the 1930s and had been rewarded for his sycophancy with an appointment as liaison officer between the foreign ministry and the intelligence services. From this position he developed his own group of informants, usually German journalists in foreign capitals or junior officers in various German embassies who reported directly and secretly to him. Likus fell from grace in the spring of 1941 when, in a lapse that infuriated Hitler and embarrassed Ribbentrop, his vaunted network failed to anticipate an anti-German coup in Yugoslavia that forced the Führer to divert attention and resources from the preparations for the invasion of Russia. Ribbentrop's favor next fell upon Andor Hencke, a colorless career officer in the ministry, who was appointed director of Informationsstelle III, a new information office that was known informally within the ministry as the Hencke Dienst. Significantly more competent and entirely more presentable than his predecessor, Hencke inherited many of the contacts who had reported to Likus.

Although the foreign ministry's special information service collected intelligence on a variety of countries, the Vatican received special attention. In early 1943, as Allied fortunes in the Mediterranean advanced and as the military threat to Italy became increasingly real, Foreign Minister Ribbentrop, who suspected papal collusion with the Americans and British, emphasized the need for more intelligence from the Vatican. Reflecting the concerns of his minister, Andor Hencke informed his operatives in Rome that special funds were available to develop new sources at the Vatican.[28]

For information on the pope and his activities, both Rudolf Likus and Andor Hencke relied on two officials at the Reich embassy to the Italian government: Harold Friedrich Leith-Jasper, a press attaché whose Anglophone name must have startled visitors to the German embassy, and Carl von Clemm-Hohenberg, a shadowy individual loosely connected to the embassy as an economic adviser. In turn, these officials cultivated sources among the self-described journalists, professional tipsters, and hangers-on who sold information to anyone with cash in the information marketplace. Sometimes these sources provided solid intelligence. In the autumn of 1942, for instance, Leithe-Jasper was able to keep the Hencke Dienst accurately informed about the general outlines of the visit to the Vatican of Myron Taylor, President Roosevelt's personal representative to the pope, who was allowed by the Italians (despite the state of war between Italy and the United States) to travel unmolested to and from Rome. On another occasion Leithe-Jasper discounted widespread reports that Pope Pius would leave Rome in the face of Allied bombing raids and correctly assured Berlin that Pius would never abandon the city.

More commonly, the information generated by the foreign ministry's secret operatives in Rome consisted of unsupported rumor or completely spurious items composed by professional fabricators and con artists who flourished in an environment where any number of intelligence services competed desperately for information on the Papacy. Veteran Vatican watchers, such as Ambassador Bergen, were wary of these sources. Once, driven to distraction by repeated requests from the Wilhelmstrasse to confirm intelligence reports that Pius intended to abandon wartime Rome for a more secure and sympathetic refuge abroad, the normally imperturbable Bergen lost his patience and tartly reminded his superiors that in recent months alone the foreign ministry's allegedly authoritative sources had the pope on the verge of departing for any number of destinations, including Switzerland, Spain, North America, Mexico, and even the Belgian Congo, but still the pope sat in his palace.[29]

Less experienced or more gullible observers, however, often fell victim to scams. For a time, Rudolf Likus was fooled into believing that he had a matchless source inside the papal secretariat of state who provided (for a price, of course) the most revealing details about the pope's secret diplomacy around the world. As if to see how much he could get away with, in October 1941, four months after Germany attacked the Soviet Union, this source sold the witless Likus a report stating that Germany and the Vatican had signed an agreement to reestablish the Catholic Church in the Soviet Union by introducing priests and bishops into Russian territories occupied by advancing German forces. This report would have been news to Likus's superiors in the foreign ministry not only because no such agreement existed but also because at a policy conference in July 1941 Hitler had made it clear that Catholic missionary activity in German-occupied Russia was out of the question. After Reinhard Heydrich, chief of the Reich security service, decreed that draconian measures were necessary to implement the Fuhrer's decision and prevent the Vatican from infiltrating priests into Russia, the German army and police arrested the handful of missionaries who tried to enter Russia behind the invading forces and executed at least one.[30]

While Ribbentrop's clandestine information services floundered in a sea of forged documents and spurious reports, a small, little-known office in a nondescript building behind the foreign ministry actually had access to authentic papal documents. Officially Z section of the ministry's division of administration and personnel, but known to the initiated as "Pers Z," the office housed the Wilhelmstrasse's cryptanalytic service. During the war the foreign ministry's codebreakers read all or part of the encrypted diplomatic communications of thirty-four countries, including the Vatican. One papal cipher had been solved in the 1930s, but it had been removed from service by the Vatican after the outbreak of war when the papal secretariat of state upgraded its communications security. A second cipher, known to the Vatican as the Cifrario Rosso (Red Cipher), had been solved by 1940 through collaboration with codebreakers in the Forschungsamt, the special communications intelligence unit that reported to Hermann Göring in the German air ministry. In addition to studying papal ciphers, the Forschungsamt also tapped the phones of the papal nunciature in Berlin, as well as the phones of German bishops.[31] The cipher cracked by the cryptanalysts at the air and foreign ministries was, however, a low-grade system used by the Vatican during the war only for routine administrative or nonconfidential messages. For secret messages the secretariat of state relied on several additional ciphers of varying degrees of complexity. One of these, the Cifrario Giallo (Yellow Cipher), may have been sufficiently reconstructed by Pers Z by 1942 that some messages were readable in whole or in part. The papal nunciature in Berlin held the Red and Yellow Ciphers, as well as two other high-grade ciphers, neither of which was cracked by German cryptanalysts. As a result of their efforts, the foreign ministry codebreakers were able to read all the routine administrative traffic in and out of the papal nunciature in Berlin, but the bulk of the more sensitive communications probably escaped their scrutiny.[32]

With neither the Abwehr nor the foreign ministry able to provide plentiful and reliable intelligence on the Vatican, the way was clear for a third organization to try its luck. In the first month of the war the various state and party police and intelligence agencies, including the Gestapo, the secret political police, and the Sicherheitsdienst, had been amalgamated into a single organization, the Reichssicherheitshauptamt, under the command of Reinhard Heydrich. Although the SD had always had a small (and largely ineffective) foreign section, during the 1930s these agencies had mainly focused on internal security and the surveillance and suppression of potential threats to the regime. With the onset of war, however, the importance of foreign intelligence rose dramatically, and the ambitious Heydrich quickly realized that power would accrue to whomever controlled the flow of such intelligence. He set out to expand his service's foreign operations, an effort that accelerated after June 1941 when Walter Schellenberg, an ambitious and energetic young officer, assumed control of Amt VI, the RSHA division responsible for foreign intelligence.

As Schellenberg settled into his new office, a veteran church intelligence officer vacated his. After the creation of the RSHA, Albert Hartl's church intelligence section was transferred to the jurisdiction of the secret political police, the Gestapo. Hartl, the SD's preeminent specialist in church affairs, had always dismissed Gestapo officers as little more than plodding gumshoes who lacked the finesse and education for serious intelligence work. This offensive attitude had not gone unnoticed by the secret police officials who were now his colleagues and superiors. The Gestapo chief, Heinrich Müller, despised his new subordinate, and this hostility represented more than a difference over investigative methods. In a leap of the imagination that would have been characterized as lunatic in any police service other than the Gestapo, Müller concluded that Hartl, a former priest, was actually a secret Jesuit and a double agent working for the Vatican inside German security.

For his part, the suspected Jesuit did little to endear himself to his new associates, who were irritated by his boasting and scandalized by his frequent sexual indiscretions with female personnel of the RSHA. In the end a clumsy attempt to seduce the wife of a senior officer in a first-class compartment of the Berlin–Vienna express proved his undoing. A gleeful Heinrich Müller promptly demoted Hartl to the enlisted ranks and assigned him to one of the extermination squads that were massacring Jews in the Soviet Union, but Reinhard Heydrich countermanded the order and sent the erring officer to the RSHA field office in Kiev with the task of monitoring public opinion in the German-occupied Ukraine. The man who had created the Nazi regime's church intelligence apparatus would never again hold an important position in German intelligence.[33]

Before the war, Nazi authorities had considered the Catholic Church an enemy of the state, and the security services had monitored German bishops, priests, and Catholic religious and lay organizations to expose and suppress real and imagined threats to the regime. This focus on the Church as largely an internal subversive threat persisted for a time after the attack on Poland. A directive concerning current intelligence priorities circulated by General Heydrich in April 1940 revealed that the RSHA was still preoccupied with the activities of the German bishops and concerned with the Papacy only to the extent of penetrating the secret courier channels that the bishops used to communicate with each other and with the Vatican.[34] By 1941, however, the RSHA was worrying more about the pope in Rome than the bishops in Berlin, Cologne, Munich, and other German cities, and its officers were scurrying to establish intelligence coverage of the Vatican. That year, for example, the agenda of a conference at Gestapo headquarters to review operations against the Catholic Church included such topics as "Vatican World Politics and Our Intelligence Tasks" in addition to old standbys such as "Intelligence Tasks in the Conflict with Political Catholicism in the Reich," and speakers discussed the need for better intelligence on the Papacy and the importance of counterespionage programs to defend the Reich against the alleged depredations of clandestine papal agents.[35] That same year General Heydrich accelerated efforts to penetrate the Vatican.

If the RSHA was to expand its foreign intelligence operations, it needed to make secure and clandestine arrangements to establish its representatives abroad. Even before the war, when he was chief only of the SD, Heydrich had sought to place his intelligence officers on the staffs of various German embassies, but the foreign ministry had successfully resisted his plan as an encroachment on its traditional responsibility for foreign political reporting. Heydrich had pressed his case and, in the fall of 1939, secured grudging permission from Ribbentrop to assign "police attachés" to certain embassies. Ostensibly these attachés were to act as liaison officers to the police services of the host country and to cooperate with those services in criminal cases and investigations of mutual interest. Their real mission, however, was to recruit agents for clandestine intelligence operations.

Although the Vatican had a small police force for patrol and traffic control, even Heydrich realized that it would be impossible to justify the assignment of a police attaché to the Reich embassy to the Holy See. By 1941, however, the increasing demand for intelligence on the Papacy required the RSHA to do something. The Vatican embassy was ideally positioned to collect intelligence, but Heydrich could not insinuate his officers into the diplomatic mission. Neither the ambassador, Diego von Bergen, nor the head of the foreign ministry's Vatican desk, Richard Haidlen, had much use for the RSHA, and the Wilhelmstrasse flatly refused to share with Heydrich's service the reports it received from Rome.

In January 1941 Heydrich approached Ribbentrop about "a very necessary intelligence apparatus against the Vatican" and requested the assignment "under some guise or another" of one of his experienced officers to the Vatican embassy. In a not so subtle reference to the obstructionism of Bergen and Haidlen, Heydrich also proposed "a change of personnel having relations with Vatican elements." Ribbentrop considered this approach an unwarranted and impertinent intrusion into the affairs of his department. To remind the pushy RSHA chief of his proper place, the foreign minister directed his staff to refuse a request from the Gestapo for a diplomatic passport for Albert Hartl, the police specialist on Catholic affairs who, in one of his last missions before his disgrace, was traveling to Rome to investigate opportunities for intelligence operations against the Vatican.[36]

Reinhard Heydrich, who had a very expansive notion of his proper place, simply changed his tactics. If he could not place his man inside the Vatican embassy, he would place his man inside the Wilhelmstrasse. In early 1942, after months of lobbying, he convinced the foreign ministry to replace Richard Haidlen, the competent but uncooperative chief of the Vatican desk, with Werner Picot, who had developed close relations with the RSHA while serving on the foreign ministry desk responsible for liaison with the security and intelligence services. Picot was clearly Heydrich's man. Shortly after assuming his new duties, he informed the RSHA representative in Rome that he would do all he could to realize Heydrich's wishes concerning intelligence coverage of the Vatican and that he would immediately take steps to improve cooperation between the foreign ministry and the RSHA in that area. Subsequently, Picot traveled several times to Rome, ostensibly to meet papal officials and his colleagues in the Reich embassy to the Holy See, but really to review intelligence operations against the Vatican.[37]

In the absence of an RSHA officer on Ambassador Bergen's staff, the principal burden for satisfying Heydrich's demand for more and better intelligence from the Vatican fell upon Major Herbert Kappler, the police attaché at the German embassy to Italy. A fanatic Nazi who proudly wore a steel ring decorated with swastikas and the death's-head and inscribed "To Herbert from his Himmler," Kappler had risen through the ranks of the Gestapo and had so impressed his superiors that he had been included in the first batch of police attachés sent abroad. In Rome he advised the ambassador on security affairs, liaised with the Fascist secret police, and maintained surveillance of Germans resident in Rome. He also ran a handful of agents against the Vatican.

Kappler's first agent was an assistant to a professor at the Gregorian, the Jesuit university in Rome. This young man had volunteered his services after reading *Mein Kampf*, Hitler's political testament, and learning the "truth" about the nefarious political influence of the Catholic Church. At the Gregorian he surreptitiously opened letters entrusted to him for mailing by professors and passed to the police attaché items from hallway and common-room conversations. Another volunteer was an administrator at the Teutonicum, a residence inside the Vatican for German ecclesiastics working or studying in Rome. A harsh critic of the current pope and an apologist for the Nazis, this priest was relatively well placed to monitor the residents of his institution and report the latest rumors inside Vatican City, but his utility proved short-lived. In 1940 he was recalled to Germany by his archbishop, Cardinal Michael von Faulhaber of Munich, at the instigation of Monsignor Kaas, who was disturbed by his vocal support for the Nazi regime. Kappler's third source was a German historian resident in Rome whose research occasionally took her to the Vatican Archive, where she chatted up other researchers and the clerks in the reading room. Her usefulness ended in September 1943 when, after the German occupation of Rome, the Vatican closed its archive and library to outside researchers.[38]

Kappler may have supplemented these meager sources, none of whom had access to significant intelligence, with information obtained through liaison with the Italian police, who had comparatively good sources inside the Vatican, but the police attaché's network was not producing the kind of intelligence required by RSHA headquarters. To improve operations, Walter Schellenberg, director of Amt VI (foreign intelligence) in the RSHA, ordered Helmut Loos to Rome as Kappler's assistant. Chief of the Vatican section in Amt VI, Loos had attracted the attention of his superiors by directing what at the time seemed to be the RSHA's best penetration of the Vatican. In 1940 he had recruited Alfred von Kageneck, the Catholic scion of minor German nobility, to go to Rome on behalf of German intelligence. In May, as German armies swept through France, Belgium, and Holland, Kageneck visited Rome and called on Father Robert Leiber, a friend of his family from prewar days. Apparently, the pope's confidential assistant was delighted to see his fellow countryman and chatted freely about life inside the Vatican. Kageneck returned to Berlin with a wealth of interesting news, including observations on Pope Pius's reaction to Germany's western offensive and information on the influence in Rome of various German cardinals and bishops. Loos's agent revisited Rome for further conversations with his friend Father Leiber in August of that year and twice in 1941, each time returning with information on the Vatican's position on a range of political topics. The intelligence convinced Amt VI that it had penetrated the most secret recesses of the Papacy, and it made Helmut Loos's reputation. Unfortunately, it was a reputation built on a weak foundation.

On his first visit to Rome, Kageneck, seized by remorse at the prospect of betraying his family's friendship with Father Leiber, had confessed to the Jesuit his connection to German intelligence and the clandestine purpose of his trip. Leiber immediately consulted the pope and the superior general of the Jesuits, and they agreed that he would continue to meet his young friend whenever he visited from Berlin, and that he would pass to the confessed spy carefully selected information. Helmut Loos's star agent was, therefore, actually a double agent operating under Vatican control and submitting reports calculated to impress German intelligence with a particular view of papal attitudes and policies.[39]

Whatever hopes Loos may have had of repeating in Rome his apparent success in Berlin soon dimmed. As others had discovered before him, reliable Vatican sources were not exactly thick on the ground. Eventually Amt VI's ace agent runner recruited a small network that included Charles Bewley, an Anglophobic Irish diplomat who had served as his country's ambassador to Germany and the Vatican before retiring to Rome, and Werner von der Schulenberg, a onetime German army officer with literary pretensions who had retired to the Eternal City, where he frequented aristocratic and intellectual circles on the pretext of promoting German-Italian cultural relations. These sources reported little beyond the current gossip in Rome and spent most of their time dunning Kappler and Loos for more money.[40]

The RSHA tried to supplement the meager intelligence from the Vatican by running independent operations against other targets. One operation involved a cooperative Czech Catholic who had extensive connections in European aristocratic and ecclesiastic circles. With financial support from Amt VI, the Czech (whose identity remains unknown) traveled frequently to Rome, Vienna, Budapest, and Prague, cultivating his connections and collecting information for his sponsors in Berlin. To ensure his welcome in ecclesiastical circles, he would occasionally pass to his clerical friends information concerning church affairs in Germany and German-occupied territories. He claimed to have picked up this information during his travels, but in fact it was fed to him by Amt VI to enhance his credibility and stature among his contacts. He was especially friendly with Father Hubert Noots, the Belgian abbot-general of the Premonstratensian Fathers, a religious order with monasteries across Europe. The Belgian priest corresponded frequently with his Czech friend and freely passed on the latest news from ecclesiastical Rome. Amt VI's agent was also close to Monsignor Giuseppe Burzio, the Vatican's diplomatic representative in Slovakia, a German client state created by the Nazis after the dismemberment of Czechoslovakia in 1938. During visits to the nunciature in Bratislava, the Slovakian capital, the agent always guided the conversation into politically important areas and occasionally induced the unsuspecting papal diplomat into indiscretions. On one occasion, for example, Burzio described to his Czech friend his procedures for communicating with the papal secretariat of state.[41]

Despite its efforts in Rome and elsewhere, the RSHA remained dissatisfied with the quality and quantity of intelligence from the Vatican. It simply could not penetrate the corridors of power inside the papal palace. Of course access is always a problem (usually *the* problem) in operations against any intelligence target, but access was a special problem at the Vatican. Unlike other governments, the Vatican did not rely on locks, alarms, walls, and guards to protect its secrecy. To be sure, it made modest efforts to improve its physical security during the war. The already high walls surrounding Vatican City were further heightened by the addition of steel railings along their tops; entry controls were tightened at the various gates; and logs were kept of all individuals entering and leaving the papal city. The pope's minuscule but decorative army took the field. At the gates to the Vatican and in the corridors of the papal palace, the famous Swiss Guards exchanged their picturesque halberds and swords for rifles and pistols. The Palatine Guards, a part-time force of Roman accountants, notaries, dentists, and shopkeepers who enjoyed dressing in military costume and presenting unloaded and antiquated rifles at papal ceremonies, were issued ammunition and bayonets and sent to patrol the perimeters of papal buildings and basilicas around Rome and at the pope's country villa at Castel Gandolfo in the Alban Hills. The papal police, a professional force whose dress uniform of fur busby, swallowtail coat, and white trousers dated back to the Napoleonic era, established a plainclothes unit for internal security and surveillance duties.

Despite these measures, papal security depended less on physical controls than on cultural and social norms. The Vatican was a very small world, and its society was almost exclusively clerical. Those who moved in that world, who understood it and knew its secrets, were priests who were set apart from outsiders by their dress, their language, their education, their rituals, and their lifestyle. It was an exclusive society, one bound by special loyalties and largely impenetrable by intelligence services (German or otherwise) that understood neither its customs nor its practices.

Reinhard Heydrich, the wily chief of the RSHA, understood the problem and concluded that the solution lay not in assaulting the target but in joining it. Rather than seeking to seduce some of the pope's men away from the Church with promises of power or fortune, German intelligence should seek to infiltrate its own men into the Church. Before the war Heydrich had developed a plan to send ideologically sound and highly motivated young Nazis into the seminaries, where, hiding their Nazi beliefs and loyalties, they would complete the course of study culminating in their ordination to the priesthood. Still concealing their real allegiances, these priests would then pursue a career in the Church, and some would eventually rise to positions of responsibility, perhaps at the Vatican. These "moles" would be well placed to serve the needs of German intelligence and, coincidentally, influence Church policies in a pro-Nazi direction. Hitler was cool to the idea, however, and the plan was not implemented.

Heydrich revived his proposal in September 1940 and specifically suggested infiltrating agents disguised as priests into Roman ecclesiastical institutions, perhaps the three German-speaking ecclesiastical colleges in Rome: Santa Maria dell'Anima (Anima), a large establishment near the Piazza Navona; the German-Hungarian College (Germanicum) on the Via San Nicola da Tolentino; and the Teutonic College and Hospice (Teutonicum) alongside St. Peter's Basilica in Vatican City itself. Opposition, this time from Ribbentrop's foreign ministry, again scuttled the plan. The ministry probably feared a crisis in German-Vatican relations should papal authorities learn of the operation. There were also doubts about the loyalties of the German colleges in Rome. During the war Berlin made no attempt to mobilize these institutions on behalf of the German intelligence or propaganda effort. The failure to utilize the Anima is particularly surprising, since the rector of this college, the Austrian bishop Alois Hudal, was known in Rome as the "Brown Bishop" because of his sympathy for the Nazi regime. Although his pro-Nazi stance made him persona non grata at the papal secretariat of state, where he was assumed (correctly) to be a German informant, Hudal was a ubiquitous figure in Roman clerical and social circles, from which he gleaned the occasional item of information for the German embassy. Despite these services, the Brown Bishop was never entirely trusted in Berlin, where some of his writings on the reconciliation of Catholicism and National Socialism were suppressed as subversive. This distrust colored official perceptions of the college of which he was rector. In 1940, for example, the Nazi ministry for church affairs vetoed a proposal to subsidize the Anima on the grounds that its rector was "not a reliable personality and is in fact very dangerous for National Socialist Germany." The veto may also have reflected displeasure with the students at the Anima, who had declined (at the Vatican's suggestion) to participate in the festivities surrounding Hitler's state visit to Rome in 1938, a snub that led German authorities to characterize the students as "unpleasant spokesmen for the [Vatican] outlook."[42] The ideological orthodoxy and patriotism of the other German ecclesiastical colleges were also in doubt. At the Teutonicum, for example, neither the students nor the staff had protested when an administrator was sacked and sent back to Germany when his vocal support for the Nazis had become an embarrassment to the Vatican.

Heydrich's plan resurfaced in the summer of 1943, although the ruthless police leader did not live to see it, having been assassinated in Prague in May 1942 by agents of the Czech government-in-exile. Now the advocate was a little-known individual who was not an officer in the RSHA. He was not even German. Michael Kedia was from Georgia, a region in the Caucasus, the mountain chain that divides Turkey and the Soviet Union. Fiercely nationalistic, he had gravitated to Berlin because he saw in Nazi Germany an instrument for reestablishing the independent nation that had been extinguished, first by the czars in the early nineteenth century, and then, after a brief revival of freedom in the ruins of the czarist empire, by the Bolsheviks, who had incorporated Georgia into the Soviet Union. A leader of the Georgian diaspora, Kedia had placed his men and resources at the service of the Third Reich. At the RSHA the Russian section of Amt VI had developed close connections with Kedia and the "research institute" he and his followers had established in Berlin; after Hitler's attack on the Soviet Union, the section considered the émigrés and their alleged clandestine connections with their distant homeland one of their more useful intelligence sources.[43]

Sometime in early 1942 Michael Kedia received a visit from a fellow countryman, Father Michael Tarchnisvili, a Catholic priest and member of an obscure Catholic religious order, the Georgian Congregation of Our Lady of Lourdes. Driven from Georgia by Soviet persecution, the order had reestablished itself in a monastery in Istanbul. In early 1941 the order had learned that it was the beneficiary of a bequest from a pious and wealthy widow who with her husband had emigrated from Georgia to Belgium to seek and find their fortune. Father Michael was teaching theology at an abbey in Bavaria when he received an instruction from his religious superior to travel to Belgium to settle the bequest and return to Istanbul with the proceeds. Belgium was now occupied by the Germans and subject to travel restrictions. When repeated requests to local German authorities for travel permits went unheeded, the priest decided to take his case to Berlin. In the Reich capital he naturally gravitated to the local Georgian community, where he met Michael Kedia. As a favor to his fellow countryman, the émigré leader used his connections to secure the necessary travel documents for Brussels. Within a few weeks the priest was back with the money and an idea.[44]

Father Michael had convinced his superior in Istanbul to use the bequest to establish a Georgian college in Rome. Almost every Catholic national group had its own college in the Eternal City, so that an ecclesiastical tour of the Italian capital might include the English College, the Irish College, the North American College, and any number of other national centers. These so-called colleges were really residences for young priests who were pursuing their studies in the papal universities, institutes, and archives. As a young seminarian, Father Michael had studied briefly in Rome, and he had long dreamed of a student residence in the city that would nurture and display the Georgian national identity and culture. Unfortunately, the bequest alone could not cover the expense of purchasing, furnishing, and maintaining such an institution. Having been impressed by Michael Kedia's influence in Berlin, Father Michael returned to the capital of the Reich to seek the advice and help of his new friend.

Kedia was immediately captivated by the idea of a Georgian college, in part because he understood its potential contribution to his homeland's cultural and religious identity, but also because he saw an opportunity to advance the cause of a free Georgia by advancing the cause of his Nazi patrons. He promised Father Michael his support and assured the priest that he knew any number of patriotic and pious Georgians who would contribute funds to such a worthy cause. He volunteered to approach these potential donors himself and urged Father Michael to go to Rome to identify a suitable site for the new institution. Kedia would send word of his progress to the German embassy in Rome, where Michael should ask for a certain Major Kappler.[45]

Overjoyed, Father Michael established himself in Rome and sought out real estate agents, while in Berlin an equally ebullient Michael Kedia sought out intelligence officers. Kedia's idea was simple: the RSHA would secretly add to the original bequest enough money to allow the Georgian Congregation of Our Lady of Lourdes to establish a college in Rome. To disguise the role of German intelligence, Father Michael and anyone else who might inquire would be told that the additional money came from an anonymous benefactor in the Georgian émigré community. In return for its covert support, the RSHA would be allowed to use the college for intelligence purposes.

Initially the RSHA was cool to the idea. In particular, Walter Schellenberg, the chief of Amt VI who found Kedia and his Georgians, with their hopeless plots to liberate their homeland, a rather tiresome lot, dismissed the plan as impractical. By the late summer of 1943, however, senior officers, particularly Ernst Kaltenbrunner, the new chief of the RSHA, were more receptive. With the Allies firmly ensconced in Sicily, Mussolini displaced from power, and Italy drained militarily and psychologically, it did not require strategic genius to anticipate an Allied invasion of the Italian peninsula in the very near future. In Berlin the demand for intelligence from Italy was increasing, and the RSHA was rushing to establish agent networks especially in Rome. What could provide better cover for a network in the Eternal City than a religious establishment, especially since, by unspoken agreement between the Vatican and the Italian police, churches, seminaries, convents, and monasteries were generally immune to search? German intelligence had long suspected (with some reason) the Allies of using such establishments to provide cover for their espionage and to shelter anti-Fascist dissidents and escaped prisoners of war. Kedia's plan offered the RSHA an opportunity to turn the tables and create for its agents a secure island in an intelligence sea that might soon be teeming with Allied troops and police. Father Michael and the Georgian College now had a silent partner.

Of course Amt VI could not merely purchase a building in Rome, put a cross on the roof, proclaim it the Georgian ecclesiastical college, and move in radios and agents. To maintain a credible cover the college would actually have to be what it purported to be: a residence for Georgian seminarians pursuing ecclesiastical studies in Rome. The administration, rules, and living arrangements would have to conform to those of similar institutions, and the intelligence component would have to be integrated unobtrusively into the setting. There would be a wireless station to maintain communications with Berlin, but it would have to be disguised or hidden. To further protect the cover story, the agents would not be Germans but young men selected from the so-called Georgian Legion, a small armed force the Nazis had recruited from Georgians living in exile or captured while serving in Soviet army units. The men would be trained in espionage in Germany, but in Rome they would wear clerical dress and pose as seminarians to divert suspicion and facilitate their penetration of ecclesiastical targets. Since Father Michael was known to many in Rome and the Vatican for his devotion and piety, his presence as rector of the new college would add the last bit of verisimilitude to the deception.

While Amt VI refined its plans, Father Michael had found a home for his college: a villa in the Monteverde Nuovo district, a sparsely settled, semi–industrial area on the northern outskirts of the city. Heeding Michael Kedia's instructions, he next called on Herbert Kappler (perhaps wondering why the embassy's police attaché should be involved in the affair) but was told by an aide, Kurt Hass, that neither instructions nor money had arrived from Berlin. It was early September 1943 and a busy time at the embassy—the Italians had just announced their armistice with the Allies, and German troops had rushed into Rome—but the aide promised to make inquiries on Father Michael's behalf and suggested that he return in a few weeks.

When Father Michael revisited the office of the police attaché in mid-October, Kurt Hass had good news. As good as his word, Michael Kedia had located a wealthy Georgian émigré who, while preferring to remain anonymous, was pleased to contribute to the original bequest sufficient funds to make the Georgian college a reality. Father Michael was overwhelmed by this news, but his joy was short-lived. After congratulating the priest on his good fortune, Hass began questioning him closely about his work and his contacts in Rome and the Vatican. Michael readily acknowledged that he was on friendly terms with several senior officials in the papal administration, including Cardinal Tisserant, the influential prefect of the Congregation for the Eastern Churches. Pleased by this response, Hass then commented that the police attaché's office might be interested in hearing what Tisserant or other papal officials had to say to him. While learned in the ecclesiastical disciplines of theology and biblical studies, Father Michael was inexperienced in the ways of the world and particularly ignorant about the shadowy corner of the world inhabited by people such as Kurt Hass. His confusion, therefore, may well have been real when he asked the German officer what he meant. Abandoning all pretense, Hass bluntly asked his visitor if he was willing to collect information on the Vatican for the Reich and allow the Germans to establish a secret radio station in the new Georgian College. The priest was aghast. What Hass had suggested was completely out of the question. Any association with espionage, but particularly espionage against the Holy Father, was contrary to the priestly vocation and the tenets of ecclesiastical law. It would be worth his soul to engage in such activity. In that case, replied Hass, Father Michael could put the matter from his mind, but he could also forget about the money for the Georgian College. The Nazi officer then unceremoniously showed the bewildered priest to the door.[46]

In his despair, Father Michael (who seems to have had an uncanny gift for falling among bad companions) turned to an old friend from his seminary days he had been surprised to encounter in Rome. Basilius Sadathieraschvili had abandoned the religious life for a prewar career of right-wing émigré politics, shady business deals, and confidence games that attracted the notice of the police in France, Germany, and Switzerland. He appeared in Rome in 1937 and began to contribute items to the *Corriere Diplomatico-Consolare*, a combination social gazette and intelligence tip sheet edited by a spurious Italian aristocrat. When he renewed his friendship with Father Michael in the fall of 1943, he was making a meager living by dealing in paintings of uncertain provenance, interpreting for the German military command that had established itself in Rome after the Italian armistice, and acting as an occasional informant for Herbert Kappler.

Knowing nothing about his old friend's shady past and dubious connections but undoubtedly impressed by his worldly manner and his alleged connections in the Georgian community, Father Michael was delighted when Basilius offered to go immediately to Berlin to speak with Michael Kedia and clear up the "misunderstanding." Basilius advised Father Michael to wait patiently in Rome and take no action until his return. He then set about betraying his friend. The unscrupulous Georgian made a quiet visit to Herbert Kappler and persuaded the police attaché that, for a price, he was just the man to bring the recalcitrant priest and his precious college to the German side. No stranger himself to duplicity and cupidity, Kappler purchased Basilius's services and sent him to Berlin to work out a solution with Kedia and the staff of Amt VI.

At RSHA headquarters there was no agreement on how to proceed. Believing that Father Michael was a good Georgian who loved his country and mourned its occupation by godless Soviet oppressors, Michael Kedia suggested another straightforward approach, but one less crude and confrontational than the earlier pitch by Kurt Hass. Perhaps a fellow countryman, speaking their native language, could bring the reluctant priest to reconsider his scruples and see that by cooperating with the Germans he would be helping his people as well as the Church, which would flourish anew in an independent Georgia. The professionals in Amt VI, however, dismissed this plan out of hand. They refused to believe that even someone as simple as Father Michael could be so naive as to believe that he was working for Georgia rather than Nazi Germany. They also seriously doubted that the unworldly priest possessed the temperament and the talent to direct an intelligence operation. Even if he agreed to cooperate, what guarantee did Amt VI have that at some future date, perhaps if and when the Allies captured Rome, he would not lose his nerve and abandon the project? Father Michael was necessary to front the operation, but someone else had to run it.

In the end the professionals prevailed. The funds held by Herbert Kappler's office in Rome would be released to Father Michael without condition. He would be allowed to purchase the villa in Monteverde Nuovo and develop his college without interference from the RSHA. He would have to be convinced, however, that the enterprise required a business manager who would supervise the financial and business affairs of the institution. Since he already had the priest's trust and was already on the RSHA payroll, Basilius was the best candidate for this role. While Father Michael busied himself with such matters as the furnishings for the chapel and devotional exercises for the students, Basilius would direct the renovation of the villa, a project that would include the preparation of two rooms for the exclusive use of the business manager. These rooms would be isolated from the rest of the facility and have their own entrance. With the assistance of a signals officer from Kappler's office, one of these rooms would be converted into a communications center with a radio set that Basilius would carry back to Rome. The second room would remain available for the use of the agents who would be sent from Berlin. Father Michael was to know nothing about the radio or the true purpose of the men from Berlin.[47]

Amt VI insisted that Basilius arrange to have the property registered in the name of the Vatican. The German officers, mistakenly believing that the Lateran Agreements that the Holy See had concluded with Italy in 1929 made all buildings owned by the Vatican extraterritorial and, therefore, immune under international law from search or seizure, concluded that papal ownership would provide another layer of security and make the Georgian College a safe haven for German agents. In fact, the Lateran Agreements guaranteed extraterritorial status and immunity only to certain basilicas and papal palaces that were identified by name in the agreement. Many churches, convents, and colleges prominently displayed signs announcing

"Property of the Holy See," but the announcement was largely a bluff, since the signs did not ensure special protection or immunity under the laws of either Italy or the Vatican. Even authentic legal immunity was only a shield against those who respected legality. During their occupation of Rome, German police searching for Jews, anti-Fascist dissidents, and escaped prisoners of war would raid several papal buildings, including the Basilica of San Paolo and the Palazzo San Calisto, both of which were explicitly identified as protected in the Lateran Agreements.

Initially, Berlin's plan went well. Father Michael, who had neither appetite nor aptitude for business affairs, readily agreed to Basilius's offer to serve as "lay administrator" of the college. Together they composed a petition to the Vatican announcing that through the generosity of the Georgian émigré community a sum of money had been collected for the purpose of establishing a national college in Rome. The petition asked the Holy Father to accept the money and use it to purchase the property in the Monteverde Nuova district in the name of the Holy See but for the use of the Georgian Congregation of Our Lady of Lourdes. The Vatican, unaware of the true source of the funds, readily agreed to the proposal. On 28 December 1943 the formalities were completed in the offices of the Vatican's Administration for Ecclesiastical Properties, and a few days later Father Michael and Basilius received notification that title to the villa had been transferred to the Holy See.

With the formalities completed, Basilius began the renovations that would convert a family villa into a respectable ecclesiastical college with a secret intelligence annex. He assumed that once the work was complete he would direct the clandestine agents operating from the college. Berlin, however, had other plans. While prepared to use Basilius temporarily because of his influence over his old school chum, Father Michael, Amt VI considered him a venal and unscrupulous adventurer who had to be watched closely to avert any "false game" on his part. Once the renovations were completed and the secret radio station installed, Amt VI intended to recall the Georgian to Berlin on a pretext and install in his place at the college a more trustworthy and experienced representative.[48]

For his part, Father Michael was no longer the innocent priest who had arrived in Rome several months earlier with a dream and a bank draft. After his unpleasant encounter with Kurt Hass, he could no longer delude himself about the "anonymous benefactor" who, apparently, found it convenient to transfer funds through the Nazi police attaché in Rome. He guessed that the money that would make his dream a reality came from the Germans, but he kept this knowledge to himself and said nothing to the Vatican. He rationalized his silence and his acceptance of the tainted money by assuring himself that throughout history a variety of governments, some rather disreputable, had financed the charitable and educational work of the Church. Surely, the obvious benefits that would accrue to the Church and the Georgian national cause justified a certain latitude when considering the moral implications of accepting German money.[49] If the good priest ever wondered why the Germans might wish to subsidize a residence for seminarians, he probably convinced himself that Berlin merely hoped to cultivate the goodwill of the Georgian nation in support of a common effort against Bolshevism. If he suspected a more insidious motive, perhaps one related to his unfortunate interview with Kurt Hass, he pushed that suspicion to the back of his mind.

Uncomfortable suspicions forced themselves forward in late February 1944 when Basilius made a brief visit to Berlin and returned unexpectedly with six young Georgian men whom he installed in a Rome hotel. He informed Father Michael that the men were good Georgian Catholics who wished to prepare for the priesthood by studying theology and philosophy in the Eternal City. Surprised, but also delighted, Michael hurried to the hotel to meet his first students. His reception was cool. The young men were surly and uncommunicative, but they assured the priest that they wanted nothing more than the chance to study in Rome. They also evidenced considerable relief when told that they would have to stay in the hotel until the renovations at the college were complete. The following day Father Michael went to the Vatican to inform Cardinal Tisserant and his deputy in the Congregation for the Eastern Churches, Monsignor Antonino Arata, of the unexpected visitors from Berlin. A grizzled veteran of twenty years in the papal diplomatic service, Monsignor Arata smelled a rat and advised the Georgian priest to send the group back to Germany. Cardinal Tisserant was less hasty, suggesting only that Michael examine the visitors individually to determine if each had the personal commitment and educational background necessary for a priestly vocation.

Accepting the cardinal's suggestion, Father Michael interviewed the young Georgians. To his consternation, he discovered that they were less interested in discussing theology than in discovering places in Rome to meet women. A cursory interview was enough to convince Michael that three of the six were completely unsuited for ecclesiastical life. He gave each a small cash gift and told them to go home. The remaining three seemed to have some potential, and Michael arranged for them to lodge temporarily at the Russicum, the Jesuit college for the preparation of priests destined for work inside the Soviet Union. After a few weeks of life in a strict religious community, two of the three gave up and returned to Germany. The last of Basilius's young men held out until the Allies captured Rome in June 1944 when he turned himself in to the liberators.[50]

Of course the six "seminarians" were imposters. They had been selected by Amt VI from the ranks of the so-called Georgian Legion, and, after some training in espionage in Berlin, they were sent to Rome to infiltrate the Vatican from the cover of the Georgian College. Father Michael's unanticipated rejection of half the team and the effective isolation of the remaining half in a Jesuit monastery threw Amt VI's plan into disarray. Worse was to follow. The relationship between Father Michael and Basilius had soured as the "lay administrator" excluded the priest from all matters involving the finances of the college. Matters reached a head when Michael discovered that without his knowledge Basilius had sealed off two rooms in the villa from the rest of the college and that one of these rooms contained a radio transmitter. There was an angry confrontation between the former friends during which Basilius tried to convince the priest that the radio was intended only to communicate with their good friend Michael Kedia in Berlin and to broadcast religious programs into Georgia. This was too much even for Father Michael. He categorically refused to allow a transmitter inside the college or on its grounds.[51]

The dispersal of the Georgian agents combined with Father Michael's refusal to cooperate dealt Operation Georgian College a mortal blow. Basilius (who may have been skimming money from the operating funds) informed Kurt Hass, his contact in the police attaché's office, that the project had run out of funds and the Italian contractor who had been hired to perform the renovations had yet to be paid. As brazen as he was corrupt, the Georgian then asked if he could have back his old job as translator for the German army and police. Hass glumly informed Berlin that it would take some time to get the operation back on track. Unfortunately, time was one of the things German intelligence did not have in the spring of 1944 as the Allies advanced on Rome.

Allied intelligence was aware of the Georgian College operation, having intercepted and decrypted messages concerning the venture as they passed between Berlin and Rome. When the Allies liberated Rome on 4 June 1944, American and British counterintelligence officers immediately rolled up the remnants of the operation. Herbert Kappler, Kurt Hass, and the staff of the police attaché's office had abandoned their premises so precipitously that they left behind many secret papers, including documents relating to the Georgian College. Basilius Sadathieraschvili was high on the Allies' list of suspected German agents, but the wily Georgian slipped through the net and disappeared into the fog of war. Undeterred by a large sign announcing "Property of the Holy See," Allied officers raided the villa in the Monteverde Nuovo neighborhood and arrested the only inhabitant, an elderly caretaker who turned out to know nothing about German spies and clandestine radios and was flabbergasted when his interrogators shoved aside a large wardrobe to reveal a door into a secret room and then pulled up a radio antenna that had been inconspicuously strung along roof tiles.

Father Michael was tracked down at a hospice for indigent priests, where he had moved when he discovered that his much-beloved college was bankrupt, his bequest squandered, and his pockets empty. The only principal in the affair actually to fall into Allied hands, the hapless priest was carried off to jail for questioning. Fearful of implicating the Vatican in the affair, Michael was initially evasive, thereby fueling the suspicions of his American and British interrogators. Eventually, however, he became more cooperative. The investigators finally concluded, "There is not sufficient evidence to hold subject for trial on espionage charges. It would be difficult to even charge subject as a collaborator of the Germans, for all the [intercepted] telegrams seem to release subject of any knowledge."[52] The investigators released Father Michael into Vatican custody with the understanding that for the duration of the war he remain within the confines of a monastery. The Allies then gave the Vatican their counterintelligence file on the Georgian College. Papal officials were angered but not surprised to learn of German plans to subvert a religious institution for intelligence purposes. For the record, the pope's secretariat of state submitted a formal protest to the German embassy, but by 1944 papal authorities were well aware that the Vatican was a prime target for hostile intelligence operations, and that Nazi Germany was not the only perpetrator of such operations.

While Germany hatched occasional plots, Fascist Italy remained the most ubiquitous and immediate intelligence threat. Vatican City was entirely surrounded by Italian territory and dependent on Italian facilities for electricity, water, sanitation, telephone, and provisioning services. In St. Peter's Square uniformed Italian police paced along the marble paving that marked the border of Vatican territory. Plainclothes detectives loitered near the gates to the papal city and haunted the neighborhood bars and cafés patronized by the clerks, gardeners, chamberlains, butlers, drivers, and police officers of the pope's tiny state. From his office in the shadow of the Vatican wall, the Commissario di Borgo monitored affairs inside papal territory through a network of informants much as his predecessors in office had been doing since Rome became the capital of a unified Italy in 1870. All phone calls and most mail in and out of the Vatican passed through

Italian switchboards and post offices, while most papal employees maintained their residences and social networks in the city of Rome. Intelligence access was further facilitated by common language, culture, and (in most cases) citizenship.[53]

Italy also had a strong motive to seek intelligence access to the Vatican. From the moment they seized power, the Fascists believed that the Catholic Church was a threat to their totalitarian vision, and, while marked by the occasional gesture of reconciliation (such as the Lateran Treaty of 1929), Church-state relations were always volatile. As Europe moved closer to war, relations became especially tense. At the conclave of 1939 to elect a successor to Pope Pius XI, the Fascist regime opposed the candidacy of Cardinal Eugenio Pacelli, fearing that the then cardinal secretary of state would be insufficiently conciliatory in his dealings with the totalitarian dictatorships. After Pacelli's election, these early reservations were fueled when it became clear that the new pope intended to rely on advisers who were highly suspect in police and intelligence circles. The secret police had long considered Father Robert Leiber, the pope's confidential assistant, a committed anti-Fascist and suspected "that odious individual" of directing a secret campaign against the regime.[54] The new cardinal secretary of state, Luigi Maglione, in the 1920s an occasional (though probably unwitting) intelligence source, was now seen as a threat because of his pro-French and anti-Fascist attitudes. During the 1930s, when Maglione was papal nuncio to France, the secret police collected accounts of "Monsignor Maglione's well-known aversion to Fascism," including a report from Paris that he had publicly referred to the Fascists as the "despoilers of the Italian people." His appointment as the new pope's foreign minister was considered a calamity for Italy and a major victory for France and the cause of anti-Fascism. With papal affairs in the hands of individuals like Robert Leiber and Luigi Maglione, the secret police concluded that the Vatican would become a center for anti-Fascist espionage and intrigue.[55] Once war broke out in September 1939, Benito Mussolini and his blackshirts were convinced that the Papacy sympathized with the Allies and secretly conspired to assist their cause. This conviction was only strengthened when, upon Mussolini's entry into the war on 10 June 1940, the embassies to the Holy See of those countries (Britain, France, and Poland) now at war with Italy were forced to abandon their offices around Rome and move into the neutral territory of Vatican City.[56]

During the war, Fascist intelligence operations against the Papacy were immeasurably facilitated by the close relationship between the Italian and papal police services. The Vatican maintained a small, uniformed police force that controlled traffic and crowds and patrolled the buildings, gardens, and courtyards of the tiny principality. Most of the pope's gendarmes were recruited from the Italian police service, and liaison between the services was frequent because the Italians provided necessary support in supervising crowds in St. Peter's Square and providing security when the pope traveled to Castel Gandolfo, his country villa in the hills outside Rome. Not surprisingly, Mussolini's agents thoroughly penetrated the papal force. Indeed, when Colonel de Mandato, the longtime commander of the Vatican police, retired early in the war, Cardinal Nicola Canali, the pro-Fascist chief administrator of Vatican City, replaced him with Colonel Soletto, an officer who also happened to be an agent for OVRA, Mussolini's secret police. Furthermore, Giovanni Fazio, the director of the papal gendarmerie's Special Section, a small, plainclothes unit that provided Vatican authorities a modest internal security and surveillance capability, had been, before his recruitment into the pope's service, an early and active member of the Fascist Party and had led black-shirted strong-arm squads against opponents of the Duce.[57] As early as the mid-1930s he began passing to Italian intelligence confidential information from the offices of the papal police.

From Giovanni Fazio, Italian intelligence received a daily report on affairs inside Vatican City, including the movements and activities of anti-regime personalities such as Count Giuseppe Dalla Torre and the staff at the Vatican newspaper, *Osservatore Romano,* and the anti-Fascist politician Alcide de Gasperi, whom the Vatican protected with a job in the papal archive and an apartment in a papal building. The pontifical police were also useful in helping the Italians monitor the activities of those Allied ambassadors to the Vatican who had moved into the papal city when their governments went to war with Italy. With their families and staffs, these ambassadors occupied cramped quarters in the Convent of Santa Marta, a pilgrim hostel on the south side of St. Peter's. Italian intelligence was convinced that from their refuge inside the Vatican these "representatives of nations at war with Italy engage in military spying against us [and] greatly endanger our armed forces which cannot move without the movement being known."[58] To expose these machinations, Italian intelligence placed agents inside Santa Marta. They also relied on their friends in the papal police.

Plainclothes officers from the Special Section maintained surveillance of Santa Marta and other buildings occupied by Allied diplomats and kept a record of those who visited them. Officers also trailed behind the representatives when they escaped their claustrophobic quarters for a brief stroll in the Vatican gardens or the Cortile del Belvedere. Lists of visitors, reports of chance encounters, and scraps of overheard conversations were reported daily to Giovanni Fazio, who routinely shared the material with Italian police intelligence. Describing for his foreign ministry the rigor of the surveillance and suggesting its motive, the French ambassador noted: "The Holy See has renounced true independence. . . . Inside the precincts of the Vatican the police of the Holy See maintain a close surveillance in collaboration, evidently, with the Fascist police. Italy has infiltrated the Vatican with the agreement, complicity, and active participation of high papal authorities, who wish to avoid difficulties with a government so close next door."[59]

In 1942, however, the collaboration between the Italian and Vatican police services was interrupted when the surveillance reports from Santa Marta ceased to appear in the daily intelligence sheet. Monsignor Giovanni Montini, the influential and anti-Fascist deputy secretary in the secretariat of state, was aware that the influence of the Italian police extended into the Vatican, and he disapproved of the apparent acquiescence of Cardinal Canali and the commanders of the papal police in this violation of Vatican neutrality. He directed Anton Call, the Special Section officer responsible for Santa Marta, to report directly to him in the secretariat of state, and not to the office of papal police. Call, who shared Montini's political sympathies, readily agreed to this rather irregular order and, when questioned by his superiors about his failure to submit reports on the Allied diplomats, merely referred them to Monsignor Montini.

As the papal authorities were trying to sort out the lines of authority in the Call affair, Cardinal Canali abruptly dismissed Giovanni Fazio from the pope's police service. For some time Allied diplomats inside Vatican City had chafed under the surveillance of Fazio's Special Section, especially since they suspected that this surveillance served the purposes of Italian intelligence. D'Arcy Osborne, the British representative, was especially insistent in protesting this activity, and the secretariat of state passed these protests to Cardinal Canali. Fazio insisted that the Allied diplomats had to be watched, since "the activity of these *enemy* diplomats is a form of disloyalty to the Holy See, because it explicitly aims to hurt Italy" (emphasis added). Cardinal Canali may have sympathized with this argument, but even a powerful protector could not save Fazio from the anti-Fascist secretariat of state, where Monsignor Montini and his superior, Cardinal Maglione, had lost patience with the prostitution of the papal police to Italian intelligence requirements.[60]

With the departure of Giovanni Fazio, the Italians lost a useful source inside the Vatican, but they revenged themselves against Anton Call, whom they were determined to punish for his refusal to cooperate in the surveillance of Allied diplomats. Mussolini's secret police placed the Special Section officer under surveillance and concocted a plan to frame him as a British agent. Call received a request from a stranger to meet inside the Vatican at the church of Santa Anna, the small chapel of the Swiss Guards. Unknown to Call, this individual was a police provocateur, who handed the papal police officer a packet of money and asked him to carry it secretly to the British ambassador, D'Arcy Osborne. Sensing a trap, Call dropped the packet and immediately left the chapel. In the end he was compromised not by Fascist tricks but by his own pro-Allied sympathies. Having escaped from an Italian prisoner-of-war camp in workman's clothes and hoping to reach the nearest neutral territory, a British sailor made his way to the Vatican and slipped through a gate while the Swiss Guards were distracted. While passing in front of Santa Marta, he was challenged by Anton Call, who was on duty outside the building. Upon discovering the nationality of the intruder, Call promptly turned him over to Osborne, who lived on the top floor of the hostel. When the Italians learned of this action, they formally protested this unneutral action by an employee of the pontiff. Although Osborne eventually managed to negotiate the seaman's exchange for an Italian prisoner held by the British, he could do nothing to protect the papal police officer. Cardinal Canali now had an excuse to allow the Italian police to arrest and interrogate Call. Released after eight days in a Roman prison, Call discovered that he had been dismissed from papal service and banned from the Vatican.[61]

Physical surveillance of Allied representatives and their quarters generated lists of visitors, contacts, and movements within the restricted confines of Vatican City but revealed little about the diplomatic activities of these representatives and the policies and intentions of the governments they served. If the British were warning the pope about Hitler's plans for Europe, or the Poles were passing the secretariat of state information concerning German atrocities in occupied territories, or (after Pearl Harbor) the Americans were urging the Vatican to stand up to Mussolini, such activities would hardly be apparent to a police agent loitering outside Santa Marta or trailing behind an ambassador and his children in the papal gardens. For hard political intelligence the Italians needed access to the instructions and reports that daily passed between the Vatican and its representatives abroad and between the embassies at the Vatican and their home governments. This required the surveillance not of people but of communications.

Under the terms of the Lateran Agreements, the pope was granted full liberty to communicate with his representatives in foreign countries. The treaty also provided that a diplomatic mission accredited to the Holy See would retain its rights and immunities under international law, including the right to maintain its quarters on Italian territory, even if its government had no diplomatic relations with Italy. When Italy entered the war, however, these guarantees were not honored. Fearing that the diplomatic missions of countries at war with Italy would serve as centers for espionage and subversion, the Fascist authorities had no intention of allowing these missions to remain on Italian territory. They had to relocate to neutral Vatican territory, where they would be contained and watched. Their communications with the outside world could also be monitored.

In violation of the Lateran Agreements, Italy refused to allow the Allied diplomats inside Vatican City to communicate freely with their home governments or even with contacts in Rome. The police monitored all telephone calls in and out of the Vatican. Ambassadors were prohibited from using their own diplomatic couriers, although they could send letters and packets through the Italian postal service. Enciphered telegrams were also prohibited, but telegrams in clear could be submitted to local cable companies. Of course no diplomat would entrust his confidential communications to such channels; Italian censors opened and read letters mailed through the post office and examined all outgoing and incoming telegrams. The Vatican had its own post office, but once the mail passed beyond the pope's walls, it reached Italian hands, where it was examined by a unit of Italian counterintelligence. Theoretically, the mail of the pope and the official communications of his secretariat of state were immune from surveillance, but this restriction was not always honored. Torn envelopes and poorly resealed flaps gave evidence of systematic, if not careful, surveillance. Vatican protests to the Fascist regime produced little beyond facile apologies and bland assurances that such "accidents" would not recur.[62]

As a courtesy the Vatican allowed its diplomatic guests to use the papal diplomatic bag to communicate with their governments. Each mission could submit to the secretariat of state a small packet of enciphered letters for inclusion in the mail destined for the papal nuncios in Bern, Lisbon, or Madrid. In these neutral capitals the nuncios would deliver the packets to the respective Allied embassies. Inside the Vatican the Allied diplomats were honor bound to restrict their dispatches to matters directly relating to their business with the Holy See. The secretariat of state wanted to give the Italian government no excuse to question Vatican neutrality by claiming that the Allied diplomats were using papal facilities to transmit espionage reports. For similar reasons the secretariat of state refused to allow (except in a few special instances) foreign diplomats to transmit or receive radiograms over Vatican Radio.

The confidential dispatches of the diplomatic guests of the Holy Father were only as secure as the papal bag that carried them and the ciphers that protected them. Under international law diplomatic bags were immune from search or seizure, but in wartime few governments could be trusted to subordinate their security interests to legal niceties. Italy was certainly not one of the few. Without a diplomatic courier organization of its own, the Vatican had, after the First World War, arranged with the Italian foreign ministry for the ministry's couriers to carry the papal diplomatic bag. By the spring of 1941 the secretariat of state had begun to suspect that its bag was opened surreptitiously and examined while in the custody of the Italians. The secretariat terminated its arrangement with the Italian foreign ministry and accepted an invitation from Bern to entrust the papal bag to the couriers of the Swiss foreign ministry.[63]

The Allied diplomats inside Vatican City trusted their ciphers to protect their correspondence even if the papal bag was intercepted and covertly opened. Their trust was misplaced. Italian military intelligence was able to read most, if not all, of the ciphers used by these diplomats. This achievement was in no small part due to the work of a small, elite unit known as the Removal Section (Sezione Prelevamento). Often assisted by suborned embassy servants, these specialists surreptitiously entered foreign missions, cracked the safes and strongboxes storing secret documents, and photographed the contents. Codebooks and cipher tables were always a priority. Before the war, the second-story artists of Sezione P successfully penetrated several embassies in Rome, including the American, British, and French missions.

When Allied missions to the pope relocated to Vatican City, Sezione P, undeterred by the pope's neutrality, simply followed them into Santa Marta. During the war Italian agents clandestinely entered several, if not all, of these Allied embassies to photograph secret documents, including ciphers.[64] Here again, friendly relations with the Vatican police probably facilitated Italian intelligence operations. Without at least the tacit cooperation of papal officers, it is unlikely that Sezione P could have pulled off what was probably its most daring stunt, the acquisition of d'Arcy Osborne's secret cipher while the British ambassador enjoyed his daily stroll in the pontifical gardens. Italian intelligence already had a spy inside the household of the British diplomat, a young Italian servant who had been suborned by the threat of immediate conscription into the army. Before the war, Osborne had been criticized for lax security by his superiors in London but apparently to little effect because his servant had no trouble removing the cipher from its cabinet and passing the material through an air shaft to Sezione P officers waiting outside Santa Marta. These officers carried the cipher to a quiet spot, perhaps outside Vatican City, photographed the pages, and then revisited Santa Marta to return the document. The secret material was so bulky and the window of opportunity so narrow (Osborne's walks rarely lasted more than half an hour) that the Italian intelligence operatives required three consecutive days to complete the operation.[65] This entire operation was completed within yards of the post maintained by the Swiss Guards and papal police at the Gate of the Bells next to St. Peter's, and at a building (Santa Marta) that was under constant surveillance by the plainclothes officers of the papal gendarmerie's Special Section.

Sezione P may not have limited its activity inside the Vatican to stealing documents from the apartments of Allied diplomats. There is some evidence that Italian agents purloined material from inside the Apostolic Palace, and may even have covertly entered the secretariat of state and its cipher office.[66] There can be little doubt that Italian intelligence was very interested in papal ciphers, and even less that Mussolini's codebreakers were able to decrypt at least some of the pope's confidential messages.

In the first winter of the war Monsignor Ambrogio Marchioni, a junior officer in the papal nunciature to Italy, was summoned to the foreign ministry by the personal assistant of the foreign minister, Galeazzo Ciano, ostensibly to discuss some minor matter concerning ecclesiastical property in Rome. To the young monsignor's surprise, the foreign minister's aide furtively took him aside and whispered that Vatican ciphers were in the hands of the Italian government and that someone had to warn the pope. Shocked by news that the Vatican's most secret communications were exposed to Fascist eyes, Monsignor Marchioni hurried across town to the Vatican, where he secured an immediate meeting with the cardinal secretary of state, Luigi Maglione. After listening to Marchioni's account, Cardinal Maglione called in his two deputies, Monsignors Domenico Tardini and Giovanni Montini. Both were skeptical about the story, Tardini going so far as to dismiss the whole thing as "rubbish." Somewhat abashed by this reaction, Monsignor Marchioni suggested a test. The secretariat would immediately send a cipher telegram to the nuncio in Lisbon concerning some innocuous subject and request a cipher reply that same day. Marchioni would then quietly call on his source in Ciano's office and ask him to produce the deciphered messages. The plan was in put in motion. Cardinal Maglione and his deputies were flabbergasted when, a few days later, Marchioni returned to the secretariat with copies of the Lisbon telegrams as deciphered by Italian intelligence.[67]

The secretariat of state soon received another shock. From a source inside the Italian government, the secretariat learned in late May or early June 1940 that the secret telegrams directing the nuncios in Brussels and The Hague to warn the Belgians and Dutch of the imminent German invasion had been intercepted and deciphered by Italian intelligence. Mussolini was outraged at this evidence of papal collusion with the Allies. Since the outbreak of war in September 1939, the Italian dictator had suspected the Vatican of sympathizing with Britain and France and covertly aiding their effort against Germany. The intercepted messages seemingly confirmed this suspicion just as the Duce was edging closer to a decision to enter the war alongside Germany. Pope Pius had been urging restraint upon the Italian leader and working behind the scenes to maintain Italian neutrality, but now the pope was seriously compromised. He was also endangered.

To punish the pope for his alleged perfidy and to cow him into submission, the Fascist regime launched a campaign of propaganda and physical intimidation. The government-controlled press directed a stream of invective against the Vatican, accusing the Papacy of betraying the interests of the Italian people just as Judas had betrayed Jesus Christ. Thugs roamed the streets of Rome, abusing priests and attacking kiosks that sold the papal newspaper, *Osservatore Romano*. The most dramatic outrage was directed at Pope Pius himself. While carrying the Holy Father to a small Roman church to say mass, the papal limousine was mobbed by gangs of Fascist youths who shouted, "Death to the Pope."[68]

Further evidence (if any was still required) that the Vatican needed to attend to its ciphers came from two other sources. In late May 1940 the nuncio to Italy, Monsignor Francesco Borgongini Duca, was surprised to discover that an Italian official with whom he was conversing seemed to know the contents of a telegram recently dispatched by the secretariat of state to papal representatives in London, Paris, Madrid, and Washington. The indiscreet official sheepishly confessed that "all telegrams in code are read." By this time the secretariat of state had also received a warning from its nunciature in Berlin. Early in the war, a conscience-stricken, young Catholic in the diplomatic section of the Forschungsamt, one of Germany's codebreaking units, sent a priest to warn the nuncio that the Germans had cracked at least one of the ciphers used by the nunciature.[69]

In the spring of 1940 the Vatican still relied on ciphers that had been in service since the 1930s. The main cipher, the Cifrario Rosso (Red Cipher), had been introduced before 1935 and was used by almost all papal diplomatic missions. Unfortunately, this system had been compromised some time before the war when the cipher office in the secretariat of state used it to transmit to all nunciatures and delegations the text of a long papal address that, subsequently, was published verbatim in various newspapers. An alert cryptanalytic service could penetrate the Cifrario Rosso by comparing the original cipher version of the address with the plain-language version in the press. By the outbreak of the war, the secretariat of state had concluded that Rosso was no longer secure, but it kept it in service for routine administrative messages that required little security. Unfortunately, this decision would lead to the compromise of yet another papal cipher. When, on 3 May 1940, the secretariat of state drafted nearly identical messages warning the nuncios in Brussels and The Hague of the impending German attack, the cipher office mistakenly encrypted one message in the insecure Rosso and the other in a more secure cipher. Once again, an alert cryptanalytic service (and most were distressingly alert) that had already solved Rosso could expose the plain-language message protected by that cipher and use the message as a crib to facilitate the penetration of the more secure cipher.[70]

Painfully aware that its secret communications had been penetrated by two countries (Germany and Italy), if not more, the Vatican set out to equip each of its nunciatures and delegations with one or more new ciphers. The preparation and distribution of new ciphers, however, would take time. One officer in the secretariat of state was solely responsible for all papal cryptography, and the new systems would have to be hand carried to their destinations by trusted priests whose itineraries and timetables would depend on the winds of war. The more important European nunciatures probably received replacement ciphers by the end of 1940. In 1941 new ciphers were distributed to papal nunciatures and delegations in the Western Hemisphere. In 1942 all but a handful of papal diplomatic missions received a new cipher, with some (Berlin, Bern, Lisbon, Madrid, Vichy, and Washington) receiving two. In 1943 the apostolic delegation in Washington received a special cipher for top secret communication with Vatican City. By the end of the war, most papal missions had three ciphers, some had four, and one (Washington) had six.[71]

In addition to new cryptosystems, the pope's representatives periodically received from the secretariat of state reminders to protect cipher material and practice secure communications procedures. Lapses were sternly admonished. The papal delegate in Tokyo received a reprimand after his secretary, in an open dispatch that might have been intercepted by Japanese intelligence, repeated word for word the plain text of an enciphered message the delegate had recently received from the Vatican. The delegate in Washington was admonished for using a code "not at all secure" for a telegram reporting the possible date of the Allied invasion of France. When the papal representative in Australia reported the name of the priest in New Guinea who was the source of information about Japanese atrocities on that island, the cipher office advised the cardinal secretary of state to warn the representative "his cipher is not entirely secure."[72]

Though always a serious security threat, the radio intercepts, phone taps, mail surveillance, and agent penetrations that characterized Nazi Germany's and Fascist Italy's aggressive intelligence operations against the Papacy during the Second World War were not a shock to papal officials. These officials were well aware that the Axis partners considered the Vatican a threat that had to be neutralized and that neither Berlin nor Rome would be constrained by moral scruple in pursuing that purpose. Furthermore, both Germany and Italy had a history of espionage at the Vatican; indeed, Italian espionage extended well back into the nineteenth century. The war merely witnessed an intensification of these intelligence activities. Of course more was at stake for all parties in the period 1939–45, but at least papal officials knew where they stood with the Axis powers. They could anticipate the threat from Berlin and Rome and take what few protective measures were available to them. They probably did not anticipate a similar threat from the Allies.

6

Between Moscow and Washington

Early one morning in May 1942, as parents ushered their children to school and merchants swept the stoops of their stores, Italian military police quietly surrounded an apartment building in the Via delle Fornaci, a modest Roman street of small shops and simple flats in the shadow of the Vatican wall. Several plainclothes officers climbed to the fifth floor of the building and forced an entry into the residence of Holger Tavornen, a Finnish business-man who had lived in Rome since July 1940. To inquisitive neigh-bors, the Finn was a friendly but quiet bachelor who had retired from business to pursue certain unspecified "studies" in the Eternal City while recuperating from a bout of tuberculosis. To the police he was the key to exposing a major enemy spy ring operating at the very heart of the Fascist empire.[1]

For some time the radio intercept station at Forte Boccea on the outskirts of Rome had been picking up certain encrypted signals that seemed to originate from the Vatican's radio transmitter, whose tower, on the highest point in Vatican City, rose within sight of the Italian listening post. For years, Italian military intelli-gence, the Servizio Informazioni Militari (SIM), had studied papal ciphers, but the mysterious signals were in a cryptosystem un-known to the codebreakers in SIM's communications intelligence section. The Italians had long suspected the Vatican of secretly col-laborating with Allied intelligence services, so at first SIM believed that the pope's secretariat of state was transmitting military and po-litical intelligence to London in a special cipher much more sophis-ticated than those normally used by the Vatican.[2] Eventually, how-ever, direction-finding techniques revealed that the transmissions emanated not from the Vatican but from a building on the nearby Via delle Fornaci. Additional "reliable information" eventually directed the police to Tavornen's apartment, where they discovered the elusive transmitter concealed in a secret compartment behind a radiator.[3]

Tavornen was neither a Finn nor a businessman. In fact, he was not even Holger Tavornen. Under interrogation he revealed that he was really Ernst Hann, a German citizen, and that he was the radio operator for a Soviet intelligence network that had been collecting information on Italy and the Vatican since 1940. The apartment on the Via delle Fornaci had been deliberately selected as the site for the network's radio because it was only steps away from Vatican City. By transmitting on or near the wavelength of Vatican Radio, the clandestine Soviet station hoped to avert discovery by "hiding" behind its ecclesiastical neighbor.

When questioned about the network's controller, Hann acknowledged that the leader lived in Rome, but he insisted that he had never met this individual. Communication was maintained by means of brief written messages folded and wedged between stones in a wall in the Borghese Gardens, a public park on the other side of the city. He did know, however, a young Italian woman whom he believed to be the mistress of the chief. Counterintelligence officers immediately arrested this woman, who promptly gave up her lover, Herman Marley, a Soviet intelligence officer living in Rome since March 1940 as Fritz Schneider, a Swiss citizen from Basel. With information extracted from Marley and Hann, the police were able to arrest the remaining members of the spy ring, including a translator for the Italian foreign ministry, a Fascist polemicist who was close to Mussolini's family, and a husband-and-wife team originally selected by Moscow for an intelligence mission in the United States, who had settled in Rome when, after Pearl Harbor, Italy's declaration of war on America ended travel between the two countries.[4]

Recognizing an opportunity to confuse the Russians and, perhaps, identify additional Soviet agents, Italian counterintelligence convinced Ernst Hann to continue to transmit to Moscow, but under the control of his captors. Through Hann, SIM fed carefully contrived items of information to Moscow and analyzed the return questions and instructions for clues to Russian intelligence operations in Italy.[5] The Italians were especially intrigued by a transmission from Moscow directing Hann to contact the occupant of an apartment on the Via Cheren, a street in a quiet residential neighborhood in northeast Rome. Moscow instructed Hann to assure this unidentified individual that everything possible was being done for him and that it was hoped he would soon have some interesting information to report. This mysterious individual was to look into the possibility of acquiring a radio transmitter, but in the meantime he was to communicate, in secret ink, with Istanbul in care of the address he already knew. Moscow ended this transmission by warning Hann that he should not be surprised to find his new contact dressed as a priest and living with a blonde woman of Russian nationality.

Looking over the shoulder of their tame radioman, Italian counterintelligence officers were excited at the prospect of uncovering yet another Soviet agent. To their surprise, they discovered that the apartment on the Via Cheren had been under recent police surveillance. The residence was occupied by Alexander Kurtna, a former seminarian employed in a sensitive position by the Vatican, and his wife, Anna Hablitz, a native of Leningrad who worked for the overseas service of Italian state radio. Before hiring Kurtna, papal officials had asked the Italians to vet their new employee, and in response the security police had, at least for a time, placed the man under surveillance. The surveillance turned up nothing untoward, but now the authorities returned to the Via Cheren with more substantial suspicions. Kurtna was away on a visit to northern Europe, but his wife was home. She was arrested. When Kurtna returned in late July 1942, two plainclothes officers were waiting for him at Rome's main railway station. For the bored officers it was just another routine arrest. Little did they suspect that the quiet man who went without protest to the headquarters of Italian counterintelligence was Moscow's most important agent inside the Vatican.[6]

Alexander Kurtna was born in 1914 into a middle-class family in Estonia, then a province of the Russian empire. After the First World War and the collapse of the czarist regime, the territory gained its independence, and young Alexander's father secured a post in the office of the Estonian president, while his mother worked as a schoolteacher. At the age of nineteen, after two years in the Estonian army during which he served as a radioman in a signals unit, Kurtna entered a seminary for Russian Orthodox priests. He soon surprised his family by abandoning the seminary and converting to Roman Catholicism. The conversion, however, did not diminish his sense of a priestly vocation. In 1935 he enrolled in the Jesuit seminary in Dubno, Poland, where he so impressed his teachers that, at the end of his first year of studies, he was called to Rome by the Jesuit superior general, Father Wladimir Ledochowski, and awarded a scholarship to the Pontifical Russian College. The Russicum had been founded in 1928 to educate priests for the dangerous mission of reestablishing Roman Catholicism in Bolshevik Russia, from which it had been driven by relentless persecution. To prepare themselves for this daunting task, the students spoke only Russian, immersed themselves in Russian culture and history, and often affected the garb and appearance of Orthodox priests, including the full beard.

Kurtna's quick intelligence and quiet demeanor, as well as his command of Estonian, Russian, Ukrainian, Polish, and German, made him a prime candidate for the Russicum's rigorous program. Despite his academic commitments, he was able to return to his homeland and to visit Latvia and Poland during a leave of absence in the summer and autumn of 1938. In 1939 he visited Estonia again and received from the government a financial grant for research in the Vatican Archive on the subject of medieval relations between the Baltic and the Papacy.[7] A protégé of the Jesuits and a brilliant student at one of the Church's elite schools, Kurtna seemed poised to embark on a glittering ecclesiastical career.

Whatever hopes the young seminarian may have had for such a career were dashed in 1940 when, for reasons that remain shrouded in mystery, the Jesuit superiors abruptly concluded that for all his intellectual talents, the young Estonian lacked an authentic vocation for the priesthood. Forced to leave the Russicum, Kurtna maintained his academic standing by enrolling as a lay student in the Vatican's school of paleography and by continuing his research in the Vatican Archive. Since he was no longer a dependent of the Jesuits, his financial status was precarious. Seeking an extension of his research stipend, Kurtna traveled to Tallinn, the Estonian capital, in September 1940. By this time Tallinn was a Soviet city. On 23 August 1939 Germany and the Soviet Union, long political enemies, had surprised the world by signing a nonaggression treaty (the so-called Molotov-Ribbentrop Pact) that effectively ensured Russia's acquiescence in the imminent German attack on Poland. Secret protocols to the treaty rewarded the Soviets for their silent collaboration by assigning parts of Poland and all of Estonia, Latvia, and (as a result of a subsequent agreement signed as Poland succumbed in late September) Lithuania to the Russian sphere of influence. In June 1940, as German troops completed the conquest of France and consolidated their occupation of Belgium and Holland, the Red Army occupied Estonia, Latvia, and Lithuania as a prelude to incorporating the Baltic republics into the Soviet Union. Upon his return to Rome in late November, Kurtna explained to his friends that the local authorities, confused and distracted by the change in regime, could tell him nothing about his scholarship and referred him to the Academy of Sciences in Moscow. He then made the long train journey to the Soviet capital, where he managed to convince the directors of the Academy of Sciences not only to continue but also to increase his research stipend. This version of his story, however, failed to mention that before visiting the academicians he had discussed his prospects with another group of Soviet officials who, in their own way, were just as interested in what a bright investigator might uncover at the Vatican.[8]

Kurtna's ability not only to move freely within the Soviet Union but also to leave the country upon the completion of his business was curious, especially when thousands of middle-class Estonians, like himself members of the old governing class, were being deported to the east by their new Russian overlords. Soviet travel and emigration controls were notoriously strict and unlikely to have been relaxed except in special circumstances for a military-age Estonian, who was now a de facto citizen of the Soviet Union. Equally curious was Kurtna's ability to extract from Moscow's Academy of Sciences a traveling scholarship to the Vatican to study the medieval Papacy even as the Soviet regime ruthlessly suppressed religious sentiment and practice and the new Communist rulers in Estonia prohibited the study of ecclesiastical subjects and destroyed theological libraries.[9]

Kurtna's story seemed to have raised eyebrows inside the Vatican, where by now the former seminarian was a familiar face in the archives as well as the cafés and restaurants patronized by papal functionaries. Official interest increased when, in early 1941, the Congregation for the Eastern Churches, the Vatican department responsible for Church affairs in the Soviet Union, hired the Estonian as a translator. After their occupation of the Baltic States, the Russians had closed all diplomatic missions, including the papal nunciatures, formerly accredited to those republics. They had also established postal and travel controls that effectively cut communication between the Baltic lands and the rest of Europe. The Vatican could no longer communicate with its bishops in Estonia, Latvia, and Lithuania and was hard-pressed to determine the condition of Catholics in the newly absorbed Soviet territories. For news it now depended on the occasional letter from a bishop or priest that, passing from hand to hand, evaded Russian and German border controls and mail surveillance and survived the long journey from the Baltic to Rome. Even less frequently, similar clandestine channels might bring some news from other parts of the Soviet Union. From the Vatican administrative directives, words of encouragement and (occasionally) sums of money secretly moved eastward into the denied regions, arriving, if at all, only months after their departure from Rome.

The meager and dismal correspondence from the Soviet Union, with its reports of arrests, deportations, and executions, found its way to desks in the Congregation for the Eastern Churches and the papal secretariat of state. As a translator for the former department, Kurtna was privy to the reports from the beleaguered Catholics in the Soviet Union and to any instructions the Vatican might send them. He would be aware of the location in Russia of the small groups of practicing Catholics who, in defiance of the secret police, maintained an underground church, and he would also know the identities of any priests who escaped police surveillance to minister secretly to their beleaguered flocks. Kurtna also moved in the small circle of priests who were responsible for Church affairs in Russia. In this way he became acquainted with Monsignor Antonino Arata, the former nuncio to Latvia and Estonia, who was the executive secretary of the Congregation for the Eastern Churches, and Monsignor Mario Brini, the desk officer for Russia in the secretariat of state who was also the personal assistant to Monsignor Giovanni Montini, the influential deputy secretary of state who saw the pope daily.

If Moscow desired details of the Vatican's policy toward the Soviet Union and papal efforts to support persecuted Catholics inside Russia, it could hardly have done better than to place an agent inside the Congregation for the Eastern Churches. Papal officials realized this, and, perhaps recalling Kurtna's curious visit to Tallinn and Moscow, they sought reassurance about his true loyalties before they offered him a position in the Congregation. Through the liaison channels that linked the papal and Italian police services, the secretariat of state, in February 1941, quietly approached the Italian government with a request for any information the intelligence services might have concerning the Jesuits' former protégé. After a review of their counterintelligence case files and watch lists, the Italians informed the Vatican that they had no reason to suspect Kurtna of working for a foreign power. As a result of the inquiry, however, the security service opened a file on the papal translator and instituted temporary surveillance of his movements to confirm that he was indeed as innocent as he seemed. It was only the following year, after the destruction of the Marley network, that the Italians discovered the truth about the mysterious Estonian.[10]

With nothing against him in Italian intelligence files, Kurtna continued his work in the Congregation for the Eastern Churches and cultivated his friends in the papal administration. Gradually, he extended his contacts into the large German community in Rome. In the spring of 1941, as German armies smashed through Yugoslavia and Greece and consolidated Axis control in the Balkans, he visited the German Historical Institute, one of the many national establishments in the Eternal City devoted to historical and archaeological studies. Ostensibly, he was seeking additional sources of financial support. The director of the institute, Dr. Ferdinand Bock, was sufficiently impressed by the apparently struggling scholar that he agreed to provide a monthly stipend from the institute's research fund.[11] It is unlikely, however, that Bock's interest was limited to Kurtna's research project. During the war the German Historical Institute was an informal arm of German intelligence in Rome, and its director maintained close connections with Major Herbert Kappler, the police attaché and Gestapo representative at the Reich embassy to Fascist Italy. By providing Kurtna with funds, Bock may have been laying the groundwork for a time when his friend, Major Kappler, would require contacts inside the Vatican.

While making new friends among the Germans, Kurtna did not neglect his Russian contacts. At least twice that spring he visited the Soviet embassy in Rome. The first visit was the result of an invitation from the cultural attaché, who ostensibly was interested in an article Kurtna had just published on the historical collections of the Hermitage, the famous state museum in Leningrad. Cardinal Eugène Tisserant, the prefect (director) of the Congregation for the Eastern Churches, had provided some help in the preparation of this article, and the Russian attaché (who was probably an intelligence officer under diplomatic cover) questioned Kurtna closely about this prelate who was rumored to be preparing to infiltrate priests secretly into the Soviet Union. Except for a brief period in 1922, when the Soviets hoped that Vatican aid would alleviate the famine that swept through Russia in the wake of revolution and civil war, the Communist authorities had waged a relentless war against Roman Catholicism in an effort to destroy a moral authority that might challenge the totalitarian aspirations of the regime. In the 1920s Moscow had uncovered and suppressed Vatican efforts to secretly consecrate new bishops and maintain an underground ecclesiastical structure. Since then, the Soviet security forces had been obsessed by the prospect of yet undetected Catholic "cells" allegedly poised to subvert the Communist regime and otherwise further the interests of potentially hostile powers such as Germany and Italy. In the 1930s, for example, the security forces had arrested Catholic nuns, students, and laypeople on charges of conspiring against the Soviet state, plotting the assassination of Stalin, and preparing a monarchist restoration under the direction of the Vatican.[12] To expose and crush these imagined conspiracies, Soviet intelligence needed information about the Vatican's intentions, especially concerning the renewal of clandestine support for persecuted Catholics in the Soviet Union.

The second visit occurred shortly before Germany's attack on the Soviet Union in June 1941. Disturbed by reports of increasing tension between Berlin and Moscow, Kurtna called at the embassy to clarify his status in the event of war between Italy, Germany's ally, and the Soviet Union. An embassy official told him to remain in Rome as long as possible and directed him to keep Moscow informed of events inside the Vatican and the Fascist capital. Kurtna agreed.[13]

Kurtna had been recruited by Soviet intelligence during his visits to Tallinn and Moscow the previous autumn.[14] Since the exposure of its informant Alexander Deubner in 1932, Soviet intelligence lacked direct access to those Vatican circles concerned with the Soviet Union. At his desk in the archives of the secretariat of state, Father Eduardo Prettner-Cippico, the other Soviet source inside the Vatican, had access to a range of diplomatic documents and may have seen the occasional paper devoted to Russian affairs, but the secretariat's Commission for Russia, once so central to the formation of papal policy toward Moscow, was by 1939 moribund. Responsibility for the supervision of the Church's interests and activities inside the Soviet Union had shifted to the Congregation for the Eastern Churches, where Alexander Kurtna worked as a translator of sensitive documents. Whether Moscow directed the Estonian to seek a position in the Congregation or his employment was fortuitous, Soviet intelligence had a spy exactly where it needed one.

Details of Alexander Kurtna's intelligence work in the months following his last visit to the Soviet embassy remain elusive. He was not a member of the ill-fated Marley network, since neither Herman Marley nor Ernst Hann betrayed his identity during their interrogations. He may have reported to another controller, or he may have been a "sleeper," and Moscow's radio instructions to Hann to contact the inhabitant of the Via Cheren were an effort to activate the Estonian. Whatever his connections with Moscow, Kurtna remained in Rome and continued his work inside the Vatican protected for the moment from the scrutiny of the Italian police by his quiet lifestyle and his ecclesiastical associations. He did not, however, escape the notice of the Gestapo.

In January 1942 Dr. Ferdinand Bock informed Kurtna that the German Historical Institute had been instructed by the Reich embassy in Rome to dismiss all non-German employees. Kurtna's monthly research stipend was immediately terminated. Apologizing profusely for this unfortunate development, Bock assured his Estonian friend that he would do everything to help him find another source of income. As good as his word, Bock, in early February, arranged for Kurtna to meet his close friend Herbert Kappler, the police attaché at the German embassy. As good fortune (or good planning) would have it, Major Kappler had a vacancy in his office and was very interested, indeed, in the Vatican translator. He hired Kurtna on the spot, ostensibly to prepare press summaries of papal affairs. In fact Kurtna was recruited as a German spy inside the Vatican.[15]

Since 1939 Herbert Kappler had been responsible for organizing intelligence penetration of the Vatican for the RSHA, the central police and security service of the Reich. After almost three years of effort, the police attaché controlled only two informants: a librarian at the Pontifical Gregorian University, across town from the Vatican, and a private researcher whose studies took her occasionally into the Vatican archives.[16] This meager "network" produced little beyond academic gossip. Berlin was not impressed. Kappler desperately needed better sources, and Kurtna, with his post in the Congregation for the Eastern Churches and his access to personnel in the secretariat of state, was a godsend.

The Estonian was especially well positioned to shed light on the Vatican's plans for Russia. With that combination of paranoia, fantasy, and plain silliness that so often characterized Nazi appreciations of the Catholic Church, General Reinhard Heydrich, the chief of the RSHA, and his senior officers had convinced themselves that the Vatican planned to use Germany's attack on the Soviet Union to infiltrate priests into Russia. Specially trained priests, disguised as soldiers or businessmen or working undercover as military chaplains, would be the shock troops for the latest stage in what Heydrich and his colleagues in Nazi intelligence circles considered a long-term Vatican project to convert Russia to Catholicism, establish the influence of the Papacy in Russian society and politics, and eventually encircle Germany with Catholic states. In this fanciful scenario Cardinal Tisserant, the director of the Congregation for the Eastern Churches, was responsible for implementing the project (known to the cognoscenti in the Nazi security apparatus as the Tisserant Plan), to which end he allegedly directed a clandestine apparatus of disciplined priests and pliant laypeople that extended across eastern Europe and into the Russian lands occupied by the German army.[17] In fact the Vatican had no such plan and no such apparatus, but Heydrich and the RSHA saw disguised Jesuits behind every bush in the Ukraine, Belorussia, and the Baltic regions.[18] To thwart this imaginary threat to the Reich, Heydrich demanded intelligence on Tisserant and Catholic activities in eastern Europe. Under pressure from Berlin, Kappler must have seen Kurtna as an opportunity to impress the fearsome Heydrich by penetrating the very heart of the Vatican conspiracy.

Kurtna also provided an opportunity to confound the Russians. The German attack into the Soviet Union had eventually stalled in front of Moscow, and in December 1941 the Russians had launched a massive counterattack that pushed the Germans back and relieved pressure on the Russian capital. Frustrated in his plan to crush the Russians in one fierce campaign, Hitler replaced generals and assumed personal command of the army. Russian affairs increasingly preoccupied German intelligence services, and this interest percolated down to intelligence stations throughout Europe. In Rome Kappler had somehow uncovered Kurtna's Soviet connections. In February 1942, the very month he recruited the Estonian, the police attaché informed Berlin that he had opened a connection to the Russian intelligence service, and in April he referred to his use of a Soviet informant from the Baltic. Kappler was probably aware that information provided to Berlin by Kurtna might also find its way to Moscow, but he intended to use his new recruit to penetrate Soviet intelligence operations in Rome and to feed disinformation to the Russians.[19]

After his recruitment of Kurtna, the police attaché's reports on the Vatican were suddenly rich with Russian news, precisely the intelligence for which Heydrich was clamoring. In February 1942, for instance, Kappler forwarded to Berlin a summary of the Vatican's Russian policy, an item on a Jesuit "information bureau" for Czech and Slovak affairs, and a report concerning alleged clandestine radio transmissions between the Vatican and the Ukraine. In March he filed items on Jesuit influence on the pope's eastern policy, the arrival of letters from Lithuania at the Vatican Information Office (an agency organized to trace prisoners of war but suspected by the Germans of performing covert intelligence functions), the identities of important Catholic personalities in eastern Europe, and the processing of clandestine mail from German-occupied eastern Europe. In one report Kappler identified the Jesuit Father Charles Bourgeois, then living in Estonia, as the author of a critical report that had secretly reached the Vatican on German policy in the former Baltic republics now occupied by German forces. Alerted by their representative in Rome, the Gestapo promptly arrested the priest and transported him to a concentration camp on the charge of clandestine communication with a foreign power (the Vatican).[20]

In June 1942 Alexander Kurtna left Rome for a visit to German-occupied Estonia. Supposedly, he was returning to his homeland to renew his research grant, but this story rings false. Although his application for travel permits was endorsed by Dr. Ferdinand Bock, the director of the German Historical Institute in Rome (and the individual who had "spotted" the Estonian for Major Kappler), it is unlikely that military and police authorities would have permitted a twenty-eight-year-old Estonian to travel across the Reich to Tallinn for *any* reason, let alone one so irrelevant to the war effort as the renewal of a small research grant. The trip could have occurred only with the support of the Gestapo representative in Rome. Kappler probably hoped to collect intelligence on Catholic activities in Poland and the Baltic States by sending to those areas an individual who was sufficiently established in the Vatican that he might be trusted by his superiors in the Congregation for the Eastern Churches to carry messages or make clandestine contact with bishops and priests in the occupied territories.[21]

It was upon his return to Rome from Estonia on 30 July 1942 that Kurtna was arrested at the train station by Italian counterintelligence officers. Knowing nothing of their prisoner's work for the Gestapo, the Italians focused on his relationship with the Russians. Suspicion of Kurtna's connections with Moscow deepened when, shortly after his arrest, SIM intercepted a letter addressed to him by a Russian woman in Istanbul who asked for the latest news. This letter appeared to connect with the earlier radio transmission from Moscow, which had instructed Kurtna to communicate with an address in Istanbul. Through fourteen months of incarceration and twenty interrogations, Kurtna steadfastly denied that he was a Soviet agent, though he eventually revealed his connection with Herbert Kappler. In the face of the damning evidence, he could only suggest that he was an innocent victim of a Russian ploy to involve him, for reasons unknown, in an intelligence scandal.

The Italians were unconvinced, although they eventually uncovered enough about Kurtna's relationship with Kappler to wonder if their prisoner's principal allegiance was to Berlin or Moscow. Noting their suspect's casual connection with Cardinal Tisserant, a former officer in the French army who was suspected by both German and Italian security services of passing information to French intelligence, some officers even speculated that the Estonian was working for France. In the end, the Italians concluded that Kurtna was a Soviet agent who had been used by Moscow to penetrate the Vatican as well as German intelligence operations in Rome.[22]

Judicial proceedings against the alleged spy were delayed by the lengthy investigation and by the administrative confusion following the dismissal and arrest of the Italian dictator, Benito Mussolini, by King Vittorio Emanuele and the army high command on 23 July 1943. The Estonian, however, did not escape his day in court. On 29 September 1943 an Italian military tribunal condemned him to death for espionage on behalf of the Russian intelligence service. Within hours of his sentencing, however, Kurtna was saved by his other employer.

Herbert Kappler had had a run of bad luck. As the senior security officer in the German embassy, he had been surprised in June 1942 when Italian counterintelligence revealed that Kurt Sauer, a cultural attaché in the embassy and a popular figure in Roman society, had been passing information to the Swiss military attaché in Rome and also to Ernst Hann, the radio operator of the Soviet spy ring rolled up by the Italians that spring.[23]

This security scandal was followed within a month by the arrest of Alexander Kurtna. Already embarrassed by the Sauer affair, Kappler was outraged by the Kurtna case, which threatened to further dull his already tarnished professional reputation. Once again, the chief of German security in Rome was confronted with the leakage of German secrets to a foreign power, a leakage that would have remained unplugged save for the efforts of the Italians. Furthermore, with the Estonian inside an Italian jail, the police attaché lost his most important source inside the Vatican, a loss for which his handful of minor sources could not compensate. Overnight the copious flow of information from inside the Vatican slowed to a trickle. Unfortunately, Berlin's appetite for intelligence on papal affairs showed no sign of abating, and Kappler now found himself in the professionally awkward position of having no intelligence product to offer his demanding customers.

Herbert Kappler's fortunes took a turn for the better on 8 September 1943 when the government of Marshall Pietro Badoglio announced an armistice with the Allies and withdrew Italy from the Axis war effort. In reaction to this "treachery," German forces occupied Rome, and Kappler, the senior German police official, effectively became the police chief of the Eternal City. With his new authority, the Gestapo officer moved quickly to reestablish his Vatican connection and punish the Italians for their impudence in arresting his most valuable agent. Upon learning of Kurtna's sentencing, Kappler ordered the immediate release of the Estonian and the removal to Gestapo headquarters on the Via Tasso of all files relating to his investigation.[24]

Kappler intended to play Kurtna back into the Vatican. With Allied armies in southern Italy and the pope suspected by Berlin of collaborating in the overthrow of Mussolini and abetting Italy's abandonment of the Axis cause, intelligence from the Vatican was more important than ever. It is, perhaps, a sign of Kappler's desperation that he was forced to use a compromised agent whose loyalties were, to say the least, problematic. Of course the Gestapo chief had no intention of relying on Kurtna's loyalty; he expected to control the Estonian through fear. Kappler reminded his erstwhile agent that he and his wife could be rearrested and deported to Germany at any time. He also had Kurtna sign a document stipulating that he would do nothing prejudicial to Germany and its war effort on pain of summary execution.[25]

The Kurtnas found a flat on the Via Cola di Rienzo, a bustling street only a few blocks from the Vatican, and Alexander returned to his job as a translator for the Congregation for the Eastern Churches. The Vatican's decision to reemploy an individual who was not only convicted of espionage for the Soviet Union but also connected with the Gestapo is, to say the least, curious. Papal officials may have been hard-pressed to find a replacement for Kurtna with the Estonian's impressive command of east European languages. Also, Vatican authorities were never very security conscious, and they had neither the appetite nor the resources for serious counterespionage. Their usual practice was to remove temptation by shifting officials suspected of improper connections or behavior to positions where they could do little damage. It is likely, therefore, that Kurtna's supervisors in the Congregation for the Eastern Churches now restricted his access to sensitive material, thereby reducing his usefulness to any intelligence service, German or Russian. It is also possible that these supervisors allowed Kurtna to handle only material the Vatican wanted Moscow or Berlin to see.

In the weeks following his rescue from Italian justice, Kurtna regularly visited the Gestapo offices on the Via Tasso, where he would be questioned about Vatican affairs and personalities by Kappler's aides, Kurt Hass and Norbert Meyer. During these visits he gradually ingratiated himself with Kappler's confidential secretary, a Fraulein Schwarzer, to whom he had been introduced by a mutual friend. This friend assured Kurtna that despite her sensitive position with the Gestapo, Schwarzer secretly nurtured Communist sympathies. Whether through personal charm or ideological affinity, the Estonian made quite an impression on the secretary, who may also have hoped to curry favor with the Russians as the advancing Red Army drew closer to her family's home in Silesia. Soon after their introduction, she agreed to remove from her boss's safe certain compromising documents concerning Kurtna's arrest and interrogation by the Italians. She also shared all the office gossip concerning personnel and operations.[26]

In January 1944 Kurtna also began reporting to Georg Elling, a former Benedictine monk who had abandoned the black robes of his religious order for the black uniform of the Sicherheitsdienst (SD), the foreign intelligence arm of the RSHA, where he served as a church specialist. Heinrich Himmler, Reichsführer SS and chief of the German Police, had arranged (over Ambassador Weizsäcker's vehement opposition) for Elling's attachment to the German embassy to the Holy See as a cultural attaché. His real assignment was to improve intelligence coverage of the Vatican and prepare "stay-behind" networks in Rome in anticipation of Allied liberation of the Eternal City. Although the main Allied advance up the Italian peninsula had stalled in fierce fighting in the rugged terrain around the famous mountaintop abbey of Montecassino 130 kilometers south of Rome, American and British troops had unexpectedly outflanked the Germans by landing at the small port of Anzio on 22 January 1944. Anzio was only 57 kilometers from the capital, and although the Germans prevented the Allied forces from breaking out, the threat to Rome could not be ignored. In the event the Allies captured the Eternal City, the German embassy to the Holy See (following the precedent set earlier by British, American, and other Allied embassies) expected to seek refuge inside Vatican City. Protected by diplomatic immunity and resident on neutral territory, Elling would be beyond the reach of Allied counterintelligence agencies. From this sanctuary he could direct his agents against Allied targets with impunity.

By the spring of 1944 Elling had established an "ecclesiastical" network to cover the Vatican and Catholic circles in Rome. Alexander Kurtna was the star of this group, which also included a priest in the Vatican Information Office (the bureau concerned with tracing prisoners of war), a monsignor in the Congregation for the Consistory (the Vatican department concerned with the appointment of bishops), two Jesuits, one assigned to the Russicum and the other to the archive at Jesuit headquarters near the Vatican, and three Benedictine monks at the order's headquarters on the Aventine Hill. Except for Kurtna, the members of this group were all Germans or Italians. Elling also recruited several journalists into a "diplomatic" network to cover political affairs in Rome after the arrival of the Allies.[27]

From the surviving evidence it is impossible to determine how Alexander Kurtna reestablished contact with Soviet intelligence after his rescue from Italian custody by Herbert Kappler. There can be no doubt, however, that the Estonian maintained his allegiance to Moscow and worked inside German intelligence as a double agent for the Soviet Union.[28] On 1 June 1944, with the Allies on the outskirts of Rome, Fraulein Schwarzer informed Kurtna that a new codebook had arrived from Berlin for Georg Elling just as that undercover agent was preparing to accompany the German embassy into Vatican City. Appealing to her secret Communist sympathies, Kurtna convinced the secretary to copy as much of the new codebook as she could. He also had her remove from Kappler's private files as many documents as possible. Schwarzer's work was abetted by the confusion surrounding the Gestapo's last hours in Rome. In the rush to evacuate their headquarters, officers grabbed whatever files were at hand and threw them into hastily collected vehicles. Confidential files were strewn about offices and hallways, and many would be abandoned. Schwarzer managed to secure for Kurtna not only a copy of Elling's new code but also a list of all the agents, including radio operators, that the Germans had organized into stay-behind networks in Rome. On 5 June, as Allied forces began to consolidate their control over the Eternal City, Kurtna wrapped the codebook and the documents into a package, which he carried to the Vatican. In a hurried meeting with his friend Monsignor Mario Brini, the Russian specialist in the secretariat of state, Kurtna asked the papal diplomat to take the package and pass it to Soviet representatives when they arrived in Rome with the Allied occupation authorities. Brini, the only Russian-speaking official in the secretariat, must have been puzzled by this strange request, but he accepted the commission, and eventually the precious information about German intelligence operations in Rome reached the Soviets.

The Estonian had provided his last service to Russian intelligence, but like so many servants of Moscow, he found his masters unappreciative. The day after his meeting with Monsignor Brini, Kurtna was taken into custody by the same Italian officers who had arrested him at the Rome train station two years earlier. Now working for the Allies, the officers delivered their prisoner to Regina Coeli jail, where he was questioned about his connections with the Germans by American and British counterintelligence officials. The Allies, however, had little interest in an apparent case of espionage against the Vatican, and they soon released the sometime papal translator. Kurtna's movements after his release are cloaked in mystery; little is known for sure except that the Estonian disappeared from Rome. According to one story, he was walking along the Via Cola di Rienzo near his apartment when he was approached by two men who then bundled him into a waiting automobile. The car drove directly to Naples, where Kurtna was taken aboard a Russian vessel that sailed within the hour for the Black Sea. In 1948 a friend from prewar days spotted him in a Soviet labor camp, where the former seminarian, who had penetrated both the Vatican and the Gestapo for Moscow, was an inmate working in the camp infirmary. Like many other wartime Russian agents, Alexander Kurtna was poorly repaid for his loyalty to the Soviet Union.[29]

Among the wartime belligerents, few governments were as active in running intelligence operations against the Vatican as Germany, Italy, or the Soviet Union. Some, such as Britain, Finland, and Hungary, intercepted papal communications and cracked one or two minor ciphers that the secretariat of state reserved for routine and nonconfidential ecclesiastical business. Other governments were content with occasional surveillance of papal representatives and other Catholic ecclesiastics within their territory. Throughout the war, for example, the French police recorded the movements of the papal nuncio, Monsignor Valerio Valeri, in obsessive detail. When, in March 1943, the nuncio traveled from Vichy to Paris for a brief visit, police agents observed his departure from the capital of occupied France; noted the number of his train compartment and the identity of his traveling companions; recorded the make, color, and license plate of the car that met him in Paris; and discreetly followed him on his visits to churches and convents in the City of Light. While such diligent surveillance resulted in lengthy, if tedious, reports for the police files, it is unlikely that it produced much in the way of useful intelligence.

Most governments with diplomatic relations with the Holy See relied on routine diplomatic reporting from their embassies for intelligence concerning papal affairs. Many governments, especially among the minor powers, considered the Vatican a sinecure for senior diplomats of long service but modest attainment, or worthy political figures who could honorably pass the years until retirement in a quiet post with few responsibilities to distract them from the attractions of Italy. However, the major powers, especially Britain, France, Germany, and the United States, were represented by responsible and intelligent diplomats who worked hard to keep their governments abreast of developments at the Vatican.

In addition to its routine contacts with the secretariat of state, the French embassy also maintained close relations with the handful of French priests who worked in the papal Curia or occupied senior positions in the religious orders. Some, such as Monsignor Jullien, an official in the Vatican tribunal responsible for marriage annulments, had little access to sensitive information, but others, such as Father Boubé, an aide to Pope Pius XII, were better situated. Commenting on Father Boubé, Ambassador Wladimir Ormesson assured his foreign ministry that "despite the discretion required by his responsibilities, the Father never forgot that he was French." The embassy considered the priest's death in October 1940 "an acute loss for the French cause."[30]

Paris's best source on Vatican affairs was probably Cardinal Eugène Tisserant, the prefect of the Congregation for the Eastern Churches. Standing literally head and shoulders above most of his colleagues in the College of Cardinals, the tall, bushy-bearded Tisserant cut a wide swath through the frescoed corridors of the papal palace, where he was known for his erudition, command of exotic languages, and somewhat imperious manner. He was also the only member of the College of Cardinals who had led cavalry into action. Though an ordained priest, Tisserant had been mobilized into the French army in 1914 and seriously wounded in the early weeks of the First World War. He later served with distinction as a cavalry officer in the Palestine campaign that culminated in the capture of Jerusalem from the Turks. The future prelate also served a stint in French military intelligence. After the war he returned to his ecclesiastical and scholarly pursuits, taking up a post in the Vatican Library, where he specialized in Near

Eastern manuscripts. As he advanced through the curial ranks, becoming a cardinal in 1936 and the prefect for the eastern churches in 1937, Tisserant developed close and apparently cooperative contacts with French diplomats in Rome. Reminding Paris of the cardinal's patriotic attitude, the ambassador to the Vatican, François Charles-Roux, could hardly restrain his enthusiasm as he praised "that excellent Frenchman, totally devoted to his country." Tisserant was especially close to the various military attachés who represented French military intelligence in the Italian capital between the wars. On at least one occasion after the German conquest of Poland in 1939, he met privately with Henri Navarre, a senior officer in French intelligence. Resolutely anti-Nazi, Tisserant had little sympathy for the collaborationist regime in Vichy that governed France after the June 1940 armistice with Germany, and his relations with the Vichy embassy in Rome were cool. After the liberation of Rome (June 1944) and Paris (August 1944), the cardinal renewed his contacts with French intelligence.[31]

Lacking confidential relations with a powerful cardinal, other governments had to rely on the skills of their diplomats at the Vatican. In this case Britain was especially fortunate. Despite a touch of hypochondria, a predilection for old paintings of uncertain provenance, and finer wine, silver, and furniture than he could afford, the British ambassador, Sir d'Arcy Godolphin Francis Osborne, a career diplomat with service in Lisbon, Rome, and Washington before his appointment to the Holy See in 1936, was especially conscientious. His efforts to keep London informed, however, were seriously constrained when, upon Italy's declaration of war against Britain on 10 June 1940, he was forced to move into Vatican City. Completely surrounded by enemy territory and lacking a radio transmitter, Osborne could communicate with London only by means of the mail. Of course all private mail was opened by Italian censors and no British diplomatic couriers could reach him, but as a courtesy the papal secretariat of state allowed Osborne to consign his dispatches to the Vatican's diplomatic pouch, which moved between Rome and Bern twice a week in the custody of Swiss couriers. In the Swiss capital a representative of the British embassy would call at the papal delegation for the sealed envelope containing Osborne's reports. The embassy would then radio to London those reports Osborne had marked (and encrypted with his cipher) for immediate transmission and would forward the remainder by pouch to the Foreign Office by means of a circuitous route through Barcelona, Madrid, and Lisbon.[32]

Osborne did not trust this communication channel. He suspected (correctly) that his cipher was not secure. He also suspected (correctly) that the papal diplomatic pouch, while theoretically protected by international law against search and seizure, was subject to clandestine surveillance by Axis intelligence services.[33] The absence of a secure communications channel seriously constrained Osborne's ability to accurately report intelligence from the Vatican. He had, for example, many evidences of papal sympathy for the Allied cause but was reluctant to report them for fear that the information would be betrayed to the Axis, who would find a way to punish the pope. In February 1941 Osborne wrote to the foreign secretary, Anthony Eden:

> I am afraid that my communications about Vatican policy (if any) and sentiments are so cautious and reticent as to confirm what I expect is your bad opinion of the general attitude of the Holy See.
>
> The fact is that there are things I would like to say that would mitigate, I think, to some extent this opinion, but I dare not either write or telegraph them for I have not entire faith in my communications by either Bag or cypher telegram. . . .
>
> I am careful not to say anything of sentiments or expressions of opinion here that might be incriminating. And my style is consequently somewhat cramped in representing the Vatican attitude.
>
> I hope that you will bear this in mind if you are inclined to condemn me for lack of precision or the Vatican for lack of understanding of what is at stake in the war.[34]

Assuming the Italians (and possibly the Germans) were reading his dispatches, Osborne decided to turn the situation to some advantage by reporting false intelligence. He began to include misleading information in his reports with the intention of fooling Axis intelligence. Particularly concerned to protect the Vatican, which he considered dangerously exposed to Axis retribution, the ambassador avoided any mention of papal sympathy for the Allies and deliberately exaggerated Vatican sympathy for the Axis. Obviously this was a risky game. Though aimed at Berlin and Rome, the ploy might backfire by inadvertently convincing London that the pope supported the dictators. Although Osborne sent one message to London alerting the Foreign Office to his disinformation scheme, it is unclear whether his contrived reports contributed to the Foreign Office's generally jaundiced view of the Vatican during the war.[35]

Among the major belligerents, the United States was the last to turn its intelligence services against the Vatican. Washington had never considered the Papacy an important intelligence target, with the result that well into the war myth and prejudice rather than information and appraisal guided (or misguided) American policy makers in their dealings with Rome. For most of the country's history these dealings had been relatively limited. Although the United States had established diplomatic relations with the old Papal States for a brief period in the mid–nineteenth century, domestic politics, particularly the tradition of separation of church and state, and persistent anti-Catholicism among segments of the population discouraged the government from engaging the Vatican on the international stage. Only in exceptional circumstances, such as the Spanish-American War and the First World War, would Washington's attention turn toward the Vatican, and in such circumstances the lack of accurate information about the Vatican and its policies often caused confusion and misunderstanding.

Attitudes in Washington began to change in the late 1930s as the Roosevelt administration came to perceive the Papacy as a potential counterweight to Italian Fascism and German Nazism. In Italy, for example, the Vatican's daily newspaper, *L'Osservatore Romano,* and Vatican Radio were the only media outlets not subject to Fascist censorship and, therefore, the only voices capable of challenging the shrill militarism and nationalism of Fascist propaganda. This circumstance led to America's first covert operation at the Vatican.

On 4 July 1937 Ambassador William Phillips hosted a large Independence Day reception at the American embassy in Rome. The guests, members of the diplomatic community and Americans resident in Rome, included Monsignor Joseph Hurley, a priest from Newburgh, Ohio, then working in the pope's secretariat of state as the desk officer for North American affairs. Phillips had never met Hurley, and that day they merely exchanged pleasantries, but the priest clearly impressed the ambassador because soon after the reception Hurley received an invitation to visit the embassy. More invitations followed, and over the next year the American priest became a familiar face at the embassy, where he and Phillips would discuss current international events and share their concern for the growing power of Nazi Germany. During these conversations, the ambassador frequently alluded to his frustration with the Fascist regime's ability, through censorship of the Italian press, to twist the facts and manipulate public opinion without challenge or contradiction.[36]

During one of Hurley's visits in early September 1938, Phillips returned to the theme of Fascist censorship. Disagreements over the status of the Sudetenland region of Czechoslovakia were pushing Berlin and Prague toward a crisis, and the ambassador complained that the Italian press completely ignored recent statements on the situation by President Franklin D. Roosevelt and his secretary of state, Cordell Hull. Phillips asked his friend if there was any chance that the Vatican newspaper might report these comments. Hurley asked for copies of the statements and took them back to the Vatican. The following day he returned to the embassy to tell Phillips that *L'Osservatore Romano* would print in full the comments by Roosevelt and Hull. Also, the American priest asked the ambassador to pass to him any additional material from Washington that deserved publicity.

Throughout 1939 Hurley worked quietly but assiduously to place pro-American and pro-democracy articles in Vatican news outlets. This was risky work, since the Fascists did not shrink from violence to silence their enemies. Phillips did what he could to protect his Vatican contact. For instance, in his dispatches to Washington concerning his special channel to the Vatican, the ambassador did not mention Hurley's name, referring only to "a certain Monsignor who is a member of the Vatican Secretariat."[37] Since the staff of the pope's secretariat of state numbered scarcely thirty, and Hurley was the only American, Phillips's oblique reference to his source was rather transparent, but at least the ambassador was aware of the danger.

It was too much to expect that Hurley's assistance to the American embassy would escape the notice of Italian intelligence. Hurley never hid his disdain for Fascism, and almost from the moment of his arrival in Rome in 1934, he had attracted the attention of the secret police, who considered the American a political threat to the regime. Now the Fascists were outraged that the Vatican newspaper would provide front-page coverage of the latest speech by Franklin Roosevelt while ignoring or downplaying the proclamations of the Duce. In July 1939 Mussolini ordered his foreign minister (and son-in-law) Galeazzo Ciano to warn the Vatican that the distribution of its newspaper in Italy would be banned unless it ended "its subtle propaganda against the Axis."[38] Neither the Vatican nor Hurley was intimidated. In September 1939, only days after the German aggression against Poland, *L'Osservatore Romano* devoted six columns of its front page to coverage of President Roosevelt's effort to revise American neutrality legislation to help Britain and France resist "the forces which assault the foundations of civilization."[39] The Fascists moved immediately against the paper. A deputy editor was arrested and jailed on charges of antiregime activities. Mussolini's own newspaper, *Il Regime Fascista*, accused the Vatican of packing the editorial staff of *L'Osservatore Romano* with anti-Fascists. There were even rumors that the secret police were targeting Vatican personalities for physical assault.

Hurley, bolstered perhaps by word from Ambassador Phillips that President Roosevelt had expressed appreciation for the effort to place his words in the papal press, remained steadfast in his labors for the American embassy. On 1 July 1940, three weeks after Mussolini brought Italy into the war alongside Germany, Hurley delivered a speech over Vatican Radio warning Catholics against conscientious objection and pacifism in the face of evil and calling on them to defend justice, if necessary with their lives. The speech, which ran as the lead story on the front page of the *Times* of London, was interpreted as a call to American Catholics to abandon isolationism in favor of Roosevelt's policy of responsible interventionism. Hurley was now walking down an increasingly dangerous path. Aware of how exposed he was, the priest noted in his diary, "The anti-Axis men at the Vatican seem to live in waiting for the axe."[40]

The ax soon fell on Hurley. On 13 August 1940 Patrick Barry, the bishop of St. Augustine, Florida, died. Usually the process of appointing a new bishop would take anywhere from six months to a year, but within three days of learning of Bishop Barry's death the Vatican announced the appointment of Monsignor Joseph Hurley as the new bishop of St. Augustine. The newly promoted monsignor immediately departed Rome for his diocese. It is unclear whether the Vatican transferred Hurley so quickly because it feared for his safety or because it hoped to placate Mussolini's regime by removing from Rome an anti-Fascist voice. Whatever the rationale, the American embassy lost an important agent of influence inside the Vatican.

Although Monsignor Hurley collaborated with the American embassy in placing information in Vatican news channels, he did not provide Ambassador Phillips intelligence on papal affairs. He was never an American spy inside the Vatican.[41] The United States had no spies inside the Vatican; in fact, it really had few spies anywhere. Between the world wars American intelligence capabilities were modest. The State Department was responsible for collecting information on foreign political developments, and it did so overtly through routine diplomatic reporting by its embassies and consulates. There was, of course, no American embassy at the Vatican, but the occasional item of news concerning the Papacy might find its way to the State Department from the embassy to Italy or other diplomatic sources. In the late 1930s, for example, the American ambassador in Poland, Anthony Drexel Biddle, passed to Washington some surprisingly accurate information concerning Vatican personalities and affairs that he obtained from a Polish nobleman whose identity and sources remain unknown.[42] The U.S. Navy's Office of Naval Intelligence and the U.S. Army's Military Intelligence Division served the intelligence requirements of their respective services and, consequently, focused on the collection of military and naval information.

The service intelligence units rarely resorted to clandestine operations, preferring to rely on open sources such as newspapers, professional journals, and the observations of army and navy attachés in American embassies. They had little reason to notice the militarily insignificant Vatican. It is unlikely that questions about the armament of the Swiss Guard or the force levels of the pontifical police would have interested even the most conscientious officer in the Military Intelligence Division.

The onset of war in September 1939 stimulated Washington's interest in the Vatican. Like most other statesmen, Roosevelt and his advisers believed that the thick walls of the Apostolic Palace protected a trove of political, economic, and military secrets assiduously collected and transmitted to Rome by faithful Catholics around the globe. Access to these secrets, the argument ran, would provide American policy makers with an insight into political developments in every country from Afghanistan to Yugoslavia. Furthermore, any effort to induce Pope Pius XII to collaborate with President Roosevelt in restraining Mussolini from marching to war alongside Hitler would require accurate information about the pope and his plans. The perceived need for more information from the Vatican contributed significantly to President Roosevelt's decision in December 1939 to send Myron Taylor as his personal representative to the pope, a decision that established, de facto if not de jure, the first American diplomatic presence at the Holy See since 1867.

For all the new interest in the Vatican, American intelligence was slow to focus on the Papacy. Even the creation of a new, civilian intelligence agency, the Coordinator of Information (COI), in July 1941 had little immediate effect on American coverage of the Vatican. During its brief life, COI was preoccupied with establishing its organizational credibility and fending off hostile takeover bids by the army and the navy, neither of which appreciated a competitor in the field of intelligence. It had little opportunity to organize intelligence operations against anyone. Although at the time of its demise in the summer of 1942 it had begun to send representatives overseas to collect information, COI relied primarily on the occasional item grudgingly shared by army or navy intelligence, careful scrutiny of open sources such as newspapers and journals, and interviews with journalists and refugees newly arrived from Europe. The fledgling intelligence service exhibited little interest in the Vatican, although news concerning Catholic organizations and affairs would sometimes surface, as when Louis Lochner, former Berlin bureau chief for the Associated Press, discussed with a COI debriefer the role of Catholics in the anti-Hitler resistance inside Germany.[43]

The Office of Strategic Services (OSS), established in July 1942 to replace COI, proved a more substantial and long-lived institution. More important, its director, William Donovan, believed that the intelligence requirements of a global war demanded an approach that abandoned the narrow and parochial focus of the military intelligence services in favor of an expansive, more inclusive outlook that recognized intelligence value in the broadest possible range of political, economic, cultural, technological, scientific, and religious questions. For Donovan, global war required a global approach to intelligence in which everything was a potential target. Bold new vision, however, did not automatically translate into bold new operations. For some time OSS maintained a rather passive attitude toward the Vatican. For several months after its foundation, Donovan's service was preoccupied by the same disagreements with the armed services that had distracted its predecessor agency, COI. During this time bureaucratic battles in Washington often required more attention than intelligence operations abroad. When OSS finally took the field in the fall of 1942, military issues predominated over diplomatic in the competition for the attention of policy makers. On the list of intelligence priorities, the Vatican was nudged lower by other targets more relevant to immediate military needs, such as preparations for the invasion of North Africa, or by special operations that caught the fancy of "Wild Bill" Donovan. As late as the summer of 1943, the Italian section of OSS devoted little effort to intelligence operations other than those in support of the Allied invasion of Sicily.[44]

Political geography was also a problem. Vatican City remained a small neutral island in a sea of Fascism. Any Allied intelligence service faced imposing problems in gaining access to papal territory and personnel. In the first year of its existence, OSS simply did not have the capability to run operations directly into Italy, let alone the Vatican, and Donovan's organization had no personnel specifically assigned to the Vatican intelligence problem.

Some information was acquired ("collected" would suggest more purpose than was present) through indirect means: press and radio reports, interviews with political exiles and travelers, and gossip from the diplomatic cocktail party circuit. There was, however, little system and even less direction in this process. Not surprisingly, the results were, at best, mixed. Most of this "intelligence" on the Vatican could not be confirmed and was, consequently, of uncertain reliability. Many of the items, such as a report that Monsignor Mario Zanin was the papal representative to China, were true but trivial. Others were almost comic in their absurdity. The same report that breathlessly announced that Monsignor Zanin was the papal delegate in

China (a piece of information so secret that it was publicly announced by the papal secretariat of state, reported by Vatican Radio and L'Osservatore Romano, and published in the papal yearbook, Annuario Pontificio) also claimed that there were ten thousand native seminarians preparing for the Catholic priesthood in China, an estimate that exaggerated the number of seminarians by a factor of ten.[45] A source who had not been in Italy since April 1941 reported in January 1943 that when he left Italy, the chief of the cipher office in the secretariat of state was an Irish priest (unidentified) who was a member of the Irish Republican Army and who exhibited his violent Anglophobia by publicly proclaiming that he praised God for every German bomb dropped on London. As an extra touch the source revealed that the papal cryptographer was a "crack golfer." In fact, no Irish priest worked in the secretariat of state in 1941. The chief of the papal cipher office was an Italian monsignor, Amadeo Finnochi, who did not play golf and almost certainly was not a member of the IRA.[46] A top secret report from April 1943 asserted that Leon Helfand, a Soviet diplomat then working under the nom de guerre "Moore," had arrived at the Vatican at the head of a secret delegation from Stalin. The story was completely fanciful. In fact, Helfand (a Russian intelligence officer as well as diplomat) had defected to the Italians in July 1940. The Italian foreign minister, Count Galeazzo Ciano, had quietly contacted the U.S. State Department and arranged for the defector and his family to receive American visas. At the time of his alleged mission to the pope, Helfand was actually somewhere in North America hiding from his former employers in the Soviet intelligence service.[47]

Perhaps the most credible of these indirect sources was "George Wood," the cover name of Fritz Kolbe, a midlevel official in the German foreign ministry who volunteered his services to American intelligence in the summer of 1943. Through a friend in the Wilhelmstrasse's courier section, Kolbe several times arranged to carry the German diplomatic pouch to Bern. During these brief visits he would pass to Allen Dulles, the OSS representative in the Swiss capital, copies of foreign ministry documents, including cables from German embassies. Occasionally, Kolbe's material would include a report forwarded to Berlin by Baron Ernst von Weizsäcker, the German ambassador to the Holy See, but these items were only as good as the information reported (or misreported) by the ambassador, and they appeared too infrequently to allow American intelligence to construct a clear picture of affairs at the Vatican.[48]

Before the fall of Rome in June 1944, Washington's most reliable information on the Vatican came not from spies or purloined documents but from a disabled American war veteran pecking away at an ancient typewriter in a cramped apartment next to St. Peter's Basilica. Harold Tittmann was a pilot in the First World War whose military career was cut short when he lost a leg and the use of a hand in a plane crash. Joining the diplomatic service, Tittmann was an officer at the American embassy in Rome when, in February 1940, he was detached to serve as assistant to Myron Taylor, President Roosevelt's representative to the pope. Constrained by domestic political considerations from establishing a formal embassy at the Vatican, but desirous of opening a channel to the Papacy, Roosevelt settled on the expedient of sending a "personal representative," a title sufficiently ambiguous to defuse any political or legal protest from Protestants in the United States. A former president of United States Steel, Myron Taylor kept a suite at the Excelsior Hotel in Rome and a villa in Tuscany, but he spent most of the war in the United States, making only flying visits to the Vatican.[49] Tittmann, however, remained in Rome. After Pearl Harbor and Italy's subsequent declaration of war against the United States, he was compelled to move into Vatican City and take up residence in the convent of Santa Marta, which was already a claustrophobic home to the diplomatic missions of several other governments at war with Italy.

Tittmann was a conscientious diplomat, and during his enforced residence in the Vatican he worked diligently to inform Washington of the attitudes and intentions of his hosts. His efforts, however, were constrained by several factors. Papal protocol and diplomatic custom limited his access to only a handful of officials: the cardinal secretary of state, Luigi Maglione; his two undersecretaries, Monsignors Domenico Tardini and Giovanni Montini; and (infrequently) the pope himself. These were of course excellent sources, but their conversations with the American diplomat were inhibited by professional discretion, by a concern for Vatican neutrality, and by a desire to focus on certain topics (Allied bombing of Rome) while avoiding others (the political situation inside Italy). Social contacts with other Vatican personalities were infrequent. There were few Americans in the papal bureaucracy, and those who might have been useful sources, such as Monsignor Walter Carroll, who had replaced Monsignor Joseph Hurley in the secretariat of state, were reluctant to compromise themselves by being seen in the company of the American diplomat.

Tittmann was also constrained by the insecurity of his communication lines to Washington. Until the liberation of Rome in June 1944, Tittmann, like his British colleague, d'Arcy Osborne, could communicate with the world beyond Vatican City only via the papal diplomatic pouch to neutral Switzerland. Since the security of the pouch could not be assured, Tittmann, again like Osborne, had to be careful about what he reported in his dispatches. His situation was especially exposed, since he had no cipher with which to encrypt his dispatches. The State Department had refused to issue a cipher to the tiny American mission to the Vatican because department regulations restricted the use of ciphers to embassies and consulates, and "The President's Personal Representative to His Holiness Pope Pius XII" did not fall into either category. Because of this bureaucratic inflexibility, Tittmann had no way to protect his reports from prying eyes.[50]

Tittmann also realized that he was under observation by the Fascist secret police, who used their contacts in the Vatican police to monitor the activities and contacts of Allied diplomats inside papal territory. Additionally, Italian intelligence suborned servants to report on their employers and purloin documents. Of course Tittmann was rarely allowed to leave the neutral territory of Vatican City and then only in the company of an Italian police officer, so he could not contact individuals or observe events beyond the walls of the papal enclave.

Fearful that any hint of espionage would embarrass the pope and compromise U.S.-Vatican relations, and aware that he and his communications were under surveillance, Tittmann limited himself to overt diplomatic representation and scrupulously avoided any suggestion of clandestine activity. Early in the war, for example, Josef Müller, the Abwehr agent who maintained liaison between the Vatican and the anti-Hitler resistance inside Germany, offered, through the father superior of a religious order in Rome, to supply Tittmann with information concerning the German army. The American diplomat adamantly refused to send the intelligence to Washington.[51]

For Washington the intelligence situation began to improve only after the Allies liberated Rome in June 1944. With Allied authorities in control of the city administration, the police, and the phone, cable, and radio facilities, the problem of access to the Vatican and its personnel lessened, and OSS quickly established in the Eternal City an intelligence station that would include the Vatican among its targets. American intelligence certainly had more reason to attend to the Papacy. With the liberation of the Italian capital, Axis diplomatic missions to the pope sought refuge inside Vatican City, in many cases occupying the same cramped apartments in Santa Marta recently vacated by their Allied opposite numbers. Just as the Germans and Italians had suspected American and British diplomats inside papal territory of espionage and subversion, so too did Allied intelligence officers decide that the Vatican's German and Japanese guests posed a security threat that demanded vigilance. Furthermore, many Fascist officials from Mussolini's now discredited regime sought refuge in monasteries and religious houses in Rome, and these fugitives required apprehension or at least surveillance.

Washington was also increasingly concerned about the Vatican's attitude toward the role the Soviet Union and Communist political parties would assume in postwar Europe. Committed to the wartime alliance with the Soviet Union and hopeful that cooperation with Moscow would ensure peace and reconstruction after the war, Washington worried about Catholic anti-Communism. The Vatican's well-founded suspicion of the "godless" regime in Moscow might complicate Great Power relations in the Catholic countries of postwar Europe, especially those such as Poland, that would find themselves in the shadow of a victorious and powerful Soviet Union. Additionally, a hostile attitude toward Russia on the part of the Vatican might have reverberations in American domestic politics as American Catholics responded to the anti-Communist cues of their leaders in Rome. In the last year of the war Washington worked assiduously to convince the Vatican that Catholicism and western Europe had nothing to fear from a powerful Soviet Union. The success of this effort depended, in part, on identifying the Vatican's specific concerns and anticipating its moves.

These issues made the Vatican an increasingly important target for American intelligence. Initially the new OSS station in Rome limited its operations against the Vatican to establishing informal contacts with papal officials who helped American intelligence monitor the movements and activities of former Fascist officials who had sought sanctuary in ecclesiastical buildings in Rome.[52] In the closing months of 1944, however, OSS launched clandestine operations that specifically targeted the Vatican.

In the fall of 1944 OSS Rome began to receive intelligence from two apparently well-placed sources inside the Vatican. Code-named Vessel, the first source had approached the Secret Intelligence branch (SI) of the Rome station in the fall of 1944 with an offer to sell copies of secret papal documents. Soon thereafter, the Counterespionage branch (X-2) of the station received a similar offer from an individual it called Dusty. Together Dusty and Vessel offered OSS a cornucopia of documents: copies of top secret telegrams exchanged between the secretariat of state and its nuncios, minutes of the pope's meetings with cardinals and bishops, confidential memorandums from various Vatican departments. The material illuminated the darkest recesses of papal diplomacy and administration. One day there would be a report that the secretariat of state had instructed the nuncio in Belgium to monitor collaboration between Catholic associations and left-wing political organizations; the next day an item revealing that the pope had recalled his delegate in Iran to prepare a plan for opening diplomatic relations with the Soviet Union; the following day a copy of a cable from the papal representative in Tokyo summarizing the political situation in Japan.[53]

OSS was ecstatic. It now had not one but two agents inside the Vatican, and the intelligence product from these sources circulated at the highest levels of American government, including the White House. Although OSS routinely shared intelligence with the British secret service, Dusty and Vessel were considered so precious that Washington decided not to pass their reports to London.[54] Many of these reports related specifically to issues that preoccupied American policy makers in the last year of the war. Concerned that Catholic anti-Communism might complicate U.S.-Soviet relations and the political reconstruction of postwar Europe, the White House and the State Department must have been relieved by Vessel/Dusty reports that the Vatican had so softened its attitude toward the Soviet Union that it was considering establishing diplomatic relations with Moscow.

Copies provided by Vessel of telegrams from Monsignor Paolo Marella, the apostolic delegate in Tokyo, especially excited policy makers. These telegrams contained details of political, military, and economic conditions inside the Japanese Empire. They included reports of Japanese military and naval movements; informed speculation about Russian policy toward Japan; appraisals of political developments in Japan, China, and Manchuria; and discussions of possible papal mediation of the Pacific war. At a time when the White House was complaining about the dearth of reports from human sources inside Japan, such a cornucopia of intelligence from inside the Vatican was a godsend. It all seemed too good to be true. It *was* too good to be true.

Dusty and Vessel were the product of the fertile imagination and skillful pen of Virgilio Scattolini—journalist, pornographer, assistant, and occasional film critic at *L'Osservatore Romano,* and the most brazen intelligence fabricator of the Second World War. As early as 1939, by which time he was already supplementing his income by spying on the anti-Fascist editors of *L'Osservatore Romano* for Mussolini's secret police, Scattolini concluded that someone with initiative and imagination could become rich by selling to interested parties accounts of personalities and events inside the Vatican.[55] Possessing both initiative and imagination in large quantities, he saw no reason why he could not be that someone. The fact that he knew absolutely nothing about the secret politics of the Vatican discouraged him not a whit. In his apartment near the Spanish Steps in the heart of old Rome, Scattolini, whose literary production until this time had tended toward salacious works about randy monks and compliant serving girls, concocted stories based on a careful scrutiny of the pope's audience schedule as published in *L'Osservatore Romano* combined with a large dose of fanciful detail concerning the alleged content and results of such audience. Gradually even the audiences became imaginary as the busy writer sought to "improve" his reporting. From creating audiences from whole cloth it was a small step to creating diplomatic telegrams and departmental memorandums. The resulting fiction would then be offered, through middlemen, to unsuspecting "clients." Dusty and Vessel were such middlemen.

The closed, secretive, and (to outsiders) mysterious world of the Vatican inadvertently abetted this confidence game by creating an audience of journalists, diplomats, and intelligence operatives starved for any information about papal affairs and by inhibiting any effort to confirm the veracity of Vessel's often dramatic revelations. Scattolini's lucrative practice was interrupted by the Italian police in 1942, but after the liberation of Rome he returned to his old stand, and his unsuspecting clients soon included newspapers, banks, embassies, and the intelligence services of several countries.[56] Bedazzled by the prospect of penetrating the very heart of the Papacy, OSS proved especially gullible; in fact, it would be some time before SI and X-2 realized that, by dealing with Dusty and Vessel, they were paying twice for the same information.

Scattolini's edifice of lies began to collapse in early 1945 when the State Department was astonished to read in a Vessel report that Myron Taylor, the president's personal representative to the pope, had met secretly with Ken Harada, the Japanese ambassador to the Holy See. This was news to the State Department. No one in Washington had authorized any such meeting, and Taylor had reported the alleged encounter to neither the White House nor the State Department. Asked to explain his irregular behavior, a surprised Taylor vehemently denied any contact with Japanese diplomats.[57]

The Taylor affair set off alarm bells in Washington and raised doubts in the minds of intelligence officials about the accuracy of the intelligence that was now known generically as Vessel. As these officials scrutinized more carefully the reports from the Vatican, checking for inconsistencies and comparing the details to reports from other sources, the doubts multiplied. Although case officers in Italy affirmed their confidence in their source, Washington was increasingly skeptical. On 17 February 1945 OSS headquarters warned its Italian outpost that the Vessel material "has earmarks of being concocted by a not too clever manufacturer of sales information. As a result, for the time being we are withholding the dissemination of most of this material." Two weeks later Washington was even more frank about its suspicions: "Whereas some unimportant items of Vessel material may be based on factual knowledge of the source, the more important items are believed to be manufactured by the source out of whole cloth or are plants."58

Despite the increasing skepticism about Vessel, the Office of Strategic Services did not immediately abandon its Vatican source. In the field, case officers were loath to admit they had been fooled by a confidence trickster, while in Washington senior officers were no more eager to wipe egg from their faces. For a time, OSS headquarters somehow convinced itself that the Vessel items dealing with Japan and the Far East were more credible than those dealing with other topics. This posture possibly reflected the service's desperate search for intelligence—any intelligence—from inside the Japanese Empire. Commenting on Vessel's summaries of reports allegedly reaching the Vatican from its representatives in the Far East, OSS admitted, "There is no other equally good source of information on current political developments in Japan. [Vessel] should therefore be retained."59 Eventually, even this faint endorsement could not be sustained. While OSS managers were concluding that Vessel's Far Eastern reports were better than nothing, the OSS office concerned with secret intelligence from Japan completed a review of five months of Vessel reports and submitted a scathing appraisal of their Vatican source. Describing the Vessel reports on Japan as confused, vague, and self-contradictory, the report commented that "such information cannot, of course, constitute valid intelligence." The conclusion was equally stark: "On the basis of this analysis of five months of cable information in which we have received hardly a shred of positive intelligence, Vessel source would seem to be of almost no value to us."60

Virgilio Scattolini could bamboozle OSS only because American intelligence had so few sources in the Vatican. Without additional contacts inside the papal administration, it was difficult, if not impossible, to confirm Vessel's reports or determine his identity.61 In fact there were other sources, although there is little evidence that OSS sought to use them to check Vessel's reports. Whatever the Vessel debacle says about OSS coverage of the Vatican, it clearly reveals that American intelligence was perfectly ignorant of the Catholic Church in general and the Vatican in particular.

Washington now paid the price for its traditional indifference toward the Papacy and its activities. Knowing nothing about administrative practices and ecclesiastical relationships inside the Vatican, intelligence officers in Rome and Washington had no basis for challenging the reports that came in from "reliable sources." They were prepared to believe anything, and the results were often ludicrous. On one occasion, for example, OSS

Rome confidently passed to Washington a Vessel report that ecclesiastical authorities were proceeding with plans to construct an airstrip in the Vatican gardens.⁶² One can only stand in awe of Scattolini's effrontery in passing this report to the Americans. By accepting this fantasy, the gullible OSS representatives demonstrated that they knew absolutely nothing about the physical, economic, or cultural geography of Vatican City, for to assign credibility to the airfield story the American agents had to believe several impossible things: that despite the deprivations of the war the Vatican could command the financial and material resources for a major construction project; that notoriously conservative and thrifty papal administrators, who were usually loath to restore the facade of a building, would suddenly embark on an expensive project to drastically alter the physical topography of Vatican City; and, most remarkably, that anyone could expect a plane to land on a runway less than one hundred yards long, laid out on the side of a hill, and surrounded by multistory buildings, including St. Peter's Basilica, the highest structure in Rome.

Amazingly, Scattolini continued to peddle his material to American intelligence until the end of 1945, months after the end of the war. Until then, some American intelligence authorities, including James Jesus Angleton, the otherwise shrewd chief of American counterintelligence in Rome, continued to express confidence in Scattolini's material. In early 1946, however, the master fabricator's lucrative relationship with American intelligence ended. A subsequent postmortem by the Central Intelligence Agency, the postwar successor to OSS, concluded that Scattolini's forgeries contributed to "misinforming and thoroughly confusing those individuals responsible for analyzing Vatican foreign policy during the period involved."⁶³

Undeterred by American disfavor, the irrepressible Scattolini simply moved on to other clients, including, apparently, the Italian Communist Party. In 1948, at the height of the electoral competition between the Communists and the pro-American Christian Democratic Party, some of Scattolini's wartime forgeries appeared in two books issued by a party publishing house, which presented the material as authentic Vatican documents. After years of putting up with the forger's escapades, the Vatican finally protested to the Italian government. Scattolini was charged and convicted in an Italian court of "creating and distributing false information concerning Vatican policy" and "hostile acts against a foreign state." The court sentenced him to a brief spell in jail. Upon his release, he slipped into quiet retirement, to the relief of any number of his former "clients" in the intelligence world.⁶⁴

While its Rome station was falling for the schemes of a con man, OSS headquarters developed another operation aimed at the Vatican. In February 1942 Phillip Rodgers, an idealistic young Catholic associated with liberal causes and then working in New York City for an organization called the Council for Democracy, had approached the coordinator of information with a proposal to use "left-Catholic" individuals and organizations in Europe and Latin America to disseminate pro-American and pro-Allied propaganda. Rodgers had also proposed to use these contacts to develop an intelligence service to collect information on the Vatican. Subsequently, Rodgers submitted to COI reports on such topics as Austrian émigré groups and Mexican politics in an effort to demonstrate the worth of his contacts, but in the desperate weeks following the attack on Pearl Harbor, American intelligence had little time for a dilettante and his memos on politically marginal topics.[65]

By the late summer of 1942, with the immediate Japanese threat repelled by the overwhelming American naval victory at the battle of Midway and the newly organized Office of Strategic Services considering the need for better sources in Europe, American intelligence had more time for Phillip Rodgers. OSS was particularly interested in his connection with a Catholic press agency called the Center of Information Pro Deo. This agency was one of several organizations that appeared in the 1930s with the tacit support of the Vatican to "infuse the spiritual into the material world" by publishing Catholic commentaries on political, economic, and social subjects. With the rise of Hitler, the Pro Deo offices in Amsterdam and Brussels, with their press contacts inside Germany, became important sources for information concerning the Nazi persecution of the churches. When Germany invaded Belgium in May 1940, the director of the Brussels office, a young Dominican priest and journalist named Felix Morlion, fled, first to Paris and then to Lisbon. In the Portuguese capital Father Morlion opened another Pro Deo office, but German pressure on the Portuguese government forced him to relocate to New York City in the summer of 1941. With the assistance of Anna Brady, a well-known journalist who after her conversion to Catholicism in 1928 had become active in Catholic propaganda and communications, Morlion established the Catholic International Press (CIP), a news service affiliated with Pro Deo and dedicated to providing a religious perspective on current political affairs.[66] Headquartered in New York City, CIP also opened offices in London and Lisbon. American authorities briefly suspected Father Morlion of pro-Fascist sympathies on the basis of several articles he researched on General Francisco Franco and the neo-Fascist Falange movement that supported the Spanish dictator, but an investigation by the Federal Bureau of Investigation concluded that the Dominican priest was anti-Fascist and anti-Communist and posed no risk to the security of the United States.[67]

Soon after establishing CIP, Father Morlion approached Phillip Rodgers for help in expanding the reach of this Catholic press service. Subsequently, Rodgers had been contacted by a representative of Britain's Ministry of Information, the wartime propaganda arm of the British government, with a request for advice on how to ensure that the British position on a range of wartime issues was fairly presented to American Catholics, especially those of Irish extraction, whose attitudes toward Britain were, at best, problematic. Recalling his conversation with Father Morlion, Rodgers suggested that the British use the CIP bureau in London to relay to CIP headquarters in New York any information His Majesty's Government hoped to disseminate among American Catholics. CIP would then distribute this information to its clients in the American Catholic press.[68]

Having established the Catholic International Press as an instrument of British propaganda, Phillip Rodgers next connected CIP with the Office of Strategic Services. It is unclear when CIP began collaborating with American intelligence, but by early 1943 OSS was receiving reports from "Hank Judah," the cover name of J. C. Maier-Hultschin, a journalist who was the CIP correspondent in London. Maier-Hultschin had been recruited with the story that the American embassy in London would be interested in any political material he picked up from his contacts in Catholic and anti-Nazi émigré circles. It is unlikely that the experienced journalist, who seems to have been more interested in money than politics, believed this charade for long. OSS officers in London forwarded the Hank Judah material to the OSS station in New York, where, after examination by intelligence analysts, it was passed to CIP. Whatever material of political interest OSS New York could extract was "from time to time" circulated as "D Reports" by the Reporting Board at OSS headquarters in Washington. For its part, CIP treated Maier-Hultschin's material as straightforward news commentary and published it as such in its newsletter, CIP Correspondence.[69]

In the summer of 1944, shortly after the liberation of Rome, American intelligence expanded its collaboration with the Catholic International Press when Father Felix Morlion moved to the Eternal City as CIP's resident correspondent. OSS hoped that the friendly friar would be able to use his journalistic and clerical credentials to insinuate himself into high ecclesiastical circles. Assigned the code name "Bernard Black," Father Morlion was run by the OSS office in New York and not by the OSS stations in Rome and Caserta, which served only as conduits for funds and reports.

Designated "Pilgrim's Progress," the new operation got off to a promising start. Arriving in Rome in the summer of 1944, Morlion immediately threw himself into the turbulent political world of the newly liberated city. He went everywhere and seemed to know everyone. A fervent anti-Communist, he became involved with individuals in Italian business, ecclesiastical, and intellectual circles that were organizing conservative Catholic opinion against the emerging influence of the Communists, whose commitment to the anti-Fascist guerrilla movement that was active in German-occupied Italy had earned the respect and often the sympathy of large numbers of Italians. This work naturally brought him into contact with the Vatican, which also viewed the growing influence of the Communists with some trepidation.

Organizing meetings, leading discussion groups, writing a newsletter, and visiting administrative offices, ecclesiastical apartments, and aristocratic salons, Morlion did not neglect his intelligence duties; indeed, the meetings, discussion groups, and newsletter were an integral part of his work for OSS. He addressed his intelligence reports to a woman in the United States identified in the surviving documents only as "A. Smith." This cutout, who was almost certainly the noted Catholic journalist Anna Brady, dealt directly with OSS, which subsidized Morlion's residence in Rome and his trips to neutral or newly liberated countries in western Europe. Through Smith OSS also provided Morlion with press clippings, pamphlets, and books to assist him in "explaining the American reaction to world events in order to receive the ideas of the people with whom he deals." 70

It is unclear to what degree Morlion considered himself a witting agent of American intelligence. He may have convinced himself that the gentlemen who so generously assisted his travels were simply pious, wealthy Americans seeking to advance the work of CIP and support a Catholic political alternative to communism in Italy. OSS representatives seem to have presented themselves to Morlion as friendly, well-intentioned people who believed that his work was worthy of support. In her communications with him (which passed along secure OSS lines), the shadowy Ms. Smith, who certainly knew who was paying the bills, never mentioned American intelligence, referring only to "the men who have taken an interest in our work."71

Witting or not, the Belgian friar was a difficult agent to run. On the one hand, his access to Vatican authorities was impressive. In his reports he freely quoted the comments of this cardinal and that, and confidently described the attitudes and activities of prominent officials in the pope's administration. For instance, from Cardinal Eugéne Tisserant, who had recently returned to Rome from an extended visit to his homeland, where he had meetings with General Charles de Gaulle, the head of the provisional government of France, Morlion elicited a lengthy appraisal of the political strength of various groups in liberated France, including the Communist Party. Morlion was also able to describe the attitudes toward Russia and postwar Europe of other influential cardinals and monsignors. In February 1945, for example, he informed his friend Ms. Smith that papal officials were divided over the possibility of détente between the Vatican and the Soviet Union. According to Morlion, Cardinal Eugéne Tisserant, the head of the department responsible for church affairs in Russia, believed that relations with Moscow could be improved, as did Cardinal Francesco Marmaggi, a career papal diplomat who had served as papal nuncio in Czechoslovakia, Poland, and Romania; Monsignor Giovanni Montini, undersecretary in the secretariat of state; and Monsignor Filippo Cortesi, a former nuncio to Poland. However, according to Morlion, the pope remained staunchly anti-Communist, and he was encouraged in his intransigence by Monsignor Domenico Tardini, the other undersecretary in the secretariat of state, and Count Enrico Galeazzi, the senior lay administrator in Vatican City.[72]

On the other hand, solid accounts of papal politics and diplomacy were few and far between. More commonly the reports would be full of trivial news or gossip: a list of the personnel of the papal secretariat of state; a report that students at the University of Rome distrust political parties; an account of Cardinal Massimo Massimi weeping upon learning of President Franklin Roosevelt's death. Morlion's controllers complained that he too often pressed his sources on topics of little interest to American intelligence, and at one point a frustrated officer in Washington insisted that the good Dominican return to his source and make the cardinal "do [his] work over again." In his meetings with high ecclesiastics the intellectual friar was inclined to pursue those subjects, such as Catholic education and social action, that were close to his own heart. The resulting reports, didactic and theoretical expositions more suited to a learned society than a wartime intelligence service, drove his controllers to distraction. Reflecting the frustration of OSS headquarters, Smith chided Morlion for submitting reports on issues of only historical and academic interest and pressed him for factual and timely information about personalities and current developments inside the Vatican. She and the OSS controllers were much more interested in the Vatican's reaction to the Yalta conference or the composition of the postwar Polish government than a review of the nineteenth-century origins of the Catholic labor union movement or the prospects for government aid to private schools in postwar Belgium.[73]

By the early spring of 1945, OSS was having second thoughts about Father Morlion. In March the controller responsible for Operation Pilgrim's Progress traveled secretly to Rome to inspect the operation on the ground. That same month, authorities at OSS headquarters in Washington launched a critical review of the operation. Expressing his own reservations about the value of Pilgrim's Progress, a senior officer on the Reporting Board, the office responsible for circulating intelligence to decision makers, asked the analysts in the Italian section for a candid assessment of Morlion's production. The response was not encouraging. Noting that the items from the Dominican friar "distort facts, draw erroneous conclusions, and sometimes even manufacture alleged fact," the Italian section concluded that the reports might seriously mislead policy makers. Both the Italian section and the Reporting Board were convinced that Morlion could not resist the temptation to introduce his own political biases into the reports, and, consequently, the items were often little more than clerical-conservative propaganda or disinformation.[74]

By April 1945 OSS had lost confidence in Pilgrim's Progress, but it hesitated to terminate the operation and cut its ties to Felix Morlion. Beyond the end of the war the frenetic friar continued to file his reports and collect his subsidies, though his customers in Washington remained underwhelmed by his product. As late as November 1945, Pilgrim's Progress was still running, although its controller acknowledged that "this project must be regarded as one that has thus far not warranted the time, money and effort spent on it," while analysts often dismissed Morlion's verbose reports as "trash," "propaganda," "rehash," or "minor vaticinations [sic]."[75] In the absence of positive results, Washington maintained Pilgrim's Progress in the hope that somehow the situation would improve and the investment in Morlion would justify itself at some later date. It also believed that a source at the Vatican, no matter how poor, was better than no source.

For a brief period in the winter of 1944–45, OSS convinced itself that it had managed to penetrate one of the hardest intelligence targets in the world: the Vatican. Vessel was reporting from the most secret chambers of the papal palace, and Pilgrim's Progress was coming on line. In January 1945, Lieutenant Colonel William Maddox, the chief of secret intelligence for the Mediterranean theater, advised OSS headquarters, "These operations are acquiring increasing importance and should be given the most careful attention. I look upon the work as one of the most significant we can perform in this theatre." To exploit this intelligence coup, Maddox asked Washington for personnel who could work full-time on the Vatican target.[76] The small OSS detachment in Rome had recruited one or two sources around the Vatican, most notably Baron Gabriel Apor, the Hungarian ambassador to the Holy See, but it was too preoccupied with operations against German and Italian targets to devote much attention to the Papacy.[77] The Vatican target deserved its own team.

Actually, OSS Rome already had a man operating full-time against the Vatican, although the results of his labors were so paltry that Lieutenant Colonel Maddox may be forgiven for believing that no one was concentrating on that target. James St. Lawrence O'Toole, an art dealer from New York City, had been in Rome since late December 1944. Posing as an art buyer, he was supposed to circulate in the so-called "black society," the close-knit network of ultra-Catholic noble families that had served the papacy for generations, fishing for sources and information among the counts and countesses, bishops and monsignors, who populated the frescoed dining rooms and tapestried ballrooms of ancient Roman palazzi. Unfortunately, O'Toole proved a poor fisherman; two months into his assignment he had yet to hook a single source. Asserting that he lacked any aptitude for undercover intelligence work, O'Toole requested a transfer back to the United States. In the belief that the green officer merely required some seasoning, the commander of the OSS detachment in Rome summoned O'Toole to his office, where he proceeded to deny the request for transfer, explain why intelligence from the Vatican was so important, arrange for the New Yorker to receive a crash course on developing and recruiting sources, and generally enjoin his subordinate to buck up and try again.

James St. Lawrence O'Toole's second attempt at espionage was no more successful than his first, and even his superiors were ready to throw in the towel. By April 1945 OSS Rome was recommending to headquarters that O'Toole be returned to the United States and released from OSS. The recommendation may have reflected more than disappointment with the hapless spy's tradecraft. Washington had learned from various sources, including the director of a major New York museum and the editor of a well-known art magazine, that before the war O'Toole had exhibited rather eccentric political tastes. Allegedly, he had pronounced Fascist sympathies and was personally connected with Fascist leaders in prewar Venice. His name was also mentioned in connection with certain shady art deals before the war. Headquarters also had reason to believe that his lack of success as an intelligence officer in Rome was more a matter of choice than of competence. During his brief tour in the Eternal City, O'Toole confided to a friend that he spent most of his time acquiring old paintings rather than new sources.[78]

Even before O'Toole's failure, Washington had dispatched another officer to spy on the Vatican. Martin Quigley, who had worked for OSS in Ireland, appeared in Rome in December 1944 under the guise of a marketing representative for the American film industry. To preserve his cover, Quigley lodged quietly with an Italian family near the Piazza Argentina and spent much of his time trying to impress film distributors with the commercial merits of American films. He never went near the OSS station, which occupied a large villa on Monte Mario, and he passed reports and received instructions only through dead-drops.

For all this discretion, the Vatican was soon aware of Quigley's true work in Rome. In a directive curiously at odds with his clandestine assignment, he had been authorized by Washington to reveal his intelligence mission to selected individuals if by doing so he could advance that mission. Shortly after arriving in Rome, Quigley revealed his OSS connection to Father Vincent McCormick, an American Jesuit attached to his order's Gregorian University who had lived in Rome since before the war, and Enrico Galeazzi, a layman and senior functionary in the Vatican who had the confidence of Pope Pius. Galeazzi undoubtedly wasted little time in revealing to the pope that the young man working as a representative of American film interests was also an intelligence officer.

Intelligent and personable, Quigley moved easily and unobtrusively through Roman ecclesiastical, social, and business circles. He cultivated a range of sources who are identified in his reports by nautical code names (BOOM, ANCHOR) or by vague references, such as "a lay Vatican official" or "an Italian lawyer with close Vatican connections." From these sources Quigley collected for Washington information on a variety of subjects, including the pope's health, the political attitudes of various cardinals, appointments to senior Vatican posts, the activities of neutral diplomats accredited to the Holy See, and the Vatican's attitude toward the Soviet Union.[79] His access to important ecclesiastics was good, in large part because his friendship with Father McCormick opened many doors. McCormick, for example, opened a channel to Father Robert Leiber, the German Jesuit who served as the pope's confidential assistant.[80] Since influential Vatican officials, such as Leiber and Galeazzi, were aware of Quigley's clandestine mission, it is likely that they revealed to the American intelligence officer only what the Vatican wanted Washington to know. On one occasion Galeazzi actually gave Quigley a Vatican document detailing anti-Catholic measures, including the execution of priests, instituted in Yugoslavia by the Communist partisan forces under Tito.[81]

In addition to his work as an intelligence officer, Martin Quigley had a special assignment whose impact on the war was potentially greater than any number of secret reports sent to Washington. Before departing for Rome, he had been summoned unexpectedly to the office of William Donovan, the director of the Office of Strategic Services. After some small talk about Quigley's work in Ireland and his assignment to Rome, Donovan got around to the reason for their meeting. The OSS chief was not sending the young officer to the Vatican just to develop a spy network. By the end of 1944, Japan was reeling from one defeat to the next, and it had little prospect of regaining its balance and forward momentum. In the spring and summer the Imperial Japanese Army had been defeated by British and British Commonwealth forces in a series of battles along the Burma–India frontier that devastated Japanese military power in the region and opened the way for the Allies eventually to recapture Burma. In October the U.S. Navy broke the back of the Imperial Japanese Navy at the battle of Leyte Gulf, while American troops began the reconquest of the Philippine Islands with landings on the island of Leyte. American submarines were ravaging the seaborne commerce on which the Japanese relied to maintain their war effort, while American heavy bombers had begun a ruthless strategic air offensive aimed at destroying Japan's principal population centers. Donovan believed that in the face of such reverses, Tokyo might soon decide to avoid total destruction by offering to surrender. If it did, the Vatican was a likely locale for the initial approach. The OSS director ordered Quigley to be alert for possible peace moves and left the young officer with the impression that he should initiate such a move should the moment seem opportune.[82]

At the Casablanca (Morocco) Conference in January 1943, President Franklin Roosevelt and Prime Minister Winston Churchill had pledged to settle for nothing less than the unconditional surrender of Germany and Japan. In view of this announced policy, Donovan's directive was breathtaking but in keeping with the OSS director's reputation for bold (some would say undisciplined) initiatives. Quigley certainly took his special mission seriously and, though more disciplined, was no less bold than his chief. In late May 1945 he decided that the time was opportune for an initiative. With the surrender of Germany on 8 May, Japan, its empire depleted, its armed forces bled white, its cities ravaged by firebombing, now faced the Allies alone. If knocked upon, the door to peace might open a crack.

Using Monsignor Egidio Vagnozzi, a friendly English-speaking officer in the papal secretariat of state, as an intermediary, Quigley passed a cryptic message to Father Benedict Tomizawa, the ecclesiastical adviser to Ken Harada, the Japanese ambassador to the Vatican. Monsignor Vagnozzi, who made it clear that he was merely a messenger and that the Vatican was not a party to the initiative, told Father Tomizawa that he had been approached by an American businessman, who was known at the Vatican and was well connected with the higher levels of American government. This businessman wanted Ambassador Harada to know that should Tokyo wish to pursue peace negotiations in or near Rome, senior American officials could be in the area in a few days. The American suggested that the terms for a settlement might include the disarmament of the Japanese army and navy and the return of territories occupied by Japan, but not necessarily the occupation of the Japanese home islands. The Japanese priest dutifully carried this message to his ambassador, who, suspecting some trickery, pondered a response for a couple of days before informing Japan's foreign ministry of the approach.

After several days passed without a reply from his superiors, Ambassador Harada sent Father Tomizawa to seek, through Monsignor Vagnozzi, more information about the American businessman and his initiative. When Tomizawa reported back, Harada sent another message to Tokyo informing the foreign ministry that the American had admitted that he had acted privately to bring the two countries together and that no official of the American government had asked to have any communication passed to Japan in the name of the United States. The response from Tokyo was once again silence. Of course Quigley's quixotic initiative never had any prospect of success. Indeed, in suggesting surrender terms and indicating that American authorities would appear to address them, he grossly exceeded his authority, which was, in fact, nil. As the following months would reveal, it would take more—much more—than an approach from an obscure, junior intelligence officer in Rome to move Japan to the peace table.

While the Office of Strategic Services developed agent networks around the Vatican, American codebreakers struggled to crack papal ciphers. During the war the U.S. Army's Signal Intelligence Service (renamed in midwar the Signal Security Agency) developed a comprehensive program to intercept and decrypt the diplomatic communications of foreign governments. At its headquarters outside Washington at Arlington Hall, a former finishing school for young women, the Signal Intelligence Service (SIS) read the communications of more than thirty-five countries: hostile, neutral, and allied. The achievements of American codebreakers produced a flood of valuable intelligence; some, such as the solution of the Japanese diplomatic cipher machine known to Arlington Hall as Purple, contributed significantly to Allied victory in the war.[83]

Shortly after the First World War, Herbert Yardley, the director of the so-called Cipher Bureau, a predecessor to the Signal Intelligence Service, had conducted a preliminary analysis of papal ciphers and concluded that they could be broken. Yardley raised the matter of Vatican ciphers during lunch with his commanding officer, who had invited him to discuss new operations for the codebreakers. Yardley had hardly begun to explain his plan to attack papal ciphers when he realized from the shocked look on the face of his commander that he was talking to a pious Catholic. Quickly shifting course and affecting no little piety of his own, the chief American codebreaker asserted that while Vatican ciphers could probably be solved, he personally believed it would be unethical to pry into the secrets of the Holy Father, and he hoped his superior would agree. Visibly relieved, the latter did indeed agree. For the time being, Vatican ciphers (and Herbert Yardley's job) remained secure.[84]

By the 1930s and the approach of a new war, self-righteousness quickly gave way to self-interest, but papal ciphers still evaded the attention of American codebreakers. The Signal Intelligence Service, which had replaced the Cipher Bureau in 1930, occasionally intercepted Vatican communications (mainly messages between the secretariat of state and its nunciatures and delegations in various countries) but for lack of staff was unable to study the encryption that protected the messages. The intercepted messages were merely filed for future reference. In a separate operation, whose details remain classified to this day, the FBI placed the mail of the apostolic delegation in Washington under surveillance. The Bureau suspected (wrongly) that Axis intelligence agents in North America used the papal diplomatic pouch to communicate with their controllers in Europe. Though the delegation's mail was closely monitored, no evidence of intelligence activity was uncovered.[85]

For some time after Pearl Harbor the FBI's operation was the only American effort to secretly read papal communications. The situation changed in September 1943 when, after Italy agreed to an armistice and abandoned the Axis coalition, Italian diplomatic traffic virtually disappeared from international communications circuits. With the cryptanalysts in its Italian section now idle, Arlington Hall had staff available for reassignment. In September 1943 the Hall quietly opened a Vatican section.[86]

Washington closely guarded the secrets of its codebreaking program because success depended in part on foreign governments remaining unaware that the ciphers that protected their most confidential communications had been cracked. In the case of the Vatican this concern was aggravated by fear of a domestic political reaction should Catholics or congressional representatives from heavily Catholic constituencies learn that their government was eavesdropping on the Holy Father. Consequently, the effort against papal ciphers was cloaked in a veil of secrecy extraordinary even by the high standards of Arlington Hall. At the Hall codebreaking teams were organized according to the country whose ciphers they were studying. The various ciphers under attack were identified by a trigraph in which the first two letters were an abbreviation of the country and the last letter an indicator of the particular cryptosystem in the sequence in which it had been taken up by the analysts. The Swiss desk, for example, might be working on SZA, SZB, and SZC, while the Turkish desk might be studying TUA and TUB.

Under this arrangement the cryptanalysts assigned to papal ciphers would normally have been organized as the Vatican desk, and their targets would have been identified as VAA, VAB, and so forth. The Papacy, however, was not a normal target. The Vatican operation was included among a handful of supersecret projects that for security purposes were identified only by color. In this scheme the Vatican team was known as "Gold" section.[87] The ciphers it studied were assigned the digraph KI, a label that gave less hint of the target government's identity than VA. Although internal memorandums and reports circulating within Arlington Hall routinely identified the countries whose ciphers were under study, no reference to the Vatican ever appeared in status reports from Gold section.

The new section began by reviewing the Vatican diplomatic messages that had accumulated in Arlington Hall's intercept folders. During the Second World War the papal secretariat of state used several ciphers, each identified by a color. Most nunciatures and delegations held two or three of these ciphers, although the more important missions might possess the entire repertoire. In 1944, for example, the apostolic delegation in Washington was using six different ciphers to communicate with Rome. Gold section first attacked a system known as the Cifrario Rosso (Red Cipher), a relatively unsophisticated cipher that had been in service since the early 1930s, a dangerously long time for a diplomatic cipher. The Vatican rightly considered this system insecure and used it only for routine administrative messages and nonconfidential matters. With assistance from the Government Code and Cypher School, the British codebreaking organization that had been working on papal ciphers since October 1941, the Americans progressed rapidly against the Red Cipher, and by the spring of 1944 most messages in this system were readable.[88]

This first success against papal ciphers was also the last because American and British codebreakers were no more able to penetrate the Vatican's high-grade ciphers than their counterparts in Germany and Italy. Arlington Hall put some of its best cryptanalysts on the problem, including two from the legendary team that had cracked Purple, Japan's high-grade cipher machine, but even they could make no headway. In the summer of 1944 Arlington Hall simply gave up. The Vatican desk became inactive, and its cryptanalysts shifted to more promising targets. Some communications intelligence on the Vatican was obtained indirectly by decrypting the messages of the Japanese, Portuguese, Spanish, and Latin American ambassadors at the Vatican as they communicated with their home capitals. Additionally, after the liberation of Rome, American intelligence (copying the practice of its Fascist counterpart) began secretly to tap all phone connections between Vatican City and the outside world, including Italy.[89]

American codebreakers were surprised by the sophistication of Vatican ciphers. In a review of their futile efforts they readily acknowledged, "The difficulties encountered showed that considerable intelligence was matched against the analysts," and they concluded that they had gone up against "a cryptographer of no mean ability."[90] Their effort was also hampered by the complete absence of compromised (stolen) cryptographic materials. In its operations against foreign cryptosystems, Arlington Hall often benefited from access to photographic copies of codebooks or cipher tables obtained from clandestine access to a courier's pouch or an embassy safe. Papal materials, however, proved difficult to steal. The secretariat of state, for example, distrusted the security of the diplomatic pouch even though under international law and custom diplomatic mail was immune from search and seizure. During the war the secretariat preferred to distribute new cryptosystems to its nunciatures by the hand of priest-couriers (usually papal diplomats traveling to their posts), who never allowed the ciphers to leave their person.

Papal diplomats also exercised strict communications discipline and kept their telegraphic traffic to a minimum. Consequently, relatively few papal messages were intercepted, a serious deficiency for codebreakers, who prefer to work with hundreds, even thousands, of messages. For example, the attack against the cipher known to Arlington Hall as KIH, a special cipher used by the Vatican to communicate with its representative in Washington, was seriously constrained by the fact that after a year of surveillance only forty-six messages thought to be in this system had been intercepted, far too few to help the cryptanalysts.

The heavy secrecy surrounding Arlington Hall's work against papal communications had an unintended impact on Washington's intelligence operations against the Vatican. The only papal cipher solved by American codebreakers was the Red Cipher. This was a low-grade cipher, and at most papal diplomatic missions it was reserved for nonconfidential messages. It was, however, the only cipher available to the apostolic delegation in Tokyo. Apparently the secretariat of state was never able during the war to arrange a secure channel for sending new, improved ciphers to the delegate in Tokyo, Monsignor Paolo Marella. All of Marella's messages to Rome were decrypted and read by Arlington Hall at the same time that OSS was purchasing Vessel reports that purported to be verbatim copies of the same messages. A comparison of the decrypted messages with the purchased versions would have immediately exposed the Vessel documents as fabrications. As reported by Vessel, Marella's messages are replete with peace maneuvers and strategic diplomacy, while the contents of the actual messages decrypted by the codebreakers were so trivial that Arlington Hall did not consider them worth including in the intelligence summaries circulated to policy makers.

The Office of Strategic Services knew nothing of the codebreakers' modest success against papal communications. Relations between OSS and Arlington Hall were distinctly cool, especially after 1943, when an OSS operation against the Japanese embassy in Lisbon caused Tokyo to consider changing its ciphers. Any such change would have been a calamity for Arlington Hall, which had managed to establish comprehensive surveillance over Japan's diplomatic communications. The work against Vatican ciphers was much too sensitive to share with other agencies, especially one as notorious for leaks and misadventures as OSS. As a result, one American intelligence service continued to swoon over elaborately detailed reports from the pope's representative in Tokyo, while another service held proof that those reports were forgeries.

Though never as extensive or aggressive as German and Italian espionage activities, American and Russian intelligence operations against the Vatican were no less a threat to the Papacy. Because they served to advance the repressive policies directed at Catholics inside the Soviet Union, the efforts of Alexander Kurtna (and, perhaps, other Soviet agents yet unidentified) were the more immediate and dangerous threat. However, for all their comic opera elements, American intelligence operations against the Vatican were more than trivial episodes in the intelligence war. The decision by Washington to consider the Papacy a legitimate target was a revealing, though perhaps unconscious, step in the evolution of American intelligence from a small-scale effort focused on military questions and limited to a handful of targets to a multifaceted, if poorly coordinated, program directed against the broadest possible range of questions and targets. While never aimed at undermining the Papacy and the Catholic Church, American intelligence operations sought to anticipate papal attitudes and policies on a range of topics from the postwar government of Italy to the future of the United Nations so as to guide or preempt those attitudes and policies. American intelligence remained always an instrument of American interests, and to the extent that those interests diverged from those of the Papacy, American intelligence could never be viewed with equanimity by papal officials.

7

"The Best Information Service in the World"

As the black car with the yellow and white pennant of the Holy See flying from its fender passed the Swiss Guards at the Gate of the Bells and entered Vatican City, Brother Edward Clancy finally relaxed. He was home, and as soon as he handed the canvas pouches that filled the backseat of the car to a functionary in the secretariat of state and signed a manifest attesting that all the pouches were present and accounted for, this mission would be over. For years Brother Edward, a member of the religious teaching order known as the Irish Christian Brothers, had been the headmaster at a Roman school, but in the summer of 1943 he had been drafted into the service of the Holy See as an occasional messenger carrying a confidential letter to Madrid or a package to Lisbon. When the Allies liberated Rome in June 1944, his journeys became more frequent. After a century and a half of entrusting its diplomatic mail to the courier services of other countries, the Vatican had decided to establish a small service of its own, and Brother Edward was among the handful of clerics assigned to this new unit. The erstwhile schoolmaster now exchanged his chalkboard for a diplomatic passport, and his book satchel for canvas mail pouches.

Brother Edward had found this latest mission especially stressful. Occasionally in the past he would set off for a European capital with only a single letter in his valise as the secretariat of state needed to transmit an especially sensitive communication to a nuncio by absolutely secure means. On this trip, however, the load had been much heavier. Detailed to collect official mail from the nunciatures in Lisbon and Madrid, Brother Edward had arrived in the Portuguese capital to find waiting for him a mound of canvas pouches, each sealed with wax, lead, and wire, and each bearing the coat of arms of the Holy See. The pouches filled a good part of the compartment on the train that carried him across Portugal and Spain. Brother Edward was reluctant to leave the bags unattended even for a moment. He assumed that they contained any number of secret items, some intended for the secretariat of state, others for the attention of the Holy Father himself. He was also well aware that several foreign intelligence services were eager for a glimpse at the contents of the Vatican's diplomatic bags, and that on more than a few occasions during the war papal diplomatic mail had been secretly diverted or opened by unauthorized hands. Brother Edward felt his responsibilities keenly, and sitting among his "children," counting and recounting them at stations to ensure that one had not gone missing, eyeing with suspicion any traveler who entered his compartment in search of a seat, he was fully prepared to endure the discomforts, the sleeplessness, and the danger in the name of doing his duty for the Holy Father. It was only several days after his return to Rome that he learned the truth about his "children." The sealed pouches for which the diplomatic courier had been prepared to risk his life contained not the confidential whispers of world leaders or the most precious secrets of wartime diplomacy but file after file of letters and testimonials from pious schoolchildren, peasants, shopkeepers, and country priests petitioning the Holy Father to elevate an obscure and long-dead Portuguese monk to the dignity of sainthood.[1]

Brother Edward Clancy's experience illuminates a striking paradox in the wartime position of the Papacy: the Vatican's access to intelligence usually fell far short of the expectations of outside observers. Throughout the war such observers assumed that the information networks of the Papacy reached into the most distant corners of the globe and that no world leader was as well-informed about world events as the Holy Father. No one was more convinced of this than the Nazis, who often seemed to believe that Roman Catholicism was nothing more than a cover organization for the private intelligence service of the pope. Senior Nazi security authorities, such as Reinhard Heydrich, were obsessed by the clandestine threat from the Vatican. A conference of German intelligence and security officers convened in 1941 to review operations against the Catholic Church explicitly articulated the collective fears. One after another, the speakers warned their audience against the machinations of the pope's countless minions. A statement that "every Catholic is practically speaking an instrument of [the pope's] intelligence operation" preceded a warning that "the Pope . . . has at his direct disposal agents committed to the Vatican who are, in some cases, officials of various states."[2] Albert Hartl, the long-serving director of

Catholic operations in the Sicherheitsdienst, the Nazi security and intelligence service, was convinced that across the globe bishops, priests, monks, and nuns systematically collected information for the Vatican, as did a small army of Catholic aristocrats, intellectuals, politicians, and industrialists who placed loyalty to the pope above loyalty to their country. Hartl warned his superiors that the pope's minions, particularly the nefarious Jesuits, were masters of conspiracy and intrigue whose clandestine operations on behalf of the political and economic interests of the Papacy extended even to non-Christian areas such as Tibet and Japan.[3]

During the Second World War the Nazis were not alone in conjuring images of papal intelligence capabilities. The Allies believed just as strongly in those capabilities, although they usually assigned a more benign intent to them than did the Nazis. The attitude of American diplomats reflected the opinion that probably prevailed among most statesmen, belligerent or neutral. In 1939 the American ambassador in Rome urged Washington to establish an embassy to the Holy See with the argument that "the resumption of diplomatic relations with the Vatican would be a new source of political information of the highest importance." Officials in the State Department concurred. Ambassador Hugh Wilson, recently returned to Washington from the embassy in Berlin, believed that the Vatican had "the best information service in Europe," while Sumner Welles, the undersecretary of state, agreed that "the detailed and accurate knowledge of the Holy See of conditions in every part of the world, particularly in the countries of Europe, is proverbial."[4]

The reality of papal intelligence capabilities fell far short of these fantasies. Since the loss of the Papal States in 1870, the Vatican had struggled, often in vain, to develop and maintain the information channels necessary to defend its interests and assert its presence in world affairs. During the Second World War few such channels were open to the Vatican, and even these sources were often compromised by the exigencies of war. Lacking both the resources and the appetite to join the intelligence war, the Papacy was often no better informed about the war than any minor power such as Mexico or Portugal. Indeed, upon their assignment to the Vatican, seasoned diplomats, such as the British ambassador to the Holy See, d'Arcy Osborne and his French counterpart, Wladimir d'Ormesson, who succeeded François Charles-Roux in the spring of 1940, were shocked to discover just how poorly informed the Vatican was about international affairs.[5]

The papal diplomatic service remained the Vatican's primary source of information during the war. At the outbreak of the war in September 1939, the Holy See maintained diplomatic relations with thirty-seven governments, to

each of which it accredited a nuncio. In another twenty-two states or territories the pope was represented by apostolic delegates. Since the First
World War the geographic scope of the papal diplomatic service had expanded significantly so that by 1939 the pope had representatives in most
parts of the globe, including Africa and Asia, and in every major capital except Moscow. On the other hand, the fortunes of war eventually forced a
contraction in the papal diplomatic network in Europe. After its occupation
of Belgium, the Netherlands, and Poland, Germany required the Vatican to
close its nunciatures in these countries, while Russia imposed a similar requirement on the nunciatures in the Baltic States when those republics
were absorbed into the Soviet Union in 1940.

Of course as a source of information a diplomatic network is only as effective as its personnel. The professionalization of the papal diplomatic service that began shortly before the First World War had continued over the
following years, with the result that during the Second World War most
nuncios and many delegates were career diplomats who had reached their
senior posts after service in junior positions in the secretariat of state and
abroad. As a group these diplomats were better trained and more experienced than the previous generation of papal representatives, although, as in
any professional group, there were some who fell short of expectations and
others who exceeded those expectations. It is probably unfair to dismiss
them collectively as "mediocre," as does one student of wartime papal diplomacy, and probably unwise to place too much credence in the temper of
the deputy secretary in the secretariat of state, the notoriously irascible
Monsignor Domenico Tardini, who decorated the margins of dispatches
from nuncios with such comments as "imbecile!" and once stormed from
his office shouting, "People always say the diplomacy of the Holy See is the
first in the world. If ours is the first, I'd like to see the second."[6]

Several factors, aside from the personal abilities of the diplomats, undermined the effectiveness of the pope's diplomatic network. The papal diplomatic service was small. The secretariat of state, the wartime nerve center
of the Vatican and the instrument of papal diplomacy, was particularly
understaffed. In the first year of the war it had only thirty-one personnel, of
which fourteen were archivists or clerks. Staff levels were remarkably low
even when compared with minor powers such as Norway or the Netherlands, whose foreign ministries in 1940 had, respectively, 119 and 80 officials.[7] The important first section, which was responsible for political relations with foreign governments, had only seven officers and three
archivists. Although the secretariat gradually added personnel over the
course of the war (the first section eventually adding seven officers), the

scope of its responsibilities, especially in such areas as refugees and prisoners of war, increased faster than the staff. Personnel were stretched thinly. Rarely was one officer responsible for a single area. In the last year of the war the office was still so understaffed that the *minutante* (chief clerk) responsible for Germany was also responsible for all of Latin America, while the *minutante* for Britain also handled anything dealing with Central Europe. In the press of work, tasks were often assigned to whichever official was available, so that one day an officer might be working on the file dealing with the Allied bombing of Rome and the next day on papers concerning the status of bishops in Japanese-occupied China. There was no office or person responsible for systematically collating and analyzing incoming information, preparing intelligence summaries, and distributing those summaries to the pope and his collaborators.[8]

The secretariat was a "flat" organization with few levels separating the highest officials from the lowest. Combined with a time-hallowed administrative custom that emphasized the authority and responsibility of the cardinal secretary of state, this organizational feature placed a heavy burden on the executive officers. When dispatches or reports arrived in the office, they were distributed immediately to the two deputy secretaries: Monsignors Tardini and Montini. As chief of the first section, Monsignor Tardini would receive documents concerning foreign affairs, while Monsignor Montini, chief of the second section ("ordinary" affairs), would receive documents dealing with routine administrative matters. In practice the lines dividing the work of the two sections and their chiefs often disappeared, and Montini frequently found himself handling diplomatic topics. The two deputies would read the papers and personally draft a response if one was required. The more delicate or serious items would receive the personal attention of the secretary of state, Cardinal Maglione. The mid- and lower-level staff, the *minutanti* and *addetti,* kept the files, produced additional documentation when requested by Maglione, Tardini, or Montini, and performed clerical and technical tasks, such as translation and cryptography. The secretariat's three senior officers were able, intelligent, and experienced officials, but they each carried an enormous workload. The burden on Tardini and Montini increased in August 1944 when Cardinal Maglione died and Pope Pius declined for the remainder of the war to appoint a successor.

The nunciatures also were understaffed. Usually a nuncio or delegate had only one junior officer to assist him. The more important posts were particularly stretched. In the first months of the war the nuncios in Berlin and Paris had but two assistants each, the delegates in London and Washington one each, and the delegate in Japan had no assistant at all. Only rarely during the war did the secretariat of state send an additional officer to a post, although some nuncios or delegates hired local priests or nuns to help with routine clerical tasks and nonconfidential ecclesiastical business. The understaffed papal missions were hard-pressed to collect additional intelligence on top of their already heavy responsibilities for representing the Holy See in routine diplomatic exchanges and supervising the health and discipline of the local Catholic Church. Intelligence capabilities were further constrained by the relatively narrow circles in which nuncios and their aides moved. They rarely traveled outside the capital city, where their contacts were usually limited to officials in the host country's foreign ministry, colleagues in the local diplomatic corps, and bishops of the local Catholic Church. Encounters with businessmen, financiers, scientists, and journalists were rare, while meetings with military personnel were even less common. The nuncio in Berlin, Monsignor Cesare Orsenigo, flatly declined all opportunities to meet military personnel except for the exchange of courtesies required at diplomatic receptions. Despite their increasing professionalism, the nuncios and their aides remained rather parochial in their perspective, thinking of themselves as bishops and priests first and diplomats only second. The primacy of their priestly vocation and culture combined with a narrow interpretation of their official responsibilities to prejudice them against developing contacts outside of official diplomatic and ecclesiastical channels and pursuing information beyond that routinely available in those channels. For its part the secretariat of state did nothing to encourage its diplomats to extend their intelligence horizons.

The information reaching the secretariat of state from its diplomatic outposts was far from comprehensive. The nuncios and delegates were inclined by training, experience, and appetite to be especially attentive to the task of monitoring the affairs of the Catholic Church in their respective area, so throughout the war the Vatican was relatively well-informed about the condition of the Church in most parts of the world except the Soviet Union, German-occupied eastern Europe (Poland and the Baltic States), and Japanese-occupied Asia (Indochina, the Dutch East Indies, the Japanese puppet state of Manchukuo, and Japanese-occupied China). On the other hand, coverage of political affairs was spotty, while reporting on military developments was practically nonexistent. Not surprisingly, the Vatican was best informed about developments in Italy, at least up to the Italian armistice and subsequent German occupation of Rome in September 1943, when the situation changed dramatically. Some of the same factors that facilitated Italian espionage against the Vatican (common language, common culture, close proximity, frequent interaction among officials) helped papal authorities stay abreast of Italian affairs. At times, Fascist officials, whether from braggadocio, moral scruple, or plain silliness, were alarmingly indiscreet. For example, the Vatican learned of Mussolini's intention to invade Greece four weeks before the actual attack when Italy's foreign minister, Count Galeazzo Ciano, could not refrain from bragging about the plan in a conversation with the papal nuncio.[9]

In addition to reports from its own representatives, the secretariat of state received information from the foreign embassies at the Vatican. Thirty-seven countries accredited ambassadors to the Holy See, but that number exaggerates the degree of diplomatic activity at the Vatican. Most of these countries were microstates (Monaco, San Marino) or minor powers (Cuba, Guatemala) that were on the periphery of wartime affairs. Many of the ambassadors did not even live in Rome because they were also accredited to other governments besides the Holy See. The ambassador from Liberia, for instance, lived in Brussels, while the representatives of Costa Rica and Nicaragua were stationed in Paris. The representatives of Bolivia, Ecuador, Haiti, and Panama were "absent" (the latter since 1929!), and their embassies were without staff, so that the missions existed only on paper. Many governments considered the Vatican a minor post that offered an honorable sinecure for elderly diplomats or politicians who could endure the years until retirement in a pleasant and undemanding post. The majority of the embassies to the Vatican, inactive or only in infrequent contact with their foreign offices, were, therefore, insignificant sources of intelligence.

During the war the major belligerents established or strengthened their representation at the Vatican in order to cultivate the goodwill and support of the Papacy and to tap the stream of intelligence they believed flowed into the papal offices from around the world. The Soviet Union was the only major power that did not have an embassy at the Vatican by the end of the war. Staffed with experienced and conscientious officers, the American, British, French, German, Italian, and Japanese embassies were potentially important sources of information, although papal authorities were well aware that information originating in these embassies was usually self-serving and one-sided. When Italy entered the war in June 1940, the Allied embassies were compelled to move into Vatican City, where their ability to communicate freely and frequently with their home governments was undermined by various controls that the Fascists, in violation of the Lateran Agreements, forced the Vatican to accept. Under these restrictions the Allied embassies were often hard-pressed to keep themselves (let alone the

Vatican) informed about wartime affairs. When the Allies liberated Rome in June 1944, it was the turn of the Axis embassies to go into Vatican City and experience similar restrictions at the hands of their enemies.

To a surprising degree the pope and his officials relied on open sources, such as newspapers and magazines, for information concerning world affairs. Unfortunately, the only newspapers available on a current basis were those of Rome, all of which were subject to Fascist or (after the liberation) Allied censorship. Swiss papers were available two or three days after publication, but newspapers from other parts of Europe and the Western Hemisphere, forwarded by the nuncios in the diplomatic pouch, arrived weeks after their publication. Alarmed at the isolation of the Papacy and hoping to improve the Vatican's timely access to non-Fascist news stories, d'Arcy Osborne began in the summer of 1940 to take notes on the daily news broadcasts of the BBC that he received on his home radio. He then organized these notes into a press summary that he sent each day to the pope and the secretariat of state. By 1941 this task had become onerous, and Osborne, assuming that by then the Vatican had improved its own access to world news, advised the pope that he would cease preparing the summaries. Pius, however, begged him to continue. The British diplomat was surprised to discover that his BBC summaries were the pope's chief source of current foreign news concerning the war.[10]

During the war both major and minor powers established organizations to monitor foreign news broadcasts for intelligence purposes. Germany, for example, had the so-called Sonderdienst Seehaus (Lake House Special Service), named for its headquarters on a bay of the Havel River in Berlin, that regularly listened to broadcasts from thirty-three countries, including the transmissions of Vatican Radio.[11] It was some time, however, before the Vatican made even rudimentary efforts in this direction. Early in the war the secretariat of state established the so-called Vatican Information Office. Despite its rather suggestive title, this unit was not a political or military intelligence service. It was created to deal with the thousands of appeals to the Holy See from anxious families seeking assistance in locating relatives missing and presumed captured by enemy armies. Working through the nuncios and the Red Cross, the office distributed hundreds of thousands of cards that allowed a prisoner of war or civilian internee to indicate his or her name, home address, and the name of an immediate family member. As these cards were returned to the secretariat of state, the names were placed on lists that were then broadcast at scheduled times on Vatican Radio. Families who tuned into the pope's radio station might learn that a missing son or father was alive and well.[12] In 1944 the information office expanded its operations by organizing a service to translate and summarize major news stories broadcast by certain foreign radio stations that were monitored by Vatican Radio. These summaries were circulated each day to the pope and a handful of top papal officials.[13]

As in the past, the extensive network of church personnel and faithful Catholics that penetrated every continent except Antarctica represented a potential source of intelligence of unparalleled importance. Writing in the second year of the war, an American diplomat noted, "It needs no flight of imagination to recognize the accumulation of information that is gathered into the hands of the high dignitaries of the Church. Through its representatives the Church has access to the thoughts of men in every chancery in Europe and in remote villages in every country."[14] In fact, this conclusion required quite a long flight of imagination, and it was a trip that many otherwise insightful observers would take during the war. The reality fell far short of the expectation. In practice the Vatican proved unwilling or unable to mobilize the tens of thousands of bishops, priests, and nuns, let alone the millions of lay Catholics, into intelligence assets.

Of course the bishops, the Church's regional managers, routinely corresponded with the Vatican on matters of ecclesiastical business. As their dioceses suffered the destruction and dislocations of war, bishops in the various war zones had much to report. Usually the initiative as to what and when to report was left to the bishop, but occasionally the secretariat of state would request specific information, as when in January 1943 Cardinal Maglione asked the archbishop of Cracow to inform the Vatican of the number of Polish priests killed or imprisoned since the onset of the war. For information concerning conditions in Germany and German-occupied territories, the Vatican relied heavily on these reports, which were transmitted through the nunciature in Berlin. Not surprisingly, the letters focused on church affairs, although occasionally they contained information of more general interest. A letter from Cardinal Michael von Faulhaber, the archbishop of Munich, reporting damage to his city's church buildings after a Royal Air Force attack on the night of 9 March 1943, provided a glimpse of the scope and effect of the Allied bombing campaign. The grim situation in Poland was apparent in the communications from the Polish bishops, such as a letter from the bishop of Katowice, who reported the imprisonment of the rector of the Warsaw seminary, the recent execution of several priests, and the death in concentration camps of two of his fellow bishops.[15]

Sometimes the Vatican would receive unsolicited information from concerned or interested Catholic priests or laypeople. In one area, the case of news concerning the Holocaust, this source would prove critical, but generally such reports were too infrequent and uncoordinated to provide more than a snapshot of an event or situation. Occasionally a report would force the Vatican to act, as when it took steps to improve its cryptography when a remorseful Italian functionary in a fit of conscience warned a papal diplomat that Italian intelligence had cracked the Vatican's ciphers. An unsolicited report might confirm information acquired through other channels, as when, in November 1939, a Benedictine monk, Dom Odo (a scion of one of Germany's most distinguished aristocratic families) startled the nuncio in Switzerland with the news that elements of the German army were plotting to overthrow Hitler, intelligence that had already reached the Vatican through Josef Müller, the representative of the Abwehr opposition circle. More frequently, the items of information, while perhaps intriguing or even alarming, had little effect on papal policy because they were uncorroborated. In all cases the Vatican was the passive recipient of such information. At no time did papal authorities direct a network of Catholic informants who were tasked with collecting political or military intelligence.

Intelligence relies on secure and reliable channels of communication. The most accurate piece of intelligence is useless unless it reaches officials in a timely manner. Furthermore, the ability of officials to respond freely and effectively to information often depends on the confidentiality of their communications. Throughout the war the Vatican was plagued by communications problems. Letters and reports that were entrusted to regular postal channels invariably passed through Italian mail facilities, where they were opened and read by Fascist and (after the liberation of Rome) Allied censorship authorities. Such channels were completely insecure and, given the disruption of international postal communications, completely unreliable. Unfortunately, communication through formal diplomatic channels was not necessarily more reliable and secure.

The Vatican communicated with its nuncios and delegates by diplomatic pouch and telegram. For most of the war the understaffed secretariat of state did not have a courier service of its own. Before the war the secretariat routinely entrusted its diplomatic pouch to the courier service of the Italian foreign ministry. When Italy entered the war in June 1940 and Italian couriers could no longer travel to many parts of the world, the secretariat accepted an offer from the Swiss foreign ministry to include the Vatican's diplomatic mail in the pouches carried by Swiss messengers. Papal authorities were also encouraged to switch to Swiss channels by evidence that Italian intelligence had been covertly opening papal diplomatic bags while they were in the custody of Italian couriers. As the war progressed, the Vatican frequently used the courier facilities of other powers.

Papal mail to and from the British Empire or areas under British influence, such as Iraq and Iran, often made at least part of the journey in the Foreign Office bag, and by the end of the war even American couriers occasionally carried the pouches, whose waxed seals bore the papal insignia of crossed keys and tiara.

By entrusting its diplomatic mail to foreign powers, the Vatican risked compromising the security of its communications. Under international law diplomatic pouches were theoretically immune from search and seizure, but legal niceties provided uncertain security against foreign intelligence services intent upon reading the pope's secrets. The Italians certainly opened the Vatican's diplomatic bag when they had the chance. German intelligence services gave high priority to determining the Vatican's procedures for moving confidential mail and organized covert operations to secure access to the papal diplomatic pouch, although the success of these operations remains uncertain.[16] Even "friendly" powers were suspect. In London, British intelligence established a secret operation to divert and open diplomatic bags entering and leaving the capital. Most mail to and from the Western Hemisphere was required to pass through Bermuda, where British censorship authorities directed a clandestine operation that opened diplomatic bags, photographed their contents, resealed them, and sent them on their way. There is little reason to assume that the pope's mail was immune from these operations. The secretariat of state certainly believed that its mail was no more secure in British hands or in British territory than in German. The papal delegation in Cairo, for example, suspected that its diplomatic pouch to and from the Vatican, which traveled by British courier on British aircraft, was covertly opened. On at least one occasion, British authorities in the Middle East actually seized several bags of papal diplomatic mail in transit to the Vatican from Baghdad, Damascus, and Beirut.[17] Even the Americans were not completely trustworthy. As we have seen, the mail of the apostolic delegation in Washington was subject to covert surveillance by the FBI. American intelligence also diverted diplomatic bags for covert examination, and while there is no specific evidence of the diversion of Vatican mail, it is curious that on at least one occasion Vatican diplomatic bags from the United States were delivered to Rome by the Office of Strategic Services, the wartime American intelligence service.[18]

Papal authorities simply assumed that papal diplomatic bags were vulnerable when in the custody of other governments. Quite naturally, these officials hesitated to entrust confidential documents to this channel. As a result, nuncios and delegates sometimes delayed writing until they could find a secure channel. Secret mail often accumulated at certain nunciatures, such as Madrid (which was a collection center for official mail from papal posts in the Western Hemisphere), until such a channel became available. The secretariat of state sometimes detached one of its officers for special courier duty, as when, in December 1942, it alerted its diplomatic missions in Bucharest (Romania) and Sofia (Bulgaria) that Monsignor Luigi Arrigoni was departing for the Balkans to deliver and collect official mail. Papal diplomats traveling to or from their posts would include packets of letters or reports in their baggage. Especially sensitive communications were never sent by diplomatic pouch but were always entrusted to special messengers. For example, a dispatch concerning the possible role of Carlo Sforza, a prewar foreign minister then living in exile, in a post-Fascist Italian government addressed to the apostolic delegate in Washington and marked "Please destroy this letter and keep nothing concerning this matter in the records" was carried to the United States by a lay official of the Holy See.[19] The situation improved slightly after the liberation of Rome, when the secretariat of state established a small courier service of its own. The handful of papal messengers, however, served mainly Spain, Portugal, and North Africa, and courier connections to the rest of Europe, North and South America, and Asia remained problematic until the end of the war.

The Vatican also communicated with its representatives abroad by telegram. Until the creation of Vatican Radio in 1931, all papal telegrams had to be handed to the Italians for transmission through Italian telegraphic facilities. After 1931 Vatican Radio transmitted these messages directly through scheduled "sessions" with government or private radio receivers in various countries. Telegraphic communication with the apostolic delegate in the United States, for example, relied on a daily exchange of messages between Vatican Radio and Mackay Radio in New York and Washington. Such messages could be intercepted by anyone with a radio receiver, a broadcast schedule, and the correct radio frequency, so the Vatican encrypted the more important or sensitive messages to protect them against prying eyes.

The pragmatic officials in the papal secretariat of state had little confidence in the ability of their ciphers to protect their communications during the war. "They read everything," a notation scribbled by a *minutante* in the margins of a report on Italian intelligence surveillance of the Vatican, suggests a prevailing fatalism, as does a bitter joke then current among papal diplomats to the effect that if the secretariat could not decipher a scrambled telegram from a nuncio, it need only apply to Italian intelligence for the correct decryption. Cardinal Secretary of State Luigi Maglione and his principal deputy, Monsignor Domenico Tardini, believed that no cipher (at least none that the Vatican could contrive) could withstand systematic attack by professional codebreakers or long avoid deliberate or accidental betrayal. In the weeks following the fall of Mussolini in the summer of 1943, as the Vatican attempted to determine American attitudes toward the new regime of Field Marshal Pietro Badoglio and the chances of disengaging Italy from the Axis, Maglione and Tardini refused to entrust their more sensitive communications with the apostolic delegate in Washington to the telegraph. Both assumed that foreign intelligence services routinely intercepted the Vatican's telegrams and cracked the ciphers that ostensibly protected these messages. When d'Arcy Osborne assured Tardini that his reports to London were fully secured by the Foreign Office cipher, the papal diplomat privately dismissed the British representative's confidence as "simpleminded."[20]

Monsignor Tardini's skepticism concerning the security of ciphers was certainly prudent. His realism stands in stark contrast to the posture of German and Japanese authorities who throughout the war maintained confidence in the security of their supposedly unbreakable cipher machines, Enigma and Purple, respectively, thereby assuring an intelligence windfall to their American and British enemies who cracked these ciphers and read Berlin's and Tokyo's most secret communications. During the war the major belligerents (and even certain neutrals) developed large and effective signals intelligence programs devoted to the interception and decryption of enciphered radio and cable messages. American codebreakers, alone, successfully attacked the ciphers of almost every country, belligerent and neutral, in the world. Ironically, the Vatican was one of the few countries whose ciphers largely resisted the attacks of foreign cryptanalysts. While several governments, including Britain, Germany, Italy, and the United States, solved one or more of the low-grade ciphers used by the papal secretariat of state for routine administrative and nonconfidential messages, apparently no government succeeded in penetrating the more complex ciphers that protected the Vatican's most secret communications during the war. In the end Monsignor Tardini's skepticism was misplaced, since papal ciphers proved to be among the most secure of the war.

During the war the Holy See discovered that communication of any sort, secure or otherwise, was difficult, if not impossible. Contact with papal representatives was denied or delayed by the vagaries of war. Belligerents on both sides often interfered with the communications of neutral powers such as the Vatican even though such communications were protected by diplomatic conventions and international law. For a time in 1941, for instance,

Britain prohibited the apostolic delegate in Egypt from communicating in cipher with the Vatican, a prohibition that was extended temporarily to the delegate in Iran in 1942.[21] For most of the war, Japan prohibited the Vatican from exchanging cipher messages with its delegates in China (Peking), Indochina (Hue), and the Philippines (Manila); indeed, the papal secretariat of state was not allowed to correspond directly with these officials in any form. The Japanese required all correspondence with these representatives to pass through the delegate in Tokyo, who could forward and receive dispatches and telegrams on behalf of his colleagues but only if the messages were not enciphered and were translated into Japanese, a requirement that exposed every message to the scrutiny of Japanese intelligence.[22]

Communication via couriers and the diplomatic pouch was especially problematic even when the belligerents did not interfere. The war devastated transportation networks in war zones as the combatants bombed, strafed, and shelled every bridge, highway, airport, and railway yard within range of aircraft, artillery, or saboteurs. Even in neutral countries transportation authorities felt the impact of war as they struggled to find the fuel and replacement parts necessary to keep their rolling stock in service and negotiated with the belligerents precarious transit agreements for passenger aircraft or steamships. Even if a courier could find a method of travel, he often could not obtain permission to travel. International law and custom agreed that diplomatic couriers should travel unimpeded, but the exigencies of war often undermined this agreement. Belligerents determined when and under what circumstances couriers could move across territory they controlled, and they often prohibited any courier service at all.[23] When the Germans occupied Rome in September 1943, the twice-weekly Swiss courier service connecting the Italian capital to Bern (upon which the Vatican relied for its communication with the world beyond Italy) became irregular, and until the liberation of Rome in June 1944 the secretariat of state experienced serious difficulty in corresponding with its nuncios and delegates in a timely manner.[24] Of course even in "normal" wartime circumstances courier communications could be slow. A dispatch from the papal nuncio in Slovakia containing early reports on the Auschwitz death camp took almost five months to reach Rome. A letter from the delegate in Tokyo dated 29 November 1941 arrived at the secretariat of state on 24 March 1942. In the last year of the war the pouch from the Berlin nunciature took up to thirty-eight days to reach the Vatican.[25]

Communication with (and, therefore, intelligence from) German-occupied areas was particularly deficient. The nunciatures in Brussels, The Hague, Riga, Vilnius, and Warsaw were closed and their responsibilities transferred to the nunciature in Berlin, where the nuncio, Monsignor Cesare Orsenigo, proved completely inadequate for the challenges of his post. Through the nuncio and his Swiss-carried diplomatic pouch, the German bishops corresponded with the Vatican throughout the war, but they could provide only the sketchiest information on events and conditions in the occupied territories. Reliable information from the east was especially scarce. Poland and the Baltic States were effectively cut off from the Vatican. The Germans prohibited official communication with these regions, so the secretariat of state had to rely on clandestine channels. Catholic chaplains and soldiers in the armies of Germany and its allies would sometimes accept a message or carry a small packet. Priests and lay Catholics might pass on a letter. Through such channels messages slowly made their way to the nunciatures in Berlin, Bratislava, and Bucharest. At best it was a makeshift and unreliable effort. A letter from the pope to the bishops of Lithuania, for example, took a full year to reach its destination. Eventually, even these efforts succumbed to the rigors and terrors of war. By 1944 the Vatican had effectively lost contact with Poland. The situation was so bad that by 1945 the secretariat of state did not even know which Polish bishops were still alive and at their posts.[26]

It is difficult to exaggerate the negative impact of poor communications on the Papacy's intelligence efforts. Unreliable or untimely communication channels meant unreliable or untimely intelligence. The problem was evident even in the Vatican's backyard. In February 1944, with the Allies in control of Sicily and much of southern Italy, Berlin radio broadcast reports that the Russian representative on the Allied advisory council for Italy had prevailed upon his American and British counterparts to prohibit sermons in Sicilian churches. These broadcasts, monitored by Vatican Radio, disturbed papal authorities, who were further alarmed by reports, again from German sources, that the Allies were allowing the Russians to send to the Soviet Union for education numerous Italian children under the age of fourteen. At the time the Vatican knew almost nothing about the situation in southern Italy. It could not communicate with its bishops across the battle lines that divided Italy below Rome, so it had no way to confirm the troubling information coming from German sources. The secretariat of state had a representative with the Allied authorities in North Africa, but it had received no communication from this officer in weeks and was not even sure of his whereabouts. Through Harold Tittmann and the apostolic delegate in Washington, the secretariat of state eventually received assurances from the United States that the stories concerning Russian activities in southern Italy were German fabrications.[27]

During the battle for Italy the Vatican was also poorly informed concerning the situation in the northern regions of the peninsula. In November 1944, at a time when the Allies had pushed into the Romagna region of north central Italy, Major Alessandro Cagiati, an American officer in the U.S. Office of Strategic Services, who had been working with the anti-Nazi Italian resistance, visited the Vatican with Father Anelli, a parish priest from Parma, who had been sent through the battle lines by the resistance to make contact with the Papacy. Father Anelli's mission was to report on Catholic resistance groups in northern Italy and secure from the Vatican support for these groups. Over the course of two days Major Cagiati and Father Anelli discussed the resistance movement with senior papal officials, including Monsignors Montini and Tardini from the secretariat of state. These discussions were a revelation to the American intelligence officer. In his report to OSS headquarters Cagiati expressed his great surprise at discovering that the Vatican was very poorly informed about events that were transpiring hardly three hundred miles north of the papal palace. It had only the most vague notion of resistance activities in the Romagna, seriously underestimated the scale of those activities, and (most surprisingly for Cagiati) was completely unaware that Catholic groups figured prominently in resistance operations. Rather than securing information concerning the resistance from papal officials, the American intelligence officer found himself providing such information to those officials, who now rushed to respond to a situation for which they were completely unprepared. Even the Holy Father was amazed by the news from the north.[28]

Clearly the "best information service in the world" was falling short of everyone's expectations. Time and again during the war the vaunted intelligence capabilities of the Vatican proved illusory. Usually the Papacy was no better informed about wartime affairs than any other government; often it was woefully uninformed. Three well-known episodes in the espionage history of the war illustrate the Vatican's comparatively modest intelligence capabilities.

At first glance the Vatican's foreknowledge of the German attack on France and the Low Countries in the spring of 1940 seems a significant intelligence coup. On 1 May 1940 Josef Müller, who on behalf of the anti-Nazi German resistance had been carrying messages back and forth between Berlin and Rome since the previous fall, arrived in the Eternal City to warn Pope Pius that the long-anticipated German offensive in the west was imminent. On 3 May the papal secretariat of state sent identical telegrams to the nuncios in Brussels and The Hague alerting them to this intelligence, and on 6 May the pope personally warned the Belgian Princess Marie, who was married to Crown Prince Umberto of Italy. The Germans attacked on 10 May, thereby confirming the accuracy of the Vatican's warnings.

The Holy See, however, was neither the first nor the only government to receive advance word of the invasion. German armies had hardly completed the occupation of Poland in late September 1939 when Hitler informed his generals of his intention to launch an offensive in the west and directed them to draw up plans for the earliest possible attack. To forestall these plans and demonstrate their good intentions to the Western democracies, the resistance circle around Colonel Hans Oster in the Abwehr betrayed the preparations to Major Gijsbertus Sas, the Dutch military attaché in Berlin, who in turn passed the intelligence to The Hague and (through his colleagues in the Belgian and French embassies in Berlin) to Brussels and Paris. The first general warning came in October 1939, but on 7 November Colonel Oster informed Major Sas that the attack would come on the twelfth of that month, news that the Dutch officer personally delivered to The Hague on the eighth. Unbeknownst to Sas, Hitler changed his timetable, and the fateful day came and went without an attack. These early warnings were followed by several further alerts as Hitler repeatedly postponed the operation. Between October 1939 and May 1940, Dutch officials received so many alerts from Major Sas that they dismissed their military attaché as an alarmist and warned their Belgian counterparts against taking the intelligence reports from Berlin too seriously.[29]

The Vatican initially learned of Hitler's intention to carry his war to western Europe in mid-November 1939, fully a month after Colonel Oster had (through Major Sas) passed word to the Belgian and Dutch governments. By that time or, perhaps, a bit later, the Italians knew the story from their military attaché in Berlin. In London, British military intelligence anticipated an attack against France, Belgium, and Holland "at the shortest possible notice" but could not be more precise as to the date. By March 1940 the Czechs and the British were receiving more detailed information from Paul Thummel, the German air ministry official working for Czech intelligence, who warned London on 1 May (the day Josef Müller arrived in Rome with the final warning and two days before the Vatican alerted its nuncios in Brussels and The Hague) that the German offensive would definitely begin on the tenth of that month.[30] In view of the intelligence available to other governments, it is difficult to consider the Vatican's awareness of German intentions toward France and the Low Countries as exceptional.

Operation Barbarossa, the German assault on the Soviet Union on 22 June 1941, was probably the most widely anticipated "surprise" attack in history. In the months preceding the attack the intelligence services of several countries, including the Soviet Union, whose services collected more than one hundred separate warnings, accumulated so much evidence of Berlin's intentions that the invasion surprised hardly anyone except the Soviet dictator, Josef Stalin, who stubbornly refused to credit the indicators.[31]

German staff officers began planning the attack as early as the summer of 1940, shortly after Hitler had subdued France and while the Royal Air Force fought the Luftwaffe over British cities and Britons watched the English Channel for German invasion craft. Almost immediately the Czechoslovakian intelligence service, now operating out of London with the Czech government-in-exile, received word of these preparations from Major Paul Thummel, the Czech service's best agent inside Germany. By December 1940 Thummel was passing to his controllers more detailed reports on German plans. These reports were shared with British and, perhaps, Russian intelligence.[32] On 18 December 1940 Hitler issued his famous "Barbarossa Directive" ordering the German armed forces to accelerate planning and the deployments, training, and logistical arrangements required for the attack. Within eleven days the Russian military attaché in Berlin had learned of the directive and alerted Moscow, a warning he would repeat with additional detail the following March. In January 1941 Japanese intelligence officers with access to German military circles were speaking of a Russo-German war in the near future. That month Harro Schulze-Boysen, an official in the Nazi air ministry who was also an agent for Soviet military intelligence, submitted to his Russian controllers the first of many reports on Barbarossa. By then Washington had acquired from a source cultivated by the commercial attaché in the American embassy in Berlin enough evidence of German intentions that President Roosevelt directed the State Department to alert the Russian ambassador in Washington. The State Department would reiterate these warnings twice in succeeding months. By February Swiss intelligence had uncovered the operation, and within a month the Greeks and the Swedes were also on to the story. By the end of March the intelligence service of the Polish government-in-exile in London was suggesting that the German attack could come as early as May.[33] From liaison with the Czechs and the Poles and through the surveillance of German communications, the British had by the late spring of 1941 collected significant evidence of German military deployments to the east, although intelligence authorities in London did not definitely conclude that these movements presaged an attack (as opposed to a bluff to extract concessions from Stalin) until early June.[34]

In the Barbarossa intelligence sweepstakes, the Papacy lagged behind most other governments. Well into the spring of 1941, by which time the Americans, British, Czechs, Greeks, Poles, Russians, Swedes, and Swiss possessed significant and often detailed information about German preparations for an attack on the Soviet Union, the Vatican had received from its nuncios and delegates only a few vague reports suggesting a deterioration in German-Russian relations. The papal secretariat of state did not receive its first solid intelligence until the end of April, when the nuncio in Switzerland, noting that diplomats in Bern were increasingly preoccupied by reports of German troop concentrations near the Russian border, reported that an official of the German embassy was speaking openly of war by July. The nuncio, however, dismissed such talk as disinformation.[35]

Additional information reached the Holy See on 15 May when the editor of *L'Osservatore Romano* informed Monsignor Tardini that one of his contacts, an Italian diplomatic courier who had just returned from Moscow, had reported that the Italian embassy in the Russian capital expected hostilities between Germany and the Soviet Union in the near future. By this time every European government had received credible intelligence of an imminent war; indeed, the Soviet military attaché in Vichy, the capital of unoccupied France, received specific warnings from his Bulgarian, Chinese, and Turkish colleagues. In June the nunciatures in Romania and Switzerland alerted the secretariat of state to the probability of a Russo-German war, although the nuncio in Bucharest somewhat sheepishly acknowledged that the "news" had already spread around the globe. On 16 June the American ambassador to Italy informed Washington that the Vatican believed that war was certain. Of course, by then so did everyone else except Stalin.[36]

The Holocaust provides, perhaps, an even better illustration of the Papacy's limited intelligence capabilities. The Nazi program to exterminate the Jews represents a rare instance in which all of the Vatican's potential sources of information became active. As we have seen, the Vatican relied primarily on its nuncios and delegates and secondarily on foreign diplomats for information concerning the war. Normally, ordinary Catholics contributed little to the intelligence picture. While accepting the authority of the pope in matters of faith and morals, the vast majority of Catholics had no sense of political allegiance to the Holy Father. They thought of themselves as *German* Catholics or *Dutch* Catholics with the emphasis as much on the national as on the religious identity. They considered themselves loyal citizens of their country and saw little conflict between the demands of their country and the demands of their religion. Most were no more inclined to pass political or military information to Rome than they were to pass such information to another state. Normally, it never occurred to them to report anything they saw or heard to the Vatican. The Holocaust, however, was not a normal event even for populations that were enduring the terrors of a second world war in a generation. Nazi extermination policies aroused such shock and revulsion, violated so many fundamental moral principles, and revealed so horrifically the abyss into which humankind could collectively tumble that normally silent voices were raised in protest and warning. Priests and laypeople who would not think to write to Rome about troop movements or armaments or political rumors now felt compelled by their faith and their humanity to alert the pope to the mass deportations, the grim trains, the shooting pits, and the gas chambers.

From the outbreak of the war there had been mass atrocities and violations of human rights. In an effort to snuff out all vestiges of Polish national identity and culture after their defeat and occupation of Poland, the Germans had displaced and persecuted the now subject population and imprisoned priests, intellectuals, and political and social leaders. In the Balkans, Croats perpetuated centuries-old ethnic and religious hatreds by massacring Serbs. Inside the Reich, Jews had been subject to increasingly harsh and violent persecution, but their systematic murder in large numbers began only with the German invasion of the Soviet Union.

Even before the invasion, Nazi leaders such as Heinrich Himmler, head of the Schutzstaffel (SS) and Reinhard Heydrich, chief of the Reichssicherheitshauptamt, had concluded that the planned campaign in the east would provide a perfect opportunity for Germany to launch the first phase of a program to liquidate its racial enemies, the Jews, under the cover of military operations.[37] "Pacification" measures behind the lines would include rounding up and killing Jews wherever they could be found as German armies moved into Russian territory, particularly the Ukraine, the former Baltic republics, and the portions of Poland occupied by the Soviet Union as a result of the Molotov-Ribbentrop agreements of 1939. The principal instruments of this deadly pacification would be specially organized Einsatzgruppen (Operational Groups), mobile RSHA killing squads that had demonstrated their prowess as mass murderers during the Polish campaign, and battalions of the Order Police, militarized units of the uniformed regular police. When Germany invaded the Soviet Union on 22 June 1941, these forces were immediately deployed behind the rapidly advancing front line. Within days of the attack more than five hundred Lithuanian Jews were massacred in the villages of Garsden, Kretinga, and Palanga. It had started.

Historians have assumed that the Vatican learned of the Final Solution at an early date and that its intelligence sources on the genocide were superior to those of other governments. Evaluating these sources, a leading student of Nazi extermination policies concluded that the Vatican "was better informed than anyone else in Europe," while another specialist has suggested that "Vatican officials, including the pope, were the first—or among the first—to learn about the Holocaust."[38] Such appraisals, however, exaggerate the intelligence capabilities of the Papacy and misperceive the scope and the timing of information reaching the Holy See.

From information shared by the Polish embassy to the Holy See and from the occasional letter that reached Rome from the Polish bishops in 1939–40, the Vatican was well aware of the brutal measures adopted by German occupation authorities in Poland, although most of the reports concerned the repression of Catholics.[39] It was only in the fall of 1941, however, that the Vatican received its first intelligence indication that the Germans were systematically killing large numbers of Jews. The information came in a dispatch dated 27 October 1941 from the papal chargé d'affaires in Slovakia, Monsignor Giuseppe Burzio, who reported that a Slovakian bishop had informed him that German police and army units were shooting large numbers of Jews in Russian territory recently occupied by German armies. Monsignor Burzio's informant had learned of the atrocities from Catholic chaplains attached to Slovakian army units that were operating in support of German forces on the Eastern Front.[40] When Burzio's report reached the secretariat of state, the killings by the Einsatzgruppen and the Order Police had been in progress for four months, and their murderous operations had already been observed by the information services of several governments.

The British were the first to learn of the atrocities. In September 1939, shortly after Germany sparked the Second World War by invading Poland, Britain's codebreakers had solved the cipher used by the German Order Police. When, a year and a half later, Order Police units moved into the Soviet Union behind the advancing German armies, British intelligence was able to read the radio traffic these units exchanged with their field headquarters and Berlin. This traffic included reports of Jews rounded up and murdered by individual detachments. By August 1941, fully two months before the Vatican received its first report of mass killings, London was well aware of the slaughter.[41] In mid-September, when German police headquarters, perhaps fearful the horrible crimes might be revealed to eavesdroppers scanning the airwaves, ordered its field units in Russia to cease reporting execution totals by radio and to forward henceforth all such reports to Berlin by courier, British radio intelligence on the executions declined precipitously. By then, however, the scope of German operations had become so apparent to British intelligence authorities that the Secret Intelligence Service (MI6), concluding that further reports would be superfluous, informed its customers in the British government that "the fact that the Police are killing all Jews that fall into their hands should by now be sufficiently well appreciated" and that MI6 would no longer report the "butcheries" unless specifically requested.[42]

Britain was not the only country to uncover the atrocities in Russia before the Vatican; indeed, by the time Monsignor Burzio's report reached Rome, at least six additional governments had significant intelligence on the subject. From partisans operating behind German lines and from refugees fleeing the invaders, the Soviet government received early reports of the executions, and by the fall of 1941 it was accumulating the evidence of German atrocities that would be released to the world in an official statement in January 1942. The Czech government-in-exile was also among the first to learn of the killings when, in the summer of 1941, Paul Thummel alerted Czech intelligence to the mass murders in the Ukraine.[43] The Polish government-in-exile in London also knew. By mid-October 1941 Polish intelligence had reported massacres in the Ukraine and the former Baltic republics of Lithuania, Latvia, and Estonia. At times this information was sufficiently detailed to suggest the scope of the German operations, as when the London Poles learned from their sources inside their country that six thousand Jews had been shot at Czyzew in what had been the zone occupied by the Russians when they divided a defeated Poland with their then Nazi allies in 1939.[44] In the United States, Jewish news agencies, such as the Jewish Telegraph Agency, had published accounts of the atrocities in the Soviet Union as early as the summer of 1941. In early October the State Department had received a report on conditions in eastern Poland that referred to "liquidation" and "extermination" of Jews, and (as Monsignor Burzio prepared his report for Rome) the New York Times carried news (based on accounts by officers in Hungarian military units fighting alongside the Germans) of mass killings in the Ukraine.[45] Finally, it is unlikely that the governments of Hungary and Slovakia remained ignorant of the terrible events attested to by their own army officers.

Various intelligence services continued to collect information on the fate of the Jews through the fall of 1941 and into 1942, and the number of informed governments grew. In November 1941, for instance, the military attaché at the American embassy in Berlin informed Washington of large-scale massacres of Jews in German-occupied Russia. About the same time, a Finnish intelligence officer returned to Helsinki from a mission to Estonia with news of the extermination of Jews in that region. The Finns, who like the Hungarians, Romanians, and Slovakians had joined Germany in the attack on the Soviet Union, may have picked up even earlier indications of what their ally was doing behind the advancing line of battle. By the end of the year, as newspapers in Britain, Sweden, and the United States reported mass murders in Russia, Swiss diplomats in Germany and Romania were receiving information on the atrocities, including eyewitness accounts of the death squads in action.[46]

Once again, the Vatican was not distinguished from other governments by its access to detailed or even timely information. After Monsignor Burzio's initial report of October 1941, the secretariat of state apparently heard nothing more about the genocide until the spring of 1942, when there was a flurry of reports. In March, Burzio confirmed his earlier report that German security forces were slaughtering Jews in Russia, and he alerted the Vatican that eighty thousand Slovakian Jews were about to be deported to what he believed was certain death. The latter news was almost immediately confirmed by similar reports from the nuncios in Hungary and Switzerland.[47] Also that month, Richard Lichtheim, the representative in Switzerland of the Jewish Agency for Palestine, and Gerhart Riegner, a representative of the World Jewish Congress, visited the nuncio in Switzerland, Monsignor Filippo Bernardini, and left with him a lengthy memorandum on the genocide. Based on evidence compiled by the World Jewish Congress and the Jewish Agency, this memorandum provided details of the deportations and deaths (such as the total of eighteen thousand Jews deported from Hungary and executed in Galicia and ninety-two thousand Jews shot in the Bessarabia region of Russia) and warned that the horrors were accelerating.

The grim news from Switzerland was soon confirmed by the Vatican's own sources. In April Monsignor Burzio reported that the deportation of Jews from Slovakia had begun. When pressed by the secretariat of state, the Slovakian ambassador to the Holy See reluctantly confirmed the accuracy of Burzio's report. In May Father Scavizzi, a chaplain on a hospital train sponsored by the Knights of Malta, returned to Italy from the Eastern Front and informed the pope that the Germans were exterminating Jews everywhere in the east and that the massacres in the Ukraine were nearly complete. Indications of disaster multiplied in the summer and fall. In July Archbishop Szeptyckyj of Lvov wrote to the secretariat of state about "horrible crimes" and the murder of more than two hundred thousand Jews in his archdiocese. That month the pope's diplomatic representative in Croatia reported that the chief of the Croatian police had informed him that as many as two million Jews were already dead. In early September Monsignor Montini in the secretariat of state learned additional details from an Italian businessman just returned from Poland. In his record of the conversation, the senior papal diplomat noted, "The massacres of the Jews have reached fearful and execrable forms and proportions. Incredible slaughter takes place every day."[48] By this time the American, Belgian, Brazilian, British, and Polish governments knew enough of what was happening to appeal to the pope to condemn the mass killings in the east, particularly the liquidation of the Warsaw ghetto. In October Father Scavizzi, just back from a second hospital tour through Poland, weighed in with another grim report, informing the secretariat of state, "The elimination of the Jews, with mass killings, is almost complete. . . . It is said that over two million Jews have been killed."[49]

There can be no doubt that the Vatican had intelligence on the Final Solution. By the fall of 1941 it had at least one alarming indication of the horror that was unfolding in Poland and German-occupied Russia. By the spring of 1942 it had certain details of that horror, and by the fall of 1942 it was aware of the scope of the genocide, although it was probably only in October or November that it received from the Polish embassy information concerning the gassings that had begun at Chelmno in December 1941 and spread to other death camps, such as Belzec and Auschwitz, by the spring of 1942.[50] There is no evidence, however, that papal intelligence on the Final Solution was consistently superior in quantity, quality, or timeliness to the information available to other governments. There were, to be sure, a few achievements. Through its diplomatic network (chiefly the indefatigable Monsignor Burzio), the Vatican was among the first to learn of the plan to deport Slovakian Jews. Only two days after the French regime in Vichy secretly ordered its prefects to prepare for deportations of Jews from unoccupied France and a full nineteen days before the raids began, the nuncio in France reported the general outline of the planned operation. More frequently, however, the Vatican's intelligence was not exceptional. Most of the information available to the Vatican was also available, sooner and in greater detail, to several other governments. The Vatican learned of the first phase of the Final Solution, the mass murders on the Eastern Front in 1941, only after the information had been available to other governments for weeks or even months. The alarming reports passed to the nuncio in Switzerland by Richard Lichtheim and Gerhart Riegner in 1942 were passed also to London, Washington, and Jerusalem at the same time. Despite the reports of Burzio, Scavizzi, and Szeptyckyj in the spring and summer of

1942, the secretariat of state possessed nothing like the details of extermination contained in the "Bund" report that reached London from inside Poland in May of that year. Prepared by the underground Jewish Socialist Party (Bund), this account surveyed German extermination programs from June 1941 to April 1942, provided data on the number of deaths throughout Poland, and indicated that thousands of Jews had been gassed in special vans.[51] Throughout 1942 the Vatican learned nothing from its own sources about the existence of a comprehensive plan for extermination, although authoritative intelligence concerning such a plan reached Geneva in August and was passed to London and Washington. Also in August, London received from Belgian sources eyewitness accounts of the infamous Riga (Latvia) massacres, word of which did not reach the Vatican from its own sources until early the following year.[52]

The modest performance of Vatican intelligence in the face of the Final Solution (precisely the kind of event likely to mobilize the full range of the Papacy's potential sources of information) was hardly that of the "best information service in the world." In the context of equally unremarkable records in the cases of Operation Barbarossa and the German assault on France and the Low Countries, that performance indicates that during the Second World War the Papacy was hard-pressed to measure up to its reputation as an intelligence powerhouse. Indeed, a survey of Vatican intelligence capabilities since the nineteenth century suggests that the reputation was always more myth than reality and that diplomats, politicians, and other professional observers consistently exaggerated the Papacy's access to secret political information.

The fifty-five years between the Congress of Vienna (1815) and the absorption of papal Rome into the kingdom of Italy (1870) were the high point for papal intelligence in the modern period. For all its shortcomings in the last decades of the Papal States, the papal administration organized and deployed intelligence resources, especially in the area of internal security, that were probably as efficient and effective as those deployed by any government of the time with the exception of Austria and, possibly, Russia. Of course after the collapse of the Papal States most of these resources disappeared while the remainder atrophied. At first no one noticed, in part because the Papacy withdrew into diplomatic isolation, and in part because the intelligence capabilities of other powers were equally modest. The deficiency would become apparent (and then only gradually) when, at the end of the nineteenth century, the Vatican tried to reclaim a significant role in world affairs only to discover that its interests and initiatives were frequently compromised by a lack of adequate intelligence.

Between 1914 and 1945 the world (especially its European and North American corners) underwent an intelligence revolution. Early signs of change were already apparent in a few places, notably Britain and France, toward the end of the nineteenth century, but the movement emerged in full form during the First World War. Accelerated by the harsh necessities of modern war, but encouraged as well by the troublesome uncertainties of modern peace, this revolution, like other upheavals, was characterized by major changes in political attitudes and structures.

Gradually government leaders came to understand that in domestic and foreign affairs information was as powerful a resource as armies, fleets, factories, and gold reserves. Generals and admirals learned (usually after painful lessons) that in modern warfare news of enemy troop movements, fleet deployments, weapons development, and strategic plans could prove more crucial to victory than brisk marches, rapid rates of fire, and dogged discipline and bravery. For their part, diplomats discovered that at international conferences polished French and exquisite finesse were no substitutes for copies of the instructions sent to other delegations by their foreign ministries. Of course it is one thing to appreciate intelligence and quite another to possess it. As authorities became increasingly aware of the importance of political and military intelligence, they began to attend more carefully to those organizations that might acquire it for them, if necessary by means of clandestine operations. Across the globe governments began to create or expand specialist organizations dedicated to the collection, analysis, and distribution of information. Some of these agencies specialized in the more arcane methods of collection, such as cryptanalysis, while others explored new areas of interest, such as scientific and industrial intelligence. By the 1930s the move toward professional intelligence establishments was so pervasive that even secondary powers such as Czechoslovakia, Poland, and the Netherlands deployed intelligence resources that fifty years earlier would have been beyond the reach and imagination of all but one or two of the major powers.

This intelligence revolution, which would dramatically influence the conduct of war and diplomacy, completely bypassed the Papacy. The specialist staffs of intelligence managers, case officers, analysts, and codebreakers that adorned the diplomatic and military establishments of most European powers had no counterparts inside the papal bureaucracy. As other governments moved to improve their ability to acquire and process intelligence by establishing intelligence services, the Vatican seemed frozen in an earlier time when political information came from newspapers and the gossip at diplomatic receptions. With the exception of the ill-fated and short-lived efforts of Monsignor Umberto Benigni before the First World War, the Vatican made no effort to create a clandestine intelligence capability after 1870. Indeed, it made hardly any effort to improve its intelligence capabilities at all. Nuncios and delegates, the Vatican's principal source of foreign intelligence in 1870, were still the principal source in 1945.

Since the intelligence sources of the Papacy often proved inadequate for the needs of the pope and his advisers, it is all the more remarkable that papal authorities did so little to improve or expand those sources. Many of these authorities (the highly competent Cardinals Secretary of State Mariano Rampolla, Pietro Gasparri, and Eugenio Pacelli come most immediately to mind) were the equals in intelligence, insight, and experience of their counterparts in secular governments, yet they declined to follow those counterparts in accepting the need for intelligence services. This reticence reflected the particular priorities of the Vatican, as well as a lack of human and financial resources.

The secretariat of state (the curial department responsible for the diplomatic and political affairs of the Holy See) was always a small organization. Before the First World War scarcely a dozen individuals worked in the secretariat; even at the height of the Second World War, the papal diplomatic service (both in Rome and abroad) numbered fewer than one hundred men. In a period when the Vatican was so hard-pressed to find qualified priests to staff its diplomatic service that many nuncios and delegates lacked assistants and secretaries, it could hardly think of diverting personnel to strictly intelligence duties. Even if it wanted to, it could not afford to. For all the fables of papal riches, the modern Papacy has always struggled to find the fluid financial resources to maintain the administrative structures required to support a global religious organization. Barely able to fund the organizations and offices it already had, the Vatican had little money available for new initiatives.

The issue of papal couriers provides a glimpse of the resource dilemma confronting papal authorities in the period 1815–1945. Officials in the Vatican were well aware that the Papacy, like any government, required secure communications. They were also aware that their communications were threatened by the interference and surveillance of other (sometimes hostile) powers. Couriers promised the greatest security, but for all the evident advantages of that method, the secretariat of state could never find the money or the personnel to support a unit of papal diplomatic couriers until the end of the Second World War. An organization that cannot find the resources to run a handful of couriers will hardly have the resources to run espionage networks.

Institutional attitudes and priorities also constrained the Vatican from pursuing a more active intelligence program. The Vatican was, above all, a *religious* institution committed primarily to the propagation of a particular faith, the maintenance of religious institutions, and the supervision and direction of believers. Personnel were recruited and educated for religious purposes, and organizational resources were overwhelmingly committed to the pursuit of religious goals. Matters relevant to those goals were given priority, while tangential matters received less attention. This focus significantly influenced the collection of information by the Vatican. For example, papal nuncios, who, like their colleagues in the secretariat of state, saw themselves as priests rather than intelligence operatives, were much more likely to take an interest in matters directly relevant to the spiritual and institutional health of the Church than in more secular matters. By establishing norms for behavior, this self-conscious religious identity also discouraged certain practices as incompatible with the religious life. Priests could no more be spies than they could be warriors. This attitude became increasingly prevalent in the decades after the loss of the Papal States as real priests gradually replaced the unconsecrated laymen in religious costume who dominated the pre-1870 papal administration. The Vatican's brief and unfortunate flirtation with an intelligence service under Umberto Benigni in the early 1900s caused nothing but scandal, and its only lasting effect was to convince papal authorities that they never wanted to walk down that path again.

Despite its intentions, the Papacy could not remain on the sidelines of the intelligence game; other countries kept pushing it onto the playing field, where it was a reluctant and ill-conditioned player. Seeking political and diplomatic advantages in peace as well as war, these countries did not hesitate to launch a variety of clandestine operations against the Vatican to intercept its communications, penetrate its offices, suborn its employees, and confound its plans. Some of these operations, such as the Gerlach affair in the First World War, seriously embarrassed the Holy See; some, such as the revelation of the so-called Roman Conversations in the Second World War, exposed the Papacy to the wrath of powerful enemies; others, such as the penetration of Bishop d'Herbigny's mission to Russia in the 1920s, compromised the Church's religious mission. Without an intelligence and counterintelligence capability of its own, the Vatican could do little but endure these threats, provocations, and disappointments.

Of course not all of these operations were successful. In many ways the Vatican was an easy target for foreign intelligence services: its security procedures were minimal, its communications channels vulnerable, its territory minuscule. These weaknesses, however, were offset by factors that made the Vatican surprisingly resistant to intelligence attack.

The predominantly ecclesiastical character of the papal administration proved an important defense. Aside from laborers, gardeners, guards, a few technicians in the museums, library, and publishing house, and a scattering of junior clerks in a few departments, all posts in the Vatican were filled by priests or members of religious orders. The ecclesiastical flavor of Vatican City was so intense that even the small pharmacy and the telephone switchboard were staffed by nuns or religious brothers. This bureaucracy of priests, brothers, and nuns formed a largely closed society distinguished by dress, education, lifestyle, and discipline from its counterpart in secular society. There was only limited interaction across the social and cultural boundaries that divided the two societies, since ecclesiastics tended to live, work, and socialize with other ecclesiastics.

The ecclesiastical citizens of the Vatican were also products of an administrative tradition and culture that emphasized prudence, secrecy, and, above all, obedience and loyalty to the Church and its pontiff. In the secretariat of state these cultural values were reinforced by oaths of office that explicitly enjoined the personnel to secrecy. These oaths, with their administrative and religious sanctions, were not taken lightly. The effect was to create a wall of silence and discretion that was very hard for foreign intelligence services to penetrate. This wall was apparent to all professional observers. A survey of the papal secretariat of state prepared for the U.S. State Department shortly after the end of the Second World War recorded the consensus of the diplomatic community in Rome that no government, with the possible exception of the Soviet Union, had a foreign office and diplomatic service as disciplined and secretive as the Papacy. American and British diplomats in Rome admitted that it was impossible to extract any information about the affairs of the secretariat of state from papal officials, even those American and British priests in papal service.[53]

Espionage operations against the Vatican were further constrained by long-standing administrative practices that tended to reserve important and confidential matters to a few senior officials. It is axiomatic in intelligence work that the security of a secret is in inverse proportion to the number of people who know that secret. Inside the Vatican, secrets were very closely held. Secrecy was further abetted by the small size of the secretariat of state, the office responsible for political and diplomatic affairs. When only two or three officials were working on an issue, the pool of potential informants was disconcertingly small.

For all its devices and desires, the Vatican might deflect the attentions of foreign intelligence services, but it could not avoid them. It could forsake clandestine intelligence but not the costs of inaccurate and inadequate information. This was the dilemma of the modern Papacy as it struggled to chart its way through the turbulent political waters of the modern world. The Vatican had to protect its interests and project its influence in an international environment where foreign powers relied increasingly on espionage and clandestine operations, but it had neither the ability nor the appetite to employ such practices itself. The Vatican never resolved this dilemma. Unable to use secret intelligence, it would always concede the advantage to those who could.

NOTES

THE ROBERT GRAHAM PAPERS

In his lifetime, Robert Graham, S.J., was the preeminent authority on the modern diplomatic history of the Papacy. His book, *Vatican Diplomacy: A Study of Church and State on the International Plane,* remains the classic introduction to the subject more than forty years after its original publication. In 1963 Father Graham was invited by the Vatican to join a team of three other Jesuit historians who had been charged with the task of reviewing the diplomatic records of the Holy See from the period of the Second World War and selecting representative documents for publication. The team eventually edited twelve volumes of documents under the title *Actes et Documents du Saint Siège relatifs à la Seconde Guerre Mondiale.* When this laborious project was completed, Father Graham remained in Rome, continuing his research into the wartime history of the Papacy and publishing his findings in various journals, magazines, and newspapers. Never content with merely the documentary record, he searched out individuals who had participated in the dramatic events of the war, especially those events that impacted the Vatican. These individuals—former German and Italian intelligence officers, retired papal diplomats, employees of Vatican offices, and associates of Pope Pius XII—were often quite frank in discussing the personalities and events of those years, and some shared with him documents they had retained from the period. The products of these interviews and researches went into files that eventually filled many boxes. Upon his retirement and return to California in 1997, these files accompanied him to his new home in the Jesuit residence in Los Gatos. Upon his death they were collected in the archive of the California Province of the Society of Jesus in Los Gatos. The intention was to index the materials, rebox the files, and make the collection available to outside researchers. These plans were interrupted, however, when the Jesuits in California received a communication from Rome directing them to pack all of Father Graham's research papers and send them to the Vatican. At the time of writing, this valuable collection is inside Vatican City in the custody of the papal secretariat of state. It is not open to researchers, and it is unclear what plans the Vatican may have for its eventual disposition.

In the course of collaborating with Robert Graham on a history of Nazi espionage against the Vatican, I had the occasion to review many of the documents in the collection. With Father Graham's permission I photocopied some (all too few) of the documents and made notes on others. Now that the Vatican has sequestered the Graham papers, these bits and pieces are all that remain available to outsiders. Where relevant, I have used this material in this book and have identified the source simply as the Robert Graham Papers.

1. THE END OF THE PAPAL STATES

1. Well into the nineteenth century, many officials in the papal administration wore clerical garb and held courtesy ecclesiastical titles, such as "monsignor," but were not priests. This was true even of the highest officers. Neither Cardinal Ercole Consalvi nor Cardinal Giacomo Antonelli, the nineteenth century's two most famous papal secretaries of state, was an ordained priest.

2. The Monti affair is recounted in Nicola Niceforo, *Cospirazioni romane, 1817–1868* (Rome: Voghera, 1899), 16–24.

3. For a survey of relations between the Papacy and France in this period, see Frank Coppa, *The Modern Papacy Since 1789* (New York: Addison Wesley Longman, 1998), chaps. 2 and 3.

4. Ibid., 61.

5. Owen Chadwick, *History of the Popes, 1830–1914* (New York: Cambridge University Press, 1998), 5–6, 58–59.

6. Ibid., 84; Coppa, *The Modern Papacy Since 1789*, 86–93.

7. Ambrogio Viviani, *Servizi segreti italiani, 1815–1985* (Rome: Kronos Libri, 1986), 48–49, 58.

8. See the selections in Segreteria di Stato (SS), Archivio Nunziatura Napoli (ANN), scatole 125–26, Archivio Segreto Vaticano (ASV), Vatican City.

9. For Salamon's adventures, see Vicomte de Richemont, *Correspondance Secrète de l'Abbe de Salamon* (Paris: Plon, Nourrit et Cie, 1898).

10. J. P. Valk, ed., *Lettres de Francesco Capaccini* (Brussels: Institut historique belge de Rome, 1983), 29–31, 315, 325; Lajos Pásztor, *La Segreteria di Stato e il suo archivio, 1814–1833* (Stuttgart: Anton Hiersemann, 1984), 2:412.

11. Carla Meneguzzi Rostagni, ed., *Il carteggio Antonelli-DeLuca, 1859–1861* (Rome: Istituto per la storia del Risorgimento italiano, 1983), 9, 19, 233.

12. Papal diplomatic missions are listed in Giuseppe De Marchi, *Le nunziature apostoliche dal 1800 al 1956* (Rome: Edizioni di storia e letteratura, 1957). In 1840 the pope maintained diplomatic relations with Austria, Bavaria, Belgium, Brazil, Colombia, France, Holland, Naples, Sardinia, Switzerland, and Tuscany.

13. On Bedini's mission, see James F. Connelly, *The Visit of Archbishop Gaetano Bedini to the United States* (Rome: Libreria Editrice dell'Università Gregoriana, 1960).

14. David Alvarez, "The Papacy in the Diplomacy of the American Civil War," *Catholic Historical Review* 69 (April 1983): 227–48.

15. For summaries of the correspondence from 1840 to 1862, see Finbar Kenneally, ed., *United States Documents in the Propaganda Fide Archives*, first series, vol. 2 (Washington, D.C.: Catholic University of America Press, 1966).

16. Ibid., 78.

17. Alvarez, "The Papacy in the Diplomacy of the American Civil War," 232–33.

18. Ibid., 240.

19. Ibid., 244.

20. For examples of political bulletins, see Segreteria di Stato (SS), 1857, rubrica 155, fascicolo 15, ASV.

21. This description of the intelligence activities of the delegates depends, unless otherwise indicated, on Sandro Scoccianti, "Apunti sul servizio informazioni pontificio

nelle Marche nel 1859–60," *Atti e memorie della deputazione di storia patria per le Marche* 88 (1983): 293–350.

22. Alessandro Roveri, *La missione Consalvi e il Congresso di Vienna* (Rome: Istituto storico italiano per l'età moderna e contemporanea, 1970), 1:82, 215; 2:226.

23. Achille Gennarelli, *Il governo pontificio e lo stato romano* (Prato: F. Alberghetti, 1860), 1:230–31.

24. Boulay de la Meurthe, ed., *Documents sur la Négociation du Concordat* (Paris: E. Leroux, 1895), 1:xxii; Ernest D'Hauterive, *La Police Secrète du Premier Empire* (Paris: Clavreuil, 1964), 5:137, 256, 378; Eugène Vaillé, *Le Cabinet Noir* (Paris: Presses Universitaires de France, 1950), 322; Mariano Gabriele, ed., *Il carteggio Antonelli-Sacconi, 1858–1860* (Rome: Istituto per la storia del Risorgimento italiano, 1962), 560.

25. Maurice-Henri Weil, *Les Dessous du Congrès de Vienne* (Paris: Librairie Payot, 1917), 1:237, 472, 646; Silvio Furlani, *La politica postale di Metternich e l'Italia* (Prato: Istituto di studi storici postali, 1987), 18; Rostagni, *Il carteggio Antonelli-DeLuca*, 50, 61, 162.

26. Valk, *Lettres de Francesco Capaccini*, 194, 312–13, 413.

27. André Denis, ed., *Relations de Voyage de Paul van der Vrecken (1777–1868): Agent Secret du Saint Siège* (Brussels: Institut historique belge de Rome, 1980), 104–13; Gabriele, *Il carteggio Antonelli-Sacconi*, 111, 560.

28. D'Hauterive, *La Police Secrète du Premier Empire*, 235, 256.

29. Roveri, *La missione Consalvi*, 37; Valk, *Lettres de Francesco Capaccini*, p. xxvi and passim; Richemont, *Correspondance Secrète de l'Abbé de Salamon*, 366, 415, 427.

30. A cipher replaces each letter in a message with a number or another letter (e.g., a = Z, b = 25). A code replaces each word or phrase in a message with a number or group of letters (e.g., Paris = 3843, messaged received = BFLC).

31. David Kahn, *The Codebreakers: The Story of Secret Writing* (New York: Macmillan, 1967), 150–51; quotation on p. 150.

32. Valk, *Lettres de Francesco Capaccini*, 256. Leo XII was pope from September 1823 to February 1829.

33. David Alvarez, "Faded Lustre: Vatican Cryptography, 1815–1920," *Cryptologia* 20 (April 1996): 108–9.

34. Ibid., 106.

35. Noel Blakiston, ed., *The Roman Question: Extracts from the Despatches of Odo Russell from Rome, 1858–1870* (Wilmington, Del.: Michael Glazier, 1962), 178.

36. Ibid., 105, 232.

37. Alessandro Luzio, *La massoneria e il Risorgimento italiano* (Bologna: N. Zanichelli, 1925), 1:314–23.

38. Viviani, *Servizi segreti italiani*, 58.

39. Bruno Ficcadenti, "Rivoluzione e reazione nelle Marche nel 1833," *Studi Urbinati* 55 (1982): 125.

40. Alan Reinerman, *Austria and the Papacy in the Age of Metternich* (Washington, D.C.: Catholic University of America Press, 1989), 2:205–15, 304ff.

41. Blakiston, *The Roman Question*, 87–88; Renato Lefevre, "Santa Sede e Russia e it colloqui dello Czar Nicolo 1 nei documenti Vaticani," in *Gregorio XVI: Miscellanea Commemorativa*, ed. Alfonso Bartoli (Rome: Pontificia Università Gregoriana, 1948), 281–88.

42. Clemente Fedele and Mario Gallenga, *Per servizio di Nostro Signore: Strade, corrieri e poste dei papi dal medioevo al 1870* (Modena: Macchi, 1988), 295, 438.

43. Roveri, *La missione Consalvi*, 2:405, 475.

44. Blakiston, *The Roman Question*, 87–88; Leo Stock, ed., *Consular Relations Between the United States and the Papal States: Instructions and Despatches* (Washington, D.C.: American Catholic Historical Association, 1945), 237.

45. John Tilley and Stephen Gaselee, *The Foreign Office* (London: Putnam's, 1933), 148.

46. Roveri, *La missione Consalvi*, 2:476; Ilario Rinieri, ed., *Corrispondenza inedita dei cardinali Consalvi e Pacca nel tempo del Congresso di Vienna, 1814–1815* (Turin: Unione tipografico-editrice, 1903), 232; Gennarelli, *Il governo pontificio*, 170–71. The encrypted Piedmontese telegrams are in Spogli: Artibani, f. 2, ASV.

47. Ficcadenti, "Rivoluzione e reazione nella Marche nel 1833," 122. For instances of Papal-Neapolitan collaboration in police and security matters, see the collection of reports in ANN, scatole 275–85, ASV.

48. Aldo Albonico, *La Mobilitazione legittimista contro il regno d'Italia: La Spagna e il brigantaggio meridionale postunitario* (Milan: Giuffrè, 1979), 134–38, 174–75.

49. Reinerman, *Austria and the Papacy in the Age of Metternich*, 1:31–33.

50. For cooperation between the Austrian and papal police, see Donald Emerson, *Metternich and the Political Police: Security and Subversion in the Hapsburg Monarchy, 1815–1830* (The Hague: Martinus Nijhoff, 1968), chap. 3.

51. *Carte segrete e atti ufficiali della polizia austriaca in Italia* (Capolago: Tip. Elvetica, 1851), 2:488.

52. Emerson, *Metternich and the Political Police*, chap. 3.

53. Gennarelli, *Il governo pontificio*, 91, 228.

54. *Carte segrete e atti ufficiali della polizia austriaca in Italia* (Capolago: Tip. Elvetica, 1851), 1:106–9; Eugenio Passamonti, "Spie mazziniane e polizia austriaca nel 1833," *Risorgimento Italiano* 19 (October–December 1926): 505–6.

55. Chadwick, *A History of the Popes*, 16–23.

56. Reinerman, *Austria and the Papacy in the Age of Metternich*, 2:191. For the evolution of the papal police, see Steven Hughes, "Fear and Loathing in Bologna and Rome: The Papal Police in Perspective," *Journal of Social History* 18 (spring 1987): 97–116.

57. Weil, *Les Dessous du Congrès de Vienne*, 1:65, 87, 136; August Fournier, *Die Geheimpolizei auf dem Wiener Kongress* (Vienna: F. Tempsky, 1913), 18.

58. Josef Karl Mayr, *Metternich's Geheimer Briefdienst* (Vienna: Verlag Adolf Nachfolger, 1935), 51–52.

59. Emerson, *Metternich and the Political Police*, 69, 85, 95.

60. Carlo Falconi, *Il Cardinale Antonelli* (Milan: Mondadori, 1983), 37.

61. Niceforo, *Cospirazioni romane*, 119–20.

62. Reinerman, *Austria and the Papacy in the Age of Metternich*, 1:131.

63. John Martin Robinson, *Cardinal Consalvi, 1757–1824* (New York: St. Martin's, 1987), 146.

64. Giustino Filippone, *La relazioni tra lo Stato Pontificio e la Francia rivoluzionaria* (Milan: Giuffre, 1961), 2:622–23; Vicente Cárcel Ortí, *Correspondencia Diplomatica del Nuncio Tiberi* (Pamplona: Ediciones Universidad de Navarra, 1976), 68; Valk, *Lettres de Francesco Capaccini*, 673–75.

65. Kahn, *The Codebreakers*, 188; Christopher Andrew, *Her Majesty's Secret Service: The Making of the British Intelligence Community* (New York: Penguin, 1987), 5. For an indication of the scope of British intelligence activities during the Napoleonic Wars, see Elizabeth Sparrow, *Secret Service: British Agents in France, 1792–1815* (Woodbridge, Suffolk: Boydell Press, 1999).

66. Douglas Porch, *The French Secret Services: A History of French Intelligence from the Dreyfus Affair to the Gulf War* (New York: Farrar, Straus and Giroux, 1995), 24–25. For evidence of the ad hoc approach to intelligence adopted by even the Great Powers, see Stephen Harris, *British Military Intelligence in the Crimean War, 1854–1856* (London: Frank Cass, 1999). I am indebted to John Ferris for several insights into intelligence practice in the nineteenth century.

67. Porch, *The French Secret Services*, 17.

68. For a negative appraisal of the papal police, see Steven Hughes, *Crime, Disorder and the Risorgimento: The Politics of Policing in Bologna* (New York: Cambridge University Press, 1994). For a description of the low standards of personal honesty and professional performance among the police of Britain and the United States in this period, see Bruce Berg, *Policing in Modern Society* (Boston: Butterworth-Heineman, 1999), 26–32.

2. PRISONER OF THE VATICAN

1. Giuseppe Manfroni, *Sulla soglia del Vaticano, 1870–1901* (Milan: Longanesi, 1971), 378–79.

2. Frank Coppa, *The Italian Wars of Independence* (New York: Longman, 1992), 139–41.

3. Ambrogio Viviani, *Servizi segreti italiani, 1815–1985* (Rome: Kronos Libri, 1986), 117.

4. Frank Coppa, *Cardinal Giacomo Antonelli and Papal Politics in European Affairs* (Albany: State University of New York Press, 1990), 165.

5. Manfroni, *Sulla soglia del Vaticano*, 55–56.

6. Carlo Fiorentino, *La questione romana intorno al 1870: Studi i documenti* (Rome: Archivio Guido Izzi, 1997), 215.

7. Manfroni, *Sulla soglia del Vaticano*, 83.

8. Fiorentino, *La questione romana intorno al 1870*, 200–203. The Italian government may have discovered that in 1871 Pius had issued a secret directive informing the cardinals that upon his death they were free to select the place to convene the conclave and implying that they should not feel bound by tradition to hold their meeting in Rome.

9. Manfroni, *Sulla soglia del Vaticano*, 104.

10. Ibid., 253–54.

11. Ibid., 161, 191–92.

12. Douglas Porch, *The French Secret Services: A History of French Intelligence from the Dreyfus Affair to the Gulf War* (New York: Farrar, Straus and Giroux, 1995), 24–25.

13. Aside from a single reference to a conversation with the French ambassador to the Vatican, Merry del Val passed to Madrid only information obtained from Cardinal Rampolla during formal interviews at the papal secretariat of state. The ambassador's reports from the Vatican during the run-up to war with the United States can be found in Archivo de embajada de España cerca de Santa Sede, expediente

1214: Cuba y los Estados Unidos, Archivo del Ministerio de Asuntos Exteriores (AMAE), Madrid.

14. Murat to the Director of Police, 17 May 1904, BA 926, Préfecture de Police, Paris.

15. Marcel Givierge, "Au service du chiffre: 18 ans de souvenirs, 1907–1925," NAF 17573–75, Bibliothèque Nationale, Paris. Douglas Porch (*The French Secret Services,* 49) asserts that the cryptanalytic service of the Sûreté (police) cracked Vatican codes, but Givierge, who was a police codebreaker for a time, is quite explicit about the lack of success: "Mais nous n'avons pas, à la Sûreté, reconstitiré les codes et traduit des télégrammes." The French foreign ministry had a separate cryptanalytic unit, but it is not known if they were successful against papal codes.

16. Porch, *The French Secret Services,* 52; Commissaire Haverna, "Note sur l'organisation et le fonctionnement du service cryptographique de la Sûreté générale," F7 14605, Archives Nationales, Paris.

17. Maurice Larkin, *Church and State After the Dreyfus Affair* (New York: Harper and Row, 1973), 144.

18. For Nava di Bontifé's dispatches, see SS, 1901, rubrica 249, fascicoli 4–5, ASV, Vatican City. On Czacki, see Yves Marchasson, *La Diplomatie Romaine et la République Française* (Paris: Beauchesne, 1974), 71–72.

19. The characterizations of Lorenzelli and Montagnini can be found in Larkin, *Church and State After the Dreyfus Affair,* 87. For comments on the weaknesses of the papal diplomatic service by a contemporary and sympathetic observer familiar with the Vatican, see Eduardo Soderini, *Leo XIII, Italy, and France* (London: Burns and Oates, 1935), 63, 131, 250. Cardinal Merry del Val was the son of the prominent Spanish diplomat who represented his country at the Vatican at the time of the Spanish-American War.

20. William Howard Taft to Helen Taft, 7 June 1902, William Howard Taft Papers, Series 2: Helen Taft, Library of Congress, Washington, D.C.

21. For the political background to the Spanish-American War, see John Offner, *An Unwanted War: The Diplomacy of the United States and Spain over Cuba, 1895–1898* (Chapel Hill: University of North Carolina Press, 1992).

22. Luigi Bruti Liberati, *La Santa Sede e le origini dell'impero americano: La guerra del 1898* (Milan: Edizioni Unicopli, 1984), 22–23, 25–26.

23. Offner, *An Unwanted War,* 163–64.

24. Ireland to Rampolla, 1 April 1898, John Ireland Papers, Archives of the Archdiocese of St. Paul, St. Paul, Minnesota.

25. For Ireland's appraisal of the delegate, see Ireland to Keane, 28 May 1898, reel 7, Denis O'Connell Papers, Records of the Diocese of Richmond, Virginia, University of Notre Dame, South Bend, Indiana.

26. Ireland to Rampolla, 1 April 1898, Ireland Papers. The Spanish ambassador at the Vatican informed his foreign ministry that President McKinley had solicited "the help of the Pope." Madrid interpreted this to mean that the president had requested papal mediation, and it foolishly leaked the report to Spanish newspapers. An embarrassed McKinley, knowing full well the political danger of seeming to defer to the pope, a figure many American Protestants viewed with deep suspicion, publicly denied that he had asked the pope for anything. This imbroglio made the

president more reserved in his dealings with Ireland. Merry del Val to the Minister of State, 2 April 1898, and Minister of State to Merry del Val, 5 April 1898, Archivio de embajada de España cerce de Santa Sede, expediente 1214, AMAE.

27. O'Connell to Ireland, 24 April 1898, Ireland Papers.

28. Unless otherwise specified, this account of the Friars' Land Question and the Taft mission to the Vatican depends on David Alvarez, "Purely a Business Matter: The Taft Mission to the Vatican," *Diplomatic History* 16 (summer 1992): 357–69.

29. Ireland to Root, 13 October 1901, Elihu Root Papers, box 160, Library of Congress, Washington, D.C.

30. Ireland to Rampolla, 12 March 1902, Spagna, 1902, posizione 975, fascicolo 369, Archivio Storico della Sacra Congregazione degli Affari Ecclesiastici Straordinari (SCAES), Vatican City.

31. Sbarretti to Rampolla, 1 April 1902, ibid.; Rampolla to Martinelli (for Sbarretti), 19 April 1902, ibid.

32. Ireland to Rampolla, 8 July 1902, Spagna, 1902, posizione 975, fascicolo 371, SCAES.

33. William Howard Taft to Helen Taft, 11 and 12 June 1902, Taft Papers.

34. As a result of the Manila negotiations, the United States agreed to purchase the friars' lands for $7,239,000, a figure within the $5 to 8 million range Taft had been prepared to negotiate in Rome. By this time the number of Spanish friars in the Philippines had been so reduced by death, retirement, and voluntary repatriation that Washington quietly dropped its demand for their expulsion.

35. Unless otherwise specified, the account of the Vatican's role in what would be known as the First Hague Peace Conference depends on David Alvarez, "The Holy See and the First Hague Peace Conference," *Archivum Historiae Pontificiae* 26 (1988): 431–38.

36. Derek Holmes, *The Triumph of the Holy See* (London: Burns and Oates, 1978), 262–66; Lester Kurtz, *The Politics of Heresy: The Modernist Crisis in Roman Catholicism* (Berkeley: University of California Press, 1986), 194–95; Anthony Rhodes, *The Power of Rome in the Twentieth Century* (New York: Franklin Watts, 1983), 193–94.

37. Quoted in Rhodes, *The Power of Rome in the Twentieth Century*, 195.

38. For Benigni's early career, see Sergio Pagano, "Documenti sul modernismo romano dal Fondo Benigni," *Ricerche per la storia religiosa di Roma* 8 (1990): 225–26.

39. Giovanni Spadolini, ed., *Il Cardinale Gasparri e la questione romana* (Florence: Felice le Monnier, 1972), 109–110.

40. Pagano, "Documenti sul modernismo romano dal Fondo Benigni," 230–32; Lorenzo Bedeschi, "Un episodio di spionaggio antimodernista," *Nuova revista storica* 56 (May–August 1972): 402 n. 67.

41. Bedeschi, "Un episodio di spionaggio antimodernista," 391–92.

42. Ibid., 393–94, 400. In 1912 Pietro Perciballi became the object of an investigation by the diocese of Rome into charges of theft and forgery. The investigation was quietly dropped, allegedly after Umberto Benigni interceded on Perciballi's behalf.

43. "Belgique-France: Modernisme," August 1910, Fondo Benigni, scatola 1, f. 360 ASV; "Université Cath. De Lille," scatola 1, f. 5, ibid.; memorandum, 12 April 1911, scatola 2, f. 224, ibid.

44. Pagano, "Documenti sul modernismo romano dal Fondo Benigni," 233–34.

45. Unsigned report, 15 October 1910, scatola 2, ff. 1–3, Fondo Benigni; unsigned report, 1 April 1911, scatola 2, f. 248, ibid.; "La persecuzione en Russia," April 1911, scatola 2, f. 315, ibid.

46. Pagano, "Documenti sul modernismo romano dal Fondo Benigni," 244–45. For letters from the Madrid nunciature, see scatola 31, Fondo Benigni.

47. Spadolini, Il Cardinale Gasparri e la questione romana, 27.

48. Pagano, "Documenti sul modernismo romano dal Fondo Benigni," 240–41. After the death of Pius X, Pietro Gasparri, by then a cardinal, testified, "Pope Pius X approved, blessed and encouraged a secret espionage association outside and above the hierarchy, which spied on the members of the hierarchy itself, even on their Eminences the Cardinals." Quoted in Holmes, The Triumph of the Holy See, 278–79.

49. Benigni's diplomatic career is reviewed in Emile Poulat, Catholicisme, Democratie et Socialisme (Tournai: Casterman, 1977), chap. 10.

50. Pagano, "Documenti sul modernismo romano dal Fondo Benigni," 230–32.

51. Pacelli to Benigni, 15 May 1912, 8 June 1912, and 7 August 1912, scatola 36, Fondo Benigni. In his letters Monsignor Pacelli made it clear that he was approaching Benigni at the explicit direction of his superior in the secretariat.

52. Bedeschi, "Un episodio di spionaggio antimodernista," 400.

53. Holmes, The Triumph of the Holy See, 282.

54. Emile Poulat, Intégrisme et Catholicisme integral (Tournai: Casterman, 1969), 88, 104–5.

55. Ibid., 143, 220, 233.

3. THE GREAT WAR

1. "Notizie Vaticano," 10 July, 13 July, 3 August, and 18 August 1914, H5, Direzione Generale della Publica Sicurezza (DGPS), Ministero dell'Interno, Archivio Centrale dello Stato (ACS), Rome.

2. John Pollard, The Unknown Pope: Benedict XV (1914–1922) and the Pursuit of Peace (London: Geoffrey Chapman, 1999), 59.

3. Stelio Marchese, La Francia ed il problema dei rapporti con la Santa Sede, 1914–1924 (Naples: Edizioni scientifiche italiane, 1969), 82 n. 26.

4. Ibid., 60–61.

5. Ferdinando Martini, Diario, 1914–1918 (Verona: Mondadori, 1966), 74.

6. Giacomo Della Chiesa held doctorates in law and theology. Before his appointment in 1907 as archbishop of Bologna, Della Chiesa had served in the papal diplomatic corps, first in the nunciature in Madrid and then in the secretariat of state, where he rose to the position of Substitute (deputy secretary). During the modernist controversy in the pontificate of Pius X, he studiously avoided any connection with the reactionary faction inside the Vatican.

In violation of the rules concerning the secrecy of the conclave, Cardinal Gustav Piffl of Vienna kept a diary in which he noted that, despite the admonitions of the Austrian government, the Austrian cardinals consistently voted for Della Chiesa.

7. Benedict first selected Cardinal Domenico Ferrata to be his secretary of state, but Ferrata died after five weeks in office.

8. Leslie Shane, *Cardinal Gasquet: A Memoir* (London: Burns and Oates, 1953), 234–35.

9. Pollard, *The Unknown Pope*, 87, 88–89.

10. Shane, *Cardinal Gasquet*, 243; Sir Henry Howard diary, 31 December 1914. A copy of the Howard diary is in the possession of the author.

11. Pollard, *The Unknown Pope*, 90, 96–97. Pollard provides an excellent summary of the Vatican's dilemma in the face of Italian belligerency.

12. For police surveillance of Erzberger, see the reports in A4. Spionaggio: Gerlach, busta 144, DGPS, ACS.

13. For the claim that Benedict inherited a treasury bankrupted by the good works and poor bookkeeping of his predecessor, see Dragan Zivojinovic, *The United States and the Vatican Policies, 1914–1918* (Boulder: Colorado Associated University Press, 1978), 12. For the claim that papal finances in 1914 were healthy, see Pollard, *The Unknown Pope*, 75.

14. Klaus Epstein, *Mathias Erzberger and the Dilemma of German Democracy* (Princeton, N.J.: Princeton University Press, 1959), 102; Georg Franz-Willing, *Die Bayerische Vatikangesandtschaft, 1803–1934* (Munich: Ehrenwirth, 1965), 132; William Renzi, *In the Shadow of the Sword: Italy's Neutrality and Entrance into the Great War, 1914–1915* (New York: Peter Lang, 1987), 156–57. Benedict was so pleased by Erzberger's efforts that he presented the German politician with gifts and a papal decoration.

15. Italian intelligence believed that when Pius X died, the papal treasury had sufficient funds to maintain the Vatican for only a month. There were rumors circulating in Rome that papal authorities were desperately trying to raise money in the United States. Martini, *Diario*, 48. German subsidies to the Vatican continued throughout the war. As late as the summer of 1918, Italian intelligence was tracing sums forwarded to the Vatican by Credit Suisse and noting that the origins of these sums was suspect because they were far in excess of the amounts normally contributed to the pope by Swiss Catholics. Renzi, *In the Shadow of the Sword*, 156–57; memorandum from the Chief of the Naval Staff to the Foreign Minister and the Director General of Public Security, 7 September 1918, reel 51, Sidney Sonnino Papers, Hoover Library, Stanford University.

16. Renzi, *In the Shadow of the Sword*, 109.

17. Howard diary, 28 January 1915; Vigiliani to Questura di Roma, 27 February 1915, A4. Spionaggio: Gerlach, busta 144, DGPS, ACS.

18. Howard diary, 23 February 1915.

19. Renzi, *In the Shadow of the Sword*, 171–72.

20. Ibid., 172; Alberto Monticone, *La Germania e la neutralità italiana, 1914–1915* (Bologna: Mulino, 1971), 539–40, 574–75.

21. Monticone, *La Germania e la neutralità italiana*, 542–43.

22. Italy did not declare war on Germany until July 1916.

23. Martini, *Diario*, 853.

24. Unsigned police report, 30 December 1916, A4. Spionaggio: Gerlach, busta 144, DGPS, ACS.

25. Thomas Hachey, *Anglo-Vatican Relations, 1914–1939: Annual Reports of the British Ministers to the Holy See* (Boston: G. K. Hall, 1972), 19.

26. Bertini to Questore di Roma, 25 November 1914, A4. Spionaggio: Gerlach, busta 144, DGPS, ACS; Questore di Roma to Direttore Generale di Pubblica Sicurezza, 27 February 1917, ibid.

27. Antonio Scottà, ed., *La conciliazione ufficiosa: Diario del Barone Carlo Monti* (Vatican City: Libreria Editrice Vaticana, 1997), 213 n. 54; Howard diary, 21 April 1915.

28. Howard diary, 1 April 1917.

29. Unsigned memorandum, 24 March 1917, Ufficio Centrale d'Investigazione, busta 3, f. 39, DGPS, ACS.

30. Memorandum by Father Genocchi, 8 May 1917, Italia. 480: Affare Gerlach, SCAES, Vatican City.

31. Tedeschini to the President of the Military Tribunal, 17 May 1917, SS, Guerra, 1914–1918, rubrica 244, f. 99, ASV, Vatican City.

32. Pro-memoria by Gerlach, 4 January 1917, Italia. 480: Affare Gerlach, SCAES.

33. In a letter to the pope justifying his behavior Gerlach asserted, "It was my right to correspond with ministers accredited to the Holy See, and *almost always* I did so with the approval of my superiors, but no force in the world can prove that these letters contained matters concerning espionage" (emphasis added). Gerlach to Benedict XV, 30 June 1917, Italia. 480: Affare Gerlach, SCAES.

34. Stewart Stehlin, "Germany and a Proposed Vatican State, 1915–1917," *Catholic Historical Review* 60 (October 1974): 421 n. 15.

35. Andre Scherer and Jacques Grunewald, *L'Allemagne et les Problèms de la Paix pendant la Première Guerre Mondiale* (Paris: PUF, 1962), 1:317–18.

36. In January 1917, for example, Gerlach was advising the papal nuncio in Germany on Berlin's attitude toward a separate peace with Belgium. Aversa to Gasparri, 25 January 1917, Guerra Europa, 1914–1918: Iniziative Pace Santa Sede, gennaio 1916–aprile 1917, SCAES.

37. Renzi, *In the Shadow of the Sword*, 174 n. 4. After the war Gerlach successfully petitioned the Vatican to release him from the priesthood, a petition that was undoubtedly facilitated by his offer to return to the Vatican certain confidential documents that he had the foresight to include in his baggage when he was expelled to Switzerland.

38. Scottà, *La conciliazione ufficiosa*, 25; Pollard, *The Unknown Pope*, 152. The Vatican had its own unofficial channel to the Italian government. Father Giovanni Gennocchi had extensive contacts in Italian political and social circles. He was often used by papal authorities to pass to his political contacts information the Vatican wanted the government to know. It is impossible to determine from the available evidence if he ever passed information on his own initiative. For examples of Gennochi at work, see Martini, *Diario*, 55, 621.

39. Giovanni Spadolini, *Giolitti e i cattolici* (Florence: Felice Le Monnier, 1960), 510–11.

40. Scottà, *La conciliazione ufficiosa*, 450; Pollard, *The Unknown Pope*, 68.

41. Spadolini, *Giolitti e i cattolici*, 502.

42. Unsigned memorandum, 12 September 1916, A4. Spionaggio: Gerlach, busta 144, DGPS, ACS; Scottà, *La conciliazione ufficiosa*, 129. In fact the commandant of the Swiss Guards seems to have assisted the Italian police in thwarting a plot to sell Italian naval ciphers to Austria.

43. "Notizie Vaticano," 22 May 1915, H5, DGPS, ACS; Spadolini, *Giolitti e i cattolici*, 503, 514–15.

44. Marchetti to Sonnino, 10 January 1918, reel 52, Sonnino Papers.

45. Hachey, *Anglo-Vatican Relations, 1914–1939*, 7.

46. Ibid.

47. Ibid., 8.

48. David Alvarez, "Vatican Communications Security, 1914–1918," *Intelligence and National Security* 7 (October 1992): 444. Dispatches for the papal representative in Constantinople, for example, would move from Rome to Bern by Swiss courier, from Bern to Vienna by Austrian courier, and on to the Bosphorus by another Austrian courier.

49. Ibid., 445.

50. Frühwirth to Gasparri, 14 May 1916, SS, Guerra 1914–1918, rubrica 244, f. 29, ASV. For a survey of Vatican cryptographic practices during the war, see David Alvarez, "Faded Lustre: Vatican Cryptography, 1815–1920," *Cryptologia* 20 (April 1996): 120–27.

51. See the collection of decrypted Vatican messages in the Sonnino Papers, particularly reel 48.

52. Gasparri to Aversa and Valfre, 23 February 1917, reel 48, Sonnino Papers.

53. Pollard, *The Unknown Pope*, 124–26.

54. Ibid., 126–27.

55. Valfre to Gasparri, 25 August 1917, reel 48, Sonnino Papers; Pacelli to Gasparri, 27 September 1917, ibid.; Italo Garzia, *La questione romana durante la prima guerra mondiale* (Naples: Edizioni scientifiche italiane, 1981), 161–64.

56. Ragonesi to Gasparri, 14 January 1918, reel 48, Sonnino Papers; Gasparri to Ogno, 15 December 1918, ibid.; Gasparri to Ogno, 20 April 1919, ibid.; Pollard, *The Unknown Pope*, 141–42; Zivojinovic, *The United States and the Vatican Policies*, 134–38.

57. Pacelli to Gasparri, 8 November 1918, reel 48, Sonnino Papers; Valfre to Gasparri, 8 November 1918, ibid.

58. Marchetti to Gasparri, 6 and 11 November 1917, ibid; Pacelli to Gasparri, 7 and 12 November 1917, ibid.

59. Denis Mack Smith, *Italy and Its Monarchy* (New Haven, Conn.: Yale University Press, 1989), 220, 227.

60. Alvarez, "Faded Lustre," 124–25.

61. Ibid., 121–22. Telegrams passing between the Vatican and its nuncio in Germany moved through German, Italian, and Swiss telegraphic facilities.

62. An enciphered code provides two levels of encryption. The plain-language message is first encoded by replacing the words or phrases with code equivalents from the codebook (message received = 2103). These code groups are then transformed (enciphered) by shuffling the arrangement of their elements according to a predetermined scheme (2103 becomes 0231) or by substituting new values for those elements by reference to cipher tables (2103 becomes 7896 where 00 = 99, 01 = 98, 02 = 97, . . . 99 = 00). The improved papal systems used the latter approach.

63. Alvarez, "Faded Lustre" 127.

64. Albert Pethö, *I servizi segreti dell'Austria-Ungheria* (Gorizia: Libreria Editrice Goriziana, 2001), 101–5. The Italians believed that the Austrians were behind the mysterious harbor explosions that sank the Italian battleships *Benedetto Brin* (1915) and *Leonardo da Vinci* (1916). Pethö repeats the rumors current at the time that plans for the *Leonardo da Vinci* were discovered by the Italian police when, during the Gerlach affair, they searched Giuseppe Ambrogetti's office. These rumors are not confirmed by Italian police records.

65. Lorenzo Bedeschi, "Un episodio di spionaggio antimodernista," *Nuova revista storica* 56 (May–August 1972): 392.

66. Emile Poulat, *Intégrisme et Catholicisme integral* (Tournai: Casterman, 1969), 524–28.

67. Zivojinovic, *The United States and the Vatican Policies,* 64. The British secret service ran few clandestine operations in Italy, relying instead on liaison with Italian intelligence for most of its secret intelligence. In 1918 Mansfield Cumming, the director of the service, admitted that he had no networks inside Italy. Alan Judd, *The Quest for C: Sir Mansfield Cumming and the Founding of the Secret Service* (New York: HarperCollins, 1999), 419. For British codebreaking successes during the war, see A. G. Denniston, "The Government Code and Cypher School Between the Wars," *Intelligence and National Security* 1 (January 1986): 54.

68. For the French tendency to see pro-German intrigues behind every pillar in St. Peter's Basilica, see Annie Lacroix-Riz, *Le Vatican, l'Europe et le Reich de la Première Guerre mondiale à la guerre froide* (Paris: Armand Colin, 1996), chap. 1.

69. See the collection of intelligence reports in dossier 6N 248, Vatican 1917–20, Service Historique de l'Armée de Terre (SHAT), Vincennes.

70. Hachey, *Anglo-Vatican Relations,* 31–32.

71. There are examples of intercepted papal messages in Europe, 1918–1929: Allemagne, vol. 370, Ministère de Affaires Étrangeres (MAE), Paris. See also Barrère to Paris, 21 and 22 February 1918, Paix, 1914–1920, MAE; Barrère to Paris, 28 January 1922, Europe: Saint Siège, 1918–1940, vol. 10, MAE. For evidence that Italian intelligence shared intercepts with friendly governments, see Buckley to War Department, 12 May 1918, Military Intelligence Division: Correspondence, box 1071, Record Group 165: National Archives (NA), Washington, D.C.

72. "Rapports recénts parvenus au Vatican," 21 May 1918, 6N 268, SHAT.

73. Hachey, *Anglo-Vatican Relations,* 7, 17–18, 32.

74. Jay (Rome) to the Secretary of State, 13 August 1918, 701.6693/6, Record Group 59: State Department Records (SD), NA; MacMurray (Peking) to the Secretary of State, 13 August 1918, 701.6693/13, ibid.; (unsigned) to the U.S. legation, Peking, 20 August 1918, Breckinridge Long Papers, box 179, Subject File: China, folder 7, Library of Congress, Washington, D.C.

75. Gasparri to Amette, 13 October 1918, FO 380/19, Public Record Office (PRO), Kew.

76. Jusserand to Lansing, 15 August 1918, 701.6693/9, SD, NA.

77. de Salis to Balfour, 26 November 1917, FO 380/16, PRO; de Salis to Balfour, 21 December 1917, ibid.; Zivojinovic, *The United States and the Vatican Policies,* 20, 71. Page also received information from Rudolfo Foa, a journalist who was sometimes used by Cardinal Gasparri to plant Vatican-inspired articles in the press.

78. When, for example, the State Department reviewed the papal peace proposal of August 1917, the "consensus of intelligent opinion" was that the initiative was inspired by Germany. William Phillips noted that "the whole thing savors too much of the Teutonic and was launched in order to create a division of opinion in enemy countries." Diary entry, 15 August 1917, William Phillips Diary, vol. 1, Harvard University.

79. Foreign Office to de Salis, 22 September, FO 380/14, PRO. The State Department's view of Bonzano was based on his successful recommendation of the auxiliary bishop of Brooklyn, George Mundelein, for the important post of archbishop of Chicago. Bonzano's support for Mundelein probably had more to do with their friendship from their years as students in Rome than with any shared sympathy for Germany. In fact, Mundelein was a native-born American (from New York City), although in the patriotic hysteria that swept the nation after the declaration of war, a German surname was sufficient to raise suspicions concerning a person's loyalty.

80. Balfour to de Salis, 6 December 1917, FO 380/14, PRO.

81. Zivojinovic, *The United States and the Vatican Policies*, 123, 131.

82. In reviewing the many files in the Vatican archives pertaining to World War I, I did not encounter a single letter, report, or memorandum from Benigni or any similar document suggesting the existence of an intelligence organization beyond the overt diplomatic service of the Holy See.

83. "Apunti presi a Vienna da mons. Pacelli," SS. Guerra, 1914–1918, rubrica 244, f. 28, ASV; Cieplak to Gasparri, 28 April 1916, Guerra Europa, 1914–1918: Iniziative Pace Santa Sede, Gennaio 1916–Aprile 1917, SCAES.

4. FACING THE DICTATORS

1. This account of Neveu's consecration depends on Hansjakob Stehle, *Eastern Politics of the Vatican, 1917–1979* (Athens: Ohio University Press, 1981), 89.

2. The Allies signed separate peace treaties with each of the former Central Powers. In September 1919 Austria signed the Treaty of St. Germain. In November Bulgaria signed the Treaty of Neuilly. Turkey's turn came in August 1920 with the Treaty of Sèvres.

3. For the Vatican's response to the peace settlement, see John Pollard, *The Unknown Pope: Benedict XV (1914–1922) and the Pursuit of Peace* (London: Geoffrey Chapman, 1999), chap. 6.

4. Dennis Dunn, *The Catholic Church and the Soviet Government, 1939–1949* (Boulder, Colo.: East European Monographs, 1977), 14–15.

5. Ibid., 35–36. Dunn suggests that the swings in Soviet religious policy between accommodation and persecution reflected the relative strength of two contending factions in the Communist Party, the fundamentalists who favored an uncompromising war against religious institutions and the pragmatists who preferred to organize and direct such institutions in support of the state.

6. Quoted in Stehle, *Eastern Politics of the Vatican*, 73–74.

7. Ibid., 50.

8. Owen Chadwick, *A History of the Popes, 1830–1914* (New York: Oxford University Press, 1998), 415–16.

9. Stehle, *Eastern Politics of the Vatican,* 83–84.

10. Ibid., 91, 94.

11. Paul Lesourd, *Entre Rome et Moscou: Le jésuite clandestine,* Mgr Michel d'Herbigny (Paris: Editions Lethielleux, 1976), 106–7.

12. Ibid., 65.

13. Stehle, *Eastern Politics of the Vatican,* 98–102.

14. Ibid., 131.

15. Ibid., 180; Dunn, *The Catholic Church and the Soviet Government,* 35.

16. Stehle, *Eastern Politics of the Vatican,* 130; Giorgio Fabre, *Roma e Mosca: Lo spionnagio fascista in URSS e il caso Guarnaschelli* (Bari: Edizioni Dedalo, 1990), 132 n. 38; Antoine Wenger, *Rome et Moscou, 1900–1950* (Paris: Desclée de Brouwer, 1987), 350–52.

17. Stehle, *Eastern Politics of the Vatican,* 166.

18. Ibid., 133. Pius would delay his most explicit condemnation of the Soviet regime until March 1937, when he issued an encyclical, *Divini Redemptoris,* that described Communism as "perverse through and through" and as a "pseudo-ideal of justice, equality and fraternity." Quoted in ibid., 170–71.

19. Ibid., 136–38; Dunn, *The Catholic Church and the Soviet Government,* 39.

20. Stehle, *Eastern Politics of the Vatican,* 147.

21. Ibid., 142.

22. Ibid., 155–56.

23. Ibid., 163–64.

24. "Servizio di informazioni dell URSS presso il Vaticano," 7 December 1933, Divisione Polizia Politica (DPP), busta 428, DGPS, Ministero dell'Interno, ACS; unsigned memorandum, 13 December 1933, ibid.

25. Divisione Polizia Politica to Divisione Generali e Riservati, 3 July 1934, ibid. After a brief stay in Paris, Deubner moved to Prague. During the Second World War he worked as a translator among Russian slave laborers in Germany. Soviet intelligence believed that during his wartime work in Germany he also served as an informant for the Gestapo. Deubner returned to Prague in early 1945 and was arrested by Soviet police when the Red Army occupied the city. His fate is unknown. Antoine Wenger, *Catholiques en Russie d'apres les archives du KGB, 1920–1960* (Paris: Desclée de Brouwer, 1998), 172–73.

26. Ibid.

27. Until his death in 1983, Monsignor Prettner-Cippico steadfastly denied any involvement with Soviet intelligence, but he never took legal action against writers who accused him in print of working for the Russians. Michel d'Herbigny, who always retained a soft spot in his heart for Alexander Deubner and could never bring himself to believe that his onetime aide would betray him, was convinced that Prettner-Cippico was the sole Russian spy inside the Commission for Russia. After Prettner-Cippico's death, the German journalist Hansjakob Stehle had access to his papers and discovered evidence of his espionage for Moscow.

28. Denis Mack Smith, *Italy and Its Monarchy* (New Haven, Conn.: Yale University Press, 1989), 245–63.

29. Quoted in Peter Kent, *The Pope and the Duce: The International Impact of the Lateran Agreements* (New York: St. Martin's, 1981), 5.

30. Frank Coppa, "Mussolini and the Concordat of 1929," in *Controversial Concordats: The Vatican's Relations with Napoleon, Mussolini, and Hitler*, ed. Frank Coppa (Washington, D.C.: Catholic University of America Press, 1999), 94–99.

31. John Pollard, *The Vatican and Italian Fascism, 1929–32* (New York: Cambridge University Press, 1985), 27–30; Coppa, "Mussolini and the Concordat of 1929," 88–90.

32. Carlo Fiorentino, *All'ombra di Pietro: La Chiesa Cattolica e lo spionaggio fascista in Vaticano, 1929–1939* (Florence: Casa Editrice le Lettere, 1999), 11, 12, 14.

33. Ibid., 16.

34. Mimmo Franzinelli, *I tentacoli dell'OVRA: Agenti, collaboratori e vittime della polizia politica fascista* (Turin: Bollati Boringhieri, 1999), 260.

35. Fiorentino, *All'ombra di Pietro*, 20, 34–35.

36. Ibid., 30.

37. Ibid., 32–33.

38. Ibid., 56–59, 66–68. For intelligence reports concerning Maglione, see his file in busta 752, DPP, DGPS, ACS.

39. For an example of Italian intelligence intercepting the telephone calls of high Vatican officials, see the unsigned memorandum, 1 December 1917, Ufficio Centrale Investigazione, busta 6, f. 73, DGPS, ACS.

40. Ugo Guspini, *L'orecchio del regime: Le intercettazioni telefoniche al tempo del fascismo* (Milan: Mursia, 1973), 92–93.

41. A copy of this letter, dated 8 March 1930, can be found in busta 752, DPP, DGPS, ACS.

42. David Alvarez, "Left in the Dust: Italian Signals Intelligence, 1915–1943," *International Journal of Intelligence and Counterintelligence* 14 (fall 2001): 392. The Vatican employed several ciphers in the 1920s and 1930s, but it is impossible to determine from the available evidence how many of these were read by Italian codebreakers. The Italians certainly read at least some encrypted papal communications.

43. David Kahn, *Hitler's Spies: German Military Intelligence in World War II* (New York: Macmillan, 1978), 224–25.

44. For Monsignor Steinmann's activities, see Stehle, *Eastern Politics of the Vatican*, 28–29, 32, 35. For Weimar-Vatican diplomatic relations, see Stewart Stehlin, *Weimar and the Vatican, 1919–1933: German-Vatican Diplomatic Relations in the Interwar Years* (Princeton, N.J.: Princeton University Press, 1983).

45. Stehle, *Eastern Politics of the Vatican*, 69, 77; Monica Biffi, *Monsignore Cesare Orsenigo: Nunzio apostolico in Germania* (Milan: NED, 1997), 99.

46. Joseph Biesinger, "The Reich Concordat of 1933," in *Controversial Concordats: The Vatican's Relations with Napoleon, Mussolini, and Hitler,* ed. Frank Coppa (Washington, D.C.: Catholic University of America Press, 1999), 124–25, 129ff.

47. In June 1933 more than one hundred priests had been imprisoned in Bavaria, some after severe beatings by the police. Ibid., 143.

48. Ernst Helmreich, *The German Churches Under Hitler* (Detroit: Wayne State University Press, 1979), 273, 278; John Conway, *The Nazi Persecution of the Churches, 1933–1945* (New York: Basic Books, 1968), 67, 95.

49. Wilhelm Höttl, *The Secret Front: The Story of Nazi Political Espionage* (New York: Praeger, 1954), 38. See also Gunther Deschner, *Heydrich: The Pursuit of Total Power* (London: Orbis, 1981), 97.

50. David Alvarez and Robert Graham, S.J., *Nothing Sacred: Nazi Espionage Against the Vatican, 1939–1945* (London: Frank Cass, 1997), 52.

51. Ibid,. 53.

52. Ibid., 54–55, 56–57.

53. John Conway, "Pope Pius XII and the German Church: An Unpublished Gestapo Report," *Canadian Journal of History* 2 (March 1967): 72–83.

54. Alvarez and Graham, *Nothing Sacred*, 56. After the Second World War, Hartl claimed that an auxiliary bishop in Bavaria had been blackmailed into cooperating with the SD. This accusation was supported by the postwar testimony of a Gestapo officer who had been his service's church specialist in Munich. The charges against this prelate were rejected by a postwar denazification court.

55. Owen Chadwick, *Britain and the Vatican During the Second World War* (New York: Cambridge University Press, 1986), 20.

56. Ibid., 35–43. For Ambassador Charles-Roux's work with the French cardinals, see the reports in Europe: Saint Siège, 1918–1940, vol. 46, MAE, Paris.

57. Chadwick, *Britain and the Vatican During the Second World War*, 45.

58. Alvarez and Graham, *Nothing Sacred*, 65–66.

59. Ibid., 66.

60. Quoted in Chadwick, *Britain and the Vatican During the Second World War*, 42.

5. MEN IN BLACK

1. Information from Father Robert Graham, S.J., who knew personally both Robert Leiber and Josef Müller. Harold Deutsch, *The Conspiracy Against Hitler in the Twilight War* (Minneapolis: University of Minnesota Press, 1968), 113–22.

2. The best account of the "Roman Conversations" remains Deutsch, *The Conspiracy Against Hitler in the Twilight War*, chap. 4. See also Owen Chadwick, *Britain and the Vatican During the Second World War* (New York: Cambridge University Press, 1986), 86–100; Klemens von Klemperer, *German Resistance Against Hitler: The Search for Allies Abroad, 1938–1945* (New York: Oxford University Press, 1992), 171ff.

3. Chadwick, *Britain and the Vatican During the Second World War*, 87.

4. Deutsch, *The Conspiracy Against Hitler in the Twilight War*, 122.

5. Christopher Andrew, *Her Majesty's Secret Service: The Making of the British Intelligence Community* (New York: Penguin, 1987), 434–39.

6. Deutsch, *The Conspiracy Against Hitler in the Twilight War*, 338–40.

7. Memorandum by Montini, 4 June 1940, SE. 641. AES 4988/40 (summary), Robert Graham, S.J., Papers, Vatican City.

8. Unless otherwise specified, information concerning the Keller affair is drawn from Deutsch, *The Conspiracy Against Hitler in the Twilight War*, 130–34.

9. Memorandum of an interview with Father Augustine Mayer, O.S.B., 17 July 1972, Graham Papers.

10. Domenico Bernabei, *Orchestra Nera* (Turin: ERI, 1991), 192.

11. Deutsch, *The Conspiracy Against Hitler in the Twilight War*, 345–46.

12. Heinz Höhne, *Canaris* (Garden City, N.Y.: Doubleday, 1979), 417–18.

13. C. G. McKay, *From Information to Intrigue: Studies in Secret Service Based on the Swedish Experience, 1939–1945* (London: Frank Cass, 1993), 168.

14. Orsenigo to Montini, 29 April 1941, Segreteria di Stato, 1941, Varie. 632, Graham Papers.

15. Ibid. Attached to the original letter was a note dated "November 1941" by an unidentified official of the secretariat of state who commented in reference to Ascher, "He is not a trustworthy person."

16. Von Korvin Krasinski, O.S.B., to Graham, 18 March 1980, Graham Papers.

17. Leiber to Montini, 24 June 1941, Graham Papers.

18. David Alvarez and Robert Graham, S.J., *Nothing Sacred: Nazi Espionage Against the Vatican, 1939–1945* (London: Frank Cass, 1997), 32; McKay, *From Information to Intrigue*, 170. Ascher's report would return to haunt the Abwehr conspirators when the Gestapo discovered it and other incriminating documents during an investigation into the attempt on Hitler's life and abortive coup of 20 July 1944. These documents helped send Wilhelm Canaris, Hans Oster, and Hans Dohnanyi to the scaffold. Josef Müller survived the war. After his mission to Rome, Gabriel Ascher returned to Sweden, where his contacts with German intelligence attracted the attention of the Swedish police. In April 1942 he was arrested and held for questioning. While never charged with a crime, he was detained pending proceedings to expel him from the country. While he was in custody, his mental condition deteriorated to the point that he was admitted to a mental institution, where he remained until 1945.

19. Memorandum of an interview with Paul Franken, 26 April 1969, Graham Papers.

20. Ibid.

21. *Actes et Documents du Saint Siège relatifs à la Seconde Guerre Mondiale (ADSS)* (Vatican City: Libreria Editrice Vaticana, 1969), 5:214–15, 396–97.

22. Osborne to Foreign Office, 25 September 1942, FO 371/37539, PRO, Kew.

23. Louis Lochner, ed., *The Goebbels Diaries* (Garden City, N.Y.: Doubleday, 1948), 409, 416. For an examination of the evidence for and against the existence of a plot against the pope, see Alvarez and Graham, *Nothing Sacred*, 85–88.

24. Memorandum of an interview with Paul Franken, 27 November 1973, Graham Papers.

25. Alvarez and Graham, *Nothing Sacred*, 3. The Germans were not alone in their frustration. In a dispatch to his foreign minister, the Japanese ambassador to the Holy See ruefully acknowledged, "Vatican officials do not tell me much."

26. Robert Graham, S.J., "La strana condotta di E. von Weizsäcker ambasciatore del Reich in Vaticano," *Civiltà Cattolica* 2 (June 1970): 455ff.

27. ADSS, 11:86.

28. Alvarez and Graham, *Nothing Sacred*, 19. Upon his promotion in the spring of 1943 to head the foreign ministry's political division, Hencke was replaced as intelligence chief by Adolf von Bieberstein.

29. Ibid., 15.

30. Ibid., 10–14. For Nazi opposition to Catholic priests in Russia, see Hansjakob Stehle, *Eastern Politics of the Vatican, 1917–1979* (Athens: Ohio University Press, 1981), 217–19.

31. Memorandum of an interview with Richard Bauer, 24 November 1973, Graham Papers.

32. David Alvarez, "No Immunity: Signals Intelligence and the European Neutrals, 1939–1945," *Intelligence and National Security* 12 (April 1997): 36–37. For Pers Z, see David Kahn, *Hitler's Spies: German Military Intelligence in World War II* (New York: Macmillan, 1978), 184–87. For a description of the various ciphers used by the Vatican during the war, see "Cryptographic Codes and Ciphers: Vatican Code Systems," Historic Cryptographic Collection, box 1284, Record Group 457: National Security Agency, NA, College Park, Maryland.

    In addition to Pers Z and the Forschungsamt, the Chiffrierabteilung (Cipher Office) of Germany's Armed Forces High Command also cracked a Vatican system, probably the Red Cipher.

33. Alvarez and Graham, *Nothing Sacred,* 63–64.

34. Ibid., 68.

35. "Bericht über die Arbeitstagung der Kirchen-Sachbearbeiter beim Reichssicherheitshauptampt am 22. und 23. September 1941," Graham Papers.

36. Alvarez and Graham, *Nothing Sacred,* 70–71; quotation on p. 71.

37. Ibid., 71–72.

38. "Interrogation Report on SS-Obersturmbannfuehrer Herbert Kappler," Graham Papers. This is a report prepared by American intelligence.

39. Alvarez and Graham, *Nothing Sacred,* 74–75.

40. "The SD (Amt VI, RSHA) in Italy," Graham Papers. This postwar American intelligence report is based on the testimony of one of Herbert Kappler's secretaries whom the Americans considered a reliable source. She dismissed Loos's sources as "for the most part corrupt, greedy and given to extravagant living."

41. Alvarez and Graham, *Nothing Sacred,* 76–77.

42. AA. St.-S. Inland I D. Vatikan. Kirche 3. T-81. roll 196. 0347308ff. NA.

43. Kedia's confidence in Germany was misplaced. In their plans for the postwar order, the Nazis had no place for an independent state in the strategically important and resource-rich Caucasus, although in their more mellow moods Nazi planners discussed the creation of several vassal states in the region with the Georgians (because of their allegedly "Aryan" qualities) given a certain primacy, albeit under strict German tutelage.

44. "Interrogation of Father Michael, 29 July 1944," Giuseppe Dosi Collection, Graham Papers. Dosi, a retired commissioner in the Italian police, was engaged by the Allies after the liberation of Rome to assist in the investigation of the Georgian College affair. He retained copies of certain of the investigative files and later gave them to Father Robert Graham.

45. Ibid.

46. Father Michael's encounters with Kurt Hass are described in "Confession of Father Michele [*sic*]," Dosi Collection, Graham Papers.

47. Berlin to Kappler, 18 November 1943, ibid.

48. Berlin to Kappler, 2 February 1944, ibid.; Hoettl to Kappler, n.d. [early February 1944], ibid.

49. "Confession of Father Michele [*sic*]," ibid.; "New declaration written by Father Michele [*sic*]," 13 August 1944, ibid.

50. Snowden to Sudakov, 16 August 1944, ibid.

51. "Confession of Father Michele [*sic*]," ibid.; Hass to Reissmann, n.d. [early March 1944], ibid.

52. "CIC Detachment, Rome Area Allied Command, Rome, Italy, 18 September 1944. Subject: Tarchnisvili, Michael, Reverend. Georgian Convent," Graham Papers.

53. Aside from the Swiss Guards, a few cardinals, and a handful of monsignors, those who worked inside Vatican City did not live there. Since Vatican citizenship was strictly limited to a small number of individuals, the vast majority of papal personnel were citizens of Italy.

54. "Echi Vaticani—del nostro informatore di palazzo," 14 November 1931, busta 710, DPP, DGPS, ACS, Rome. Father Leiber's anti-Fascist and anti-Nazi sentiments were known to a few of his close friends. Information from Eva Kuttner, who, with her husband, befriended Leiber in the 1930s and had the papal aide to dinner almost weekly until they departed Rome in 1940.

55. Unsigned memorandums, 26 January 1931, 27 September 1931, 12 March 1939, and 14 March 1941, busta 752 (Luigi Maglione), DPP, DGPS, ACS.

56. The Belgian ambassador to the Holy See moved into the Vatican in June 1940, although Belgium did not declare war on Italy until November of that year. As other countries entered the war against the Axis, their embassies to the Vatican also relocated to papal territory. When Italy declared war on the United States on 11 December 1941, Harold Tittmann of the office of the President's Special Representative to the Pope moved with his family into Vatican City.

57. Chadwick, *Britain and the Vatican During the Second World War*, 168–70.

58. Quoted in ibid., 174.

59. French embassy to the Holy See to the Ministry of Foreign Affairs (Paris), 18 August 1940, Guerre, 1939–1945, Vichy-Europe: Saint Siège, vol. 545, MAE, Paris; Report from the Commissariato di Borgo, 4 August 1941, busta 35, DGPS, ACS.

60. Chadwick, *Britain and the Vatican During the Second World War*, 170. Noting that Italian police files contain accusations that Fazio had developed a friendship with Osborne, Count Dalla Torre, and other anti-Fascists inside the Vatican, Chadwick suggests that the police officer had switched loyalties and that his dismissal was orchestrated by Italian intelligence. This is unlikely because after his dismissal Fazio continued to exhibit a commitment to Fascism. Shortly after his removal from office and arrest in July 1943, Benito Mussolini was rescued by German special forces and removed to northern Italy, where he established under German protection a rump Fascist government known as the Republic of Salò. Die-hard Fascists followed their leader to the north. Fazio was among these. In February 1944 he wrote to Mussolini from Turin (then in the Axis-controlled zone of Italy) reminding the Duce of his many services to Italian intelligence and requesting as compensation a business license in Turin. These are not the actions of someone who has turned his back on Fascism. For a copy of Fazio's letter to Mussolini, see Carlo Fiorentino, *All'ombra di Pietro: La Chiesa Cattolica e lo spionaggio facista in Vaticano, 1929–1939* (Florence: Casa Editrice Le Lettere, 1999), 34 n. 94.

61. Chadwick, *Britain and the Vatican During the Second World War*, 170–72.

62. Ibid., 152–53. For Italian supervision of Vatican mail and phone communications, see busta 204: Città del Vaticano, DPP, DGPS, ACS.

63. British embassy, Lisbon, to Foreign Office Communications Department, 31 March 1941, FO 371/30190, PRO.
64. Carlo De Risio, *Generali, servizi segreti e fascismo* (Milan: Mondadori, 1978), 183.
65. Chadwick, *Britain and the Vatican During the Second World War*, 167. Chadwick expresses some doubt as to whether this theft really occurred, but the story has been confirmed by Osborne's American and Yugoslavian colleagues inside Vatican City. Costa Zoukitch to Robert Graham, 16 September 1975, Graham Papers; interview with Harold Tittmann, 19 March 1972, ibid.
66. "SIM. Brigadier General Amè, Cesare," 12 October 1944, entry 108A, box 205, Record Group 226: Office of Strategic Services (OSS), NA.
67. Interview with Monsignor Ambrogio Marchioni, 10 May 1979, Graham Papers.
68. *ADSS*, 1:436 n. 2; Chadwick, *Britain and the Vatican During the Second World War*, 112–14.
69. *ADSS*, 1:473–74; Ernst Nienhaus to Robert Graham, 18 March 1966, Graham Papers. Nienhaus was the Forschungsamt officer in question.
70. Note of a conversation with Federico Alessandrini, Graham Papers.
71. "Cryptographic Codes and Ciphers: Vatican Code Systems," NA.
72. *ADSS*, 10:131–33; note from the cipher office attached to Panico to Secretariat of State, 21 March 1942, Graham Papers.

6. BETWEEN MOSCOW AND WASHINGTON

1. Questore di Roma to Direzione Generale di Pubblica Sicurezza, n.d., A4. Spionaggio, busta 203: Alessandro Kurtna, DGPS, ACS.
2. As early as November 1941, the Vatican had been warned by a source in the Italian foreign ministry that SIM suspected that Vatican Radio was transmitting intelligence to the Allies. *Actes et Documents du Saint Siège relatifs à la Seconde Guerre Mondiale (ADSS)* (Vatican City: Libreria Editrice Vaticana, 1969), 5:229.
3. Memorandum by General (ret.) Eugenio Piccardo, 22 March 1974, Graham Papers. Piccardo was a wartime counterintelligence officer in SIM.
4. Ibid.
5. Ibid.
6. Ibid.
7. "Interrogation Report on Aleksander Kurtna," Graham Papers.
8. Ibid.; Houghton to Dunn, Weekly Summary no. 23, 26 August 1944, entry 210, box 9, Record Group 226: OSS, NA.
9. For the antireligious measures in Soviet-occupied Estonia, see Toivo Raun, *Estonia and the Russians* (Stanford, Calif.: Hoover Institution Press, 1987), 154–55.
10. Senise to Attolico, 12 February 1941, A4. Spionaggio, busta 203: Alessandro Kurtna, DGPS, ACS; Divisione Polizia Politica to Questore di Roma, 11 March 1941, ibid.
11. "Interrogation Report on Aleksander Kurtna," Graham Papers.
12. Antoine Wenger, *Catholiques en Russie d'apres les archives du KGB, 1920–1960* (Paris: Desclée et Brouwer, 1998), 78–79.
13. Memorandum by General (ret.) Eugenio Piccardo, 22 March 1974, Graham Papers; "German Espionage Organization," Counter-Intelligence Corps, Detachment

6750th Headquarters Company, Rome Allied Command, 11 July 1944, Case No. 242, Graham Papers.

14. After the liberation of Rome, Kurtna admitted to American counterintelligence officers that the Russians allowed him to return to Rome on the condition that he collect political and diplomatic intelligence for Moscow. Houghton to Dunn, Weekly Summary no. 23, 26 August 1944, Entry 210, box 9, OSS, NA.

15. "Interrogation Report of Aleksander Kurtna," Graham Papers.

16. "Interrogation Report on SS Obersturmbannfuehrer Herbert Kappler," Graham Papers. During his postwar interrogation, Kappler recalled that his librarian worked at the Russicum, but the informant, a native-born German, was employed only at the Gregorian University, another Jesuit school. A third source, a priest employed at the Teutonicum, a residence for German priests working or studying in the Vatican, was sent back to Germany by his religious superiors in 1940.

17. For Heydrich's fears concerning Vatican penetration of the Soviet Union, see chapter 5.

18. Rather than waiting for an opportunity to implement a prepared plan with a priestly force in readiness, the papal secretariat of state did not even consider sending one or more priests into Russia behind the German armies until a week after Germany's invasion of the Soviet Union. When the idea was raised, the Vatican discovered that it had no priests prepared for such a mission, although the secretariat of state knew of one priest who was possibly suitable. By 4 July 1941 the Vatican had proceeded no farther than deciding to dispatch one priest to Slovakia to study the possibility of sending some priests into Russia. *Actes et Documents du Saint Siège relatifs à la Seconde Guerre Mondiale (ADSS)* (Vatican City: Libreria Editrice Vaticana, 1967), 4:593; *ADSS*, 5:71–72.

19. "Interrogation Report on SS Obersturmbannfuehrer Herbert Kappler," Graham Papers. In his interrogation Kappler referred to Kurtna as "an ex-Soviet agent."

20. David Alvarez and Robert Graham, S.J., *Nothing Sacred: Nazi Espionage Against the Vatican, 1939–1945* (London: Frank Cass, 1997), 122, 124.

21. Ibid., 124–25. The authors asserted that Kurtna was away only seven days. Italian intelligence documents make it clear that he was, in fact, absent for more than a month.

22. Memorandum by General (ret.) Eugenio Piccardo, 22 March 1944, Graham Papers.

23. Sauer had been exposed when Italian agents secretly entered the Swiss embassy and burgled the safe of the military attaché. The agents discovered documents that incriminated the German diplomat. Interview with General (ret.) Giulio Fettarappa-Sandri, Graham Papers.

24. Questore di Roma to Direzione Generale di Pubblica Sicurezza, 1 October 1943, A4. Spionaggio, busta 203: Alessandro Kurtna, DGPS, ACS. Kappler's anger over Kurtna's arrest touched individual Italian officers. Lieutenant Colonel Manfredo Talamo, the counterintelligence officer responsible for the Kurtna investigation, was among those executed under Kappler's authority at the Ardeatine caves outside Rome on 24 March 1944.

25. "Interrogation Report on Aleksander Kurtna," Graham Papers.

26. Ibid.; Houghton to Dunn, Weekly Summary no. 23, 26 August 1944, Entry 210, box 9, OSS, NA.

27. The informants are identified in a handwritten list from the files of Herbert Kappler. There is a photocopy of the list in the Graham Papers.

28. Houghton to Dunn, Weekly Summary no. 23, 26 August 1944, Entry 210, box 9, OSS, NA.

29. Walter Ciszek, S.J., *With God in Russia* (New York: McGraw-Hill, 1964), 207–8. Father Ciszek, an American Jesuit who had briefly studied with Alexander Kurtna at the prewar Russicum in Rome, had been arrested inside Russia in 1940 and imprisoned for practicing his ministry. He encountered his old schoolmate in the labor camp, but Kurtna declined to say how he came to be in the camp. In his memoirs Ciszek refers to Kurtna by the pseudonym "Misha."

30. Ormesson to Baudouin, 28 October 1940, Guerre 1939–1945, Vichy-Europe: Saint Siège, vol. 557, MAE.

31. Annie Lacroix-Riz, *Le Vatican, l'Europe et le Reich de la Première Guerre mondiale à la guerre froide* (Paris: Armand Colin, 1996), 377; Roger Faligot and Rémi Kauffer, *Éminences Grises* (Paris: Fayard, 1992), 62–74.

32. Owen Chadwick, *Britain and the Vatican During the Second World War* (New York: Cambridge University Press, 1986), 181. This book provides an excellent account of Osborne's travails during the war.

33. Ibid., 182. For evidence of the Foreign Office's concern for the security of Osborne's cipher, see Dunlop to Dixon, FO 380/74, PRO.

34. Quoted in Chadwick, *Britain and the Vatican During the Second World War,* 182–83.

35. Ibid., 185.

36. Charles Gallagher, "Cassock and Dagger: Monsignor Joseph P. Hurley and American Anti-Fascism in Mussolini's Italy, 1938–1940" (paper presented at the meeting of the American Catholic Historical Association, Indianapolis, 28 March 1998). My account of the Hurley operation depends upon this paper.

37. Quoted in ibid., 7.

38. Quoted in ibid., 8.

39. Quoted in ibid., 9.

40. Quoted in ibid., 13.

41. Information from Charles Gallagher.

42. Ibid.

43. Bradley Smith, *The Shadow Warriors: OSS and the Origins of the CIA* (New York: Basic Books, 1983), 93–94; memorandum of an interview with Louis Lochner, 6 June 1942, box 66, folder 26, OSS, NA. I am indebted to Margot Sempreora for the Lochner reference.

44. "OSS Italian Activities, January 1943–June 1945," entry 210, box 80, OSS, NA.

45. "Zanin, Msgr. Mario," 23 June 1943, Rome-X2-OP-2, box 1, reel 6, OSS, NA. After the war a survey of ecclesiastical personnel in China recorded that there were 803 native seminarians in the country. Louis Wei Tsing-sing, *Le Saint Siège et la Chine* (Paris: Editions A. Allais, 1968), 187.

46. "Vatican Priest," January 1943, Rome-X2-OP-2, box 1, reel 6, OSS, NA.

47. "Helfand," 30 April 1943, ibid. Information from Brian Sullivan.

48. On Fritz Kolbe, see Neal Petersen, "From Hitler's Doorstep: Allen Dulles and the Penetration of Nazi Germany," in *The Secrets War: The Office of Strategic Services in World War II*, ed. George Chalou (Washington, D.C.: National Archives and Records Administration, 1992), 278–79. For an example of a Weizsäcker report, see Boston Series No. 10, "Events at the Vatican," entry 210, box 442, OSS, NA.

49. Despite the state of war between Italy and the United States, the Italian government allowed Myron Taylor to travel between Washington and Vatican City in fulfillment of his diplomatic mission to the pope. Taylor flew to Rome from neutral Spain and then transferred to Vatican City in a curtained car under police escort.

50. Interview with Harold Tittmann, 19 March 1972, Graham Papers.

51. Strategic Services Unit (Rome) to Washington, 6 December 1945, entry 216, box 6, OSS, NA.

52. Max Corvo, *The OSS in Italy, 1942–1945: A Personal Memoir* (New York: Praeger, 1990), 220.

53. Report no. 104311, 14 November 1944, box 1178, Research and Analysis Branch, Intelligence Reports, OSS; Report no. L49138, 25 November 1944, box 414, ibid.; Report no. L51213, 11 December 1944, box 421, ibid.

54. Technically, Vessel was the name not of the source but of an Italian intermediary who on behalf of the source physically passed the documents to an American contact. The intelligence product, however, was known as Vessel, as was the operation, so the code word is used here to describe both the source and the product.

55. For Scattolini's prewar connections with the Fascist secret police, see Mimmo Franzinelli, *I tentacoli dell'OVRA: Agenti, collaboratori e vittime della polizia politica fascista* (Turin: Bollati Boringhieri, 1999), 483.

56. Alvarez and Graham, *Nothing Sacred*, 16–17.

57. Long after the war the Japanese ambassador confirmed that he never spoke to Myron Taylor during the war. Harada to Quigley, 26 December 1969, box 1, folder 77, Martin Quigley Papers, Georgetown University.

58. Joyce to Magruder, 26 January 1945, entry 190, box 163, folder 1148, OSS, NA; Magruder and Shepardson to Caserta Station, 17 February 1945, entry 90, box 6, folder 73, OSS, NA; Magruder to Caserta Station, 3 March 1945, entry 90, box 6, folder 73, OSS, NA.

59. "Vessel Reports," 6 June 1945, entry 92, box 595, folder 6, OSS, NA.

60. "Analysis of Vessel Cables," 8 June 1945, entry 210, box 437, OSS, NA.

61. Timothy Naftali, "ARTIFICE: James Angleton and X-2 Operations in Italy," in *The Secrets War: The Office of Strategic Services in World War II*, ed. George Chalou (Washington, D.C.: National Archives and Records Administration, 1992), 232.

62. Caserta Station to OSS (Magruder), 22 January 1945, entry 90, box 6, folder 63, OSS, NA.

63. Naftali, "ARTIFICE: James Angleton and X-2 Operations in Italy," 233.

64. Robert Graham, S.J., *Il Vaticano e il nazismo* (Rome: Cinque Lune, 1975), 267.

65. Vanderbilt to McBaine, 7 February 1942, entry 217, box 2, OSS, NA.

66. There is some uncertainty as to the meaning of the acronym "CIP." Some documents maintain that the initials are an acronym for Catholic International Press, while others state that the letters stand for Center for Information ProDeo.

67. Federal Bureau of Investigation File 100-HQ-93828, Subject: Felix Morlion. This file was released to the author by the FBI under the provisions of the Freedom of Information Act.
68. O'Keefe to Hughes, 15 August 1942, entry 217, box 2, OSS, NA.
69. Dolbeare to Hall, 25 April 1945, entry 210, box 424, OSS, NA. Maier-Hultschin is identified as "Hank Judah" in Horton to Maddox, 12 April 1945, entry 210, box 386, OSS, NA.
70. Dolbeare to Van der Hoef, n.d., Field Station Files (Caserta), box 121, folder 483, OSS, NA; ABBOTT to DIANE, 5 April 1945, Field Station Files (Caserta), box 121, folder 481, OSS, NA.
71. A.S. no. 21, 29 March 1945, Field Station Files (Caserta), box 121, folder 481, OSS, NA.
72. Bernard to Smith, 18 February 1945, Field Station Files (Caserta), box 121, folder 481, OSS, NA.
73. Dolbeare to Mayer, 16 March 1945, entry 210, box 424, OSS, NA; A.S. to Black, 15 February 1945, Field Station Files (Caserta), box 121, folder 481, OSS, NA.
74. Houck to Ogle, 31 March 1945, entry 210, box 424, OSS, NA; Ogle to Houck, 4 April 1945, entry 210, box 424, OSS, NA.
75. "A Brief Report on the Pilgrim's Progress Project," 15 November 1945, entry 216, box 2, OSS, NA.
76. Maddox to Shepardson, 13 January 1945, entry 210, box 386, OSS, NA.
77. Chapin to Chief, Secret Intelligence, 17 December 1944, entry 210, box 386, OSS, NA. Ambassador Apor, an anti-Nazi, switched his allegiance to the Allies after Germany occupied Hungary in the spring of 1944. Information from Charles Fenyvesi.
78. Scamporino to Maddox, 6 April 1945, entry 210, box 386, OSS, NA; Sawyer to Blain, 26 April 1945, entry 215, box 10, OSS, NA.
79. Several of Quigley's reports are in box 2, folders 72–75, Quigley Papers.
80. McCormick's diary entry for 19 February 1945 records "P[adre] Leiber in A.M.— talk on Russia, etc. for Martin Q." Extracts from the McCormick diary are in box 2, folder 32, Quigley Papers.
81. Martin Quigley, *Peace Without Hiroshima: Secret Action at the Vatican in the Spring of 1945* (Lanham, Md.: Madison Books, 1991), 28.
82. Ibid., 80.
83. For details of this program, see David Alvarez, *Secret Messages: Codebreaking and American Diplomacy, 1930–1945* (Lawrence: University Press of Kansas, 2000).
84. Herbert Yardley, *The American Black Chamber* (reprint, Laguna Hills, Calif.: Aegean Park Press, n.d.), 333.
85. Memorandum for the Director from Edward Tamm, 28 September 1942, and "Allegations of the Misuse of the Washington Papal Embassy Diplomatic Pouch" (date and name of author withheld). These documents were released to the author by the FBI under the provisions of the Freedom of Information Act.
86. Unless otherwise noted, this discussion of American work against papal ciphers depends on "Vatican Code Systems," box 1284, Historic Cryptographic Collection, Record Group 457: National Security Agency, NA.
87. A highly sensitive project to crack the ciphers of the Soviet Union, one of Washington's principal allies, was known as "Blue."

88. For British work against papal ciphers, see "Minutes of the Third Meeting of the Directing Subcommittee of Research Section," 24 October 1941, HW 14/21, PRO; "Minutes of the Meeting of Heads of Section," 1 April 1942, HW 14/33, PRO.

89. Christie to CinC, Allied Armies in Italy, "Vatican City Communications," 22 August 1944, box 47, Record Group 84: Foreign Service Post Files, NA.

90. "Vatican Code Systems," 57, 59.

7. "THE BEST INFORMATION SERVICE IN THE WORLD"

1. Information from Brother Edward Clancy as recounted to Father Robert Graham.

2. Quotations in David Alvarez and Robert Graham, S.J., *Nothing Sacred: Nazi Espionage Against the Vatican, 1939–1945* (London: Frank Cass, 1997), 60–61.

3. Ibid., 61.

4. *Foreign Relations of the United States, 1939* (Washington, D.C.: Government Printing Office, 1956), 2:869 n. 4; Hugh Wilson, *Diplomat Between the Wars* (New York: Longmans, 1941), 27; Sumner Welles, *Time for Decision* (New York: Harper Brothers, 1944), 142.

5. Owen Chadwick, *Britain and the Vatican During the Second World War* (New York: Cambridge University Press, 1986), 201.

6. Ibid., 55; Paul Hofmann, *O Vatican!* (New York: Congdon and Weed, 1984), 111.

7. Numbers for the secretariat of state are drawn from the personnel roster in *Annuario Pontificio* (Vatican City: Libreria Editrice Vaticana, 1939), 745–47. Numbers for the Dutch and Norwegian foreign ministries are drawn from Zara Steiner, ed., *The Times Survey of Foreign Ministries of the World* (London: Times Books, 1982), 80, 399.

8. "The Men and Offices of the Vatican Secretariat of State," 15 April 1945, entry 210, box 424, Record Group 226: OSS, NA.

9. *Actes et Documents du Saint Siège relatifs à la Seconde Guerre Mondiale (ADSS)* (Vatican City: Libreria Editrice Vaticana, 1967), 4:162–63.

10. Chadwick, *Britain and the Vatican During the Second World War*, 202.

11. David Kahn, *Hitler's Spies: German Military Intelligence in World War II* (New York: Macmillan, 1978), 162–63.

12. Carlo Gasbarri, *Quando il Vaticano confinava con il Terzo Reich* (Padua: Edizioni Messaggero, 1984), 99–101.

13. "The Men and the Offices of the Vatican Secretariat of State," entry 210, box 424, OSS, NA.

14. Wilson, *Diplomat Between the Wars*, 28.

15. *ADSS*, 8:265–66; *ADSS*, 3:728ff.

16. Houghton to Dunn, 4 December 1944, Weekly Summary no. 37, entry 210, box 9, OSS, NA.

17. Letter to the author from Cardinal Silvio Oddi, 1 November 1994. During the war the then Monsignor Oddi was a young officer in the apostolic delegation in Cairo.

18. Montante to Scamporino, 28 April 1945, entry 210, box 269, OSS, NA.

19. *ADSS*, 7:131, 167.

20. Ibid., 576, 594; *ADSS*, 5:460.

21. FO 371/28695, PRO.

22. *ADSS*, 11:240, 631.

23. For an instance of British authorities prohibiting Spanish diplomatic couriers from traveling in the Near East in 1941, see Foreign Office to the Spanish Ambassador, 20 May 1941, FO 371/28698 PRO.

24. "Comment on plan proposed for handling communications to and from Vatican City," n.d. [summer 1944], box 47, Record Group 84: Foreign Service Post Files: Records of the Political Advisor to the Supreme Allied Commander (RPA), Mediterranean, NA.

25. ADSS, 10:5; ADSS, 2:25; ADSS, 5:320.

26. ADSS, 3:14–15, 897.

27. Stettinius to the Political Advisor, 28 February 1944, box 47, RPA, NA.

28. "OSS Italian Activities, January 1943–June 1945: Report of Major Alessandro Cagiati," entry 210, box 80, OSS, NA.

29. Harold Deutsch, The Conspiracy Against Hitler in the Twilight War (Minneapolis: University of Minnesota Press, 1968), 95, 319; Douglas Porch, The French Secret Services: A History of French Intelligence from the Dreyfus Affair to the Gulf War (New York: Farrar, Straus and Giroux, 1995), 165.

30. Macgregor Knox, Mussolini Unleashed, 1939–1941: Politics and Strategy in Fascist Italy's Last War (New York: Cambridge University Press, 1982), 63; Christopher Andrew, Her Majesty's Secret Service: The Making of the British Intelligence Community (New York: Penguin, 1987), 445.

31. Christopher Andrew and Vasili Mitrokhin, The Sword and the Shield: The Mitrokhin Archive and the Secret History of the KGB (New York: Basic Books, 1999), 92. For a survey of the many intelligence indicators preceding the attack, see Barton Whaley, Codeword Barbarossa (Cambridge, Mass.: MIT Press, 1973).

32. James Barros and Richard Gregor, Double Deception: Stalin, Hitler and the Invasion of Russia (DeKalb: Northern Illinois University Press, 1995), 28–29, 34; F. H. Hinsley, British Intelligence in the Second World War, abridged edition (New York: Cambridge University Press, 1993), 90.

33. Barros and Gregor, Double Deception, 36–37, 43, 45; Hinsley, British Intelligence, 101.

34. Andrew, Her Majesty's Secret Service, 484.

35. ADSS, 4:473–74.

36. Ibid., 549–51. In 1946 Pope Pius told Monsignor Tardini of the papal secretariat of state that he had received word of the German attack from the same source that had alerted him to the German attack on France and the Low Countries, i.e., the anti-Nazi resistance circle in the Abwehr. Tardini made a note of this revelation but did not indicate when the pope received the information concerning Barbarossa. In a conversation with the American historian Harold Deutsch in 1966, Father Robert Leiber, the pope's confidential assistant, recalled that the pope received several notices of German plans concerning Russia, and though unsure of the timing, Leiber thought the first might have been as early as the end of 1940. By the time of this conversation with Deutsch, Father Leiber had suffered a stroke, and his memory seemed to have been impaired. He had no recollection, for example, of the Abwehr warning the pope of a German attack on Denmark and Norway, although there is ample evidence of such warning. Deutsch, The Conspiracy Against Hitler in the Twilight War, 35 n. 10, 351.

37. Richard Breitman, *Official Secrets: What the Nazis Planned, What the British and Americans Knew* (New York: Hill and Wang, 1998), 34–35.

38. Walter Laqueur, *The Terrible Secret* (Boston: Little, Brown, 1980), 55; Michael Phayer, *The Catholic Church and the Holocaust, 1930–1965* (Bloomington: Indiana University Press, 2000), 42; Raul Hilberg, *The Destruction of the European Jews* (New York: Octagon Books, 1978), 469–70; Saul Friedlander, *Pius XII and the Third Reich* (New York: Knopf, 1966), 104.

39. John Morley, *Vatican Diplomacy and the Jews During the Holocaust, 1939–1943* (New York: KTAV Publishing, 1980), 133–34; Alessandro Duce, *Pio XII e la Polonia* (Rome: Edizioni Studium, 1997), 151–52, 155–59.

40. Susan Zuccotti, *Under His Very Windows: The Vatican and the Holocaust in Italy* (New Haven, Conn.: Yale University Press, 2000), 97–98.

41. Breitman, *Official Secrets*, 92.

42. Ibid., 96.

43. Ibid., 95.

44. Ibid., 100; Laqueur, *The Terrible Secret*, 67, 109–10. David Engel suggests that Polish intelligence representatives in German-occupied Warsaw learned of the mass killings in the east by October 1941 but that their reports would have taken some time to reach the Polish government-in-exile in London. David Engel, *In the Shadow of Auschwitz: The Polish Government-in-Exile and the Jews, 1939–1942* (Chapel Hill: University of North Carolina Press, 1987), 175.

45. Laqueur, *The Terrible Secret*, 94; David Wyman, *The Abandonment of the Jews: America and the Holocaust, 1941–1945* (New York: Pantheon, 1984), 20.

46. Breitman, *Official Secrets*, 124; Laqueur, *The Terrible Secret*, 36, 42, 61.

47. Phayer, *The Catholic Church and the Holocaust*, 47; Zuccotti, *Under His Very Windows*, 99.

48. Quoted in Zuccotti, *Under His Very Windows*, 104.

49. Quoted in ibid., 105.

50. Ibid., 102, 107. Kurt Gerstein, a German Protestant who joined the SS to investigate rumors of atrocities, personally witnessed the gassing of Jews at Belzec in August 1942. That same month he described his experience to a Swedish diplomat, who soon after returned to Stockholm with word of "corpse factories." After his encounter with the Swede, Gerstein attempted to contact the nuncio in Berlin but was turned away from the nunciature because he was in military uniform. Gerstein gave his information to the assistant of the Catholic bishop of Berlin with the request that it be forwarded to the Vatican. From the information currently available to historians, it is impossible to determine when the information reached the Vatican.

51. Martin Gilbert, *Auschwitz and the Allies* (New York: Henry Holt, 1981), 39–44. By July 1942 press and radio accounts of the Bund report had appeared in Britain and the United States.

52. Ibid., 56, 63; Wyman, *The Abandonment of the Jews*, 43.

53. Memorandum by McFadden, 5 December 1947, box 17, Political-General, Record Group 59: State Department Records: Records of the Personal Representative of the President to Pope Pius XII (PRP), NA; memorandum by Parsons, 22 May 1948, box 19, Memoranda-Confidential, PRP, NA.

BIBLIOGRAPHY

ARCHIVAL SOURCES
Archives Nationales, Paris
   C 7376-86   Enquete sur les papiers de la nonciature
   F7 14605   Commissaire Haverna, "Note sur l'organisation et le fonctionnement du
           service cryptographique de la Sûreté générale"
Archivio degli Affari Ecclesiastici Straordinari, Vatican City
   Guerra Europa, 1914–1918
   Germania
   Italia
   Spagna
Archivio Centrale dello Stato, Rome
   Ministero dell'Interno
      Direzione Generale della Pubblica Sicurezza
      Divisione Polizia Politica
Archivo del Ministerio de Asuntos Exteriores, Madrid
   Archivo de embajada de España cerca de Santa Sede
Archivio Segreto Vaticano, Vatican City
   Fondo Benigni
   Segreteria di Stato
Bibliothèque Nationale, Paris
   Marcel Givierge, "Au service du chiffre: 18 ans de souvenirs, 1907–1925," NAF
   17573–75
Ministère des Affaires Étrangères, Paris
   Paix, 1914–1920
   Europe: Allemagne, 1918–1940
   Europe: Saint Siège, 1918–1940
   Guerre, 1939–1945. Vichy-Europe: Saint Siège
   Papiers d'agents, archives privées: Charles-Roux
National Archives and Records Administration, College Park, Maryland
   Record Group 59   State Department Records
   Record Group 84   Foreign Service Post Files
   Record Group 165   War Department General and Special Staffs
   Record Group 226   Office of Strategic Services
   Record Group 457   National Security Agency
Préfecture de Police, Paris
   BA 926   Benedetto Lorenzelli
   BA 1579   Carlo Montagnini
   BA 2196   Vatican

Private Papers
   Robert Graham, S.J., Papers, Vatican City
   Henry Howard Diary. Copy in possession of the author
   John Ireland Papers. Archives of the Archdiocese of St. Paul, Minnesota
   Denis O'Connell Papers. University of Notre Dame
   William Phillips Diary. Harvard University
   Martin Quigley Papers. Georgetown University
   Elihu Root Papers. Library of Congress
   Sidney Sonnino Papers. Hoover Library, Stanford University
   William Howard Taft Papers. Library of Congress
Public Record Office, Kew
   Foreign Office
      371   Political Department, General Correspondence
      380   Legation, Vatican
Service Historique de l'Armée de Terre, Vincennes
      6 N 248 Vatican, 1917–1920

SECONDARY SOURCES

Actes et Documents du Saint Siège relatifs à la Seconde Guerre Mondiale. 12 vols. Vatican City: Libreria Editrice Vaticana, 1965–81.

Albonico, Aldo. *La Mobilitazione legittimista contro il regno d'Italia: La Spagna e il brigantaggio meridionale postunitario.* Milan: Giuffre, 1979.

Alvarez, David. "The Papacy in the Diplomacy of the American Civil War." *Catholic Historical Review* 69 (April 1983): 227–48.

———. "The Professionalization of the Papal Diplomatic Service, 1909–1967. *Catholic Historical Review* 72 (April 1989): 233–48.

———. "Purely a Business Matter: The Taft Mission to the Vatican." *Diplomatic History* 16 (summer 1992): 357–69.

———. "Faded Lustre: Vatican Cryptography, 1815–1920." *Cryptologia* 20 (April 1996): 97–131.

———. *Secret Messages: Codebreaking and American Diplomacy, 1930–1945.* Lawrence: University Press of Kansas, 2000.

Alvarez, David, and Robert Graham. *Nothing Sacred: Nazi Espionage Against the Vatican, 1939–1945.* London: Frank Cass, 1997.

Amè, Cesare. *Guerra segreta in Italia, 1940–1943.* Rome: Gherado Casini, 1954.

Andrew, Christopher. *Her Majesty's Secret Service: The Making of the British Intelligence Community.* New York: Penguin, 1987.

Andrew, Christopher, and Oleg Gordievsky. *KGB: The Inside Story of Its Foreign Operations from Lenin to Gorbachev.* New York: HarperCollins, 1990.

Andrew, Christopher, and Vasili Mitrokhin. *The Sword and the Shield: The Mitrokhin Archive and the Secret History of the KGB.* New York: Basic Books, 1999.

Aston, Nigel. *Religion and Revolution in France, 1780–1804.* Washington, D.C.: Catholic University of America Press, 2000.

Barros, James, and Richard Gregor. *Double Deception: Stalin, Hitler and the Invasion of Russia.* De Kalb: Northern Illinois University Press, 1995.

Bedeschi, Lorenzo. "Un episodio di spionaggio antimodernista." *Nuova revista storica* 56 (May–August 1972): 389–423.

Berg, Bruce. *Policing in Modern Society.* Boston: Butterworth-Heineman, 1999.

Bernabei, Domenico. *Orchestra Nera.* Turin: ERI, 1991.

Biffi, Monica. *Monsignore Cesare Orsenigo: Nuncio Apostolico in Germania.* Milan: NED, 1997.

Blakiston, Noel, ed. *The Roman Question: Extracts from the Despatches of Odo Russell from Rome, 1858–1870.* Wilmington, Del.: Michael Glazier, 1962.

Blet, Pierre, S.J. *Pius XII and the Second World War.* New York: Paulist Press, 1999.

Breitman, Richard. *Official Secrets: What the Nazis Planned, What the British and Americans Knew.* New York: Hill and Wang, 1998.

Browder, George. *Foundations of the Nazi Police State: The Formation of Sipo and SD.* Lexington: University Press of Kentucky, 1990.

Canosa, Romano. *I Servizi Segreti del Duce: I persecutori e le vittime.* Milan: Mondadori, 2000.

Chadwick, Owen. *Britain and the Vatican During the Second World War.* New York: Cambridge University Press, 1986.

———. *A History of the Popes, 1830–1914.* New York: Oxford University Press, 1998.

Chalou, George, ed. *The Secrets War: The Office of Strategic Services in World War II.* Washington, D.C.: National Archives and Records Administration, 1992.

Connelly, James F. *The Visit of Archbishop Gaetano Bedini to the United States.* Rome: Libreria Editrice dell'Università Gregoriana, 1960.

Conway, John. "Pope Pius XII and the German Church: An Unpublished Gestapo Report." *Canadian Journal of History* 2 (March 1967): 72–83.

———. *The Nazi Persecution of the Churches, 1933–1945.* New York: Basic Books, 1968.

Coppa, Frank. *Cardinal Giacomo Antonelli and Papal Politics in European Affairs.* Albany: State University of New York Press, 1990.

———. *The Italian Wars of Independence.* New York: Longman, 1992.

———. *The Modern Papacy Since 1789.* New York: Addison Wesley Longman, 1998.

———, ed. *Controversial Concordats: The Vatican's Relations with Napoleon, Mussolini, and Hitler.* Washington, D.C.: Catholic University of America Press, 1999.

Corvo, Max. *The OSS in Italy, 1942–1945: A Personal Memoir.* New York: Praeger, 1990.

Delmer, Sefton. *Black Boomerang.* New York: Viking, 1962.

De Marchi, Giuseppe. *Le nunziature apostoliche dal 1800 al 1956.* Rome: Edizioni di storia e letteratura, 1957.

Denis, André, ed.. *Relations de Voyage de Paul van der Vrecken (1777–1868): Agent Secret du Saint Siège.* Brussels: Institut historique belge de Rome, 1980.

De Risio, Carlo. *Generali, servizi segreti e fascismo.* Milan: Mondadori, 1978.

Deschner, Gunther. *Heydrich: The Pursuit of Total Power.* London: Orbis, 1981.

Deutsch, Harold. *The Conspiracy Against Hitler in the Twilight War.* Minneapolis: University of Minnesota Press, 1968.

D'Hauterive, Ernest. *La Police Secrète du Premier Empire.* Paris: Clavreuil, 1964.

Duce, Alessandro. *Pio XII e la Polonia (1939–1945).* Rome: Edizioni Studium, 1997.

Dunn, Dennis. *The Catholic Church and the Soviet Government, 1939–1949.* Boulder, Colo.: East European Monographs, 1977.

Emerson, Donald. *Metternich and the Political Police: Security and Subversion in the Hapsburg Monarchy, 1815–1830.* The Hague: Martinus Nijhoff, 1968.

Engel, David. *In the Shadow of Auschwitz: The Polish Government-in-Exile and the Jews, 1939–1942.* Chapel Hill: University of North Carolina Press, 1987.

Epstein, Klaus. *Mathias Erzberger and the Dilemma of German Democracy.* Princeton, N.J.: Princeton University Press, 1959.

Fabre, Giorgio. *Roma e Mosca: Lo spionnagio fascista in URSS e il caso Guarnaschelli.* Bari: Edizioni Dedalo, 1990.

Falconi, Carlo. *Il Cardinale Antonelli.* Milan: Mondadori, 1983.

Faligot, Roger, and Rémi Kauffer. *Éminences Grises.* Paris: Fayard, 1992.

Fattorini, Emma. *Germania e Santa Sede: Le nunziatura di Pacelli tra la Grande Guerra e la Repubblica di Weimar.* Bologna: Mulino, 1992.

Fedele, Clemente, and Mario Gallenga. *Per servizio di Nostro Signore: Strade, corrieri e poste dei papi dal medioevo al 1870.* Modena: Macchi, 1988.

Ficcadenti, Bruno. "Rivoluzione e reazione nelle Marche nel 1833." *Studi Urbinati* 55 (1982): 118–135.

Filippone, Giustino. *Le relazioni tra lo Stato Pontificio e la Francia revoluzionaria.* 2 vols. Milan: Giuffre, 1961.

Fiorentino, Carlo. *La questione romana intorno al 1870: Studi e documenti.* Rome: Archivio Guido Izzi, 1997.

———. *All'ombra di Pietro: La Chiesa Cattolica e lo spionaggio fascista in Vaticano, 1929–1939.* Florence: Casa Editrice le Lettere, 1999.

Fournier, August. *Die Geheimpolizei auf dem Wiener Kongress.* Vienna: F. Tempsky, 1913.

Franzinelli, Mimmo. *I tentacoli dell'OVRA: Agenti, collaboratori e vittime della polizia politica fascista.* Turin: Bollati Boringhieri, 1999.

Friedlander, Saul. *Pius XII and the Third Reich.* New York: Knopf, 1966.

Furlani, Silvio. *La politica postale di Metternich e l'Italia.* Prato: Istituto di studi storici postali, 1987.

Gabriele, Mariano, ed. *Il carteggio Antonelli-Sacconi, 1858–1860.* Rome: Instituto per la storia del Risorgimento italiano, 1962.

Gallagher, Charles. "Cassock and Dagger: Monsignor Joseph P. Hurley and American Anti-Fascism in Mussolini's Italy, 1938–1940." Paper presented at the meeting of the American Catholic Historical Association, Indianapolis, 28 March 1998.

Garzia, Italo. *La questione romana durante la prima guerra mondiale.* Naples: Edizioni scientifiche italiane, 1981.

Gasbarri, Carlo. *Quando il Vaticano confinava con il Terzo Reich.* Padua: Edizioni Messaggero, 1984.

Gennarelli, Achille. *Il governo pontificio e lo stato romano.* 2 vols. Prato: F. Alberghetti, 1860.

Gilbert, Martin. *Auschwitz and the Allies.* New York: Henry Holt, 1981.

Gorodetsky, Gabriel. *Grand Illusion: Stalin and the German Invasion of Russia.* New Haven, Conn.: Yale University Press, 1999.

Graham, Robert, S.J. "Spie naziste attorno al Vaticano durante la seconda guerra mondiale." *Civiltà Cattolica* 1 (January 1970): 21–31.

———. "La strana condotta di E. von Weizsäcker ambasciatore del Reich in Vaticano." *Civiltà Cattolica* 2 (June 1970): 455–71.

————. "Voleva Hitler allontanare da Roma Pio XII?" *Civiltà Cattolica* 1 (February 1972): 319–27.

————. "Il vaticanista falsario: L'incredibile successo di Virgilio Scattolini." *Civiltà Cattolica* 3 (September 1973): 46/–78.

Guspini, Ugo. *L'orecchio del regime: Le intercettazioni telefoniche al tempo del fascismo.* Milan: Mursia, 1973.

Hachey, Thomas, ed. *Anglo-Vatican Relations, 1914–1939: Annual Reports of the British Ministers to the Holy See.* Boston: G. K. Hall, 1972.

Harris, Stephen. *British Military Intelligence in the Crimean War, 1854–1856.* London: Frank Cass, 1999.

Helmreich, Ernst. *The German Churches Under Hitler.* Detroit: Wayne State University Press, 1979.

Hilberg, Raul. *The Destruction of the European Jews.* New York: Octagon Books, 1978.

Hill, Leonidas. "The Vatican Embassy of Ernst von Weizsäcker, 1943–1945." *Journal of Modern History* 39 (June 1967): 138–59.

Hinsley, F. H. *British Intelligence in the Second World War.* Abridged edition. New York: Cambridge University Press, 1993.

Holmes, Derek. *The Triumph of the Holy See.* London: Burns and Oates, 1978.

Hughes, Steven. "Fear and Loathing in Bologna and Rome: The Papal Police in Perspective." *Journal of Social History* 18 (spring 1987): 97–116.

————. *Crime, Disorder and the Risorgimento: The Politics of Policing in Bologna.* New York: Cambridge University Press, 1994.

Judd, Alan. *The Quest for C: Sir Mansfield Cumming and the Founding of the Secret Service.* New York: HarperCollins, 1999.

Kahn, David. *The Codebreakers: The Story of Secret Writing.* New York: Macmillan, 1967.

————. *Hitler's Spies: German Military Intelligence in World War II.* New York: Macmillan, 1978.

Kent, Peter. *The Pope and the Duce: The International Impact of the Lateran Agreements.* New York: St. Martin's, 1981.

Klemperer, Klemens von. *German Resistance Against Hitler: The Search for Allies Abroad, 1938–1945.* New York: Oxford University Press, 1992.

Knox, Macgregor. *Mussolini Unleashed, 1939–1941: Politics and Strategy in Fascist Italy's Last War.* New York: Cambridge University Press, 1982.

Kurtz, Lester. *The Politics of Heresy: The Modernist Crisis in Roman Catholicism.* Berkeley and Los Angeles: University of California Press, 1986.

Lacroix-Riz, Annie. *Le Vatican, l'Europe et le Reich de la Première Guerre mondiale à la guerre froide.* Paris: Armand Colin, 1996.

Laqueur, Walter. *The Terrible Secret.* Boston: Little, Brown, 1980.

Larkin, Maurice. *Church and State After the Dreyfus Affair.* New York: Harper and Row, 1973.

Leslie, Shane. *Cardinal Gasquet: A Memoir.* London: Burns and Oates, 1953.

Lesourd, Paul. *Entre Rome et Moscou: Le jésuite clandestine, Mgr Michel d'Herbigny.* Paris: Editions Lethielleux, 1976.

Levine, Paul. *From Indifference to Activism: Swedish Diplomacy and the Holocaust, 1938–1944.* Uppsala: Acta Universitatis Upsaliensis, 1998.

Lian, His-Huey. *The Rise of Modern Police and the European State System from Metternich to the Second World War*. New York: Cambridge University Press, 1992.

Liberati, Luigi Bruti. *La Santa Sede e le origini dell'impero americano: La guerra del 1898*. Milan: Edizioni Unicopli, 1984.

Manfroni, Giuseppe. *Sulla soglia del Vaticano, 1870–1901*. Milan: Longanesi, 1971.

Marchasson, Yves. *La Diplomatie Romaine et la République Française*. Paris: Beauchesne, 1974.

Marchese, Stelio. *La Francia ed il problema dei rapporti con la Santa Sede, 1914–1924*. Naples: Edizioni scientifiche italiane, 1969.

Marchetti, Odoardo. *Il servizio informazione dell'esercito italiano nella Grande Guerra*. Rome: Tipografia Regionale, 1937.

Martini, Ferdinando. *Diario, 1914–1918*. Verona: Mondadori, 1966.

Mayr, Josef Karl. *Metternich's Geheimer Briefdienst*. Vienna: Verlag Adolf Nachfolger, 1935.

McKay, C. G. *From Information to Intrigue: Studies in Secret Service Based on the Swedish Experience, 1939–1945*. London: Frank Cass, 1993.

Monticone, Alberto. *La Germania e la neutralità italiana, 1914–1915*. Bologna: Mulino, 1971.

Morley, John. *Vatican Diplomacy and the Jews During the Holocaust, 1939–1943*. New York: KTAV Publishing, 1980.

Moseley, Ray. *Mussolini's Shadow: The Double Life of Count Galeazzo Ciano*. New Haven, Conn.: Yale University Press, 1999.

Naftali, Timothy. "ARTIFICE: James Angleton and X-2 Operations in Italy." In *The Secrets War: The Office of Strategic Services in World War II*, edited by George C. Chalou, 218–45. Washington, D.C.: National Archives and Records Administration, 1992.

Niceforo, Nicola. *Cospirazioni romane, 1817–1868*. Rome: Voghera, 1899.

Offner, John. *An Unwanted War: The Diplomacy of the United States and Spain over Cuba, 1895–1898*. Chapel Hill: University of North Carolina Press, 1992.

Pagano, Sergio. "Documenti sul modernismo romano dal Fondo Benigni." *Ricerche per la storia religiosa di Roma* 8 (1990): 223–300.

Pásztor, Lajos. *La Segreteria di Stato e il suo archivio, 1814–1833*. Stuttgart: Anton Hiersemann, 1984.

Persico, Joseph. *Roosevelt's Secret War: FDR and World War II Espionage*. New York: Random House, 2001.

Pethö, Albert. *I servizi segreti dell'Austria-Ungheria*. Gorizia: Librera Editrice Goriziana, 2001.

Phayer, Michael. *The Catholic Church and the Holocaust, 1930–1965*. Bloomington: Indiana University Press, 2000.

Pollard, John. *The Vatican and Italian Fascism, 1929–32*. New York: Cambridge University Press, 1985.

———. *The Unknown Pope: Benedict XV (1914–1922) and the Pursuit of Peace*. London: Geoffrey Chapman, 1999.

Porch, Douglas. *The French Secret Services: A History of French Intelligence from the Dreyfus Affair to the Gulf War*. New York: Farrar, Straus and Giroux, 1995.

Poulat, Emile. *Intégrisme et Catholicisme integral*. Tournai: Casterman, 1969.

———. *Catholicisme, Democratie et Socialisme*. Tournai: Casterman, 1977.

Quigley, Martin. *Peace Without Hiroshima: Secret Action at the Vatican in the Spring of 1945.* Lanham, Md.: Madison Books, 1991.

Reinerman, Alan. *Austria and the Papacy in the Age of Metternich.* 2 vols. Washington, D.C.: Catholic University of America Press, 1979–89.

Renzi, William. *In the Shadow of the Sword: Italy's Neutrality and Entrance into the Great War, 1914–1915.* New York: Peter Lang, 1987.

Rhodes, Anthony. *The Vatican in the Age of the Dictators.* New York: Holt Rinehart and Winston, 1973.

———. *The Power of Rome in the Twentieth Century.* New York: Franklin Watts, 1983.

Richemont, Vicomte de. *Correspondance Secrète de l'Abbe Salamon.* Paris: Plon, Nourrit et Cie, 1898.

Rinieri, Ilario, ed. *Corrispondenza inedita dei cardinali Consalvi e Pacca nel tempo del Congresso di Vienna, 1814–1815.* Turin: Unione tipografico-editrice, 1903.

Robinson, John Martin. *Cardinal Consalvi, 1757–1824.* New York: St. Martin's, 1987.

Rostagni, Carla Meneguzzi, ed. *Il carteggio Antonelli-DeLuca, 1859–1861.* Rome: Istituto per la storia del Risorgimento italiano, 1983.

Roveri, Alessandro. *La missione Consalvi e il Congresso di Vienna.* 2 vols. Rome: Istituto storico italiano per l'età moderna e contemporanea, 1970.

Rumi, Giorgio, ed. *Benedetto XV e la pace, 1918.* Brescia: Editrice Morcelliana, 1990.

Sánchez, José. *Pius XII and the Holocaust: Understanding the Controversy.* Washington, D.C.: Catholic University of America Press, 2002.

Scoccianti, Sandro. "Apunti sul servizio informazioni pontificio nelle Marche nel 1859–60." *Atti e memorie della deputazione di storia patria per le Marche* 88 (1983): 293–350.

Scottà, Antonio. *La conciliazione ufficiosa: Diario del Barone Carlo Monti.* Vatican City: Libreria Editrice Vaticana, 1997.

Smith, Bradley. *The Shadow Warriors: OSS and the Origins of the CIA.* New York: Basic Books, 1983.

Smith, Denis Mack. *Italy and Its Monarchy.* New Haven, Conn.: Yale University Press, 1989.

Spadolini, Giovanni. *Giolitti e i cattolici.* Florence: Felice le Monnier, 1960.

———, ed. *Il Cardinale Gasparri e la questione romana.* Florence: Felice le Monnier, 1972.

Sparrow, Elizabeth. *Secret Service: British Agents in France, 1792–1815.* Woodbridge, Suffolk: Boydell Press, 1999.

Stehle, Hansjakob. *Eastern Politics of the Vatican, 1917–1979.* Athens: Ohio University Press, 1981.

Stehlin, Stewart. *Weimar and the Vatican, 1919–1933: German-Vatican Diplomatic Relations in the Interwar Years.* Princeton, N.J.: Princeton University Press, 1983.

Stock, Leo, ed. *Consular Relations Between the United States and the Papal States: Instructions and Despatches.* Washington, D.C.: American Catholic Historical Association, 1945.

Tilley, John, and Stephen Gaselee. *The Foreign Office.* London: Putnam's, 1933.

Vaillé, Eugène. *Le Cabinet Noir.* Paris: Presses Universitaires de France, 1950.

Valk, J. P. *Lettres de Francesco Capaccini.* Brussels: Institut historique belge de Rome, 1983.

Viviani, Ambrogio. *Servizi segreti italiani, 1815–1985.* Rome: Kronos Libri, 1986.

Weil, Maurice-Henri. *Les Dessous du Congrès de Vienne*. Paris: Librairie Payot, 1917.

Weinberg, Gerhard. *The World at Arms: A Global History of World War II*. New York: Cambridge University Press, 1994.

Welles, Sumner. *Time for Decision*. New York: Harper Brothers, 1944.

Wenger, Antoine. *Rome et Moscou, 1900–1950*. Paris: Desclée de Brouwer, 1987.

———. *Catholiques en Russie d'apres les archives du KGB, 1920–1960*. Paris: Desclée de Brouwer, 1998.

Whaley, Barton. *Codeword Barbarossa*. Cambridge, Mass.: MIT Press, 1973.

Wilson, Hugh. *Diplomat Between the Wars*. New York: Longmans, 1941.

Wyman, David. *The Abandonment of the Jews: America and the Holocaust, 1941–1945*. New York: Pantheon, 1984.

Zivojinovic, Dragan. *The United States and the Vatican Policies, 1914–1918*. Boulder: Colorado Associated University Press, 1978.

Zuccotti, Susan. *Under His Very Windows: The Vatican and the Holocaust in Italy*. New Haven, Conn.: Yale University Press, 2000.

INDEX

Della Chiesa, Cardinal Giacomo, 87, 88, 97, 98–99, 115. *See also* Benedict XV
Della Somaglia, Cardinal Giulio, 31
De Luca, Msgr. Antonino, 16
De Stefano, Antonio, 78
Deubner, Alexander, 146, 147–51
Directory, 7
Dohnanyi, Major Hans, 174, 175, 184, 188
Donovan, William, 244, 260
Dulles, Allen, 245
Dusty (code name), 248–49
Duvoin, Bertaud, 27

Ecuador, 59
Elling, Georg, 234–35
Erzberger, Mathias, 91–93, 101, 102, 103, 106
Estonia, 225, 226, 231

Faulhaber, Cardinal Michael von, 198, 275
Fay, Cyril, 125
Fazio, Giovanni, 157, 158, 213, 214
Fedeltà e Mistero, 22
Ferrari, Cardinal Andrea, 79
Ferrata, Cardinal Domenico, 87
Ferry, Jules, 56, 88
Fesch, Cardinal Joseph, 35, 42
Final Solution, 285–91
Finland, 236
Finnochi, Msgr. Amadeo, 245
Fonck, Fr., 94
Fossati, Cardinal Maurilio, 170, 171
Foster, Elizabeth, 43
France, 3, 7, 45, 49, 55, 58, 60, 79, 81, 111, 158, 176, 256, 283, 290, 292
  anticlericalism, 14–15, 56, 117–18
  Austria-Hungary, 13, 16
  disinformation, 119–23
  election of Benedict XV, 87, 88
  election of Pius XII, 169
  intervenes in Papal States, 8, 12
  monitors papal mail, 24–25, 27, 28
  Piedmont, 13, 16
  sources at Vatican, 43, 117–19, 128, 237
  studies papal ciphers, 57
  surveillance of nuncios, 56–57, 236–37
Francesco II, 37

Franco, General Francisco, 253
Franken, Paul, 185–86, 188, 189
Franz Ferdinand, Archduke, 85
Freddi-Battilori, Ludovico, 41
Frison, Bishop Alexander, 131, 139, 140, 142, 143
Fritsch, General Werner von, 180
Frühwirth, Cardinal Andrea, 98

Galeazzi, Enrico, 256, 259
Garibaldi, Giuseppe, 24, 37, 44, 55
Gasparri, Cardinal Pietro, 75, 76, 79, 81, 88, 90, 93, 100, 102, 112, 115, 118, 126, 127, 128, 131, 153, 157, 159, 163, 293
Gasperi, Alcide de, 213
Gasquet, Cardinal Aidan, 88, 89, 123
Gehrmann, Fr. Eduard, 136, 147–48, 162
Gemelli, Fr. Agostino, 158
George V, 112
Georgian College, 203–11
Georgian Legion, 205, 210
Gerlach, Msgr. Rudolf, 98–99, 101–3, 106
German Historical Institute, 227, 229
German-Hungarian College, 201
Germany, 3, 4, 68, 70, 81, 230, 236, 240, 260, 270
  Abwehr, 173, 178, 184, 188, 195
  anti-Nazi resistance, 174–75, 185–86, 243
  Austria-Hungary, 91
  concordat with Vatican, 163
  election of Benedict XV, 86, 87
  election of Pius XII, 169–70
  embassy at Vatican, 88, 90, 96, 102, 189–90, 197, 235
  Final Solution, 286–87, 289–90
  Forschungsamt, 180, 194, 219
  funds for Vatican, 92
  Gestapo, 165, 175, 188, 195, 231, 235
  Italian neutrality, 98
  monitors Vatican mail, 108, 115
  Nazis and Catholic Church, 162–64
  Pers Z, 194, 195
  reads Vatican ciphers, 114, 115, 194–95, 219
  Reichsicherheitshauptamt (RSHA), 179, 188, 195, 196, 200, 204, 207

Morlion, Fr. Felix, 253–57
Muckermann, Fr. Friedrich, 181–82
Mühlberg, Otto von, 88
Müller, Heinrich, 195, 196
Müller, Bishop Johannes, 182
Müller, Josef, 173, 175–77, 178, 179, 180–81, 183–84, 188, 247, 282
Murat, Joachim, 35
Murri, Romolo, 72
Mussolini, Benito, 151, 152, 153–54, 155, 186, 212, 219, 232, 241, 273

Naples, Kingdom of, 12, 17, 37, 43, 44, 45
Nava di Bontifé, Msgr. Giuseppe, 60
Navarre, Henri, 238
Nebe, Arthur, 180
Netherlands, 3, 28, 68, 176, 270, 283, 292
Neveu, Bishop Pie Eugene, 131, 138, 140, 141, 143, 144
Nicholas I, 35
Nicholas II, 67
Nieuwenhuys, Adrien, 177, 180, 181
Non abbiamo bisogno, 155, 161
Noots, Abbot Hubert, 174, 200
Norway, 270

O'Connell, Msgr. Denis, 64
Odo, Dom, 276
O'Gorman, Bishop Thomas, 66, 67
Orlando, Vittorio, 157
d'Ormesson, Wladimir, 237, 269
Orsenigo, Msgr. Cesare, 182, 272, 281
Osborne, d'Arcy, 169, 176, 178, 214, 215, 238–39, 246, 269, 274, 279
Osservatore Romano, 81, 83, 189, 219, 240, 241, 245
Oster, Colonel Hans, 174, 175, 184, 188, 283
O'Toole, James, 258
Ott, Alice, 131, 139
Ottaviani, Msgr. Alfredo, 160

Pacca, Cardinal Bartolomeo, 42
Pacca, Msgr. Tiberio, 6, 22, 42
Pacelli, Msgr. Eugenio, 82, 111, 112, 127, 135, 139, 163, 169, 171, 293. *See also* Pius XII

Page, Thomas Nelson, 124
Palatine Guards, 200
Papal intelligence sources
  bishops and priests, 19–22
  consuls, 18–19
  mail surveillance, 35–37
  nuncios, 13–17
  other governments, 37–40
  police, 22, 37, 40–41, 46–47, 58
  provincial delegates, 22–23, 58
Papal States, 5, 7
  administration, 9, 10, 291
  Austria-Hungary, 38–40
  codes and ciphers, 28–31
  communications, 25–28
  couriers, 26–27
  diplomatic service, 17–18
  foreign intelligence, 17–18, 24, 31–32, 45–46
  internal security, 32–34, 46–47
  Naples, 37
  Piedmont, 13, 43–45, 47
  revolutionary activity, 5, 10–11, 15, 44
  secretariat of state, 31, 37
  United States, 19, 20–21, 36
  See also Papal intelligence sources
Paraguay, 59
Parma, 38, 43
Partito Populare Italiano, 154
Patin, Wilhelm, 164
Perciballi, Fr. Pietro, 78
Peru, 59
Peter's Pence, 92
Petrelli, Msgr. Giuseppe, 121, 122
Philippines, 64, 66
Phillips, William, 240–41
Phipps, Eric, 169
Pichon, Stephen, 57
Picot, Werner, 197–98
Piedmont, Kingdom of, 17, 36
  Austria-Hungary, 23, 43, 44
  espionage against Papacy, 37–38, 43
  France, 13, 16
  monitors papal mail, 25
  Papal States, 13, 43–45, 47
Pierce, Franklin, 17
Piffle, Cardinal Gustav, 79

Vatican Archive, 3, 4, 198
Vatican Information Office, 231, 235, 274–75
Vatican intelligence sources
  bishops, priests, and laypeople, 77, 127, 136, 275–76, 285–86
  foreign diplomats, 273
  nuncios, 59–60, 77, 112, 113, 126, 270, 285, 293
  press and radio, 274–75
Vatican Radio, 216, 222, 240, 245, 275, 278, 281
Verdesi, Fr. Gustavo, 78
Vessel (code name), 248–49, 251, 252, 265
Vittorio Emanuele II, 49, 50, 61
Vittorio Emanuele III, 152, 186, 232
Vives y Tuto, Cardinal Jose, 80
Vrecken, Paul van der, 26–27

Walsh, Fr. Edmund, 134, 136
Weizsäcker, Ernst von, 190–92, 234, 245
Welles, Sumner, 269
Wilberforce, Robert, 125
Wilson, Hugh, 269
Wilson, President Woodrow, 111, 124
Wolff, Martin, 164

Yardley, Herbert, 261–62
Young Italy (Giovane Italia), 9, 33, 37
Yugoslavia, 158, 259

Zanin, Msgr. Mario, 244
Zeiger, Fr. Ivo, 178, 185
Zerr, Bishop, 135
Zetkin, Clara, 147